Rick Steves'
SPAIN & PORTUGAL
2002

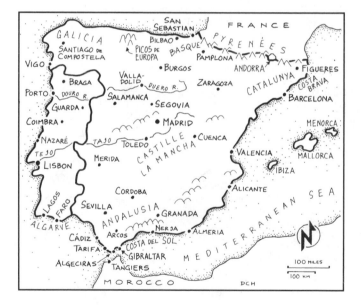

AVALON
TRAVEL

Other ATP travel guidebooks by Rick Steves

Rick Steves' Best of Europe
Rick Steves' Europe 101: History and Art for the Traveler
    (with Gene Openshaw)
Rick Steves' Europe Through the Back Door
Rick Steves' Mona Winks: Self-Guided Tours of Europe's Top Museums
    (with Gene Openshaw)
Rick Steves' Postcards from Europe
Rick Steves' France, Belgium & the Netherlands (with Steve Smith)
Rick Steves' Germany, Austria & Switzerland
Rick Steves' Great Britain
Rick Steves' Ireland (with Pat O'Connor)
Rick Steves' Italy
Rick Steves' Scandinavia
Rick Steves' London (with Gene Openshaw)
Rick Steves' Florence (with Gene Openshaw)
Rick Steves' Paris (with Steve Smith and Gene Openshaw)
Rick Steves' Rome (with Gene Openshaw)
Rick Steves' Venice (with Gene Openshaw)
Rick Steves' Phrase Books: German, Italian, French, Spanish/Portuguese,
    and French/Italian/German

Seventh Edition. First printing January 2002
Printed in the United States of America by R. R. Donnelley

For the latest on Rick Steves' lectures, guidebooks, tours, and
public-television series, contact Europe Through the Back Door,
Box 2009, Edmonds, WA 98020, tel. 425/771-8303, fax 425/771-0833,
www.ricksteves.com, or e-mail: rick@ricksteves.com.

ISBN 1-56691-358-6
ISSN 1084-4414

Europe Through the Back Door Editor: Risa Laib
Avalon Travel Publishing Editor: Kate Willis
Copy Editor: Chris Hayhurst
Research Assistance: Risa Laib, Carlos Galvin, Norman Bell
Production & Typesetting: Kathleen Sparkes, White Hart Design
Design: Linda Braun
Cover Design: Janine Lehmann
Maps: David C. Hoerlein
Cover Photo: Giralda Tower and Cathedral, Sevilla, Spain;
    copyright © Blaine Harrington III

CONTENTS

Top Destinations in Spain and Portugal

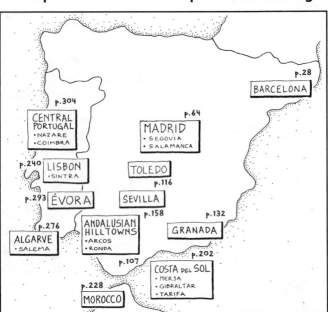

INTRODUCTION

Like a grandpa bouncing a baby on his knee, Iberia is a mix of old and new, modern and traditional. Spain and Portugal can fill your travel days with world-class art treasures, folk life, exotic foods, sunshine, friendly people, and castles where the winds of the past still howl. And, in spite of its recent economic boom, Iberia (particularly Portugal) remains Europe's bargain basement. Tourism is huge here. Spain, with 40 million inhabitants, entertains 50 million visitors annually. Iberia is very popular—and you're about to learn why.

This book breaks Spain and Portugal into their top big-city, small-town, and rural destinations. It then gives you all the information and opinions necessary to wring the maximum value out of your limited time and money. If you plan a month or less in Iberia, this lean and mean little book is all you need.

Experiencing Spain and Portugal's culture, people, and natural wonders economically and hassle-free has been my goal for 25 years of traveling, tour guiding, and writing. With this book, I pass on to you the lessons I've learned, updated for 2002.

Rick Steves' Spain & Portugal is a tour guide in your pocket, with a balanced, comfortable mix of exciting cities and cozy towns topped off with an exotic dollop of Morocco. It covers the predictable biggies and stirs in a healthy dose of Back Door intimacy. Along with seeing a bullfight, the Prado, and flamenco, you'll buy cookies from cloistered nuns in a sun-parched Andalusian town and recharge your solar cells in an Algarve fishing village. You'll eat barnacles with green wine in village Portugal and scramble the ramparts of an ancient Moorish castle. I've been selective, including only the most exciting sights and experiences. For example, there are countless whitewashed Andalusian hill towns; I recommend the best two—Arcos and Ronda.

The best is, of course, only my opinion. But after two busy decades of travel writing, lecturing, and tour guiding, I've developed a sixth sense for what tickles the traveler's fancy.

This Information Is Accurate and Up-to-Date

This book is updated every year. Most publishers of guidebooks that cover a region from top to bottom can afford an update only every two or three years, and then the research is often by letter. Since this book is selective, covering only the places I think make the best month or so in Iberia, it can be personally updated each summer. Even with annual updates, things change. But if you're traveling with the current edition of this book, I guarantee you're using the most up-to-date information available (for the latest, see www.ricksteves.com/update). Trust me, you'll regret trying to save a few bucks by traveling with old information. If you're packing an old book, you'll quickly learn the seriousness of your mistake...

in Europe. Your trip costs about $10 per waking hour. Your time is valuable. This guidebook saves lots of time.

Planning Your Trip

This book is organized by destinations. Each destination is covered as a mini-vacation on its own, filled with exciting sights and homey, affordable places to stay. In each chapter, you'll find the following:

Planning Your Time, a suggested schedule with thoughts on how best to use your limited time.

Orientation, including tourist information, city transportation, and an easy-to-read map designed to make the text clear and your arrival smooth.

Sights with ratings: ▲▲▲—Don't miss; **▲▲**—Try hard to see; **▲**—Worthwhile if you can make it; no rating—Worth knowing about.

Sleeping and **Eating**, with addresses and phone numbers of my favorite budget hotels and restaurants.

Transportation Connections to nearby destinations by train, bus, or car, with recommended roadside attractions for drivers.

The **appendix** is a traveler's tool kit, with telephone tips, a climate chart, a list of festivals, and cultural background.

Browse through this book, choose your favorite destinations, and link them up. Then have a great trip! You'll travel as a temporary local, getting the absolute most out of every mile, minute, and dollar. You won't waste time on mediocre sights because, unlike other guidebooks, this one covers only the best. Since your major financial pitfall is lousy, expensive hotels, I've worked hard to assemble the best accommodations values for each stop. And, as you travel the route I know and love, I'm happy you'll be meeting some of my favorite Spanish and Portuguese people.

Trip Costs

Five components make up your trip cost: airfare, surface transportation, room and board, sightseeing/entertainment, and shopping/miscellany.

Airfare: Don't try to sort through the mess yourself. Get and use a good travel agent. A basic round-trip flight from the United States to Madrid or Lisbon should cost $700 to $1,000 (even cheaper in winter), depending on where you fly from and when. Always consider saving time and money by flying "open-jaw" (into one city and out of another, e.g., into Barcelona and out of Lisbon).

Surface Transportation: For a three-week whirlwind trip linking all of my recommended destinations, allow $350 per person for second-class trains and buses ($500 for first-class trains) or $600 per person (based on 2 people sharing) for a three-week car rental, tolls, gas, and insurance. Car rental is cheapest to arrange from home in the United States. Train passes, easily purchased outside of Europe, are also available at some of the larger European train stations. You may save money, however, by simply buying tickets as you go (see "Transportation," below).

Room and Board: While most will spend more (because they've got it and it's fun), you can thrive in Iberia on $50 a day per person for room and board. A $50-a-day budget allows $5 for lunch, $15 for dinner, and $30 for lodging (based on 2 people splitting the cost of a $60 double room that includes breakfast). That's doable. Students and tightwads will do it on $30 ($15 per bed, $15 for meals and snacks). But budget sleeping and eating require the skills and information covered below (or more extensively in *Rick Steves' Europe Through the Back Door*).

Sightseeing and Entertainment: In big cities, figure $3 to $4 per major sight (Prado, Picasso Museum), $2 for minor ones (climbing church towers), and $25 for splurge experiences (flamenco, bullfights). An overall average of $10 a day works for most. Don't skimp here. After all, this category directly powers most of the experiences all the other expenses are designed to make possible.

Shopping and Miscellany: Figure $1 per coffee, beer, ice-cream cone, and postcard. Shopping can vary in cost from nearly nothing to a small fortune. Good budget travelers find that this category has little to do with assembling a trip full of lifelong and wonderful memories.

Exchange Rates
I list prices in euros throughout the book. Both Spain and Portugal have adopted the euro currency.

$1 equals about €1.10.   €1 = about $0.90.

To roughly convert prices in euros into dollars, take 10 percent off the price in euros: €10 = about $9, and €25 = about $22, and €140 = about $125.

For the first two months of 2002, Spanish pesetas (roughly 200 ptas = $1) and Portuguese escudos (approximately 240$ = $1) will be in dual circulation with the euro. For more on the euro, check www.euro.ecb.int.

Prices, Times, and Discounts
The telephone numbers and hours of sights listed in this book are accurate as of mid-2001. Iberia is always changing, and I know you'll understand that this, like any other guidebook, starts to yellow even before it's printed—especially this transition year, when the euro materializes into bills and coins. Because it's possible that everyone might adjust prices a bit in 2002—depending on current exchange rates, the prices in this book are approximate.

In Europe—and in this book—you'll be using the 24-hour clock. After 12:00 noon, keep going—13:00, 14:00, and so on. For anything over 12, subtract 12 and add p.m. (14:00 is 2:00 p.m.).

In peak season, May through September, sightseeing attractions are wide open. Off-season, roughly October through April, expect shorter hours, more lunchtime breaks, and fewer activities. Confirm your sightseeing plans locally, especially when traveling off-season.

Portuguese time is usually one hour earlier than Spanish time (due to daylight saving time). Moroccan time can be up to two hours earlier than Spanish time.

While discounts for sightseeing and transportation are not listed in this book, seniors (60 and over), students (with International Student Identity Cards), and youths (under 18) sometimes get discounts—but only if they ask.

When to Go

Spring and fall offer the best combination of good weather, light crowds, long days, and plenty of tourist and cultural activities. Summer and winter travel both have their predictable pros and cons. July and August are most crowded and expensive in coastal areas, less crowded but uncomfortably hot and dusty in the interior. For weather specifics, see the climate chart in the appendix. Whenever you anticipate crowds, particularly in summer, call hotels in advance (call from one hotel to the next, with the help of your fluent receptionist) and try to arrive early in the day.

Sightseeing Priorities

Depending on the length of your trip, here are my recommended priorities.

3 days:	Madrid, Toledo
5 days, add:	Barcelona
7 days, add:	Lisbon
10 days, add:	Andalucía, Sevilla
14 days, add:	Granada, Algarve
17 days, add:	Costa del Sol, Morocco
20 days, add:	Coimbra, Nazaré
22 days, add:	Salamanca, Segovia

Red Tape, Business Hours, and Banking

You currently need a passport but no visa and no shots to travel in Spain, Portugal, and Morocco.

For visitors, Iberia is a land of strange and frustrating schedules. Most businesses respect the afternoon siesta. When it's 100 degrees in the shade, you'll understand why.

In Spain and Portugal, shops are generally open from 9:00 to 13:00 and from 15:00 (or 16:00 in Spain) to 19:00 (or 20:00 in

Spain), longer in touristy places. Small shops are often open on Saturday only in the morning and are closed all day Sunday. The biggest museums stay open all day. Smaller ones often close for a siesta.

Banking: Bring a Visa or MasterCard with a four-digit PIN so you can use the same card to withdraw cash from ATMs and to charge any expensive items. Both Spain and Portugal have easily available, easy-to-use 24-hour ATMs with English instructions. They'll save you time and money (on commission fees). I traveled painlessly throughout Spain and Portugal in 2001 with my Visa debit card. Get details at your bank and bring an extra copy of your card (or another of your cards) just in case once gets demagnetized or gobbled up by a machine. Pack along some cash or a few traveler's checks as a backup. If you're planning on getting cash advances from your regular credit card, be sure to ask the card company about fees before you leave.

Banks are generally open Monday through Friday nonstop from 9:00 to 14:00 in Spain, and in Portugal from 8:30 to 15:00, often with a lunch break.

Spanish banks charge acceptable commissions for changing traveler's checks. American Express offices (found only in big cities) offer mediocre rates but change any type of traveler's check without a commission. Portugal's banks charge outrageous, unregulated commissions ($8–15). Shop around. Sometimes the hole-in-the-wall exchange offices offer better deals than the bank. Look for the rare American Express office. Better yet, use a cash machine.

Language Barrier

For me, nowhere in Europe is the language barrier more frustrating than in Iberia. Learn the key phrases. Here, a phrase book comes in handy, particularly if you want to interact with local people. You'll find that doors open quicker and with more smiles when you can speak a few words of the language.

Spanish is easier than Portuguese to learn and pronounce. Try to learn the pleasantries. Fortunately, in Portugal's big cities and along the Algarve, people in the tourist business generally speak English. Otherwise, Spanish, French, or sign language come in handy.

My Spanish and Portuguese phrase book, which includes a traveler's dictionary, will help you hurdle the language barrier. You'll find the Survival Phrases in the appendix of this book useful as well.

Travel Smart

Reread this book as you travel and visit local tourist information offices. Buy a phone card and use it for reservations and confirmations. Use taxis in the big cities, bring along a water bottle, and

Whirlwind Three-Week Tour

linger in the shade. Connect with the cultures. Set up your own
quest for the best cream cake, cloister, fish soup, or whatever.

Enjoy the friendliness of the local people. Ask questions.
Most locals are eager to point you in their idea of the right
direction. Wear your money belt, pack a pocket-size notepad
to organize your thoughts, and practice the virtue of simplicity.
Those who expect to travel smart, do.

Design an itinerary that enables you to hit the festivals, bullfights, and museums on the right days. As you read this book, note
the problem days: Mondays, when many museums are closed, and
Sundays, when public transportation is meager. Treat Saturday as
a weekday (though transportation connections can be less frequent
than those Mon–Fri).

Plan ahead for banking, laundry, post-office chores, and picnics. Maximize rootedness by minimizing one-night stands. Mix
intense and relaxed periods. Every trip (and every traveler) needs
at least a few slack days. Pace yourself. Assume you will return.

Reservations for Granada's Alhambra: The only Iberian
sight you might want to reserve tickets for in advance is this
remarkable Moorish hilltop stronghold, consisting of palaces,

Spain & Portugal's Best Three-Week Trip

Day	Plan	Sleep in
1	Arrive in Madrid	Madrid
2	Madrid	Madrid
3	El Escorial, Valley of Fallen, Segovia	Segovia
4	Segovia and Salamanca	Salamanca
5	Salamanca, Coimbra	Coimbra
6	Coimbra, Batalha, Fatima, Nazaré	Nazaré
7	Beach day in Nazaré, Alcobaça side trip	Nazaré
8	Nazaré, Lisbon	Lisbon
9	Lisbon	Lisbon
10	Lisbon side trip to Belém and Sintra	Lisbon
11	Lisbon to the Algarve	Salema
12	Free beach day, Sagres	Salema
13	Across Algarve, Sevilla	Sevilla
14	Sevilla	Sevilla
15	Andalucía's Route of White Villages	Arcos
16	Arcos, Jerez, Tarifa	Tarifa
17	A day in Morocco	Tarifa
18	Gibraltar, Costa del Sol	Nerja
19	Nerja to Granada	Granada
20	Granada	Granada
21	Through La Mancha to Toledo	Toledo
22	Toledo	Toledo/Madrid/fly

While this itinerary is designed to be done by car, it can be done by train and bus (7–8 bus days and 4–5 train days). For three weeks without a car, I'd modify it to start in Barcelona and finish in Lisbon. From Barcelona, fly or take the night train to Madrid (see Toledo, Segovia, and El Escorial as side trips); take the night train to Granada; bus along Costa del Sol to Tarifa (visit Morocco—likely from nearby Algeciras); bus to Arcos, Sevilla, and Algarve; and take the train to Lisbon. This skips Coimbra and Salamanca and assumes you'll fly open-jaw into Barcelona and fly out of Lisbon. If you're catching the train from Lisbon back to Madrid, you can sightsee your way in three days (via Coimbra and Salamanca) or simply catch the night train to Madrid. Note that transportation connections are easier from Coimbra to Salamanca than vice versa.

gardens, a fortress, and a rich history. You can make reservations for the Alhambra upon arrival in Spain (ideally before you reach Granada), but I mention it here for those who like to have things nailed down before they leave. For more information, check the Granada chapter (see "Sights—The Alhambra," page 136).

Warning: Tourists are targeted by thieves throughout Spain and Portugal, especially in Barcelona, Madrid, Sevilla, and Lisbon. While hotel rooms are generally safe, cars are commonly broken into, purses are snatched, and pockets are picked. Be on guard, wear a money belt, and treat any commotion around you as a smoke screen for theft. Don't believe any "police officers" looking for counterfeit bills. Drivers should park carefully and leave nothing of value in the car; locals leave their cars empty and unlocked. When traveling by train, keep your rucksack in sight and get a *couchette* (bed in an attendant-monitored sleeping car) for safety on overnight trips.

Tourist Information

Your best first stop in a new city is the Turismo (tourist information office—abbreviated as TI in this book). Get a city map and advice on public transportation (including bus and train schedules), special events, and recommendations for nightlife. Many Turismos have information on the entire country. When you visit a Turismo (TI), try to pick up maps for towns you'll be visiting later in your trip.

While the TI has listings of all lodgings and is eager to book you a room, use its room-finding service only as a last resort (bloated prices, fees, no opinions, and they take a cut from your host). You'll get a far better value by using the listings in this book and going direct.

The national tourist offices in the United States are a wealth of information. Before your trip, get their free general information packet and request any specific information you want, such as city maps and schedules of upcoming festivals.

Tourist Office of Spain: Check these Web sites (www .okspain.org or www.tourspain.es) and contact the nearest office.

In New York: 666 5th Ave., 35th floor, New York, NY 10103, tel. 212/265-8822, fax 212/265-8864, e-mail: oetny@tourspain.es.

In Illinois: 845 N. Michigan Ave. #915E, Chicago, IL 60611, tel. 312/642-1992, fax 312/642-9817, e-mail: chicago@tourspain.es.

In Florida: 1221 Brickell Ave. #1850, Miami, FL 33131, tel. 305/358-1992, fax 305/358-8223, e-mail: oetmiami@tourspain.es.

In California: 8383 Wilshire Blvd. #960, Beverly Hills, CA 90211, tel. 323/658-7188, fax 323/658-1061, e-mail: espanalax @aol.com.

Portuguese National Tourist Office: 590 5th Ave., 4th floor, New York, NY 10036, tel. 800/PORTUGAL or 212/354-4403,

fax 212/764-6137, www.portugalinsite.com, e-mail: tourism
@portugal.org. Videotapes, maps, and information on regions,
castles, and beach resorts. Very helpful.

Moroccan National Tourist Office: 20 E. 46th St. #1201,
New York, NY 10017, tel. 212/557-2520, fax 212/949-8148, www
.tourism-in-morocco.com. Good country map. Information on cities
and regions.

Gibraltar Information Bureau: 1156 15th St. N.W., Suite
1100, Washington, D.C. 20005, tel. 202/452-1108, fax 202/452-1109.

Recommended Guidebooks

You may want some supplemental travel guidebooks, especially
if you are traveling beyond my recommended destinations. When
you consider the improvement it will make in your $3,000 vaca-
tion, $25 or $35 for extra maps and books is money well spent.
For several people traveling by car, the extra weight and expense
of a small trip library are negligible.

Lonely Planet's guides to Spain and Portugal are thorough,
well-researched, and packed with good maps and hotel recommendations for low- to moderate-budget travelers, but they're
not updated annually. Students and vagabonds will like the hip
Rough Guide: Spain and *Rough Guide: Portugal* (written by insight-
ful British researchers, but not updated annually) and the highly
opinionated *Let's Go: Spain and Portugal* (by Harvard students,
thorough hostel listings, updated annually, includes Morocco).
Let's Go is best for backpackers with a train pass interested in the
youth and night scene. Older travelers enjoy Frommer's Spain/
Morocco and Portugal guides even though they, like the Fodor
guides, ignore alternatives that enable travelers to save money by
dirtying their fingers in the local culture. The popular, skinny
Michelin Green Guides to Spain and Portugal are excellent,
especially if you're driving. They're known for their city and
sightseeing maps, dry but concise and helpful information on
all major sights, and good cultural and historical background.
English editions are sold in Iberia. The well-written and thought-
ful Cadogan guides to Spain and Portugal are excellent for "A"
students on the road. The encyclopedic Blue Guides to Spain and
Portugal are dry as the plains in Spain but just right for some.

The Eyewitness series has editions covering Spain, Barcelona,
Madrid, Sevilla/Andalucía, Portugal, and Lisbon (published by
Dorling Kindersley, sold in the United States or Iberia). It's
extremely popular for its fine graphics, 3-D cutaways of buildings,
aerial-view maps of historic neighborhoods, and cultural background. I use and like them, but they're heavy, and if you pull
out the art, the print that's left is pretty skimpy.

Juan Lalaguna's *Spain: A Traveler's History* provides a readable
background on this country's tumultuous history. John Hopper's

The New Spaniards provides an interesting look at Spain today. Portuguese history is mentioned (but not thoroughly covered) in various guidebooks, such as Cadogan, Eyewitness, and the Michelin Green Guide.

Rick Steves' Books and Videos

Rick Steves' Europe Through the Back Door 2002 gives you budget travel tips on minimizing jet lag, packing light, planning your itinerary, traveling by car or train, finding beds without reservations, changing money, outsmarting thieves, avoiding rip-offs, hurdling the language barrier, staying healthy, taking great photographs, using your bidet, and much more. The book also includes chapters on 35 of my favorite "Back Doors," three of which are in Iberia.

My **Country Guides**, a series of eight guidebooks including this book, cover the Best of Europe, Great Britain, Ireland, France/ Belgium/Netherlands, Italy, Scandinavia, and Germany/Austria/ Switzerland. All are updated annually and come out in January.

My **City Guides** feature London, Paris, Rome, and—new for 2002—Venice and Florence. These easy-to-read guides are updated annually (London, Paris, and Rome available in January, Venice and Florence available in March), and offer thorough coverage of the best of these grand cities. Enjoy self-guided, illustrated tours of top sights, with a focus on great art.

Rick Steves' Europe 101: History and Art for the Traveler (with Gene Openshaw, 2000) tells the story of Europe's peoples, history, and art. Written for smart people who were sleeping in their history and art classes before they knew they were going to Europe, *101* really helps Europe's sights come alive.

Rick Steves' Mona Winks (with Gene Openshaw, 2001) provides fun, easy-to-follow, self-guided tours of Europe's top 25 museums and cultural sites in London, Paris, Rome, Venice, Florence, and Madrid. Madrid's Prado is the thickest tour in the book.

Rick Steves' Spanish & Portuguese Phrase Book gives you the words and survival phrases necessary to communicate your way through a smooth and inexpensive trip.

My new public television series, *Rick Steves' Europe*, includes a show on Lisbon. My original series, *Travels in Europe with Rick Steves*, has six half-hour shows on Spain and Portugal. These earlier shows still air on public television throughout the United States. They are also available in information-packed home videos, along with my two-hour slide-show lecture on Spain and Portugal (call us at 425/771-8303 for our free newsletter/catalog).

Rick Steves' Postcards from Europe, my autobiographical book, packs 25 years of travel anecdotes and insights into the ultimate 3,000-mile European adventure. Through my guidebooks I share my favorite European discoveries with you. *Postcards* introduces you to my favorite European friends.

All of my books are published by Avalon Travel Publishing (www.travelmatters.com).

Maps

The maps in this book, drawn by Dave Hoerlein, are concise and simple. Dave, who is well-traveled in Spain and Portugal, has designed the maps to help you locate recommended places and get to the TIs, where you'll find more in-depth, free maps of the cities or regions.

Don't skimp on maps. For an overall Europe trip, consider my *Rick Steves' Europe Planning Map*, geared for the traveler with sight-seeing destinations prominent (call us at 425/771-8303 for our free newsletter/catalog). Excellent Michelin maps are available—and cheaper than in the United States—throughout Iberia in bookstores, newsstands, and gas stations. Train travelers can do fine with a simple rail map (such as the one that comes with your train pass) and city maps from the TIs. Drivers should invest in good 1:400,000 maps and learn the keys to maximize the sightseeing value.

Tours of Spain and Portugal

Travel agents can tell you about all the normal tours, but they won't tell you about ours.

At Europe Through the Back Door, we offer 17-day tours of Spain and Portugal featuring most of the highlights in this book (departures April–Oct). We have fully-guided tours (24 people on a big roomy bus with two great guides) and cheaper BBB—bus, bed, and breakfast—tours (27 people with an escort, ideal for families and independent travelers). For details, call 425/771-8303 or see www.ricksteves.com.

Transportation

By Car or Train?

Cars are best for three or more traveling together (especially families with small kids), those packing heavy, and those scouring the countryside. Trains and buses are best for solo travelers, blitz tourists, and city-to-city travelers.

Overview of Trains and Buses

Public transportation in Spain is becoming as slick, modern, and efficient as in northern Europe. Portugal is straggling in train service but offers excellent bus transportation. The best public transportation option is to mix bus and train travel. Always verify bus or train schedules before your departure. Never leave a station without your next day's schedule options in hand. In either Spain or Portugal, to ask for a schedule at an information window, say, "*Horario para* _____–_____ [fill in names of cities], *por favor*."

Cost of Public Transportation

Prices listed are for 2001. For 2002 prices, get my free *Rick Steves' 2002 Guide to European Railpasses*—call 425/771-8303 or visit www.ricksteves.com/rail after 12/15/01 (you can order most passes online).

SPAIN FLEXIPASS

	1st class	2nd class
Any 3 days in 2 months	$200	$155
Extra rail days (max. 7)	35	30

IBERIC FLEXIPASS

Covers both Spain and Portugal. 1st class: Any 3 days in 2 months for $205. Extra rail days (7 max.): $45.

Spain & Iberic Flexipass holders pay a supplement (included w/reservation) for the fast Talgo and AVE trains. For $85-$235, take a "Night Talgo" sleeper train from Madrid or Barcelona to Lisbon, Paris, Zurich, or Milan.

PORTUGUESE FLEXIPASS

1st class: Any 4 days out of 15 for $105.

EURAIL SELECTPASS

This pass covers travel in three adjacent countries. For 2002 prices and details, visit www.ricksteves.com/rail or see *Rick Steves' 2002 Guide to European Railpasses.*

	1st class Selectpass	1st class Saverpass	2nd class Youthpass
5 days in 2 months	$328	$280	$230
6 days in 2 months	360	306	252
8 days in 2 months	420	358	294
10 days in 2 months	476	406	334

Saverpass prices are per person for 2 or more people traveling together. Prices are subject to change.

SPAIN RAIL & DRIVE PASS

Any 3 rail days and 2 car days in 2 months.

	1st class	extra car day
Economy car	$239	$39
Compact car	249	49
Intermediate car	259	59
Compact automatic	265	59

Prices are approximate per person for 2 traveling together. Solo travelers pay about $75 extra. 3rd and 4th persons sharing car buy only the railpass. Extra rail days (2 max.) cost $36. To order Rail & Drive passes, call DER at 800/549-3737 or Rail Europe at 800/438-7245.

Iberia: Map shows approximate point-to-point one-way 2nd class rail fares in $US. Add up fares for your itinerary to see whether a railpass will save you money.

(The local TI will sometimes have schedules available for you to take or copy.) To study train schedules in advance, see www.renfe .es (Spain), www.cp.pt (Portugal), or www.reiseauskunft.bahn.de/ bin/query.exe/en (Germany's Europe-wide timetable).

Trains

While you could save money by purchasing tickets as you go, you may find the convenience of a railpass worth the extra cost. Iberia, Spain, and Portugal offer "flexi" railpasses that allow travel for a given number of days over a longer period of time. Of the

Public Transportation Routes

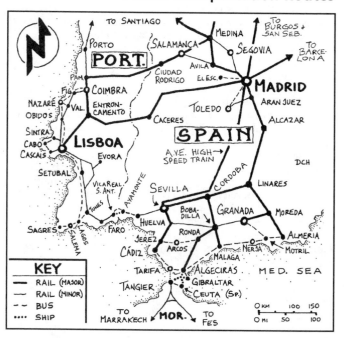

various Eurailpass options, the best choice for an Iberian jaunt is the Eurail Selectpass (see chart on page 12). Spain also offers a rail-and-drive pass, which gives you the ease of big-city train hops and the flexibility of a car for rural areas such as the Andalusian hill towns. Remember, you'll be making a lot of connections by buses, which are not covered by railpasses.

Spain: The long second-class train rides from Madrid to Barcelona, Lisbon, Sevilla, and Granada cost about $50 each. First class costs 50 percent more—often as much as a domestic flight. Using a railpass to cover these trips can be a good value.

If you're buying point-to-point tickets, note that round-trip tickets are 20 percent cheaper than two one-way tickets. You can get a round-trip discount even if you start with a one-way ticket—as long as you save the ticket and make a return trip. For example, if you buy a one-way ticket from Barcelona to Madrid, visit Madrid, then decide to return to Barcelona, you can bring your one-way Barcelona-Madrid ticket to the train station and get a 40 percent discount on your return trip (this equals a total 20 percent discount for the round-trip). Travelers under age 26 can buy cheap train tickets in Wasteels offices in most major train stations.

RENFE (the acronym for the Spanish national train system) used to be "Relatively Exasperating, and Not For Everyone," but it is getting better. To save time in Spain, consider buying tickets or reservations at the RENFE offices located in over 100 city centers. These are more central and less crowded/confusing than the train station. Or, for information and reservations, dial RENFE's national number (tel. 90-224-0202) from anywhere in Spain.

Spain categorizes trains this way:

The high-speed train called the **AVE** (Alta Velocidad Española) whisks travelers between Madrid and Sevilla in less than three hours. AVE is almost entirely covered by the Eurailpass (Madrid to Sevilla costs Eurailers about €14 in second class; €29 for first class includes meal). Franco left Spain a train system that didn't fit Europe's gauge. AVE trains run on European-gauge tracks.

The **Talgo** is fast, air-conditioned, and expensive, and runs on AVE rails. **Intercity** and **Electro** trains fall just behind Talgo in speed, comfort, and expense. **Rapido**, **Tranvia**, **Semi-directo**, and **Expreso** trains are generally slower. **Cercania** are commuter trains for big-city workers and small-town tourists. **Regional** and **Correo** trains are slow, small-town milk runs. Trains get more expensive as they pick up speed, but all are cheaper per mile than their northern European counterparts.

Long-distance fast trains can be priced differently according to their time of departure. Peak hours (*punta*) are most expensive, followed by *llano* and *valle* (quietest and cheapest times).

In Spain, *salidas* means "departures" and *llegadas* is "arrivals." On train schedules, "LMXJVSD" are the days of the week, starting with Monday. A train that runs "LMXJV-D" doesn't run on Saturdays. *Laborables* can mean Monday through Friday or Monday through Saturday. Most train stations have handy luggage lockers.

Overnight Trains in Iberia: Overnight trains (and buses) are usually less expensive and slower than the daytime rides. Most overnight trains have berths and beds that you can rent (not included in the cost of your train ticket or railpass). Sleeping berths (*litera*) cost $15. A *coche-cama*, or bed in a classy quad compartment, costs $20; and a bed in a double costs $25. For long trips I go overnight on the train or fly (domestic shuttle flights are generally under $100). Travelers with first-class reservations are entitled to the use of comfortable "Intercity" lounges in train stations in Spain's major cities.

The overnight train between Lisbon and Madrid is a pricey Hotel Train called the "Lusitania" (fares listed in Lisbon chapter under Transportation Connections; discounts with railpass; for info on Hotel Trains, see below). No cheaper rail option exists between Iberia's capital cities. You can save money by taking a bus, or save time by taking a plane.

Overnight Trains to/from Europe: Expensive Hotel

Trains connect France, Italy, and Switzerland with Spain. These fancy overnight trains (known collectively as Talgo Night) all have fancy names: Francisco de Goya (Madrid-Paris), Joan Miro (Barcelona-Paris), Pau Casals (Barcelona-Zurich), and Salvador Dali (Barcelona-Milan). These trains are not covered by railpasses, but railpass holders (of Eurail, Euro, Eurail Select, Spain, Iberic, France, and consecutive-day Swiss passes) can get discounted fares on routes within their pass boundaries; you'll give up a flexi-day and pay about half the full fare, which ranges from an $85 second-class quad *couchette* to a posh $235 Gran Class single compartment. (Full fares range from $153 in a quad to a $375 Gran Class single.) If you can easily afford to take a Hotel Train, consider flying instead to save time.

To avoid the expensive luxury of a Hotel Train, change trains at the Spanish border (at Irun on Paris runs, at Cerbère on the eastern side). You'll connect to a normal night train with $20 *couchettes* on one leg of the trip. This plan is more time-consuming, and may take two days of a flexipass.

Portugal: Portugal has mostly slow milk-run trains and an occasional Expreso. Departures and arrivals are *partidas* and *chegadas*, respectively. On Portuguese train schedules, *diario* means "daily," *mudanca de comboio* means "change trains," *so* means "only," and *não* means "not." This is a typical qualifier: *"Não se efectua aos sabados, domingos, e feriados oficiais"* (not effective on Saturdays, Sundays, and official holidays). Or *"So se efectua aos..."* ("only effective on...").

Buses

In either Spain or Portugal, ask at the tourist office about travel agencies that sell bus tickets to save you time if the bus station is not central. Don't leave a bus station to explore a city without checking your departure options and buying a ticket in advance if necessary (and possible). Bus service on holidays, Saturdays, and especially Sundays can be dismal.

You can (and most likely will be required to) stow your luggage under the bus. For longer rides, give some thought to which side of the bus will get the most sun, and sit on the opposite side. Even if a bus is air-conditioned and has curtains, direct sunlight can still get unpleasantly hot.

Iberian drivers and station personnel rarely speak English. Buses usually lack WCs but stop every two hours or so for a break (usually 15 min, but can be up to 30). In either Spain or Portugal, ask the driver "How many minutes here?" (*"¿Cuantos minutos aquí?"*) so you know if you have time to get out. Bus stations have WCs (rarely with toilet paper) and cafés offering quick and cheap food.

Both Spain and Portugal have a number of different bus companies, sometimes running buses to the same destinations and using the same transfer points. If you have to transfer, make sure to look for a bus with the same name/logo as the company you bought the ticket from.

A few buses are entirely nonsmoking; others are nonsmoking only in the front. When you buy your ticket for a long-distance bus (8 hours or more), ask for nonsmoking (*no fumadores* in Spanish, *não fumador* in Portuguese). It's usually pointless, since passengers ignore the signs, but it's a statement.

Your ride will likely come with a soundtrack: taped music (usually American pop in Portugal, Spanish pop in Spain), a radio, or sometimes videos. If you prefer silence, bring earplugs.

Portugal: Off the main Lisbon–Porto–Coimbra train lines, buses are usually a better bet. In cases where buses and trains serve the same destination, the bus is often more efficient, offering more frequent connections and sometimes a more central location.

Bus schedules in Portugal are clearly posted at each major station. Look for "*Partidas*" (departures), not "*Chegadas*" (arrivals). On schedules, exceptions are noted, such as "*Excepto sabados e domingos*" (Except Saturdays and Sundays). More key Portuguese "fine-print" words: Both *as* and *aos* mean "on." *De* means "from," as in "from this date to that date." *Feriado* means "holiday." *Directo* is "direct." *Ruta* buses are slower because they make many stops en route. Posted schedules list most, but not all, destinations. If your intended destination isn't listed, check at the ticket/info window for the most complete schedule information. For long trips your ticket might include an assigned seat.

Spain: Spain's bus system is more confusing than Portugal's because it has more bus companies (though they're usually clustered within one building). The larger stations have an information desk with all the schedules. In smaller stations, check the destinations and schedules posted on each office window.

Taxis

Most taxis are reliable and cheap. Drivers generally respond kindly to the request, "How much is it to ____, more or less?" (Spanish: "*¿Cuanto cuesta a ____, mas o menos?*" Portuguese: "*Quanto cuesta a ____, mais o menos?*"); if there's a long line-up of taxis, ask this question of one of the taxi drivers stuck farther back in line who has time (rather than ask at the head of the line where you might feel pressured to get in the cab and go). Spanish taxis have more extra add-ons (luggage, nighttime, Sundays, train-station or airport pickup, and so on). Rounding the fare up to the nearest large coin (maximum of 10 percent) is adequate for a tip. City rides cost $3 to $5. Keep a map in your hand so the cabby knows (or thinks) you know where you're going. Big cities have plenty of taxis. In many cases, couples travel by cab for little more than two bus or subway tickets.

Standard European Road Signs

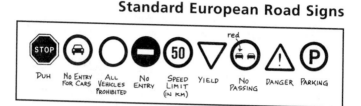

| STOP | NO ENTRY FOR CARS | ALL VEHICLES PROHIBITED | NO ENTRY | SPEED LIMIT (IN KM) | YIELD | NO PASSING | DANGER | PARKING |

Car Rental

It's cheapest to rent a car through your travel agent well before your departure. You'll want a weekly rate with unlimited mileage. Figure about $200 a week. For three weeks or longer, it's cheaper to lease; you'll save money on taxes and insurance.

Comparison shop through your agent. Beware of cheap weekly rates followed by very expensive daily costs. Remember, you can turn in your car at any office on any day (normally with credit for early turn-in or extra charge for extension). Also remember that rental offices usually close midday Saturday until Monday.

I normally rent a small economy model. For peace of mind, I splurge for the CDW insurance (Collision Damage Waiver, about $15 a day). A few "gold" credit cards cover CDW insurance; quiz your credit-card company on the worst-case scenario. Travel Guard offers CDW for $6 a day (U.S. tel. 800/826-1300, www .travelguard.com). With the luxury of CDW you'll enjoy Iberia's highways, knowing you can bring back the car in an unrecognizable shambles and just say, "S-s-s-sorry."

Driving

Driving in Iberia is great—sparse traffic and generally good roads. While the International Driver's License is officially required (cheap and easy to obtain from AAA; bring 2 photos and $10), I drive in Iberia with only my U.S. driver's license. (The Spanish version of AAA is the Real Automobil Club; Portugal's is the Automobil Clube de Portugal.)

Good maps are available and inexpensive throughout Iberia. Freeways in Spain and Portugal come with tolls (about $4 per hour) but save huge amounts of time. On freeways, navigate by direction (*norte, oeste, sur, este*). Also, since road numbers can be confusing and inconsistent, navigate by city names.

Drive defensively. If you're involved in an accident, you will be blamed and in for a monumental headache. Seat belts are required by law. Expect to be stopped for a routine check by the police (be sure your car-insurance form is up to date). There are plenty of speed traps. Tickets are issued and paid for on the spot. Portugal is statistically one of Europe's most dangerous places to drive. You'll see lots of ambulances on the road.

Gas and diesel prices are controlled and the same everywhere—around $3.50 a gallon for gas, less for diesel. *Gasolina* is either normal or super; unleaded is now widely available. Note that diesel is called *gasoleo*.

Get used to metric. A liter is about a quart, four to a gallon; a kilometer is six-tenths of a mile. To convert kilometers to miles, drop the last digit, then multiply by six (90 km: 9 x 6 = 54 mph; 120 km/hr: 12 x 6 = 72 mph).

If possible, make a copy of your key for safety and convenience. Choose parking places carefully. Leave valuables in the trunk during the day and leave nothing worth stealing in the car overnight. While you should avoid parking lots with twinkly asphalt, thieves break car windows anywhere, even at stoplights. Police recommend leaving the glove compartment open and your car unlocked at night. If it's a hatchback, take the trunk cover off at night so thieves can look in without breaking in. Parking attendants all over Spain holler, "*Nada en el coche*" ("Nothing in the car"). And they mean it. Ask at your hotel for advice on parking. In cities you can park safely but expensively in guarded lots.

Telephones, Cell Phones, Mail, and E-mail

You cannot travel smartly in Iberia without using the telephone—to reserve and confirm hotel rooms, check sightseeing plans, and call home. A few tips will minimize frustration.

At a phone booth, make calls by using a phone card (*tarjeta telefónica* in Spanish, *cartão telefónico* in Portuguese) rather than feeding in a bunch of coins. There are two types of phone cards you can buy: The kind you insert in a phone (sold at post offices and many newsstand kiosks) and a new PIN card that's not inserted into a phone. You can use a PIN card from almost any phone (even from your hotel room, unless it has an older touch-tone phone). You dial the access number, listed on the card, then follow the prompts, dialing your scratch-off Personal Identification Number and finally the number you want to call. PIN cards, made by numerous different (sometimes fly-by-night) companies, are sold at newsstand kiosks and tobacco shops; ask for an international calling card. PIN cards offer cheaper per-minute rates (particularly for international calls), but they don't consistently work as well as the insertable cards. In Portugal, I bought one that advertised in English, "Call Home!" but it worked only for calls within Portugal. Try to confirm that the card will work for calls to America (the salesclerk may not know), and buy a lower-denomination card in case the card is defective.

Either type of phone card works only in the country it's purchased in. If you have any time left on your card when you're about to leave a country, blow any remaining credit on a call home (about 50 cents/minute from any phone booth to the United States).

To use an insertable card, simply stick it into the slot on the phone, wait for a dial tone and digital readout to show how much value remains on your card, and dial your local, long-distance, or international call; the cost of the call is automatically deducted from your card. Portuguese phone cards usually don't tell you your balance until after you dial, but they do beep for 15 seconds before dying. This gives you plenty of time to sign off or push the eject button (look at the directions on the phone beforehand) and slip in a new card.

Portuguese phones are even-tempered, but Spanish phones refuse to be rushed. After you "*inserta*" your "*tarjeta*" (phone card) into the Spanish phone, wait until the digital display says "*Marque numero*" and then dial. Dial slowly and deliberately. Push the square "R" button to get a dial tone for a new call. Remember to retrieve your card. Neither in Spain nor Portugal will you get a reminder beep to remove it.

Dialing Direct: All phone numbers in Spain and Portugal are nine-digit numbers (without area codes) that can be dialed direct throughout each country; for example, in Madrid you dial a nine-digit number whether you're calling across the street or calling Barcelona. To dial international calls direct, you'll need the international access codes and country codes (see the appendix). European time is six/nine hours ahead of the east/west coast of the United States. Midnight in Seattle is breakfast in Madrid. Remember that if you're calling to make hotel reservations from the United States.

USA Direct Services: Since direct-dialing rates have dropped, calling cards (offered by AT&T, MCI, and Sprint) are no longer the good value they used to be. Still, calling the United States from any kind of phone (even your hotel room) is easy with a calling card. Each card company has a toll-free number in each European country that puts you in touch with an English-speaking operator who takes your card number and the number you want to call, puts you through, and bills your home phone number for the call. Sprint is the priciest, costing $3 for the first minute with a $4.50 connection fee; if you get an answering machine, it'll cost you $7.50 to say "Sorry I missed you." For less than 25 cents, call first with a coin or European phone card to see if the answering machine is off or if the right person's at home. For a list of AT&T, MCI, and Sprint calling-card operators, see the appendix. It's a rip-off to use USA Direct for calls between European countries (it costs more than calling the U.S.); instead call direct using a European phone card.

Cell Phones: Affluent travelers like to buy cell phones in Europe (about $60 on up) to use for making local and international calls. The cheaper phones generally work only if you're making calls from the country where you purchased it (e.g., a phone bought in Spain won't work in Portugal). Pricier phones allow you to call from any country but it'll cost you about $40 to outfit the phone per country with the necessary chip and prepaid phone time. If you're interested, stop by any European shop that sells cell phones (you'll see an array of phones prominently displayed in the store window). Depending on your trip and budget, ask for a phone that works only in that country or one that can be used throughout Europe. And if you're really on a budget, skip cell phones and use PIN cards instead.

Mail: To arrange for mail delivery, reserve a few hotels along your route in advance and give their addresses to friends or use American Express Company's mail services (available to anyone who has at least one American Express traveler's check). Allow 10 days for a letter to arrive. Phoning is so easy that I've dispensed with mail stops altogether.

E-mail: E-mail use among Iberian hoteliers is increasing. I've listed e-mail addresses when possible. Some family-run pensions can become overwhelmed by the volume of e-mail they receive, so please be patient if you don't get an immediate response. Cybercafés and little hole-in-the-wall Internet access shops (offering a few computers, no food, and cheap prices) are becoming popular in most cities.

Sleeping

In the interest of smart use of your time, I favor hotels (and restaurants) handy to your sightseeing activities. Rather than list hotels scattered throughout a city, I describe my favorite couple of neighborhoods and recommend the best accommodations values in each, from $10 bunks to $180 doubles.

Spain and Portugal offer some of the best accommodations values in Europe. Most places are government-regulated, with posted prices. While prices are low, street noise is high (Spaniards are notorious night owls). Always ask to see your room first. Check the price posted on the door, consider potential night-noise problems, ask for another room, or bargain down the price. You can request either *con vista* (with view) or *tranquilo* (*calado* in Portuguese). In most cases the view comes with street noise. Breakfast may or may not be included in your room cost. It is often used as a bargaining chip. Ask before accepting a room. Most of the year, prices are soft.

All rooms have sinks with hot and cold water. Rooms with private bathrooms are often bigger and renovated, while the cheaper rooms without bathrooms often will be dingier and/or on the top floor. Any room without a bathroom has access to a bathroom on the corridor. Towels aren't routinely replaced every day, so you should drip-dry and conserve.

It's officially prohibited for hotels to use central heat before November 1 and after April 1 (unless it's unusually cold); prepare

Sleep Code

To give maximum information in a minimum of space, I use this code to describe accommodations listed in this book. Prices listed are per room, not per person. When there is a range of prices in one category, the price will fluctuate with the season; these seasons are posted at the hotel desk. Especially in resort areas, prices go way up in July and August. In Spain, some hotels include the 7 percent I.V.A. tax in the room price, others tack it onto your bill. Hotel breakfasts, while rarely included in Spain, are often included in Portugal.

S = Single room (or price for one person in a double).

D = Double or twin. Double beds are usually big enough for nonromantic couples.

T = Triple (often a double bed with a single bed moved in).

Q = Quad (an extra child's bed is usually cheaper).

b = Private bathroom with toilet and shower or tub.

s = Private shower or tub only (the toilet is down the hall).

CC = Accepts credit cards (Visa and Mastercard, rarely American Express).

no CC = Does not accept credit cards; pay in local cash.

SE = Speaks English. This code is used only when it seems predictable that you'll encounter English-speaking staff.

NSE = Does not speak English. Used only when it's unlikely you'll encounter English-speaking staff.

According to this code, a couple staying at a "Db-€90, CC, SE" hotel would pay a total of €90 (about $77) for a double room with a private bathroom. The hotel accepts accepts credit cards or cash in payment, and the staff speaks English.

for cool evenings if you travel in spring and fall. Summer can be extremely hot. Consider air-conditioning, fans, and noise (since you'll want your window open), and don't be shy about asking for ice at the fancier hotels. Many rooms come with mini-refrigerators (if it's noisy at night, unplug it).

Don't judge hotels by their bleak and dirty entryways. Landlords, stuck with rent control, often stand firmly in the way of hardworking hoteliers who'd like to brighten up their buildings.

Any regulated place will have a complaint book (*libro de*

reclamaciones in Spanish and *livro de reclamações* in Portuguese). A request for this book will generally solve any problem you have in a jiffy.

Rooms in Private Homes: In both Spain and Portugal you'll find rooms in private homes, usually in touristy areas where locals decide to open up a spare room and make a little money on the side. These rooms are private, often with separate entries. Especially in resort towns, the rooms might be in small apartment-type buildings. Ask for a *cama, habitacion,* or *casa particulare* in Spain and a *quarto* in Portugal. They're cheap ($10–25 per bed without breakfast) and usually a good experience.

Historic Inns: Spain and Portugal also have luxurious, government-sponsored, historic inns. These *paradores* (Spain) and *pousadas* (Portugal) are often renovated castles, palaces, or monasteries, many with great views and stately atmospheres. These can be a very good value (doubles $80-200), especially for younger people (30 and under) and seniors (60 and over), who often get discounted rates; for details and family deals, see www.parador.es (Spain) and www.pousadas.pt (Portugal). If you're not eligible for any deals, you'll get a better value by sleeping in what I call "poor-man's paradors"—elegant normal places that offer double the warmth and Old World intimacy for half the price.

Hostels and Campgrounds: Both Spain and Portugal have plenty of youth hostels and campgrounds, but considering the great bargains on other accommodations, I don't think they're worth the trouble and don't cover them in this book. Hotels and *pensiónes* are easy to find, inexpensive, and, when chosen properly, a fun part of the Spanish and Portuguese cultural experience. If you're on a starvation budget or just prefer camping or hosteling, plenty of information is available in the backpacker guidebooks, through the national tourist offices, and at local tourist information offices.

Making Reservations
Even though Easter, July, and August are often crowded, you can travel at any time of year without reservations. But given the high stakes, erratic accommodations values, and the quality of the gems I've found for this book, I'd highly recommend calling ahead for rooms. In peak times or for big cities, you can reserve long in advance. Otherwise, simply call several days in advance as you travel. For maximum flexibility—especially off-season—you might make a habit of calling between 9:00 and 10:00 on the day you plan to arrive, when the hotel knows who'll be checking out and just which rooms will be available. Use the telephone and the convenient phone cards. Most hotels listed are accustomed to English-only speakers. A hotel receptionist will trust you and hold a room until 16:00 without a deposit, though some will ask for a credit-card number. Honor (or cancel by phone) your reservations.

Long distance is cheap and easy from public phone booths. Don't let these people down—I promised you'd call and cancel if for some reason you won't show up. Don't needlessly confirm rooms through the tourist office; they'll take a commission.

Those on a tight budget save pocketfuls of euros by traveling with no reservations and taking advantage of the discounted prices that hotels offer when it's clear they'll have empty rooms that day. Also, in the case of the places offering a 10 percent discount to those booking direct with this guidebook (as noted in hotel listings), remember to negotiate your best deal and only then claim the discount.

If you know exactly which dates you need and really want a particular place, reserve a room well in advance before you leave home. To reserve from home, call, fax, or e-mail the hotel. Simple English usually works. To fax, use the handy form in the appendix (online at www.ricksteves.com/reservation).

If you're writing, add the zip code and confirm the need and method for a deposit. A two-night stay in August would be "16/8/02 to 18/8/02" (Europeans write the date day/month/year, and hotel jargon uses your day of departure). You'll often receive a letter back requesting one night's deposit. A credit card will usually be accepted as a deposit. If your credit card is the deposit, you can pay with your card or cash when you arrive; if you don't show up, you'll be billed for one night. Reconfirm your reservations a day or two in advance for safety. If you have hotel confirmations in writing, bring them along.

Eating in Spain

Spaniards eat to live, not vice versa. Their cuisine is hearty and served in big, inexpensive portions. You can get good $10 meals in restaurants.

Although not fancy, there is an endless variety of regional specialties. Two famous Spanish dishes are paella and gazpacho. Paella features saffron-flavored rice as a background for whatever the chef wants to mix in—seafood, sausage, chicken, peppers, and so on. Considered a heavy meal, paella usually is served at midday rather than in the evening. Gazpacho, an Andalusian specialty, is a chilled soup of tomatoes, bread chunks, and spices—refreshing on a hot day and commonly available in the summer. Spanish cooks love garlic and olive oil.

People tip at restaurants. When you pay your bill, leave some coins, rounding the bill up to the next big bill (up to 10 percent).

The Spanish eating schedule frustrates many visitors. First off, many restaurants close during August. Secondly, when restaurants are open, they serve meals "late." Because most Spaniards work until 19:30, supper (*cena*) is usually served around 21:00 or 22:00. Lunch (*almuerzo*), also served late (13:00–16:00), is the

Tapas Tips

Here are some typical tapas:

aceitunas—olives
alinos—salads
bacalao—cod
boquerones—fresh anchovies
calamares fritos—fried
    squid rings
caracoles—snails
    (May–Sept)
chacinas—cold cuts
champinones—mushrooms
chorizo—spicy sausage
colo de toro or *rabo de toro*—
    bull-tail stew
ensaladilla—Russian salad
espinacas—spinach with
    chick peas
fritos—fried fish and meat
gambas—shrimp

gambas a la plancha—
    grilled shrimp
guiso—stew
jamón iberico—the best ham,
    from acorn-fed baby
    pigs
jamón serrano—cured ham
mejillones—mussels
pisto—mixed sautéed
    vegetables
pulpo—octopus
queso—cheese
queso manchego—sheep cheese
tabla serrana—could be a
    hearty plate of moun-
    tain meat and cheese.
tortilla española—Spanish
    potato omelet

largest meal of the day. Don't buck this system. Generally, no good restaurant serves meals at American hours.

The alternative to this late schedule, and my choice for a quick dinner, is to eat in tapas bars. Tapas are small portions, like appetizers, of all kinds of foods—seafood, salads, meat-filled pastries, deep-fried tasties, and on and on—normally displayed under glass at the bar (from about $1–10 for seafood). Confirm the price before you order (point and ask "*¿Quanto cuesta un tapa?*"). *Pinchos* are bite-size portions (not always available), tapas are snack-size, and *raciónes* are larger portions—half a meal. A *montadito* is a tiny open-faced sandwich (common at tapas bars; as in "*monta-dito de* . . . ," meaning "little sandwiches of . . . "). *Bocadillos* (sandwiches) are cheap and basic. A ham sandwich is just that—ham on bread, period.

For a budget meal in a restaurant, try a *plato combinado* (combination plate), which usually includes portions of one or two main dishes, a vegetable, and bread for a reasonable price; or the *menu del día* (menu of the day), a substantial three- to four-course meal that usually comes with a carafe of house wine. Flan (caramel custard) is the standard dessert. *Helado* (ice cream) is popular, as is *blanco y negro*, a vanilla-ice-cream-and-coffee float.

Eating and drinking at a bar is usually cheapest if you eat or drink at the counter (*barra*). You may pay a little more to eat sitting at a table (*mesa*) and still more for an outdoor table (*terraza*). Locate the price list (posted in fine type on a wall somewhere) to know the menu options and price tiers. In the right place, a quiet coffee break on the town square is well worth the extra charge. But the cheapest seats sometimes get the best show. Sit at the bar and study your bartender—he's an artist.

When searching for a good bar, I look for the noisy places with piles of napkins and food debris on the floor, lots of locals, and the TV blaring. Popular television shows include bullfights and soccer games, American sitcoms, and Spanish interpretations of soaps and silly game shows (you'll see Vanna Blanco).

Spain produces some excellent wine, both red (*tinto*) and white (*blanco*). Major wine regions include Valdepeñas, Penedès, Rioja, and Ribera del Duero. Sherry, a fortified wine from the Jerez region, ranges from dry (*fino*) to sweet (*dulce*)—Spaniards drink the fino and export the *dulce*. *Cava* is Spain's answer to champagne. *Sangría* (red wine mixed with fruit juice) is popular and refreshing. To get a small draft beer, ask for a *caña*. Spain's bars often serve orange juice (*zumo de naranja*), also available in boxes at grocery stores. For something completely different, try *horchata de chufa*, a sweet, milky beverage made from earth almonds.

For a quick and substantial breakfast, order *tortilla española* (potato omelet) with your *café solo* (black) or *café con leche* (with milk) in any café. The town market hall always has a colorful café filled with locals eating cheap breakfasts.

Eating in Portugal

The Portuguese meal schedule, while still late, is less cruel than Spain's. Lunch (*almoço*) is the big meal, served between noon and 14:00, while supper (*jantar*) is from 20:00 to 22:00. Tapas, therefore, are not such a big deal. You'll eat well in restaurants for $8.

Eat seafood in Portugal. Fish soup (*sopa de peixe*) and shellfish soup (*sopa de mariscos*) are worth seeking out. *Caldo verde* is a popular vegetable soup. *Frango no churrasco* is roast chicken; ask for *piri-piri* sauce if you like it hot and spicy. *Porco a alentejana* is an interesting combination of pork and clams. As in Spain, garlic and olive oil are big. *Meia dose* means half portion, while *prato do dia* is the daily special. If appetizers (such as olives or bread) are brought to your table before you order, they are not free. If you don't want the unordered food, ask to have it removed—or you'll end up paying for it.

For a quick snack, remember that cafés are usually cheaper than bars. *Sandes* (sandwiches) are everywhere. The Portuguese breakfast (*pequeno almoço*) is just *café com leite* and a sweet roll, but due to the large ex-pat English community, a full British "fry" is available in most touristy areas. A standard, wonderful local pastry is the cream tart, *pastel de Nata* (called *pastel de Belém* in Lisbon).

Portuguese wines are cheap and decent. *Vinho da casa* is the house wine. *Vinho verde* is a young, light wine from the north that goes well with seafood. The Dão region produces the best red wines. And if you like port wine, what better place to sample it than its birthplace? Beer (*cerveja*) is also popular—for a small draft beer, ask for *uma imperial*. Freshly squeezed orange juice (*sumo de laranja*), mineral water (*agua mineral*), and soft drinks are widely available.

As in Spain, it's good to tip, leaving the coins from your change. Rounding things up to the next big bill is considered generous.

Stranger in a Strange Land

We travel all the way to Europe to enjoy differences—to become temporary locals. You'll experience frustrations. Certain truths that we find "God-given" or "self-evident," such as cold beer, ice in drinks, bottomless cups of coffee, hot showers, body odor smelling bad, and bigger being better, are suddenly not so true. One of the benefits of travel is the eye-opening realization that there are logical, civil, and even better alternatives. A willingness to go local ensures that you'll enjoy a full dose of European hospitality.

If there is a negative aspect to the European image of Americans, it is that we are big, loud, aggressive, impolite, rich, and a bit naive. While Europeans look bemusedly at some of our Yankee excesses—and worriedly at others—they nearly always afford us individual travelers all the warmth we deserve.

Back Door Manners

While updating this book, I heard over and over again that my readers are considerate and fun to have as guests. Thank you for traveling as temporary locals who are sensitive to the culture. It's fun to follow you in my travels.

Send Me a Postcard, Drop Me a Line

If you enjoy a successful trip with the help of this book and would like to share your discoveries, please fill out and send the survey at the end of this book to me at Europe Through the Back Door, Box 2009, Edmonds, WA 98020. I personally read and value all feedback.

For our latest travel information, visit **www.ricksteves.com**. For any updates to this book, check www.ricksteves.com/update. My e-mail address is rick@ricksteves.com. Anyone is welcome to request a free issue of our *Back Door* quarterly newsletter.

Judging from the happy postcards I receive from travelers, it's safe to assume you're on your way to a great, affordable vacation—with the finesse of an independent, experienced traveler. Thanks, and *buen viaje*!

BACK DOOR TRAVEL PHILOSOPHY
As Taught in *Rick Steves' Europe Through the Back Door*

Travel is intensified living—maximum thrills per minute and one of the last great sources of legal adventure. Travel is freedom. It's recess, and we need it.

Experiencing the real Europe requires catching it by surprise, going casual ... "Through the Back Door."

Affording travel is a matter of priorities. (Make do with the old car.) You can travel—simply, safely, and comfortably—anywhere in Europe for $80 a day plus transportation costs. In many ways, spending more money only builds a thicker wall between you and what you came to see. Europe is a cultural carnival, and, time after time, you'll find that its best acts are free and the best seats are the cheap ones.

A tight budget forces you to travel close to the ground, meeting and communicating with the people, not relying on service with a purchased smile. Never sacrifice sleep, nutrition, safety, or cleanliness in the name of budget. Simply enjoy the local-style alternatives to expensive hotels and restaurants.

Extroverts have more fun. If your trip is low on magic moments, kick yourself and make things happen. If you don't enjoy a place, maybe you don't know enough about it. Seek the truth. Recognize tourist traps. Give a culture the benefit of your open mind. See things as different but not better or worse. Any culture has much to share.

Of course, travel, like the world, is a series of hills and valleys. Be fanatically positive and militantly optimistic. If something's not to your liking, change your liking. Travel is addictive. It can make you a happier American as well as a citizen of the world. Our Earth is home to 6 billion equally important people. It's humbling to travel and find that people don't envy Americans. They like us, but with all due respect, they wouldn't trade passports.

Globe-trotting destroys ethnocentricity. It helps you understand and appreciate different cultures. Travel changes people. It broadens perspectives and teaches new ways to measure quality of life. Many travelers toss aside their hometown blinders. Their prized souvenirs are the strands of different cultures they decide to knit into their own character. The world is a cultural yarn shop. And Back Door travelers are weaving the ultimate tapestry. Come on, join in!

BARCELONA

Barcelona is Spain's second city and the capital of the proud and distinct region of Catalunya. With Franco's fascism now history, Catalan flags wave once again. Language and culture are on a roll in Spain's most cosmopolitan and European corner.

Barcelona bubbles with life in its narrow Gothic Quarter alleys, along the grand boulevards, and throughout the chic, grid-planned new town. While Barcelona had an illustrious past as a Roman colony, Visigothic capital, 14th-century maritime power, and, in more modern times, a top Mediterranean trading and manufacturing center, it's most enjoyable to throw out the history books and just drift through the city. If you're in the mood to surrender to a city's charms, let it be in Barcelona.

Planning Your Time

Sandwich Barcelona between flights or overnight train rides. There's little of earth-shaking importance within eight hours by train. It's as easy to fly into Barcelona as into Madrid, Lisbon, or Paris for most travelers from the United States. Those renting a car can cleverly start here, sleep on the train or fly to Madrid, see Madrid and Toledo, and pick up the car as they leave Madrid.

On the shortest visit, Barcelona is worth one night, one day, and an overnight train out. The Ramblas is two different streets by day and by night. Stroll it from top to bottom at night and again the next morning, grabbing breakfast on a stool in a market café. Wander the Gothic Quarter, see the cathedral, and have lunch in Eixample (eye-SHAM-plah). The top two sights in town, Gaudí's Sacred Family Church and the Picasso Museum, are usually open until 20:00. The illuminated fountains (on Montjuïc, near Plaça Espanya) are a good finale for your day.

Barcelona

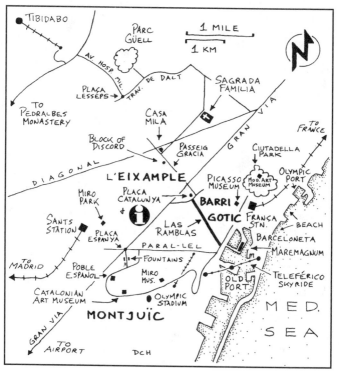

Of course, Barcelona in a day is insane. To better appreciate the city's ample charm, spread your visit over two or three days.

Orientation

Orient yourself mentally by locating these essentials on the map: Barri Gòtic/Ramblas (old town), Eixample (fashionable modern town), Montjuïc (hill covered with sights and parks), and Sants Station (train to Madrid). The soul of Barcelona is in its compact core—the Barri Gòtic (Gothic Quarter) and the Ramblas (main boulevard). This is your strolling, shopping, and people-watching nucleus. The city's sights are widely scattered, but with a map and a willingness to figure out the sleek subway system (or a few dollars for taxis), all is manageable.

Tourist Information

There are four useful **TIs** in Barcelona: at the **airport** (daily 9:30-20:30, tel. 93-478-4704), at the **Sants train station** (daily

8:00–20:00, near track 6), on **Plaça de Catalunya** (daily 9:00–
21:00, on main square near recommended hotels, look for red
sign, Gothic Quarter walking tours in English Sat–Sun at 10:00
from TI, €6.60, 2 hrs, call to reserve, tel. 93-304-3232; fair rates
at TI exchange desk; room-finding service; half-price ticket booth
from 3 hrs before show time; www.barcelonaturisme.com), and an
all-Catalunya office at **Passeig de Gràcia** 107 (Mon–Sat 10:00–
19:00, Sun 10:00–13:00, tel. 93-238-4000). Pick up the large city
map, brochure on public transport, and the free quarterly "See
Barcelona" guide with practical information on museum hours,
restaurants, transportation, history, festivals, and so on.

Arrival in Barcelona

By Train: Although many international trains use the França Station, all domestic (and some international) trains use Sants Station.
Both França and Sants have baggage lockers and subway stations:
França's is "Barceloneta" (2 blocks away), and Sants' is "Sants
Estacio" (under the station). Sants Station has a good TI, a world
of handy shops and eateries, and a classy, quiet "Sala Euromed"
lounge for travelers with first-class reservations (TV, free drinks,
study tables, and coffee bar). Subway or taxi to your hotel. Most
trains to/from France stop at the subway station Passeig de Gràcia,
just a short walk from the center (Plaça de Catalunya, TI, hotels).

    By Plane: Barcelona's El Prat de Llobregat Airport is 12 kilo-
meters southwest of town and connected cheaply and quickly by
Aerobus (immediately in front of arrivals lobby, 4/hr until 24:00,
20 min to Plaça de Catalunya, buy €3.25 ticket from driver, tel.
93-412-0000) or by RENFE train (walk the tunnel overpass from
airport to station, 2/hr at :13 and :43, 20 min to Sants Station and
Plaça de Catalunya, €2). A taxi to or from the airport costs under
€18. The airport has a post office, pharmacy, left luggage, and
ATMs (far-left end of arrival hall as you face the street). Airport
info: tel. 93-298-3838.

Getting around Barcelona

Subway: Barcelona's Metro, among Europe's best, connects just
about every place you'll visit. It has five color-coded lines (L1 is
red, L2 is lilac, L3 is green, L4 is yellow, L5 is blue). Rides cost
€1. The new T-10 Card for €5.30 gives you 10 tickets good for
all local bus and Metro lines as well as the separate FGC line and
RENFE train lines. Pick up the TI's guide to public transport.
One-, two-, and five-day passes are available.

    Hop-on hop-off bus: The handy Tourist Bus (*Bus Turistic*)
offers two multi-stop circuits in colorful double-decker buses
(red route covers north Barcelona—most Gaudí sights; blue route
covers south—Barri Gótic, Montjuïc) with multilingual guides
(April–Dec 9:00–21:30, buses run every 10–20 min, buy tickets on

bus). Ask for a brochure at the TI. One-day (€13.25) and two-day (€16.75) tickets include discounts on the city's major sights.

Taxis: Barcelona is one of Europe's best taxi towns. Taxis are plentiful and honest (€1.90 drop charge, €0.70/km, extras posted in window). Save time by hopping a cab (Ramblas to Sants Station—€3.60, luggage—€0.60/piece).

Helpful Hints

Theft Alert: You're more likely to be pickpocketed here—especially on the Ramblas—than about anywhere else in Europe. Most of the crime is non-violent, but muggings do occur. Be on guard. Leave valuables in your hotel, and wear a money belt.

Here are a few common street scams, easy to avoid if you recognize them. Most common is the too-friendly local who tries to engage you in conversation by asking for the time, whether you speak English, and so on. If you suspect the person is more interested in your money than your time, ignore him and move on. A common street gambling scam is the pea-and-carrot game, a variation on the shell game. The people winning are all ringers and you can be sure that you'll lose if you play. Also beware of groups of women aggressively selling carnations, people offering to clean off a stain from your shirt, and people picking things up in front of you on escalators. If you stop for any commotion or show on the Ramblas, put your hands in your pockets before someone else does.

American Express: AmEx offices are at Passeig de Gràcia 101 (Mon–Fri 9:30–18:00, Sat 10:00–12:00, Metro: Diagonal, tel. 93-415-2371) and at La Ramblas 74 opposite the Liceu Metro station (daily 9:00–24:00, tel. 93-301-1166).

U.S. Consulate: Passeig Reina Elisenda 23 (tel. 93-280-2227).

Emergency Phone Numbers: Police—092, Emergency—061.

Pharmacy: At the corner of Ramblas and Carrer de la Portaferrissa (daily 9:00–22:00, 24-hour info line: tel. 010).

Local Guides: The Barcelona Guide Bureau is a co-op with plenty of excellent local guides who give personalized four-hour tours for €150 (Via Laietana 54, tel. 93-310-7778).

Internet Access: A handy choice among the many Internet cafés is Cybermundo Internet Center, a block off Plaça de Catalunya (Mon–Fri 9:00–24:00, Sat 10:00–24:00, Sun 11:00–24:00, no line likely in morning, Carrer Bergara 3, tel. 93-317-7142).

Introductory Walk: From Plaça de Catalunya down the Ramblas

A ▲▲▲ sight, Barcelona's central square and main drag exert a powerful pull as many visitors spend a major part of their time here doing laps on the Ramblas. Here's an orientation walk:

Plaça de Catalunya—This vast central square—littered with statues of Catalan heroes—divides old and new Barcelona and is the

"You're not in Spain, You're in Catalunya!"

This is a popular pro-nationalist refrain you might see on T-shirts or stickers around town. Catalunya is *not* the land of bullfighting and flamenco that many visitors envision when they think of Spain (best to wait until you're in Madrid or Sevilla for those).

The region of Catalunya—with Barcelona as its capital—has its own language, history, and culture, and the people have a proud independent spirit. Historically, Catalunya has often been at odds with the central Spanish government in Madrid. The Catalan language and culture have been repressed or outlawed at various times in Spanish history, most recently during the Franco Era. Three of Barcelona's monuments are reminders of that suppression: The Parc de la Ciutadella was originally a much-despised military citadel, constructed in the 18th century to keep locals in line. The Castle of Montjuïc, built for similar reasons, has been the site of numerous political executions, including hundreds during the Franco Era. The Sacred Heart Church atop Tibidabo, completed under Franco, was meant to atone for the sins of Barcelonans during the Spanish Civil War—the main sin being opposition to Franco. Although rivalry between Barcelona and Madrid has calmed down in recent times, it rages any time the football clubs from both cities meet.

To see real Catalan culture, look for the Sardana dance (mentioned in "Sights" below) or an exhibition of Castellers. These teams of human castle builders come together for festivals

hub for the Metro, bus, airport shuttle, and both hop-on and hop-off buses (red/northern route leaves from El Corte Inglés, blue/southern route from west side of Plaça). The grass around its fountain is the best public place in town for serious necking. Overlooking the square, the huge El Corte Inglés department store offers everything from bonsai trees to a travel agency, plus one-hour photo developing, haircuts, and cheap souvenirs (Mon–Sat 10:00–22:00, closed Sun, supermarket in basement, 9th-floor terrace cafeteria with great city view—take elevator from near entrance, tel. 93-306-3800). Four great boulevards start from Plaça de Catalunya: the Ramblas, the fashionable Passeig de Gràcia, the cozier but still fashionable Rambla Catalunya, and the stubby, shop-filled, pedestrian-only Portal de L'Angel. Home-sick Americans even have a Hard Rock Café. Locals traditionally start or end a downtown rendezvous at the venerable Café Zurich (cross street from café to reach . . .).

throughout the year to build towers that can reach over 15 meters (50 feet) high, topped off by the bravest member of the team—a child! The Gràcia festival in August and the Mercè festival in September are good times to catch the Castellers.

The Catalan language is irrevocably tied to the history and spirit of the people here. Since the end of the Franco Era in the mid-1970s, the language has made a huge resurgence. Now most school-aged children learn Catalan first and Spanish second. Although Spanish is understood here (and the basic survival words are the same), Barcelona speaks Catalan. Here are the essential Catalan phrases:

Hello	*Hola*	(OH-lah)
Please	*Si us plau*	(see oos plow)
Thank you	*Gracies*	(GRAH-see-es)
Goodbye	*Adeu*	(ah-DAY-oo)
Exit	*Sordida*	(sor-DEE-dah)
Long live Catalunya!	*Visca Catalunya!*	(BEE-skah...)

Most place-names in this chapter are listed in Catalan. Here is a pronunciation guide:

Barcelona	barth-ah-LOH-nah
Plaça de Catalunya	PLAS-sah duh cat-ah-LOON-yah
Eixample	eye-SHAM-plah
Passeig de Gràcia	PAH-sage duh grass-EE-ah
Catedral	CAH-tah-dral
Barri Gòtic	BAH-rrree GAH-teek
Montjuïc	MOHN-jew-eek

Ramblas Walk Stop #1: The top of the Ramblas—Begin your ramble 20 meters down at the ornate fountain (near #129). Grab a chair—a man will collect €0.30—and observe.

More than a Champs-Élysées, this grand boulevard takes you from rich at the top to rough at the port in a 1.5-kilometer, 20-minute walk. You'll raft the river of Barcelonan life past a grand opera house, elegant cafés, plain prostitutes, pickpockets, con men, artists, street mimes, an outdoor bird market, great shopping, and people looking to charge more for a shoeshine than you paid for the shoes. When Hans Christian Andersen saw this street he wrote there's no doubt Barcelona is a great city.

Rambla means "stream" in Arabic. The Ramblas used to be a drainage ditch along the medieval wall that once defined what's now called the Gothic Quarter. The boulevard consists of five separately named segments, but address numbers treat it as a single long street.

From Plaça de Catalunya down the Ramblas

Open up your map and read some history into it: You're about to walk right across medieval Barcelona from Plaça de Catalunya to the harbor. Notice how the higgledy-piggledy street plan of the medieval town was contained within the old town walls—now gone but traced by a series of roads named Ronda (meaning "to go around"). The five-pronged lampposts—midway down the Ramblas—mark where the gateways to the old city used to be. Find the Roman town, occupying about 10 percent of what became the medieval town—with tighter roads yet around the cathedral. The sprawling modern grid plan beyond the Ronda roads is from the 19th century. Breaks in this urban waffle show where a little town was consumed by the growing city. The popular Passeig de Gràcia boulevard was literally the road to Gràcia (once a town, now a characteristic Barcelona neighborhood).

"Las Ramblas" is plural, a succession of streets. You're at Rambla Canaletes, named for the fountain. The black-and-gold Fountain of Canaletes is the beginning point for celebrations and demonstrations. Legend says that one drink from the fountain ensures that you'll return to Barcelona one day. (Take a gulp!) All along the Ramblas you'll see newspaper stands (open 24 hours, selling phone cards) and ONCE booths (selling lottery tickets which support Spain's organization of the blind, a powerful advocate for the needs of disabled people).

Got some change? As you wander downhill, drop coins into the cans of the human statues (the money often kicks them into entertaining gear). Warning: Wherever people stop to gawk, pickpockets are at work.

Walk 100 meters downhill to #115 and...

Ramblas Walk Stop #2: Rambla of the Little Birds—Traditionally kids bring their parents here to buy pets, especially on Sundays. Apartment-dwellers find birds, turtles, and fish easier to handle than dogs and cats. Balconies with flowers are generally living spaces, those with air-conditioning are generally offices. The Academy of Science's clock (at #115) marks official Barcelona time—synchronize. The Champion supermarket (at #113) has cheap groceries and a handy deli with cooked food to go. A newly-discovered Roman necropolis is in a park across the street, 50 meters behind the big modern Citadines Hotel (go through the passageway at #122). Local apartment-dwellers blew the whistle on contractors who hoped they could finish their building before anyone noticed the antiquities they had unearthed. Imagine the tomb-lined road leading into the Roman city of Barcino 2,000 years ago.

Another hundred meters takes you to Carrer del Carme (at #2), and...

Ramblas Walk Stop #3: Baroque Church—The big plain church lining the boulevard is Baroque, rare in Barcelona. While Barcelona's Gothic age was rich (with buildings to prove it), the

Baroque age hardly left a mark (the city's importance dropped when New World discoveries shifted lucrative trade to ports on the Atlantic). The Bagues jewelry shop across Carrer del Carme from the church is known for its Art Nouveau jewelry (from the molds of Masriera, displayed in the window). At the shop's side entrance, step on the old-fashioned scales (free, in kilos) and head down the lane opposite (behind the church, 30 meters) to a place expert in making you heavier. Café Granja Viader (see "Eating," below) has specialized in baked and dairy delights since 1870.

Stroll through the Ramblas of Flowers to the subway stop marked by the red M (near #100), and...

Ramblas Walk Stop #4: La Boqueria—This lively produce market is an explosion of chicken legs, bags of live snails, stiff fish, delicious oranges, and sleeping dogs (#91, Mon–Sat 8:00–20:00, best mornings after 9:00, closed Sun). The Conserves shop sells 25 kinds of olives (straight in, near back on right, 100-gram minimum, €0.20–0.40). Full legs of ham (*jamón serrano*) abound; *Paleta Iberica de Bellota* are best and cost about €120 each. Beware: *Huevos de toro* are bull testicles—surprisingly inexpensive...but oh so good. Drop by Mario and Alex's Café Central for an *espresso con leche* (far end of main aisle on left) or breakfast. Ask for Mario's "breakfast special" (potato omelet with whatever's fresh). For lunch and dinner options, try La Garduña, located at the back of the market (See "Eating," below).

The Museum of Erotica (€7.20, daily 10:00–24:00, shorter hours in winter, across from market at #96) is your standard European sex museum—neat if you like nudes and a chance to hear phone sex in four languages.

At #100, Gimeno sells cigars (appreciate the dying art of cigar boxes). Go ahead...buy a Cuban cigar (singles from €0.60). Tobacco shops sell stamps.

Farther down the Ramblas at #83, the Art Nouveau Escriba Café—an ornate world of pastries, little sandwiches, and fine coffee—still looks like it did on opening day in 1906 (daily 8:30–21:00, indoor/outdoor seating, tel. 93-301-6027).

A much-trod-upon mosaic created by noted abstract artist Joan Miró marks the midpoint of the Ramblas. From here, walk down to the Liceu Opera House (reopened after a 1994 fire, tickets on sale Mon–Fri 14:00–20:30, tel. 90-233-2211; tours in English Mon–Fri 9:30–11:00, reserve in advance, tel. 93-485-9900). From the Opera House, cross the Ramblas to Café de l'Opera for a beverage (#74, tel. 93-317-7585). This bustling café, with modernist decor and a historic atmosphere, boasts it's been open since 1929, even during the Spanish Civil War. Continue to #46; turn left down an arcaded lane to a square filled with palm trees...

Ramblas Walk Stop #5: Plaça Reial—This elegant neoclassical square comes complete with old-fashioned taverns, modern bars with patio seating, a Sunday coin and stamp market (10:00–14:00), Gaudi's first public works (the 2 helmeted lampposts), and characters who don't need the palm trees to be shady. Herbolari Ferran is a fine and aromatic shop of herbs, with fun souvenirs such as top-quality saffron or *safra* (Mon–Sat 9:30–14:00, 16:30–20:00, closed Sun, downstairs at Plaça Reial 18). The small streets stretching toward the water from the square are intriguing, seedy, and dangerous.

Back across the Ramblas, the **Palau Güell** offers an enjoyable look at a Gaudí interior (€2.40, usually open Mon–Sat 10:00–13:00, 16:00–19:00, Carrer Nou de la Rambla 3–5, tel. 93-317-3974). If you'll see Casa Milà, skip the climb to this rooftop.

Farther downhill, on the right-hand side, is…

Ramblas Walk Stop #6: Chinatown—This is the world's only Chinatown with nothing even remotely Chinese in or near it. Named for the prejudiced notion that Chinese immigrants go hand in hand with poverty, prostitution, and drug dealing, the actual inhabitants are poor Spanish, Arab, and Gypsy people. At night the Barri Xines features prostitutes, many of them transvestites, who cater to sailors wandering up from the port. A nighttime visit gets you a street-corner massage—look out.

During the day, the bottom of the Ramblas is crowded with commercial artists selling their wares—look hard to find something original, or get a personal portrait. On weekends and holidays, look for the Nova Artesania arts-and-crafts market at the very bottom. This is your chance to buy jewelry and artwork directly from locals. At the bottom of the Ramblas is the Columbus Monument.

Or, from the Drassanes Metro stop, you can take a quick detour to the Fairy Forest pub (El Bosc de les Fades). To get there, cross the Ramblas on the left, walk through Pasatge de la Banca toward the Wax Museum (Museu de Cera), and turn right. This pub lives up to its name, decorated with elaborate Brothers' Grimm–style trees, elves, and waterfalls. Stop here for a drink or just a peek (Sun–Thu 10:30–24:00, Sat–Sun 10:30–24:00, Pasatge de la Banca, tel. 93-317-2649). Walk out the other end of the passageway and you'll see your next stop, the Columbus Monument.

Ramblas Sights at the Harbor

Columbus Monument (Monument a Colóm)—Marking the point where the Ramblas hits the harbor, this 50-meter-tall monument built for an 1888 exposition offers an elevator-assisted view from its top (€1.80, daily 9:00–20:30, off-season 10:00–13:30, 15:30–19:30, the harbor cable car offers a better—if less handy—view). It's interesting that Barcelona would so honor the man whose discoveries ultimately led to its downfall as a great trading power. It was here in Barcelona that Ferdinand and Isabel welcomed Columbus home after his first trip to America.

Maritime Museum (Museo Maritim)—This museum—housed in the old royal shipyards—covers the salty history of ships and navigation from the 13th to 20th centuries, showing off the Catalan role in the development of maritime technology (e.g., the first submarine is claimed to be Catalan). With fleets of seemingly unimportant replicas of old boats explained in Catalan and Spanish, landlubbers may find it dull—but the free audioguide livens it up for sailors (€5.40, daily 10:00–19:00, closed Mon off-season). For just €0.60 more, visit the old-fashioned sailing ship *Santa Eulàlia*, docked in the harbor across the street.

Golondrinas—Little tourist boats at the foot of the Columbus Monument offer 30-minute harbor tours (€3.20, daily 11:00–20:00). A glass-bottom catamaran makes longer tours up the coast (€8 for 75 min, 4/day, daily 11:30–18:30.) For a picnic place, consider one of these rides or the harbor steps.

La Rambla de Mar—This "Rambla of the Sea" is a modern extension of the boulevard into the harbor. A popular wooden pedestrian bridge—with waves like the sea—leads to Maremagnum, a soulless Spanish mall with a cinema, huge aquarium, restaurants, and piles of people out for the night.

Sights—Gothic Quarter (Barri Gòtic)

The Barri Gòtic is a bustling world of shops, bars, and nightlife packed between hard-to-be-thrilled-about 14th- and 15th-century buildings. The area around the port is seedy. But the area around the cathedral is a tangled yet inviting grab bag of undiscovered courtyards, grand squares, schoolyards, Art Nouveau storefronts, baby flea markets, musty junk shops, classy antique shops, street musicians strumming Catalan folk songs, and balconies with domestic jungles behind wrought-iron bars. Go on a cultural scavenger hunt. Write a poem.

▲**Cathedral**—As you stand in the square facing the cathedral, you're facing what was Roman Barcelona. To your right, letters spell out BARCINO—the city's Roman name. The three towers on the building to the right are mostly Roman (wander inside for good Roman Wall views).

The colossal **cathedral**, started in about 1300, took 600 years to complete. Rather than stretching toward heaven, it makes a point to be simply massive (similar to the Gothic churches of Italy). The west front, while built according to the original plan, is only 100 years old (cathedral: daily 8:00–13:30, 17:00–19:30; cloisters: daily 9:00–13:00, 17:00–19:00; tel. 93-315-1554).

The spacious interior—characteristic of Catalan Gothic—was supported by buttresses. These provided walls for 28 richly ornamented chapels. While the main part of the church is fairly plain, the chapels—sponsored by local guilds—show great wealth. Located in the community's most high-profile space, they provided

Barcelona's Gothic Quarter

❶	Hotel Catalonia Albinoni	⓭	Quatre Gats
❷	Hotel Catalunya Plaza	⓮	Meson Castilla
❸	Hotel Barcelona	⓯	La Dolca Herminia
❹	Nouvel Hotel	⓰	Restaurante Agut
❺	Hotel Toledano, Capitol & Cont.	⓱	Rest. Egipte
❻	Hotel Lloret	⓲	Self Naturista
❼	Hotel Jardi	⓳	Bio Center
❽	Hotel Condes Barcelona	⓴	Citadines Ramblas Aparthotel
❾	Hotel Regente	㉑	La Taverneta
❿	Hotel Duques Bergara	㉒	Cafe Granja Viader
⓫	Hosteria Grau	㉓	La Fonda
⓬	Taverna Basca Irati	㉔	Tapas Street

a kind of advertising to illiterate worshipers. Find logos and symbols of the various trades represented. The Indians Columbus brought to town were supposedly baptized in the first chapel on the left.

The **chapels** ring a finely carved 15th-century choir (*coro*). Pay €0.90 for a close-up look (with the lights on) at the ornately carved stalls and the emblems representing the various Knights of the Golden Fleece who once sat here. The chairs were folded up, giving VIPs stools to lean on during the standing parts of the Mass. Each was creatively carved and—since you couldn't sit on sacred things—the artists were free to enjoy some secular fun here. Study the upper tier of carvings.

The **high altar** sits upon the tomb of Barcelona's patron saint, Eulàlia. She was a 13-year-old local girl tortured 13 times by Romans for her faith and finally crucified on an X-shaped cross. Her X symbol is carved on the pews.

Ride the **elevator** to the roof and climb a tight spiral staircase up the spire for a commanding view (€1.40, Mon–Fri 10:30–12:30, 16:30–18:00, start from chapel left of high altar).

Enter the **cloister** (through arch, right of high altar). In the cloister, look back at the arch, an impressive mix of Romanesque and Gothic. A tiny statue of St. George slaying the dragon stands in the garden. Jordi (George) is one of the patron saints of Catalunya and by far the most popular boy's name here. While cloisters are generally found in monasteries, this church added it to accommodate more chapels—good for business. Again, notice the symbols of the trades or guilds. Even the pavement is filled with symbols—similar to Americans getting their name on a brick for helping to pay for something.

Long ago the resident geese—there are always 13 in memory of Eulàlia—functioned as an alarm system. Any commotion would get them honking, alerting the monk in charge.

From St. Jordi, circle to the right (past a WC). The skippable little €0.60 **museum** (far corner) is one plush room with a dozen old religious paintings. In the corner the dark, barrel-vaulted Romanesque Chapel of Santa Lucia was a small church predating the cathedral and built into the cloister. The candles outside were left by people hoping for good eyesight (Santa Lucia's specialty). Farther along, the Chapel of Santa Rita (in charge of impossible causes) usually has the most candles. Complete the circle and exit at the door just before the place you entered.

Walk uphill, following the church. From the end of the apse turn right 50 meters up Carrer del Paradis to the **Roman Temple** (Temple Roma d' August). In the corner a sign above a millstone in the pavement marks "Mont Tabor, 16.9 meters." Step into the courtyard for a peek at a surviving corner of the imposing temple which once stood here on the city's highest hill, keeping a protective watch over Barcino (free, daily 10:00–14:00, 16:00–20:00).

Barcelona's Cathedral

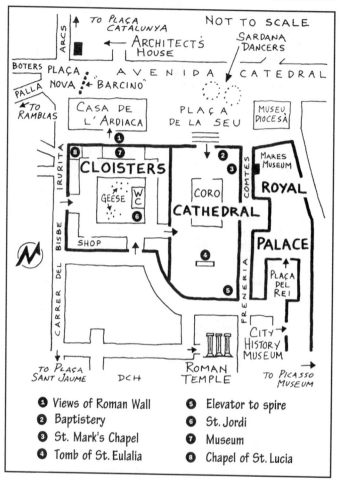

TO PLAÇA CATALUNYA
NOT TO SCALE
ARCHITECT'S HOUSE
SARDANA DANCERS
ARCS
BOTERS PLAÇA
NOVA "BARCINO"
AVENIDA CATEDRAL
PALLA
TO RAMBLAS
CASA DE L'ARDIACA
PLAÇA DE LA SEU
MUSEU DIOCESÀ
❶
❽ ❼
CLOISTERS
GEESE WC
❻
❷
❸
COMTES
MARES MUSEUM
ROYAL
CORO
CATHEDRAL
SHOP
IRURITA
BISBE
CARRER DEL BISBE
❹
❺
FRENERIA
PALACE
PLAÇA DEL REI
CITY HISTORY MUSEUM
TO PLAÇA SANT JAUME
DCH
ROMAN TEMPLE
TO PICASSO MUSEUM

❶ Views of Roman Wall
❷ Baptistery
❸ St. Mark's Chapel
❹ Tomb of St. Eulalia
❺ Elevator to spire
❻ St. Jordi
❼ Museum
❽ Chapel of St. Lucia

Plaza del Rei—The Royal Palace sat on King's Square (a block from the cathedral) until Catalunya became part of Spain in the 15th century. Then it was the headquarters of the local inquisition. Columbus came here to show King Ferdinand his souvenirs from what he thought was India.

▲**City History Museum**—After a multimedia presentation on the history of the city, take an elevator down 20 meters (and 2,000 years) to walk the streets of Roman Barcelona. You'll see sewers, models of domestic life, and bits of an early Christian church. Nearly nothing remains of the Royal Palace (€4.80 includes museum, presentation, and visits to Pedralbes Monastery and Verdaguer House Museum, see museum pamphlet for details; Tue–Sat 10:00–14:00, 16:00–20:00, Sun 10:00–14:00, closed Mon, Plaça del Rei, tel. 93-315-1111).

Frederic Mares Museum—This classy collection combines medieval religious art with a quirky bundle of more modern artifacts—old pipes, pinups, toys, and so on (Tue–Sun 10:00–15:00, closed Mon, Carrer del Comtes, off Plaça de la Seu, next to cathedral).

▲**Sardana Dances**—The patriotic Sardana dances are held at the cathedral (often at 18:00 and most Sun at 12:00) and at Plaça de Sant Jaume (often on Sun at 18:00 in spring and summer, 18:30 in fall and winter). Locals of all ages seem to spontaneously appear. They gather in circles after putting their things in the center—symbolic of community and sharing (and the ever-present risk of theft). Then they raise and hold hands as they hop and sway gracefully to the band. The band (*cobla*) consists of a long flute, tenor and soprano oboes, strange-looking brass instruments, and a tiny bongolike drum (*tambori*). The rest of Spain mocks this lazy circle dance, but it is a stirring display of local pride and patriotism.

Shoe Museum (Museu del Calçat)—Shoe-lovers enjoy this two-room shoe museum (with a we-try-harder attendant) on the delightful Plaça Sant Felip Neri (€1.20, Tue–Sun 11:00–14:00, closed Mon, 1 block beyond outside door of cathedral cloister, behind Plaça de G. Bachs, tel. 93-301-4533). The huge shoe at the entry is designed to fit the foot of the Columbus Monument at the bottom of the Ramblas.

Plaça de Sant Jaume—On this stately central square of the Gothic Quarter, two of the top governmental buildings in Catalunya face each other: The Barcelona city hall (Ajuntament, free Sun 10:00–13:30) and the seat of the autonomous government of Catalunya (Palau de la Generalitat). Sardana dances take place here many Sundays at 18:00 or 18:30, depending on the season (see "Sardana Dances," above).

▲▲▲**Picasso Museum**—This is the best collection of Picasso's (1881–1973) work in Spain, and the best collection of his early works anywhere. It's scattered through two Gothic palaces, six blocks from the cathedral.

Picasso's personal secretary, Sabartes, amassed a huge collection of his work and bequeathed it to the city. Picasso, happy to have a fine museum showing off his work in the city of his youth, added to the collection throughout his life. (Sadly, since Picasso vowed never to set foot in a fascist Spain, and he died 2 years before Franco, the artist never saw the museum.)

This is a great chance to see Picasso's earliest art and better understand his genius (€4.80, free on first Sun of month, Tue–Sat

10:00–20:00, Sun 10:00–15:00, closed Mon, free and required bag check, Montcada 15–19, Metro: Jaume, tel. 93-319-6310).

There's no English information inside but the art is presented chronologically. If you follow the rooms in numerical order and take this quick room-by-room tour, you can see Picasso's art evolve:

Room 4 (1895): With this earliest art, a budding genius emerges at age 12.

Room 6 (1896): Pablo moves to Barcelona and gets serious about art. The portraits (left as you enter, Padre del Artista) are of Pablo's first teacher, his father. The glass case is filled with what you do at art school. Every time Pablo starts breaking rules, he's sent back to the standard classic style.

Room 9 (1896)—reached through room 4: More school assignments. The goal: Sketch models to capture human anatomy accurately.

Room 10 (1896): On the left you see three self-portraits with a self-awareness of his genius showing in his eyes. The woman (Retrato de la Madre del Artista) is Pablo's mother. Fifteen-year-old Pablo is working on the fine details and gradients of white in her blouse. Pablo was closer to his mom than his dad. Spaniards keep both parents' surnames: Pablo Ruiz Picasso. Eventually he kept just his mom's name.

Room 11: During a short trip to Málaga, Picasso dabbles in Impressionism (unknown in Spain at the time).

Room 12: As a 15-year-old, Pablo does his first big painting for a fine-arts exhibition in Barcelona. While forced to show a religious subject (First Communion), Pablo uses it as an excuse to paint his family.

Room 13: *Science and Charity*, a prize-winning fine-arts exhibition piece, got Picasso the chance to study in Madrid. His little sister (perhaps portrayed in the arms of the nun) had just died. Here for the first time we see Picasso conveying real feeling. The doctor (Pablo's father) represents science. The nun represents charity and religion. But nothing can help and the woman is clearly dead (notice her face and lifeless hand). Pablo painted a little trick: Notice how the bed stretches and shrinks as you walk across the room. Four small studies for this painting hang in the back of the room.

Room 14: Fine-arts school in stuffy Madrid was boring. But Pablo enjoyed hanging out in the Prado Gallery and copying the masters (such as Velázquez's portrait of Phillip IV).

Room 15 (1900): Back in Barcelona, Art Nouveau is the rage. Upsetting his dad, Pablo quits art school and falls in with the avant-garde crowd. These bohemians congregate daily at the Four Cats (slang for "a few crazy people"—see "Eating," below). Picasso declares his artistic freedom by painting portraits of his new friends, and nothing more of his family.

Room 17 (1900): Picasso goes to Paris, a city bursting with life, light, and love.

Room 18: Dropping the surname Ruiz, Pablo establishes his commercial brand name: "Picasso." Here we see the explorer Picasso befriending prostitutes and painting like Toulouse-Lautrec. La Espera (Margot)—with her bold outline and strong gaze—pops out from the Impressionistic background. Painting a dwarf (*La Nana*), Picasso, like Velázquez and Toulouse-Lautrec, sees "the beauty in ugliness."

Room 19 (1902): The bleak weather and poverty Picasso experienced in Paris leads to his "Blue Period." He cranks out piles of blue art just to stay housed and fed. With blue—the coldest color—backgrounds and depressing subjects, this period was revolutionary in art history. Now the artist is painting not what he sees but what he feels.

Room 20 (1902)—across the hall, through two glass doors: Back home in Barcelona, Picasso paints his hometown at night from rooftops (*Terrats de Barcelona*). Still blue, here we see proto-cubism...five years before the first real cubist painting. The woman in pink (*Retrato de la Sra. Canals*), painted with classic "Spanish melancholy," finally lifts Picasso out of his funk, replacing the blue period with the happier pink period (of which this museum has only one painting).

Room 21 (1917): Jumping 15 years, we see Picasso is a painter of many styles. In the age of the camera, the cubist gives just the basics (a man with a bowl of fruit) and lets you finish it. We see a little post-Impressionistic Pointillism and a portrait that looks like a classical statue (inspired by a trip to Rome). The chrome-framed painting of a spool of cable (between the information sheets on the wall) is remarkably realistic. The expressionist horse symbolizes to Spaniards the innocent victim. In bull-fights, the horse—clad with blinders and who is pummeled by the bull—has nothing to do with the fight. Picasso used the horse—guts spilling out near the bull's horn—to show the suffering of war. (This shows up again in his future masterpiece, *Guernica*, which you can see in Madrid.)

Room 22 (1957): Notice the print of Velázquez's *Las Meninas* to the left of the doorway. Picasso, who had great respect for Velázquez, painted 60 interpretations of the painting many consider the greatest painting by anyone ever (it's in Madrid's Prado). In the big black-and-white canvas, Picasso plays with perspectives within the painting. The king and queen (reflected in the mirror in the back of the room) are hardly seen while the self-portrait of the painter towers above everyone. The two women of the court on the right look like they're in a tomb—but they're wearing party shoes. In this room and room 23, see the fun Picasso had playing paddleball with Velázquez's masterpiece.

Rooms 24 and 26 (1957): All his life Picasso said, "Paintings are like windows open to the world." Here we see the French Riviera. As a child, Picasso was forced to paint as an adult. Now, at age 60 (with little kids of his own and an also-childish artist Matisse for a friend), he paints like a child.

To exit, hike up the stairs through rooms 28 to 32 and lots of Picasso etchings and engravings, and out.

Textile and Garment Museum (Museu Textil i de la Indumentaria)—If fabrics from the 4th to 16th centuries leave you cold, have a *café con leche* on the museum's beautiful patio (€2.40, Tue–Sat 10:00–20:00, Sun 10:00–15:00, closed Mon, free entrance to patio, which is outside museum but within the walls, 30 meters from Picasso Museum at Montcada 12–14).

▲▲Catalana Concert Hall (Palau de la Música Catalana)—This concert hall, finished in 1908, features the best modernist interior in town. Inviting arches lead you into the 2,000-seat hall. A kaleidoscopic skylight features a choir singing around the sun while playful carvings and mosaics celebrate music and Catalan culture. Admission is by tour only and starts with a relaxing 20-minute video (€4.20, 1 hr, in English, daily on the hour 10:00–15:00, maybe later, tel. 93-268-1000). Ask about concerts (300 per year, inexpensive tickets).

Sights—Eixample

Uptown Barcelona is a unique variation on the common grid-plan city. Barcelona snipped off the building corners to create light and spacious eight-sided squares at every intersection. Wide sidewalks, hardy shade trees, chic shops, and plenty of Art Nouveau fun make the Eixample a refreshing break from the old town. For the best Eixample example, ramble Rambla Catalunya (unrelated to the more famous Ramblas) and pass through Passeig de Gràcia (described below, Metro: Passeig de Gràcia for Block of Discord or Diagonal for Casa Milà).

The 19th century was a boom time for Barcelona. By 1850 the city was busting out of its medieval walls. A new town was planned to follow a gridlike layout. The intersection of three major thoroughfares—Gran Vía, Diagonal, and Meridiana—would shift the city's focus uptown.

The Eixample, or "Expansion," was a progressive plan in which everything was made accessible to everyone. Each 20-block-square district would have its own hospital and large park, each 10-block-square area would have its own market and general services, and each five-block-square grid would house its own schools and day-care centers. The hollow space found inside each "block" of apartments would form a neighborhood park.

While much of that vision never quite panned out, the Eixample was an urban success. Rich and artsy big shots bought plots along the grid. The richest landowners built as close to the center as possible. For this reason, the best buildings are near the Passeig de Gràcia. Adhering to the height, width, and depth limitations, they built as they pleased—often in the trendy new modernist style.

Sights—Gaudí's Art and Architecture

Barcelona is an architectural scrapbook of the galloping gables and organic curves of hometown boy Antonio Gaudí. A devoted Catalan and Catholic, he immersed himself in each project, often living on-site. He called Parc Güell, La Pedrera, and the Sagrada Familia all home.

▲▲**Sagrada Familia (Sacred Family) Church**—Gaudí's most famous and persistent work is this unfinished landmark. He worked on the church from 1883 to 1926. Since then, construction has moved forward in fits and starts. Even today, the half-finished church is not expected to be completed for another 20 years. One reason it's taking so long is that the temple is funded exclusively by private donations and entry fees. Your admission helps pay for the ongoing construction (€5.10, daily 9:00–20:00, Nov–March 9:00–18:00; €3 extra for tours in English: 4/day April–Oct, 2/day Nov–March; Metro: Sagrada Familia, tel. 93-207-3031. www.sagradafamilia.org).

When the church is finished, 12 100-meter spires (representing the apostles) will stand in groups of four and mark the three ends of the building. The center tower (honoring Jesus), reaching 170 meters up, will be flanked by 125-meter-tall towers of Mary and the four evangelists. A unique exterior ambulatory will circle the building like a cloister turned inside out.

The nativity facade really shows the vision of Gaudí. It was finished in 1904, before Gaudí's death, and shows scenes from the birth and childhood of Jesus along with angels playing musical instruments. (Because of ongoing construction, you may need to access this area—opposite the entrance, viewed from outside—by walking through the museum. Don't miss it.)

The little on-site **museum** displays physical models used for the church's construction. Gaudí lived on the site for more than a decade and is buried in the crypt. When he died in 1926, only the stubs of four spires stood above the building site. Judge for yourself how the recently-completed and controversial Passion facade by Josep Maria Subirachs fits in with Gaudí's original formulation.

With the cranking cranes, rusty forests of rebar, and scaffolding requiring a powerful faith, the Sagrada Familia Church offers a fun look at a living, growing, bigger-than-life building. Take the lift on the Passion side (€1.20) or the stairs on the Nativity side (free but often miserably congested) up to the dizzy lookout bridging two spires. You'll get a great view of the city and a gargoyle's-eye

Gaudí & Moderniste Sights

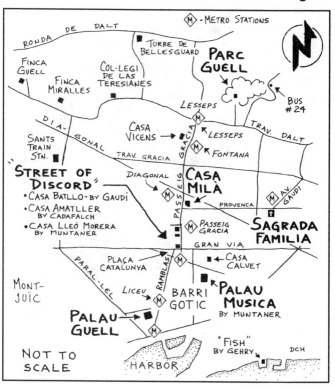

perspective of the loopy church. If there's any building on earth I'd like to see, it's the Sagrada Familia... finished.

▲**Palau Güell**—This is a good chance to enjoy a Gaudí interior (see "Introductory Tour," above). Curvy.

▲▲**Casa Milà (La Pedrera)**—This Gaudí exterior laughs down on the crowds filling Passeig de Gràcia. Casa Milà, also called La Pedrera (the Quarry), has a much-photographed roller coaster of melting-ice-cream eaves. This is Barcelona's quintessential modernist building.

Visits come in three parts: apartment, attic, and rooftop. Buy the €6 ticket to see all three. Starting with the apartment, an elevator whisks you to the *Life in Barcelona 1905–1929* exhibit (well-described in English). Then you walk through a sumptuously furnished Art Nouveau apartment. Upstairs in the attic, wander under brick arches—enjoying a multimedia exhibit of models, photos, and videos of Gaudí's works. From there a stairway leads

Modernisme

The Renaixensa (Catalan cultural revival) gave birth to Modernisme (Catalan Art Nouveau) at the end of the 19th century. Barcelona is its capital. Its Eixample neighborhood shimmers with the colorful, leafy, flowing, blooming shapes of Modernisme in doorways, entrances, facades, and ceilings. Meaning "a taste for what is modern," this free-flowing organic style lasted from 1888 to 1906. Breaking with tradition, artists experimented with glass, tile, iron, and brick. Decoration became structural. It comes with three influences: nature, exotic (e.g., Chinese), and a fanciful Gothic twist to celebrate Catalan's medieval glory days. It was a way of life as Barcelona burst into the 20th century.

Antoni Gaudí is the most famous modernist artist. From four generations of metalworkers, a lineage of which he was quite proud, he incorporated his ironwork into his architecture and came up with novel approaches to architectural structure and space.

The year 2002 is "International Gaudi Year," marking the 150th anniversary of Gaudí's birth. Barcelona celebrates with exhibitions, "Gaudinian" festivals, and more (tel. 93-316-1000, www.gaudi2002.bcn.es).

Two more modernist architects famous for their unique style are Lluís Domènech i Muntaner and Josep Puig i Cadafalch. You'll see their work on "The Block of Discord."

to the fanciful rooftop where chimneys play volleyball with the clouds. From here, you can see Gaudí's other principal works, the Sagrada Familia, Casa Batllo, and Parc Güell (daily 10:00–20:00; free tours in English Mon–Fri at 17:30, Sat–Sun and holidays at 11:00; Passeig de Gràcia 92, Metro: Diagonal, tel. 93-484-5995). At the ground level of Casa Milà is the original entrance courtyard for the Fundacio Caixa de Catalunya, dreamily painted in pastels (free). The first floor hosts free art exhibits. During the summer, a concert series called "Pedrera by Night" features jazz, flamenco, tango, or other classy live music, a glass of champagne, and the chance to see the rooftop illuminated (€9, July–Sept Fri–Sat at 22:00, tel. 93-484-5900).

▲The Block of Discord—Four blocks from Casa Milà you can survey a noisy block of competing early-19th-century facades. Several of Barcelona's top modernist mansions line Passeig de Gràcia (Metro: Passeig de Gràcia). Because the structures look as though they are trying to outdo each other in creative twists, locals nicknamed the block between Consell de Cent and Arago, "The Block of Discord." First (at #43) and most famous is Gaudí's Casa Batlló, with skull-like balconies and a tile roof that suggests a cresting dragon's back (Gaudí based the work on the popular St. Jordi-slays-the-dragon legend). By the way, if you're tempted to frame your photos from the middle of the street, be careful—Gaudí died under a streetcar.

Next door, at Casa Amatller (#41, desk sells Modernist Route combo tickets), check out architect Puig i Cadafalch's creative mix of Moorish and Gothic and iron grillwork. At the desk inside is the only place in town you can purchase Modernist Route combo tickets. For €3.60, you get a 50 percent discount to 10 of the most important modernist sights in Barcelona (valid for 1 month). Even if you only have time to see Sagrada Familia and Casa Milà, you'll save money with this ticket.

On the corner (at #35) is Casa Lleo Morera (by Lluís Dom-ènech i Muntaner, who did the Catalana Concert Hall—you'll see similarities). The perfume shop halfway down the street has a free and interesting little perfume museum in the back. The Hostal de Rita restaurant, just around the corner on Calle Arago, serves a fine three-course lunch for a great price at 13:00 (see "Eating," below).

Park Güell—Gaudí fans find the artist's magic in this colorful park (free, daily 9:00–20:00) and small Gaudí Museum (€2.50, daily 10:00–20:00, closes off-season at 18:00, Metro: Vallcarca but easier by bus #24 from Plaça de Catalunya; €6 by taxi). Gaudí intended this to be a planned garden city rather than a park. As a high-income housing project, it flopped. As a park...even after I reminded myself that Gaudí's work is a careful rhythm of color, shapes, and space, it was disappointing. Still, some find the pan-oramic view of Barcelona worth the trip. Only the hill of Tibidabo offers a better city view (see below).

More Sights—Barcelona

Tibidabo—Tibidabo comes from the Latin for "to thee I shall give," the words the devil used when he was trying to tempt Christ. It's still an enticing offer: At the top of Barcelona's highest peak, you'll find the city's oldest fun-fair, the neo-Gothic Sacred Heart Church, and—if the weather and air quality are good—a near-limitless view of the city and the Mediterranean.

Getting there is part of the fun: Start by taking the FGC line—similar to but separate from the Metro, also covered by the T-10 ticket—from the Plaça Catalunya station (under Café Zurich) to the Tibidabo stop. The red Tourist Bus stops here, too. Then take Barcelona's only remaining tram—the Tramvia Blau—from Plaça John F. Kennedy to Plaça Dr. Andreu (€2.40, 2–4/hr). From there, take the cable car to the top (€2.40, tel. 90-642-7017.)

Ciutadella Park (Parc de la Ciutadella)—Barcelona's biggest, greenest park, originally the site of a much-hated military citadel, was transformed in 1888 for a World's Fair (Universal Exhibition). The stately Triumphal Arch at the top of the park was built as the main entrance. Inside you'll find wide pathways, plenty of trees and grass, the zoo, the Geology and Zoology Museums, and the Modern Art Museum (see below). In Barcelona, which suffers from a lack of real green space, this park is a haven. Enjoy the ornamental fountain that the young Antoni Gaudí helped design, and consider a spin in a rowboat on the lake in the center of the park (€1.20/person for 30 min). Check out the tropical *Umbracle* greenhouse and the *Hivernacle* winter garden, which has a pleasant café-bar (daily 8:00–20:00, Metro: Arc de Triomf, east of França train station).

Modern Art Museum (Museu d'Art Modern)—This manageable museum in Ciutadella Park exhibits Catalan sculpture, painting, glass, and furniture by Gaudí, Casas, Llimona, and more (€3, Tue–Sat 10:00–19:00, Thu until 21:00, Sun 10:00–14:30, closed Mon).

Barcelona's Beach—Take the trek through the charming Barceloneta neighborhood to the tip of this man-made peninsula. The beaches begin here and stretch for four kilometers up the coast to the Olympic Port and beyond. Everything you see here— palm trees, cement walkways, and tons of sand—was installed in the mid-1980s in an effort to shape up the city for the 1992 Olympic Games. The beaches are fine for sunbathing (beach chair rental—€3/day), but the water quality is questionable for swimming. Take a lazy stroll down the seafront promenade to the Olympic Port, where you'll find bars, restaurants, and at night, dance clubs.

Sights—Barcelona's Montjuïc

The Montjuïc (Mount of the Jews), overlooking Barcelona's hazy port, has always been a show-off. Ages ago it had the impressive fortress. In 1929 it hosted an international fair, from which most of today's sights originated. And in 1992 the Summer Olympics directed the world's attention to this pincushion of attractions.

There are many ways to reach Montjuïc: on the blue Tourist Bus route (see "Getting around Barcelona," above); or bus #50 from the corner of Gran Vía and Passeig de Gràcia (€0.90, every 10 min); or subway to Metro: Parallel and catch the funicular (€1.70 one-way, €2.40 round-trip, Mon–Sat 10:45–20:00, closed Sun); or taxi (about €6.60). The first three options leave you at the *teleférico* (cable car), which you can take to the Castle of Montjuïc (€2.90 one-way, €4.10 round-trip, daily 11:00–22:00, less off-season, tel. 93-443-0859). Alternatively, from the same spot, you can walk uphill 20 minutes through the pleasant park. Only a taxi gets you doorstep delivery. From the port, the fastest and most scenic way to Montjuïc is via the 1929 Trasbordador Aereo (at tower in port, ride elevator up to catch dangling gondola, €7.20 round-trip, 4/hr, daily 10:30–19:00, tel. 93-443-0859).

Castle of Montjuïc—This offers great city views and a military museum (€1.20, Tue–Sun 9:30–20:00, closed Mon). The seemingly endless museum houses a dull collection of guns, swords, and toy soldiers. An interesting section on the Spanish-American War covers Spain's valiant fight against American aggression (from its perspective). Unfortunately, there are no English descriptions. Those interested in Jewish history will find a fascinating collection of ninth-century Jewish tombstones. The castle itself has a facist past. It was built in the 18th century by the central Spanish government to keep an eye on Barcelona and stifle citizen revolt. When Franco was in power, the castle was the site of hundreds of political assassinations.

▲**Fountains (Font Magica)**—Music, colored lights, and huge amounts of water make an artistic and coordinated splash on summer nights (Fri–Sun, 20-min shows start on the half-hour, 21:30–24:00, in summer Thu eve, too, from Metro: Plaça Espanya, walk toward towering National Palace).

Spanish Village (Poble Espanyol)—This tacky five-acre model village uses fake traditional architecture from all over Spain as a shell to contain gift shops. Craftspeople do their clichéd thing only in the morning (not worth your time or €5.70). After hours it becomes a popular local nightspot.

▲▲**Catalan Art Museum (Museo Nacional d'Art de Catalunya)**—Often called "the Prado of Romanesque art," this is a rare, world-class collection of Romanesque art taken mostly from remote Catalunyan village churches in the Pyrenees (saved from unscrupulous art dealers—many American).

The Romanesque wing features frescoes, painted wooden altar fronts, and ornate statuary. This classic Romanesque art— with flat 2-D scenes, each saint holding his symbol, and Jesus (easy to identify by the cross in his halo)—is impressively displayed on replicas of the original church ceilings.

In the Gothic wing, fresco murals give way to vivid 14th-century paintings of Bible stories on wood. A roomful of paintings by the Catalan master Jaume Huguet (1412–1492) deserves a close look.

Before you leave, ice skate under the huge dome over to the air-conditioned cafeteria. This was the prime ceremony room and dance hall for the 1929 International Exposition (museum-€4.80, Tue–Sat 10:00–19:00, Thu until 21:00, Sun 10:00–14:30, closed Mon, tel. 93-622-0375). The museum is in the massive National Palace building above the fountains, near Plaça Espanya (Metro: Plaça Espanya, then hike up or ride the bus; the blue Tourist Bus and bus #50 stop close by).

▲**Fundació Joan Miró**—For something more up-to-date, this

museum showcases the modern-art talents of yet another Catalan artist and is considered the best collection of Joan Miró art anywhere. You'll also see works by other modern Spanish artists; don't miss the *Mercury Fountain* by Alexander Calder. This museum leaves those who don't like abstract art scratching their heads (€4.80, July–Sept Tue–Sat 10:00–20:00, Thu until 21:30, Sun 10:00–14:30, closed Mon, Oct–June closes at 19:00 Tue–Sat).

Sleeping in Barcelona
(€1.10 = about $1, country code: 34)
Sleep Code: **S** = Single, **D** = Double/Twin, **T** = Triple, **Q** = Quad, **b** = bathroom, **s** = shower only, **CC** = Credit Cards accepted, **no CC** = Credit Cards not accepted, **SE** = Speaks English, **NSE** = No English.

Book ahead. If necessary, the TI at Plaça de Catalunya has a room-finding service. Barcelona is Spain's most expensive city. Still, it has reasonable rooms. Cheap places are more crowded in summer; fancier business-class places fill up in winter and offer discounts on weekends and in summer. Prices listed do not include the 7 percent tax or breakfast (ranging from simple €3 spreads to €13.25 buffets) unless otherwise noted. While many recommended places are on pedestrian streets, night noise is a problem almost everywhere (especially in cheap places with single-pane windows). For a quiet night, ask for "*tranquilo*" rather than "*con vista.*"

Sleeping in Eixample
For an elegant and boulevardian neighborhood, sleep in Eixample, a 10-minute walk from the Ramblas action.

Hotel Condes de Barcelona, a four-star business hotel in a grand modernist building, rents 183 stylish and spacious rooms with all the comforts (Db-€201, extra bed-€42, CC, air con, smoke-free floor, elevator, Internet access in rooms, Gaudí-pleasing rooftop sun garden with Jacuzzi, intersection of Mallorca and Passeig de Gracia at Passeig de Gracia 73-75, 08008 Barcelona, tel. 93-467-4780, fax 93-467-4781, www.condesdebarcelona.com, e-mail: reservas @condesdebarcelona.com). Note that the hotel has two buildings. One is a 115-year-old modernist hotel (#75) and the other is new. For more charm, ask for a room in the old building when making reservations.

Hotel Regente, another big four-star place, is a notch below Condes de Barcelona but still a fine splurge (80 rooms, Db-€150, less June–Aug, CC, air con, elevator, roof terrace, Rambla Catalunya 76, 08008 Barcelona, tel. 93-487-5989, fax 93-487-3227, e-mail: regente@hoteles-centro-ciudad.es).

Hotel Gran Vía, filling a palatial mansion built in the 1870s, offers Botticelli and chandeliers in the public rooms; a sprawling, peaceful sun garden; and 54 spacious, comfy, air-conditioned rooms. It's an excellent value (Sb-€69, Db-€94 with this book through 2002—only valid with phone or faxed reservations, CC, Internet access, elevator, quiet, Gran Vía de les Corts Catalanes 642, 08007 Barcelona, tel. 93-318-1900, fax 93-318-9997, e-mail: hgranvia@nnhotels.es).

Hotel Residencia Neutral, with a classic Eixample address and 35 basic rooms, is popular with backpackers (tiny Sb-€22.80, Ds-€33, Db-€39, extra bed-€9, CC, elevator, thin walls and some street noise, elegantly located 2 blocks north of Gran Vía at Rambla Catalunya 42, 08007 Barcelona, tel. 93-487-6390, fax 93-487-6848).

Sleeping near Plaça de Catalunya and at the top of the Ramblas
(zip code: 08002 unless otherwise noted)

The first five places are on big but quiet streets within two blocks of Barcelona's exuberant central square. The next are on or near the top of the Ramblas, also just off Plaça de Catalunya. The last is buried in the Gothic Quarter. For location, see map on page 39.

Hotel Duques de Bergara boasts four stars with splashy public spaces, slick marble and hardwood floors, 150 comfortable rooms, and a garden courtyard with a pool a world away from the big-city noise (Sb-€138, Db-€168, extra bed-€18, CC, air con, elevator, a half block off Plaça de Catalunya at Bergara 11, tel. 93-301-5151, fax 93-317-3442, www.hoteles-catalonia.es, e-mail: cataloni@hoteles-catalonia.es).

Hotel Occidental Reding, a five-minute walk west of the Ramblas and Plaça de Catalunya action on a quiet street, keeps business travelers fat and happy with 44 modern rooms (Db-€114, extra bed-€32, CC, air con, elevator, near University Metro stop at Gravina 5, 08001 Barcelona, tel. 93-412-1097, fax 93-268-3482, e-mail: reding@occidental-hoteles.com).

Hotel Catalonia Albinoni (formerly Hotel Allegro) elegantly fills a renovated old palace with wide halls, hardwood floors, and modern rooms with all the comforts. It overlooks a thriving pedestrian boulevard. Front rooms have views. Balcony rooms on the back are quiet and come with sun terraces (Db-€162, extra bed-€18, CC, family rooms, air con, elevator, a block down from Plaça de Catalunya at Portal de l'Angel 17, tel. 93-318-4141, fax 93-301-2631).

Catalunya Plaza, an impersonal business hotel right on the square, has all the air-conditioning and minibar comforts (Sb-€120, Db-€144, includes breakfast, CC, elevator, ask for free nuts and a welcome glass of champagne at the desk, Plaça de Catalunya 7, tel. 93-317-7171, fax 93-317-7855, e-mail: catalunya@city-hotels.es).

Hotel Barcelona is another big, American-style hotel with bright, prefab, and comfy rooms (Sb-€114, Db-€162, Db with terrace-€204, CC, air con, elevator, a block from Plaça de Catalunya at Caspe 1–13, tel. 93-302-5858, fax 93-301-8674, e-mail: hotelbarcelona@husa.es).

Nouvel Hotel, an elegant Victorian-style building on a fine pedestrian street, has royal lounges and 71 comfy rooms (Sb-€79, Db-€120, includes breakfast, manager Gabriel promises 10 percent discount with this book, CC, air con, Carrer de Santa Ana 18, tel. 93-301-8274, fax 93-301-8370).

Hotel Toledano, overlooking the Ramblas, is suitable for backpackers and popular with dust-bunnies. Small, folksy, and borderline dumpy, it's warmly run by Juan Sanz, his son Albert, and trusty Daniel on the nightshift (Sb-€27.50, Db-€47, Tb-€60, Qb-€66, cheaper off-season, CC, not all rooms have air con—request it when you call; Rambla de Canaletas 138, tel. 93-301-0872, fax 93-412-3142, www.hoteltoledano.com, e-mail: toledano @ibernet.com). They run **Hostal Residencia Capitol** one floor above—quiet, plain, cheaper, and also appropriate for backpackers (S-€20.50, D-€32, Ds-€36, cheap 5-bed room).

Hotel Continental has comfortable rooms, double-thick mattresses, and wildly clashing carpets and wallpaper. To celebrate 100 years in the family, José includes a free breakfast and an all-day complimentary coffee bar. Choose a Ramblas-view balcony or quiet back room (Db-€61–84, includes tax, extra bed-€12, special family room, CC, fans in rooms, elevator, Internet access, Ramblas 138, tel. 93-301-2570, fax 93-302-7360, www.hotelcontinental.com, e-mail: ramblas@hotelcontinental.com).

Hotel Lloret is a big, dark, old-world place on the Ramblas with plain neon-lit rooms (Sb-€42, Db-€66, Tb-€78, extra bed-€6, choose a noisy Ramblas balcony or *tranquilo* in the back, CC, air con in summer, elevator dominates stairwell, Rambla de Canaletas 125, tel. 93-317-3366, fax 93-301-9283).

Hosteria Grau is a homey, almost alpine place, family-run with 27 clean and woody rooms just far enough off the Ramblas (S-€27, D-€39, Ds-€45, Db-€51, family suites with 2 bedrooms-€102, €6 extra charged July–Sept, CC, fans, 200 meters up Calle Tallers from the Ramblas at Ramelleres 27, 08001 Barcelona, tel. 93-301-8135, fax 93-317-6825, www.intercom.es/grau, e-mail: hgrau@lix.intercom.es, Monica SE).

Meson Castilla is clean, comfy, and handy, but it's also pricey, a bit sterile, and in all the American guidebooks. It's three blocks off the Ramblas in an appealing university neighborhood (56 rooms, Sb-€75, Db-€96, Tb-€129, Qb apartment-€153, includes buffet breakfast, CC, air con, elevator, Valldoncella 5, 08001 Barcelona, tel. 93-318-2182, fax 93-412-4020, e-mail: hmesoncastilla@teleline.es).

Citadines Ramblas Aparthotel is a clever concept offering apartments by the day in a bright modern building right on the Ramblas. Prices range with the seasonal demand and rooms come in three categories (studio apartment for 2 with sofa bed and kitchenette-€114–150, hotel room for 2 with real bed-€132–144, apartment with real bed and sofa bed for up to 4 people-€171–195, includes tax, CC, laundry, Ramblas 122, tel. 93-270-1111, fax 93-412-7421, e-mail: barca@citadines.com).

Hotel Jardi is a hardworking, clean, and newly-remodeled place on the happiest little square in the Gothic Quarter. Balcony rooms overlooking the peaceful leafy square are most expensive (Sb-€48, Db-€60, extra bed-€9, includes tax, 10 percent off with cash, CC if bill totals at least €90, air con, elevator, halfway between Ramblas and cathedral on Plaça Sant Josep Oriol #1, tel. 93-301-5900, fax 93-318-3664, e-mail: sgs110sa@retemail.es, Albert SE). Rooms with balconies enjoy an almost Parisian ambience and minimal noise.

Humble Places Buried in Gothic Quarter with Youth-Hostel Prices

Pensio Vitoria has loose tile floors and 12 basic rooms, each with a tiny balcony. It's more dumpy than homey, but consider the price (D-€24, Db-€33, cheaper off-season, CC, a block off day-dreamy Plaça dei Pi at Carrer la Palla 8, tel. & fax 93-302-0834).

Hostal Campi—big, quiet, and ramshackle—is a few doors off the Ramblas (D-€36, Db-€42, T-€48, no CC, Canuda 4, tel. & fax 93-301-3545). **Huéspedes Santa Ana** is plain and claustrophobic, with head-to-toe twins (S-€18, D-€36, Db-€48, T-€45, no CC, Carrer de Santa Ana 23, tel. 93-301-2246). **Hostal Residencia Lausanne**, filled with backpackers, has only its location and price going for it (S-€24, D-€36, Ds-€42-45, Db-€51, no CC, TV room, Avenida Portal de l'Angel 24, tel. & fax 93-302-1139, friendly Javier SE). **Hostal Rembrandt** keeps backpackers happy with 26 simple rooms and a good location (S-€21, Sb-€28.25, D-€33, Ds-€36, Db-€40–46, Tb-€66, no CC, Porta-ferrisa 23, tel. & fax 93-318-1011). **Pension Fina**, next to Hostal Rembrandt, offers more cheap sleeps (S-€24, D-€39, Db-€45, no CC, Portaferrissa 11, tel. & fax 93-317-9787).

Eating in Barcelona

Barcelona, the capital of Catalunyan cuisine, offers a tremendous variety of colorful places to eat. Many restaurants are closed in August (or sometimes July), when the owners are on vacation.

Eating near the Ramblas and in the Gothic Quarter

Taverna Basca Irati serves 25 kinds of hot and cold Basque *pintxos* for €0.90 each. These are open-faced sandwiches—like Basque sushi but on bread. Muscle in through the hungry local crowd. Get an empty plate from the waiter, then help yourself. It's a Basque honor system: You'll be charged by the number of toothpicks left on your plate when you're done. Wash it down with *sidra* (apple wine, €0.90) poured from on high to bring out the flavor (Tue–Sat 12:00–15:00, 19:00–23:00, Sun 12:00–15:00, closed Mon, a block off the Ramblas, behind arcade at Calle Cardenal Casanyes 17, near Metro: Liceu, tel. 93-302-3084). **Juicy Jones**, next door, is a tutti-frutti vegetarian place with a hip menu and a stunning array of fresh-squeezed juices (#7, lunch menu-€7, daily 10:00–24:30).

Ria de Vigo III, a nondescript local eatery, is filled with blue-collar workers and cheap, no-nonsense food (open until 21:30, closed Sun, 3 blocks off the Ramblas at Carrer Tallers 69, tel. 93-318-4724).

La Taverneta, an artists' bistro, brags it doesn't cater to tourists. It serves good Catalan food seasoned in the evenings with live music (lunch menu-€7.20, Mon–Sat 13:00–16:30, 19:00–24:00, closed Sun, 2 blocks off the Ramblas near Plaza Villa de Madrid at Pasatge Duque de la Victoria 3, tel. 93-302-6152).

Café Granja Viader is a quaint time trip, family-run since 1870. This feminine place—specializing in baked and dairy delights, toasted sandwiches, and light meals—is ideal for a traditional breakfast (note the "Esmorzars" specials posted). Try a glass of *orxata* (horchata—almond milk, summer only), Llet Mallorquina (Majorca-style milk with cinnamon, lemon, and sugar), or Suis (literally Switzerland, hot chocolate with a snowcap of whipped cream). It's a block off the Ramblas behind El Carme church (Mon 17:00–20:45, Tue–Sat 9:00–13:45, 17:00–20:45, closed Sun, Xucla 4, tel. 93-318-3486).

Egipte offers decent food, indifferent service, and late-19th-century ambience on the Ramblas (daily 13:00–16:00, 20:00–24:00, Ramblas 79, downhill from Boqueria, tel. 93-317-7480). **La Garduña,** located at the back of the La Boqueria market, offers tasty meat and seafood meals made with fresh ingredients bought directly from the market (€8 lunch menus include wine and bread, €10.75 dinner menus don't include wine, Mon–Sat 13:00–16:00, 20:00–24:00, closed Sun, Calle Jerusalem 18, tel. 93-302-4323).

Consider **La Poma** for a good pizza at the top of the Ramblas (Ramblas 117). For focaccia bread and good desserts, try **Buenas Migas** (Plaça Bonsuccés 6, take second right off the Ramblas and go 50 meters, tel. 93-412-1686; another location behind cathedral at Bajada Santa Clara 2, tel. 93-319-1380).

Homesick tourists flock to the **The Bagel Shop**, which offers fresh bagels, brownies, and a rare-in-Barcelona Sunday brunch of pancakes, fried eggs, and bacon (Mon–Sat 9:30–21:30, Sun 11:00–16:00, Calle Canuda 25, tel. 93-302-4161).

For **groceries**, it's El Corte Inglés (Mon–Sat 10:00–22:00, closed Sun, supermarket in basement, Plaça de Catalunya) and Champion Supermarket (Mon–Sat 9:00–22:00, closed Sun, Ramblas 113).

Restaurants in the Gothic Quarter

A chain of three bright, modern restaurants with high-quality traditional cuisine in classy bistro settings with great prices has stormed Barcelona. Each can be crowded so arrive early if you can: **La Fonda** (daily 13:00–15:30, 20:30–23:30, a block from Plaça Reial at Escudellers 10, tel. 93-301-7515), **La Dolca Herminia** (2 blocks toward the Ramblas from Catalan Concert Hall at Magdalenes 27, tel. 93-317-0676), and **Les Quinze Nits** (on trendy La Plaça Reial at #6—you'll see the line, €6.60 lunch menu, tel. 93-317-3075).

Els Quatre Gats, Picasso's hangout, still has a bohemian feel in spite of its tourist crowds. Before the place was founded in 1897, the idea of a café for artists was mocked as a place where only *quatre gats* ("four cats," meaning only crazies) would go (€27 meals, Mon–Sat 8:30–24:00, Sun 17:00–24:00, live piano Mon–Sat from 21:00, Sun from 20:00, CC, Montsio 3, tel. 93-302-4140).

Restaurante Agut, buried deep in the Gothic Quarter four blocks off the harbor, is a fine place for local-style food in a local-style setting (Tue–Sat 21:00–24:00, closed Sun, Mon, and July or Aug, Calle Gignas 16, tel. 93-315-1709).

Vegetarian near Plaça de Catalunya

Self Naturista is a quick, no-stress buffet that will make vegetarians and health-food lovers feel right at home. Others may find a few unidentifiable plates and drinks. The food seems tired—pick what you like and microwave it (Mon–Sat 11:30–22:00, closed Sun, near several recommended hotels, just off the top of Ramblas at Carrer de Santa Ana 11–17).

Bio Center, a Catalan soup-and-salad place popular with local vegetarians, is better but not as handy (Mon–Sat 13:00–17:00, closed Sun, Pintor Fortuny 25, Metro: Catalunya, tel. 93-318-0343). This street has several other good vegetarian places.

Eating in the Eixample

The people-packed boulevards of the Eixample (Passeig de Gràcia and Rambla Catalunya) are lined with appetizing places with breezy outdoor seating. Many trendy and touristic tapas bars offer a cheery welcome and slam out the appetizers.

La Bodegueta is an unbelievably atmospheric below-street-level bodega serving hearty wines and *flautas*—sandwiches made with flute-thin baguettes (Mon–Sat 7:00–24:00, Sun 19:00–24:00, Rambla Catalunya 100, at intersection with Provenza, Metro: Diagonal, tel. 93-215-4894).

El Hostal de Rita is a fresh and dressy little place serving Catalan cuisine near the street of Discord. Their three-course-with-wine lunch (€6.60, Mon–Fri at 13:00) and dinner (€12, daily from 20:30) specials are a great value (Arago 279, tel. 93-487-2376).

The classy **Quasi Queviures** serves upscale tapas, sandwiches, or the whole nine yards—classic food with modern decor (Passeig de Gràcia 24).

El Café de Internet provides an easy way to munch a sandwich while sending e-mail messages to Mom (€1.50/30 min, €2.40/hr Mon–Fri 8:00–22:00, Sat–Sun 16:00–22:00, closed Sun, Gran Vía 656, Metro: Passeig de Gràcia, tel. 93-412-1915, www.cafeinternet.es).

Sandwich Shops

Bright, clean and inexpensive sandwich shops are proudly holding the cultural line against the fast-food invasion hamburgerizing the rest of Europe. You'll find great sandwiches at **Pans & Company** and **Bocatta**, two chains with outlets all over town. Catalan sandwiches are made to order with crunchy French bread. Rather than butter, locals prefer *pa amb tomaquet* (pah ahm too-MAH-kaht), a mix of crushed tomato and olive oil. Study the instructive multilingual menu fliers to understand your options.

Eating near the Harbor in Barceloneta

Barceloneta is a charming beach suburb of the big city. A grid plan of long, narrow, laundry-strewn streets surrounds the central Plaça Poeta Boscan. For an entertaining evening, wander around this corner. Drop by the two places listed here or find your own restaurant (15-min walk or Metro: Barceloneta). During the day a lively produce market fills one end of the square. At night kids play soccer and Ping-Pong.

Cova Fumada is the neighborhood eatery. Josep Maria and his family serve famously fresh fish (Mon–Fri 17:30–20:30, closed July, Carrer del Baluarte 56, on the corner at Carrer Sant Carles, tel. 93-221-4061). Their *sardinas a la plancha* (grilled sardines, €2.10) are fresh and tasty. *Bombas* (potato croquets with pork, €0.90) are the house specialty. It's macho to have it *picante* (spicy with chili sauce); gentler taste buds prefer it *alioli*, with garlic cream. Catalunyan *bruschetta* is *pan tostado* (toast with oil and garlic, €0.80). Wash it down with *vino tinto* (house red wine, €0.50).

At **Bar Electricidad**, Arturo Jordana Barba is the neighborhood source for cheap wine. Drop in. It's €1.10 per liter; the empty plastic water bottles are for takeaway. Try a €0.50 glass of Torroja Tinto, the best local red, or Priorato Dulce, a wonderfully sweet red (Mon–Sat 8:00–13:00, 15:00–19:00, across the square from Cova Fumada, Plaça del Poeta Bosca 61, NSE).

The Olympic Port, a swanky marina district, is lined with harborside restaurants and people enjoying what locals claim is the freshest fish in town (a short taxi ride from the center past Barceloneta).

Tapas on Carrer Merce in the Gothic Quarter

Tapas aren't as popular in Catalunya as they are in the rest of Spain, but Barcelona boasts great *tascas*—colorful local tapas bars. Get small plates (for maximum sampling) by asking for "*tapas*," not "*raciones*."

While trendy uptown places are safer, better lit, and come with English menus and less grease, these places will stain your journal.

From the bottom of the Ramblas (near the Columbus Monument), hike east along Carrer Clave. Then follow the small street that runs along the right side of the church (Carrer Merce), stopping at the *tascas* that look fun.

La Jarra is known for its tender *jamón canario con patatas* (baked ham with salty potatoes). Across the street, **La Pulperia** serves up fried fish. A block down the street, **Tasca El Corral** makes one of the neighborhood's best chorizo *al diablo* (hell sausage), which you sauté yourself. It's great with the regional specialty, *pan con tomate*. Across the street, **La Plata** keeps things wonderfully simple, serving extremely cheap plates of sardines and small glasses of keg wine. **Tascael Corral** serves northern Spain mountain favorites such as *queso de cabrales* (very moldy cheese) with *sidra* (apple wine). Have a chat with the parrot at **Bar la Choza del Sopas**. At the end of Carrer Merce, **Bar Vendimia** serves up tasty clams and mussels. Carrer Ample and Carrer Gignas, the streets paralleling Carrer Merce inland, have more refined barhopping possibilities.

Transportation Connections—Barcelona

By train to: Lisbon (1/day, 17 hrs with change in Madrid, €107), **Madrid** (7/day, 7–9 hrs, €31–41), **Paris** (3/day, 11–15 hrs, €72–102, night train, reservation required), **Sevilla** (3/day, 11 hrs, €38), **Granada** (2/day, 12 hrs, €46), **Málaga** (2/day, 14 hrs, €39), **Nice** (1/day, 12 hrs, €58, change in Cerbère), **Avignon** (5/day, 6–9 hrs, €38). Train info: tel. 90-224-0202.

By bus to: Madrid (12/day, 8 hrs, half the price of a train ticket, departs from station Barcelona Nord at Metro: Marina).

By plane: To avoid 10-hour train trips, check the reasonable flights from Barcelona to Sevilla or Madrid. Iberia Air (tel. 93-412-5667) and Air Europe (tel. 90-224-0042) offer $80 flights to Madrid. Airport info: tel. 93-298-3838.

NEAR BARCELONA: FIGUERES, CADAQUES, SITGES, AND MONTSERRAT

Four fine sights are day-trip temptations from Barcelona. For the ultimate in surrealism and a classy but sleepy port-town getaway, consider a day or two in Cadaques with a stop at the Dalí Museum in Figueres. Figueres is an hour from Cadaques and two hours from Barcelona. For the consummate day at the beach, head 45 minutes south to the charming and popular resort town, Sitges. Pilgrims with hiking boots head an hour into the mountains for the most sacred spot in Catalunya—Montserrat.

Figueres

▲▲▲**Dalí Museum**—This is the essential Dalí sight. Inaugurated
in 1974, the museum is a work of art in itself. Dalí personally
conceptualized, designed, decorated, and painted it, intending to
showcase his life's work. Highlights include the epic Palace of the
Wind ceiling, the larger-than-life Mae West room (complete with
fireplaces for nostrils), fun mechanical interactive art (Dalí was
into action; bring lots of coins), and the famous squint-to-see
Abraham Lincoln. Other major and fantastic works include the
tiny *Le Spectre Du Sex-Appeal*, *Soft Self Portrait*, and the red-shoe
riddle of *Zapato y Vaso de Leche*. The only real historical context
provided is on the easy-to-miss and unlabeled earphone info
boxes in the Mae West room. A bizarre video (near the exit)
shows every half hour. While not in English, it's plenty entertaining (€7.20, daily 9:00–19:45, off-season daily 10:30–17:45, last
entry 45 min before closing, free bag check has your bag waiting
for you at the exit, tel. 97-267-7500). Dalí, who was born in
Figueres in 1905, is buried in the museum. From the train station,
follow "Museu Dalí" signs to the museum.

Connections: Figueres is an easy daytrip from Barcelona or
a stopover (trains from France stop in Figueres; lockers at station).
Trains from Barcelona depart Sants Station or the RENFE station
at Metro: Passeig de Gràcia (hrly, 2 hrs, €14.25 round-trip).

Cadaques

Since the late 1800s, Cadaques has served as a haven for intellectuals
and artists alike. Salvador Dalí, raised in nearby Figueres, brought
international fame to this sleepy Catalan port in the 1920s. He and
his wife, Gala, set up home and studio at the adjacent Port Lligat.
Cadaques inspired surrealists such as Eluard, Magritte, Duchamp,
Man Ray, Buñuel, and García Lorca. Even Picasso was drawn to
this enchanting coastal *cala* (cove), and he painted some of his
cubist works here.

In spite of its fame, Cadaques is laid-back and feels off the
beaten path. If you want a peaceful beach-town escape near Barcelona, there's no better place. From the moment you descend
into the town, taking in whitewashed buildings and deep blue
waters, you'll be struck by the port's tranquility and beauty. Have
a glass of *vino tinto* or *cremat* (a traditional brandy-and-coffee drink
served flambé style) at one of the seaside cafés and savor the lap-
ping waves, brilliant sun, and gentle breeze.

The **Casa Museu Salvador Dalí**, once Dalí's home, gives
fans a chance to explore his labyrinthine compound (€7.80, Tue–
Sun 10:30–21:00, summer, closed Mon, closes spring and fall
at 18:00, closed in winter, 15-min walk over the hill from Cadaques to Port Lligat, limited visits, call to reserve a time, tel.
97-267-7500).

Sights Near Barcelona

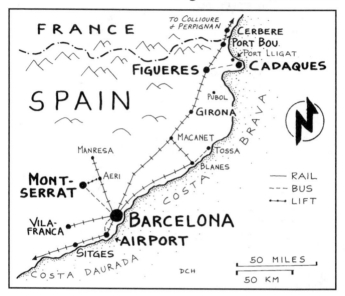

The **TI** is at Carrer Cotxe 2 (Mon–Sat 9:00–14:00, 16:00–21:00, Sun 10:00–13:00, shorter hours off-season, tel. 97-225-8315).

Sleeping and Eating: These affordable options are conveniently located in the main plaza, around the corner from the TI and across from the beach: **Hostal Marina** (D-€27, Ds-€33, Db-€48, breakfast-€3, CC, Riera 3, tel. & fax 97-225-8199) and **Hostal Cristina** (D-€24, Ds-€36, Db-€48, CC, La Riera, tel. 97-225-8138).

For a fine dinner, try **Casa Anita**, down a narrow street from La Residencia. Sitting with others around a big table, you'll enjoy house specialties like *calamars a la plancha* (grilled squid) and homemade *helado* (ice cream). Muscatel from a glass *porron* finishes off the tasty meal (Juan and family, tel. 97-225-8471).

Connections: Cadaques is reached by Sarfa buses from Figueres (3/day, 50 min, €3) or from Barcelona (5/day, 2.5 hrs, €10.50, less frequent off-season, tel. 93-265-6508).

Sitges

Sitges is one of Catalunya's most popular resort towns and a world-renowned vacation destination among the gay community. Despite jet-setting status, its old town has managed to retain its charm. Nine beaches extend about 1.5 kilometers southward from town. Stroll down the seaside promenade, which stretches from the town to the end of the beaches. About halfway down, the crowds thin out, and the beaches become more intimate and cove-like. Along the way, restaurants and *chiringuitos* (beachfront bars) serve tapas, paella, and drinks. Take time to explore the old town's streets and shops. On the waterfront, you'll see the 17th-century Sant Bartomeu i Santa Tecla Church. It's a quick hike up for a view of town, sea, and beaches.

Connections: Southbound trains depart from Sants Station and at the RENFE station at Plaça Catalunya (hrly, €4.20 round-trip).

Montserrat

Montserrat, with its unique rock formations and mountain mon-astery, is a popular daytrip from Barcelona (53 km). This has been Catalunya's most important pilgrimage site for a thousand years. Hymns ascribe this "serrated mountain" to little angels who carved the rocks with golden saws. Geologists blame 10 million years of nature at work.

Montserrat's top attraction is *La Moreneta*, the statue of the Black Virgin, which you'll find within the basilica (daily 8:00–10:30, 12:00–18:30). The Moreneta, one of the patron saints of Catalunya, is the most revered religious symbol in the province.

Inside the basilica, be sure to see the Virgin close-up (behind the altar). Pilgrims touch her orb; the rest is protected behind glass. Then descend into the prayer room for a view of the Moreneta from behind. Pilgrims dip a memento of their journey into the holy water or even leave a personal belonging here (like a motorcycle helmet for safety) to soak up more blessings.

Stop by the new audiovisual center for some cultural and historical perspective. The interactive exhibition, which includes CD-ROM screens and a short video, covers the mountain's history and gives a glimpse into the daily lives of the monastery's resident monks (€1, daily 9:00–18:00, tel. 93-877-7701).

The first hermit monks built huts at Montserrat around A.D. 900. By 1025 a monastery was founded. A choir school soon followed. The **Montserrat Escolania**, or choir school, is consid-ered to be the oldest music school in Europe. Fifty young boys, who live and study in the monastery itself, make up the choir, which performs Mon–Sat at 13:00 and 18:45 and Sun at 12:00 (choir on vacation in July). Note: Catch the early show. If you attend the evening performance, you'll miss the last funicular down the mountain.

The **Museu de Montserrat** offers prehistoric tools, religious art, ancient artifacts, and a few paintings by masters such as El Greco, Caravaggio, Monet, Picasso, and Dalí (€3.60, July–Sept daily 9:30–19:00, Oct–June Mon–Fri 10:00–18:00, Sat–Sun 9:30–18:30).

The Moreneta was originally located in the **Santa Cova** (holy cave), a 40-minute hike down from the monastery. The path is lined with statues depicting scenes from the life of Christ. While the original Black Virgin statue is now in the basilica, a replica sits in the cave. A three-minute funicular ride cuts 20 minutes off the hike (€1.50 one-way, €2.40 round-trip).

The **Sant Joan funicular** (see below) continues another 250 meters above the monastery (3.70 one-way, 5.90 round-trip). At the top of the funicular, a 20-minute walk takes you to the Sant Joan chapel and the starting point of numerous hikes, described in the TI's "Six Itineraries from the Monastery" brochure.

Sleeping: You can sleep in the **old monks' cloister**—now equipped with hotel and apartment facilities—far more comfortably than did its original inhabitants (D-€66, fine restaurant attached, tel. 93-877-7701).

Connections: Ferrocarriles Catalanes trains leave hourly for Montserrat from Barcelona's Plaça Espanya (€11.25 round-trip, cash only, Eurailpass not valid, tel. 93-205-1515). The new Trans-Montserrat ticket includes the train trip, cable-car ride, and unlimited funicular rides (€17.75). The TotMontserrat ticket includes all of this, plus the museum and a self-serve lunch (€32). If you plan to do it all, you'll save a little money (roughly €1.80) with either ticket (buy at Plaça Espanya or TI). If you don't plan on taking either funicular, it's cheaper to buy just the train ticket (includes cable car).

Enter the Plaça Espanya Metro station next to the Plaza Hotel. Follow signs to the "FF de la Generalitat" underground station, then look for train line R5 (direction Manresa, departures at :36 past each hour, 45 min). Get off at the Aeri de Montserrat stop at the base of the mountain, where the cable car awaits (the round-trip from Barcelona includes cable-car ride, 4/hr). Returning, you'll find departures at :15 past the hour make the trains leaving at :36 past the hour. For efficiency, leave by 18:15 at the latest. The last cable-car departs the monastery at 18:45 (17:45 in off-season), entailing a 45-minute wait for the train.

MADRID

Today's Madrid is upbeat and vibrant, still enjoying a post-Franco renaissance. You'll feel it. Even the statue-maker beggars have a twinkle in their eyes.

Madrid is the hub of Spain. This modern capital—Europe's highest, at more than 615 meters (2,000 feet)—has a population of more than four million and is young by European standards. Only 400 years ago, King Philip II decided to move the capital of his empire from Toledo to Madrid. One hundred years ago Madrid had only 400,000 people, so 90 percent of the city is modern sprawl surrounding an intact, easy-to-navigate historic core.

Dive headlong into the grandeur and intimate charm of Madrid. The lavish Royal Palace, with its gilded rooms and frescoed ceilings, rivals Versailles. The Prado has Europe's top collection of paintings. The city's huge Retiro Park invites you for a shady siesta and a hopscotch through a mosaic of lovers, families, skateboarders, pets walking their masters, and expert bench-sitters. Make time for Madrid's elegant shops and people-friendly pedestrian zones. Enjoy the shade in an arcade. On Sundays, cheer for the bull at a bullfight or bargain like mad at a mega–flea market. Lively Madrid has enough street singing, barhopping, and people-watching vitality to give any visitor a boost of youth.

Planning Your Time

Madrid's top two sights, the Prado and the palace, are each worth a half day. On a Sunday (Easter–Oct), consider allotting extra time for a bullfight. Ideally, give Madrid two days and spend them this way:
Day 1: Breakfast of *churros* (see "Eating," below) before a brisk, good-morning-Madrid walk for 20 minutes from Puerta del Sol to the Prado; 9:00–12:00 at the Prado; afternoon siesta in Retiro

Park or modern art at Centro Reina Sofía (Guernica) and/or Thyssen-Bornemisza Museum; dinner at 8:00, with tapas around Plaza Santa Ana.

Day 2: Follow this book's "Puerta del Sol to Royal Palace Walk" (see below); tour the Royal Palace, lunch near Plaza Mayor; afternoon free for other sights, shopping, or side trip to El Escorial (open until 19:00). Be out at the magic hour—before sunset—when beautifully lit people fill Madrid.

Note that the Prado, Thyssen-Bornemisza Museum, and El Escorial are closed on Monday. For day-trip possibilities from Madrid, see the next two chapters ("Northwest of Madrid" and "Toledo").

Orientation

The historic center is enjoyably covered on foot. No major sight is more than a 20-minute walk or a €3.50 taxi ride from Puerta del Sol, Madrid's central square. Divide your time between the city's two major sights—the Royal Palace and the Prado—and its barhopping, contemporary scene.

The Puerta del Sol, which marks the center of Madrid and of Spain itself, contains the "kilometer zero" marker from which all of Spain is surveyed (for its exact location, see "Introductory Walk," below). The Royal Palace to the west and the Prado Museum and Retiro Park to the east frame Madrid's historic center.

Southwest of Puerta del Sol is a 17th-century district with the slow-down-and-smell-the-cobbles Plaza Mayor and memories of pre-industrial Spain.

North of Puerta del Sol runs Gran Vía, and between the two are lively pedestrian shopping streets. Gran Vía, bubbling with expensive shops and cinemas, leads to the modern Plaza de España. North of Gran Vía is the gritty Malasana quarter, with its colorful small houses, shoemakers' shops, sleazy-looking hombres, milk vendors, bars, and hip night scene.

Tourist Information

Madrid has five TIs: **Plaza Mayor** at #3 (Mon–Sat 10:00–20:00, Sun 10:00–15:00, tel. 91-588-1636); **near the Prado Museum** (behind Palace Hotel, Mon–Fri 9:00–19:00, Sat 9:00–13:00, Duque de Medinaceli 2, tel. 91-429-4951); and smaller offices at the **Chamartin** train station (Mon–Fri 8:00–20:00, Sat 9:00–13:00, tel. 91-315-9976), **Atocha** train station (Mon–Fri 9:00–21:00, closed Sat–Sun), and at the **airport** (Mon–Fri 8:00–20:00, Sat 9:00–13:00, closed Sun, tel. 91-305-8656). The general tourist info number is tel. 902-100-107 (www.munimadrid.es). During the summer small temporary stands with yellow umbrellas and yellow-shirted student guides pop up (at places such as Puerta del Sol), happy to help out lost tourists. Confirm your sightseeing plans and pick up a city map

Madrid

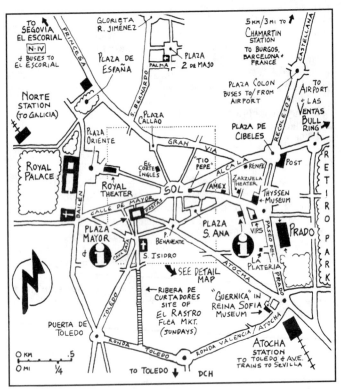

and *Enjoy Madrid*. If interested, ask at the TI about bullfights and zarzuela (the local light opera).

For entertainment listings, the TI's free *En Madrid* is not as good as the easy-to-decipher Spanish weekly entertainment guide *Guía del Ocio* (€0.90, sold at newsstands), which lists events, restaurants, and movies ("v.o." means a movie is in its original language rather than dubbed).

If you're heading to other destinations in this book, ask any Madrid TI for free maps and brochures (ideally in English). Since many small-town TIs keep erratic hours and run out of these pamphlets, get what you can here. You can get schedules for buses and some trains, avoiding unnecessary trips to the various stations. The TI's free and amazingly informative *Mapa de Comunicaciones España* lists all the Turismos and highway SOS numbers with a road map of Spain. (If they're out, ask for the Paradores Hotel chain-sponsored route map.)

Arrival in Madrid

By Train: Madrid's two train stations, Atocha and Chamartin, are
both on subway lines with easy access to downtown Madrid. Each
station has all the services. Chamartin handles most international
trains. Atocha generally covers southern Spain and runs AVE trains
to Sevilla. Both stations offer long-distance trains (*largo recorrido*) as
well as smaller, local trains (*regionales* and *cercanías*) to nearby destinations. To travel between Chamartin and Atocha, don't hassle with
the subway (which involves a transfer)—the *cercanías* trains are faster
(6/hr, 12 min, €1.20, free with railpass—show it at ticket window
in the middle of the turnstiles). These trains depart from Atocha's
track 2. At Chamartin, it's usually track 2 or 3, but check the Salidas
Immediatas board for the next departure.

Chamartin: The TI is opposite track 19. The impressively
large *Centro de Viajes/Travel Center* customer-service office is in the
middle of the building. You can use the Club Intercity lounge if
you have a first-class railpass and first-class seat or sleeper reservations. The *cercanías* platforms cluster around track 5. The station's
Metro stop is Chamartin. (If you arrive by Metro at Chamartin,
follow signs to *Información* to get to the lobby rather than *Vías*,
which sends you directly to the platforms.)

Atocha: Atocha is split into two halves, connected by a corridor
of shops. On one side are the slick AVE trains, some Talgo trains,
and a botanical garden (in the soaringly high old-station building,
complete with birds, places to sit, and a cafeteria). On the other side
of the station you'll find the local *cercanías*, *regionales*, some Talgos,
and the Metro stop (named Atocha RENFE—not simply Atocha,
which is a different Metro stop in Madrid). Each side of the station
has separate schedules; this can be confusing if you're in the wrong
side of the building. You'll find a tiny TI that handles tourist info
only—not train info (Mon–Fri 9:00–21:00, closed Sat–Sun, 50
meters straight ahead of the Metro's turnstiles, ground floor). For
train info, try the customer-service office called *Atención al Cliente*
(daily 7:00–23:00); although there's one office for each half of the
building, the office on the AVE side (just off the botanical garden)
is more likely to speak English.

Atocha's Club AVE is a lounge reserved solely for AVE business or first-class ticket-holders or Eurailers with a reservation
(daily 6:30–22:30, upstairs on AVE side of station, free drinks,
newspapers, showers, and info service).

To buy tickets at Atocha for the local *cercanías* trains (e.g., to
Toledo), go to the middle of the *cercanías* side and get your ticket
from ticket windows in the small rectangular offices (marked *Venta
de Billetes sin reserva*). You can buy AVE and other long-distance
train tickets in the bigger ticket offices in either half of the building; the airier *Taquillas* office on the AVE side (next to *Atención al
Cliente* off the botanical garden) is more pleasant. Station ticket

offices can get really crowded (mid-morning and late afternoon are usually peaceful). It's often quicker to buy your ticket at an English-speaking travel agency (such as in El Corte Inglés) or at the downtown RENFE office, which offers train information, reservations, tickets, and minimal English (Mon–Fri 9:30–20:00, CC, go in person, 2 blocks north of the Prado at Calle Alcala 44, tel. 902-240-202, www.renfe.es).

By Bus: Madrid's three key bus stations, all connected by Metro, are: Larrea (for Segovia, Metro: Príncipe Pío), Estación Sur Autobuses (for Toledo, Àvila, and Granada, on top of Metro stop: Méndez Alvaro, tel. 91-468-4200), and Estación Intercambiador (for El Escorial, in the Metro: Moncloa). For details, see "Transportation Connections" at the end of this chapter.

By Plane: For information on Madrid's Barajas Airport, see "Transportation Connections" at the end of this chapter.

Getting around Madrid

By Subway: Madrid's subway is simple, speedy, and cheap (€0.90/ride, runs 6:00–01:30). The €4.60, 10-ride Metrobus ticket can be shared by several travelers and works on both the Metro and buses (available at kiosks or tobacco shops or in Metro). The city's broad streets can be hot and exhausting. A subway trip of even a stop or two might save time and energy. Most stations offer free maps (*navegamadrid*; www.metromadrid.es). Navigate by subway stops (shown on city maps). To transfer, follow signs to the next subway line (numbered and color-coded). End stops are used to indicate directions. Insert your ticket in the turnstile, then retrieve it as you pass through. Green *Salida* signs point to the exit. Using neighborhood maps and street signs to exit smartly can save lots of walking.

By Bus: City buses, while not as easy as the Metro, can be useful (bus maps at TI or info booth on Puerta del Sol, €0.90 tickets sold on bus, or €4.60 for a 10-ride Metrobus—see "By Subway," above; buses run 6:00–24:00).

By Taxi: Madrid's 15,000 taxis are easy to hail and reasonable (€1.10 drop, €0.60 per km; supplements for airport, train/bus stations, bags, Sunday, and night service). Threesomes travel as cheaply by taxi as by subway. A ride from the Royal Palace to the Prado costs about €3.50.

Helpful Hints

Theft Alert: Be wary of pickpockets, anywhere, anytime, but particularly on Puerta del Sol (main square), the subway, and crowded streets. Wear your money belt. The small streets north of Gran Vía are particularly dangerous, even before nightfall. Muggings occur, but are rare.

Travel Agencies and Free Maps: The grand department store, El Corte Inglés, has two travel agencies (on first and seventh floors, Mon–Sat 10:00–22:00, just off Puerta del Sol) and gives out free Madrid maps (at the information desk, immediately inside the door, just off Puerta del Sol at intersection of Preciados and Tetuan; supermarket in basement). El Corte Inglés is taking over the entire intersection; the main store is the tallest building with the biggest sign.

Books: For books in English, try the oddly-named **Fnac Callao** (Mon–Sat 10:00–21:30, Sun 12:00–21:30, second floor, Calle Preciados 8, tel. 91-595-6190), **Casa del Libro** (Mon–Sat 9:30–21:30, Sun 11:00–21:00, English on ground floor in back, Gran Vía 29, tel. 91-521-2219), and **El Cortes Inglés** (guide-books and some fiction, in its Libreria branch kitty-corner from main store, see listing within "Travel Agency," above).

American Express: The AmEx office at Plaza Cortes 2 sells train and plane tickets, and even accepts Visa and Mastercard (opposite Palace Hotel, 2 blocks from Metro: Banco de España, Mon–Fri 9:00–17:30, Sat 10:00–14:00, tel. 91-322-5445).

Embassies: The U.S. Embassy is at Serrano 75 (tel. 91-587-2200); the Canadian Embassy is at Nuñez de Balboa 35 (tel. 91-423-3250).

Laundromat: The self-service Lavamatique is the most central, just west of the Prado (Mon–Sat 9:00–20:00, closed Sun, Cervantes 1).

Internet Access: You'll find lots of computer terminals at NavegaWeb, centrally located at Gran Vía 30 (daily 9:00–24:00). Zahara's Internet café is at the corner of Gran Vía and Mesoneros (Mon–Fri 9:00–24:00, Sat–Sun 9:00–24:00).

Tours of Madrid

Hop-On Hop-Off Bus Tours—Several companies offer virtually identical 15-stop 75-minute circuits of the city with two or three buses per hour allowing you to hop on and off all day at the various sights, including the Royal Palace and Prado. The easiest place to catch any of the buses is at the south side of Puerta del Sol. Before you commit, ask if the bus has live or tape-recorded commentary; if the ticket is valid for one day or two (sometimes this is a bonus, sometimes it costs extra); and if discounts are offered for youth and seniors (about €9.50, daily 10:00–18:00, until 20:00 in summer). It's possible that in 2002 only one company, maybe Grayline, will offer these tours, depending on a ruling from the city government.

Walking Tours—British expatriate Stephen Drake-Jones gives entertaining, informative walks of historic old Madrid almost nightly (along with more specialized walks, such as "Hemingway," "Civil War," and "Bloody Madrid"). A historian with a passion for the memory of Wellington (the man who stopped Napoleon), Stephen is the founder of the Wellington Society. For €25 you become a member of the society for one year and get a free two-hour tour that includes stops at two bars for local drinks and tapas. Eccentric Stephen takes you back in time to sort out Madrid's Hapsburg and Bourbon history. Stephen likes his wine. If that's a problem, skip the tour. Tours start at the statue on Puerta del Sol (maximum 10 people, tel. 60-914-3203—a cell-phone number that will cost you €0.60—to confirm tour and reserve a spot, www .wellsoc.org, e-mail: sdrakejones@hotmail.com). Members of the Wellington Society can take advantage of Stephen's helpline (if you're in a Spanish jam, call him to translate and intervene) and assistance via e-mail (for questions on Spain, your itinerary, and so on). Stephen also does inexpensive private tours and daytrips for small groups.

Introductory Walk: From Madrid's Puerta del Sol to the Royal Palace

Connect the sights with the following walking tour. Allow an hour for this one-kilomter walk, not including your palace visit.

▲▲**Puerta del Sol**—Named for a long-gone medieval gate with the sun carved onto it, Puerta del Sol is ground zero for Madrid. It's a hub for the Metro, buses, and pickpockets.

Stand by the statue of King Charles III and survey the square. Because of his enlightened urban policies, Charles III (who ruled until 1788) is affectionately called the "best mayor of Madrid." He decorated the city squares with fine fountains, got those meddlesome Jesuits out of city government, established the public school system, made the Retiro a public park rather than a royal retreat, and generally cleaned up Madrid.

Look behind the king. The statue of the bear pawing the strawberry bush and the Madrono trees in the big planter boxes are symbols of the city. Bears used to live in the royal hunting grounds outside Madrid.

The king faces a red-and-white building with a bell tower. This was Madrid's first post office, established by Charles in the 1760s. Today it's the governor's office, though it's notorious for being Franco's police headquarters. An amazing number of those detained and interrogated by the Franco police "tried to escape" by flying out the windows to their deaths. Notice the hats of the civil guardsmen at the entry. It's said the hats have square backsides so they can lean against the wall while enjoying a cigarette.

Crowds fill the square on New Year's Eve as the rest of Madrid watches the action on TV. As Spain's "Big Ben" atop the governor's office chimes 12 times, Madrileños eat one grape for each ring to bring good luck through the coming year.

Cross Calle Mayor. Look at the curb directly in front of the entrance of the governor's office. The scuffed-up marker is the center of Spain. To the right of the entrance, the plaque on the wall

Heart of Madrid

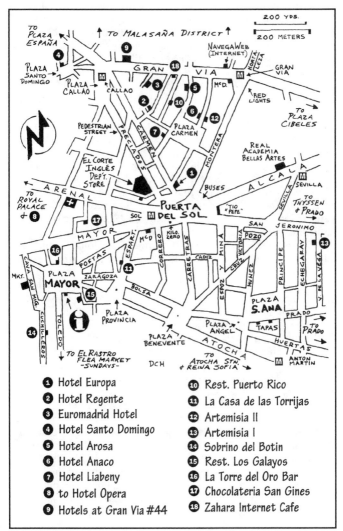

① Hotel Europa
② Hotel Regente
③ Euromadrid Hotel
④ Hotel Santo Domingo
⑤ Hotel Arosa
⑥ Hotel Anaco
⑦ Hotel Liabeny
⑧ to Hotel Opera
⑨ Hotels at Gran Via #44
⑩ Rest. Puerto Rico
⑪ La Casa de las Torrijas
⑫ Artemisia II
⑬ Artemisia I
⑭ Sobrino del Botin
⑮ Rest. Los Galayos
⑯ La Torre del Oro Bar
⑰ Chocolateria San Gines
⑱ Zahara Internet Cafe

marks the spot where the war against Napoleon started. Napoleon wanted his brother to be king of Spain. Trying to finagle this, Napoleon brought nearly the entire Spanish royal family to France for negotiations. An anxious crowd gathered outside this building awaiting word of the fate of their royal family. This was just after the French Revolution, and there was a general nervousness between France and Spain. When the French guard appeared, on May 2, 1808, the massacre took place. Goya, who worked just up the street, observed the event and captured the tragedy in his paintings *2nd of May, 1808*, and *3rd of May, 1808*, now in the Prado.

Walking from Puerta del Sol to Plaza Mayor: On the corner of Calle Mayor and Puerta del Sol, across from McDonald's, is the busy *confiteria*, Salon la Mallorquina (daily 9:00–21:15). Cross Calle Mayor to go inside. The shop is famous for its sweet Napolitana cream-filled pastry (€0.75) and savory, beef-filled *agujas* pastries (€1.20)—if you can't finish yours, the beggar at the front door would love to. See the racks with goodies hot out of the oven. Look back toward the entrance and notice the tile above the door with the 18th-century view of the Puerta del Sol. Compare this with the view out the door. This was before the square was widened, when a church stood where the Tío Pepe sign stands today. The French used this church to detain local patriots awaiting execution. (That venerable sign, advertising a famous sherry for over 100 years, is Madrid's first billboard.)

Cross busy Calle Mayor (again), round McDonald's, and veer left up the pedestrian alley called Calle de Postas. The street sign shows the post coach heading for that famous first post office. Medieval street signs came with pictures so the illiterate could "read" them. After 50 meters, take a left up Calle San Cristobal. Within two blocks, you'll pass the local feminist bookshop (Libreria Mujeres—on the left—appropriately) and reach a small square. At the square notice the big brick 17th-century Ministry of Foreign Affairs building (with the pointed spire)—originally a prison for rich prisoners who could afford the best cells. Turn right and walk down Calle de Zaragoza under the arcade into…

Plaza Mayor—This square, built in 1619, is a vast, cobbled, traffic-free chunk of 17th-century Spain. Each side of the square is uniform, as if a grand palace were turned inside out. The statue is of Philip III, who ordered the square's construction. Upon this stage, much Spanish history was played out: bullfights, fires, royal pageantry, and events of the gruesome Inquisition. Reliefs serving as seatbacks under the lampposts tell the story. During the Inquisition, many were tried here. The guilty would parade around the square (bleachers were built for bigger audiences, the wealthy rented balconies) with billboards listing their many sins. They were then burned. Some were slowly strangled with a *garrotte*; they'd hold a crucifix and hear the reassuring words of a priest as this life was squeezed out of them. The square is painted a democratic shade of burgundy—the result of a citywide vote. Since Franco's 1975 death, there's been a passion for voting here. Three different colors were painted as samples on the walls of this square, and the city voted for its favorite.

From Plaza Mayor to the Royal Palace

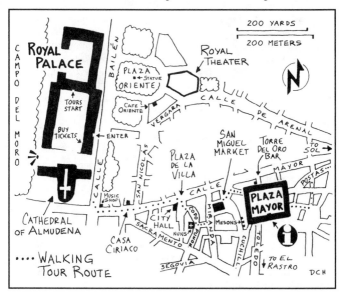

A stamp-and-coin market bustles here on Sundays from 10:00 to 14:00, and on any day it's a colorful and affordable place to enjoy a cup of coffee. Throughout Spain, lesser *plazas mayores* provide peaceful pools for the river of Spanish life. The TI is at #3, on the south side of the square. The building decorated with painted figures, on the north side of the square, is the Casa de la Panadería, which used to house the Bakers' Guild. To the left of it is . . .

The Torre del Oro Bar Andalu (northwest corner of square) is a good place for a drink to finish off your Plaza Mayor visit. This bar is a temple to bullfighting. Warning: They push expensive tapas on tourists. A *caña* (small beer) shouldn't cost more than €1.20. The bar's ambience is "Andalu" . . . Andalusian. Look under the stuffed head of "Barbero" the bull. At eye level you'll see a *puntilla*, the knife used to put a bull out of its misery at the arena. This was the knife used to kill Barbero.

Notice the incredible action caught in the bar's many photographs. At the end of the bar in a glass case is the "suit of lights" El Cordobes wore in his ill-fated 1967 fight. With Franco in attendance, El Cordobes went on and on, long after he could have ended the fight, until finally the bull gored him. El Cordobes survived; the bull didn't. Find Franco with El Cordobes at the far end (to the left of Segador the Bull). Under the bull is a photo of El Cordobes' illegitimate son, El Cordobes, kissing a bull. Disowned by El Cordobes and using his dad's famous name after a court battle, El Cordobes is one of this generation's top fighters.

Walking from Plaza Mayor to the Royal Palace: Leave Plaza Mayor on Calle Cuidad Rodrigo (far right corner from where you entered the square, and to your right as you exit Torre del Oro). You'll pass a series of fine turn-of-the-20th-century storefronts and shops such as the recommended Casa Rua, famous for their cheap *bocadillos calamares*—fried squid-ring sandwiches.

From the archway you'll see the covered Mercado de San Miguel (green iron posts, on left). Before you enter the market, look left down the street Cava de San Miguel. If you like sangria and singing, come back tonight around 21:00 and visit one of the *mesons* (such as Guitarra, Tortilla, or Boqueron) that you'll find just down the street. These cave-like bars stretch way back and get packed with locals who—emboldened by sangria, the setting, and Spain—might suddenly just start singing. It's a fun scene, best on Fridays and Saturdays.

Wander through the newly-renovated produce market and consider buying some fruit (Mon–Fri 9:00–14:30, 17:15–20:15, Sat 9:00–14:30, closed Sun). Leave it on the opposite (downhill) side and follow the pedestrian lane left. You'll pass Taberna San Miguel, which makes good *churros* in the morning. At the first corner, turn right, and cross the small plaza to the modern brick convent. The door on the right says *venta de dulces;* to buy inexpensive sweets from cloistered nuns, buzz the *monjas* button, wait patiently for the sister to respond over the intercom, and say *dulces* (dool-thays) when she does (Mon–Sat 9:30–13:00, 16:00–18:30). When the lock buzzes, push open the door and follow the sign to *torno*, the lazy Susan which lets the sisters sell their baked goods without being seen (smallest quantities: half or *medio* kilo). Of the many choices (all good), consider *pastas de Almendra* (crumbly) or *manteados de yema* (moist and eggy).

Follow Calle del Codo (see the street sign—where those in need of bits of armor shopped) around the convent to Plaza de la Villa, the city-hall square. Ahead the flags of city, state, and nation grace the city hall. The statue in the garden is of Don Bazan—mastermind of the Christian victory over the Muslims at the naval battle of Lepanto in 1571. This pivotal battle ended the Muslim threat to Christian Europe. The mayor's office is behind Don.

From here, busy Calle Mayor leads downhill a couple more blocks to the Royal Palace. Halfway down (on the left) there's a tiny square opposite the recommended Casa Ciriaco restaurant (#84). The statue memorializes the 1906 anarchist bombing that killed 23 people as the royal couple paraded by on their wedding day. While the crowd was throwing flowers, an anarchist threw a bouquet lashed to a bomb from a balcony of #84 (which was a hotel at the time). Amazing photos of the event hang just inside the door in the back room of the restaurant.

Continue down Calle Mayor. Within a couple of blocks you'll come to a busy street, Calle de Bailen. (On the corner—to your right—is the Garrido-Bailen music store, a handy place to stock up on castanets, unusual flutes, and Galatian bagpipes.)

Across the busy street is the **Cathedral of Almudena**, Madrid's new cathedral. It's worth a look while you're here. Built between 1883 and 1993, its exterior is a contemporary mix and its interior is neo-Gothic with a colorful ceiling. Next to the cathedral is the...

▲▲**Royal Palace (Palacio Real)**—Europe's third-greatest palace (after Versailles and Vienna's Schonbrunn) is packed with tourists and royal antiques. After a fortress burned down on this site, King Phillip V commissioned this huge 18th-century palace as a replacement. How big is it? Over 2,000 rooms with tons of lavish tapestries, a king's ransom of chandeliers, priceless porcelain, paintings, and lots of clocks (Charles IV was a huge collector). While the royal family lives in a mansion a few kilometers away, the place still functions as a royal palace and is used for formal state receptions and tourist daydreams.

A simple one-floor, 24-room, one-way circuit is open to the public. You can wander on your own or join an English tour (get time of next tour and decide as you buy your ticket; tours depart about every 20 min). The tour guides, like the museum guidebook, show a passion for meaningless data (€6 without a tour, €7 with a tour, April–Sept Mon–Sat 9:00–19:00, Sun 9:00–16:00; Oct–March Mon–Sat 9:30–18:00, Sun 9:00–15:00, last tickets sold an hour before closing, palace can close without warning if needed for a royal function; cafeteria; Metro: Opera, tel. 91-559-7404 or 91-454-8800). Your ticket includes the armory and the pharmacy, both on the courtyard.

If you tour on your own, here are a few details you won't find on the little English descriptions posted in each room:

The Grand Stairs: Fancy carpets are rolled down (notice the little metal bar-holding hooks) for formal occasions. At the top of the first landing, the blue and red coat of arms is of the current—and popular—constitutional monarch, Juan Carlos. While Franco chose him to be the next dictator, J.C. knew Spain was ripe for democracy. Rather than become "Juan the Brief" (as some were nicknaming him), he turned real power over to the parliament. At the top of the stairs (before entering first room, right of door) is a bust of J.C.'s great-great-g-g-g-great-grandfather Phillip V. The grandson of France's King Louis XIV, he began the Bourbon dynasty in 1700. The dynasty survives today with Juan Carlos.

Throne Room: Red velvet walls, lions, and frescoes of

Spanish scenes symbolize the monarchy in this rococo riot. The chandeliers are the best in the house. The thrones are only from 1977. This is where ambassadors give their credentials to the king, who receives them relatively informally...standing rather than seated in the throne.

Gasparini Anteroom (2 rooms after the throne room): The paintings are of King Charles IV and his wife—all by Goya. Velázquez's masterpiece *Las Meninas* originally hung here.

Gasparini Room: This was the royal dressing room, hinting of the Asian influence popular at the time. Dressing, for a divine monarch, was a public affair. The court bigwigs would assemble here as the king, standing on a platform—notice the height of the mirrors—would pull on his leotards. In the next room, the silk wallpaper is new—notice the J.C.S. initials of the king and Sofia (the queen).

Gala Dining Room: Five or six times a year the king entertains up to 150 guests at this bowling lane–sized table. The table in the next room would be lined with an exorbitantly caloric dessert buffet. In the next room you can ogle at glass cases filled with the silver tableware used for these functions.

Stradivarius Room: The queen likes classical music and when you perform for her, do it with these precious 300-year-old violins. About 300 Antonius Stradivarius–made instruments survive. This is the only matching quartet: two violins, a viola, and a cello.

Royal Chapel: The Royal Chapel is used only for baptisms and funerals. The royal tomb sits here before making the sad trip to El Escorial to join the rest of Spain's past royalty.

Billiards and Smoking Rooms: The billiards room and the smoking room were for men only. The porcelain and silk of the smoking room imitates a Chinese opium den.

Queen's Boudoir: The next room was for the ladies, decorated just after Pompeii was excavated and therefore in fanciful ancient-Roman style. You'll exit down the same grand stairway you climbed 24 rooms ago. Near the exit is a cafeteria and bookstore, which has a variety of books on Spanish history.

The **armory**, recently renovated, displays the armor and swords of El Cid, Ferdinand, Charles V, and Phillip II.

After you finish your visit, consider walking a few minutes farther up the length of the palace to Plaza de Oriente. With your back to the palace, face the equestrian statue of Philip IV. To your far left is the Torre de Madrid skyscraper, with statues of Don Quixote and Sancho at its base (not visible from your vantage point). Behind the equestian statue of Philip IV is the Royal Theater (*Teatro Real*). Many theater-goers stop by Café de Oriente before or after the performance (using a clock as a compass, the café is at 1:00). Walk in front of the Royal Theater. Cross the square and take Calle Arenal back to Puerta del Sol.

Sights—Madrid's Museum Neighborhood

These three worthwhile museums are in east Madrid. From Prado to the Thyssen-Bornemisza Museum is a five-minute walk; Prado to Centro Reina Sofia is a 10-minute walk.

Museum Pass: If you plan to visit all three museums, you'll save 25 percent by buying the Paseo del Arte pass (€7.75, sold at each museum, valid for a year—but good for only one visit per site). Note that the Prado and Centro Reina Sofia museums are free on Saturday afternoon and Sunday (and May 18, Oct 12, Dec 6, and anytime for those under 18 and over 65); the Prado and Thyssen-Bornemisza are closed Monday; and the Reina Sofia is closed Tuesday.

▲▲▲**Prado Museum**—The Prado holds my favorite collection of paintings anywhere. With more than 3,000 canvases, including entire rooms of masterpieces by Velázquez, Goya, El Greco, and Bosch, it's overwhelming. Take a tour or buy a guidebook (or bring along the Prado chapter from *Rick Steves' Mona Winks*). Focus on the Flemish and northern (Bosch, Dürer, Rubens), the Italian (Fra Angelico, Raphael, Titian), and the Spanish art (El Greco, Velázquez, Goya).

Follow Goya through his stages, from cheery (*The Parasol*) to political (*2nd of May, 1808* and *3rd of May, 1808*) to dark ("Negras de Goya": e.g., *Saturn Devouring His Children*). In each stage, Goya asserted his independence from artistic conventions. Even the standard court portraits from his "first" stage reflect his politically liberal viewpoint, subtly showing the vanity and stupidity of his royal patrons by the looks in their goony eyes. His political stage, with paintings such as the *3rd of May, 1808*, depicting a massacre of Spaniards by Napoleon's troops, makes him one of the first artists with a social conscience. Finally, in his gloomy "dark stage," Goya probed the inner world of fears and nightmares, anticipating our modern-day preoccupation with dreams.

Also, seek out Bosch's *The Garden of Earthly Delights*—a three-paneled altarpiece showing creation, the "transparency of earthly pleasures," and the resulting hell. Bosch's self-portrait looks out from hell (with the birds leading naked people around the brim of his hat) surrounded by people suffering eternal punishments appropriate for their primary earthly excesses.

The art is constantly rearranged by the Prado's management, so even the Prado's own maps and guidebooks are out of date. Regardless of the latest location, most art is grouped by painter, and better guards can point you in the right direction if you say "*¿Dónde está…?*" and the painter's name as Españoled as you can (e.g., Titian is "Ticiano" and Bosch is "El Bosco"). The Murillo entrance—at the end closest to the Atocha train station—usually has shorter lines. Lunchtime, from 14:00 to 16:00, is least crowded (€3, free on Sat afternoon after 14:30, all day Sun, and to anyone

Madrid's Museum Neighborhood

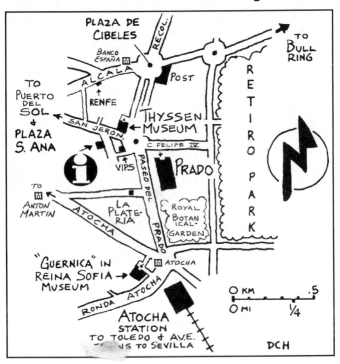

under 18 and over 65; Tue–Sat 9:00–19:00, Sun 9:00–14:00, closed Mon, last entry 30 min before closing; ticket valid for one visit—no in-and-out privileges; free, mandatory baggage check after your things are scanned just like at the airport; can't bring water bottle inside; photos are allowed without a flash; cafeteria at Murillo end; Paseo de Prado, Metro: Banco de España or Atocha—each a 15-min walk from the museum, tel. 91-330-2800, http://museoprado.mcu.es).

While you're in the neighborhood, consider a visit to the Charles III Botanical Garden (listed under "More Sights," below).

▲▲**Thyssen-Bornemisza Museum**—Locals call this stunning museum simply the Thyssen (tee-sun). It displays the impressive collection that Baron Thyssen (a wealthy German married to a former Miss Spain) sold to Spain for $350 million. It's basically minor works by major artists and major works by minor artists (the real big guns are over at the Prado). But art lovers appreciate how the good baron's art complements the Prado's collection by filling in where the Prado is weak (Impressionism). For a delightful walk through art history, ride the elevator to the top floor and do the rooms in numerical order. It's kitty-corner from the Prado at Paseo del Prado 8 in Palacio de Villahermosa (€4.75, or €6.50 to add current exhibition, free for accompanied children under 12, Tue–Sun 10:00–19:00, closed Mon, ticket office closes at 18:30, audioguide-€3, free baggage check, café, shop, no photos or videotaping allowed, Metro: Banco de España or Atocha, tel. 91-420-3944, www .museothyssen.org). If you're tired, hail a cab at the gate and zip straight to Centro Reina Sofia.

▲▲**Centro Reina Sofia**—In this exceptional modern-art museum, ride the elevator to the second floor and follow the room numbers for art from 1900 to 1950. The fourth floor continues the collection from 1950 to 1980. The museum is most famous for Picasso's *Guernica*, a massive painting showing the horror of modern war. Guernica, a village in northern Spain, was the target of the world's first saturation-bombing raid, approved by Franco and carried out by Hitler. Notice the two rooms of studies for *Guernica* filled with iron-nail tears and screaming mouths. *Guernica* was exiled in America until Franco's death, and now it reigns as Spain's national piece of art.

The museum also houses an easy-to-enjoy collection of other modern artists, including more of Picasso (3 rooms divided among his pre-civil-war work, *Guernica*, and his post-civil-war art) and a mind-bending room of Dalís. Enjoy a break in the shady courtyard before leaving (€3, free Sat afternoon after 14:30 and all day Sun, always free to the under-18 and over-65 crowd, Mon and Wed–Sat 10:00–21:00, Sun 10:00–14:30, closed Tue, good brochure, no photos or videos allowed, no tours in English—yet, free baggage check, Santa Isabel 52, Metro: Atocha, across from Atocha train station, look for exterior glass elevators, tel. 91-467-5062, http://museoreinasofia.mcu.es).

More Sights—Madrid

Chapel San Antonio de la Florida—Goya's tomb stares up at a splendid cupola filled with his own frescoes. On June 13, local ladies line up here to ask St. Anthony for a boyfriend, while outside a festival rages, with street musicians, food, and fun (€1.80, Tue–Fri 10:00–14:00, 16:00–20:00, Sat–Sun 10:00–14:00, closed Mon, July and Aug only 10:00–14:00, Glorieta de San Antonio de la Florida, Metro: Príncipe Pío, tel. 91-542-0722). This chapel is near the bus station that covers Segovia. If you're daytripping to Segovia, it's easy to stop by the chapel before or after your trip.

Next door to the chapel is Restaurante Casa Mingo, popular for its cheap chicken, chorizo, and *cabrales* cheese served with cider. Ask the waiter to pour the cider for you. For dessert, try *tarta de Santiago*—almond cake (daily 11:00–24:00, Paseo de la Florida 34, tel. 91-547-7918).

Royal Tapestry Factory (Real Fabrica de Tapices)—Have a look at the traditional making of tapestries (€1.80, some English tours, Mon–Fri 10:00–14:00, closed Aug, Calle Fuenterrabia 2, Metro: Menendez Pelayo, take Gutenberg exit, tel. 91-434-0551).

▲**Retiro Park**—Siesta in this 350-acre green and breezy escape from the city. At midday on Saturday and Sunday, the area around the lake becomes a street carnival, with jugglers, puppeteers, and lots of local color. These peaceful gardens offer great picnicking and people watching. From the Retiro Metro stop, walk to the big lake (El Estanque), where you can cheaply rent a rowboat. Past the lake, a grand boulevard of statues leads to the Prado.

Charles III's Botanical Garden (Real Jardín Botánico)—After your Prado visit, you can take a lush and fragrant break in this sculpted park wandering among trees from around the world (entry just opposite Prado's Murillo entry, €1.50, daily 10:00–20:00, until 18:00 in winter, Plaza de Murillo 2).

Moncloa Tower (Faro de Moncloa)—This tower's elevator zips you up 92 meters to the best skyscraper view in town (€1.20, Tue–Fri 10:00–14:00, 17:00–19:00, Sat–Sun 10:30–17:30, closed Mon, Metro: Moncloa, tel. 91-544-8106). If you're going to El Escorial by bus, this is a convenient sight near the bus station.

Teleferico—For a break from the big city, ride this cable car from downtown over Madrid's sprawling city park to Casa de Campo (€2.60 one-way, €3.60 round-trip, daily from 11:00, fall and winter from 12:00, departs from Paseo del Pintor Rosales, Metro: Arguelles, tel. 91-541-7450, www.teleferico.com. At Casa de Campo, you can rent a rowboat, picnic, and visit the zoo and amusement park.

Shopping

Shoppers focus on the colorful pedestrian area between Gran Vía and Puerta del Sol. The giant Spanish department store, El Corte Inglés, is a block off Puerta del Sol and a handy place to pick up just about anything you need (Mon–Sat 10:00–21:30, closed Sun, free maps at info desk, supermarket in basement).

▲**El Rastro**—Europe's biggest flea market, held on Sundays and holidays, is a field day for shoppers, people watchers, and thieves (9:00–15:00, best before 12:00). Thousands of stalls titillate more than a million browsers with mostly new junk. If you brake for garage sales, you'll pull a U-turn for El Rastro. Start at the Plaza Mayor and head south or take the subway to Tirso de Molina. Hang on to your wallet. Munch on a *pepito* (meat-filled pastry). Europe's biggest stamp market thrives simultaneously on Plaza Mayor.

Nightlife

▲▲▲**Bullfight**—Madrid's Plaza de Toros hosts Spain's top bull-fights on most Sundays and holidays from Easter through October and nearly every day from May through early June. Top fights sell out in advance. Fights start punctually at 19:00. Tickets range from €3.30–102. There are no bad seats at Plaza de Toros; paying more gets you in the shade and/or closer to the gore. To be close to the action, choose areas 8, 9, and 10; for shade: 1, 2, 9, 10; for shade/sun: 3, 8; for the sun and cheapest seats: 4, 5, 6, 7. Hotels and booking offices such as the one at Plaza Carmen 3 (daily 9:30–13:30, 16:00–19:00, tel. 91-531-2732) are convenient but they add 20 percent and don't sell the cheap seats. If you want to save money, stand in the bullring ticket line. A thousand tickets are held back to be sold on the five days leading up to a fight, including the day of the fight. The bullring is at Calle Alcala 237 (Metro: Ventas, tel. 91-356-2200, www.las-ventas.com). The bullfighting museum (Museo Taurino) is at the back of the bullring (free, 9:30–14:30, closed Sat and Mon and early on fight days, Calle Alcala 237, tel. 91-725-1857). See the appendix for more on the "art" of bullfighting.

▲▲**Zarzuela**—For a delightful look at Spanish light opera that even English speakers can enjoy, try zarzuela. Guitar-strumming Napoleons in red capes; buxom women with masks, fans, and castanets; Spanish-speaking pharaohs; melodramatic spotlights; and aficionados clapping and singing along from the cheap seats where the acoustics are best—this is zarzuela ...the people's opera. Originating in Madrid, zarzuela is known for its satiric humor and surprisingly good music. The season, which runs from mid-December through June, features a mix of zarzuela, traditional opera, and dance. You can buy tickets at Theater Zarzuela (€7–27, box office open 12:00–18:00 or until showtime, Jovellanos 4, near the Prado, Metro: Banco de España, tel. 91-524-5400, www.teatrozarzuela.mcu.es). The TI's monthly guide has a special zarzuela listing.

Flamenco—Save this for Sevilla if you can. In Madrid, Taberna Casa Patas is small, intimate, smoky, and powerful, with one drink included and no hassling after that (tickets around €18, shows at 22:00, Canizares 10, 3 blocks south of Plaza Santa Ana, reservations tel. 91-369-0496). Café de Chinitas is more touristy (Calle Torija 7, just off Plaza Mayor).

Sleeping in Madrid
(€1.10 = about $1, country code: 34)
Sleep Code: **S** = Single, **D** = Double/Twin, **T** = Triple, **Q** = Quad, **b** = bathroom, **s** = shower only, **CC** = Credit Cards accepted, **no CC** = Credit Cards not accepted, **SE** = Speaks English, **NSE** = No English. Breakfast is not included unless noted. In Madrid, the 7 percent IVA tax is sometimes included in the price.

Madrid has plenty of centrally located budget hotels and *pensiónes*. You'll have no trouble finding a sleepable double for $30, a good double for $60, and a modern air-conditioned double with all the comforts for $100. Prices are the same throughout the year, and it's almost always easy to find a place. Anticipate full hotels May 15 to May 25 (the festival of Madrid's patron Saint Isidro) and the last week in September (conventions). The accommodations I've listed are within a few minutes' walk of Puerta del Sol.

Sleeping in the Pedestrian Zone between Puerta del Sol and Gran Vía
(zip code: 28013)

Predictable and away from the seediness, these are good values for those wanting to spend a little more. Their formal prices may be inflated, and some offer weekend and summer discounts whenever it's slow. Use Metro: Sol for all but the last. See map on page 71 for location.

Hotel Europa has red-carpet charm: a royal salon, plush halls with happy Muzak, polished wood floors, attentive staff, and 80 squeaky-clean rooms with balconies overlooking the pedestrian zone or an inner courtyard (Sb-€48, Db-€60, Tb-€85, Qb-€100, Quint/b-€115, tax not included, breakfast-€5, fine lounge on 2nd floor, elevator, fans, easy phone reservations with credit card, CC, Calle del Carmen 4, tel. 91-521-2900, fax 91-521-4696, www .hoteleuropa.net, e-mail: info@hoteleuropa.net, Antonio and Fernando Garaban and their helpful staff SE). The convenient Europa cafeteria/restaurant next door is a great scene and a fine value any time of day.

Hotel Regente is a big, traditional, and impersonal place with 145 plain but comfortable air-conditioned rooms and a great location (Sb-€45, Db-€78, Tb-€87, tax not included, breakfast-€3.90, CC, midway between Puerta del Sol and Plaza del Callao at Mesonero Romanos 9, tel. 91-521-2941, fax 91-532-3014, e-mail: info@hotelregente.com).

Euromadrid Hotel is like a cross between a Motel 6 and a hospital, with 43 white rooms in a modern but well-worn shell (Sb-€54, Db-€75, Tb-€84, includes buffet breakfast but not tax, CC, air con, discounted rate for parking-€8.75/day, Mesonero Romanos 7, tel. 91-521-7200, fax 91-521-4582, e-mail: clasit@infonegocio.com).

Hotel Santo Domingo is a fancy, worthwhile splurge— for its artsy paintings, inviting lounge, and 120 great rooms, each decorated differently (Sb-€114, Db-€168, pricier superior rooms are not necessary, CC, air con, elevator, Plaza de Santo Domingo 13, tel. 91-547-9800, fax 91-547-5995, www.hotelsantodomingo .com). Prices drop—and breakfast is included—on weekends (Fri, Sat, and Sun) and July through August.

Hotel Arosa charges the same for all of its 134 rooms, whether they're sleekly remodeled art-deco or just aging gracefully. Ask for a remodeled room with a terrace (Sb-€101, Db-€154, cheaper July–Aug, taxes not included, breakfast-€10.75, CC, air con, memorably tiny triangular elevator, Calle Salud 21, a block off Plaza del Carmen, tel. 91-532-1600, reservations number in Spain: tel. 90-099-3900, fax 91-531-3127).

A block away, the more basic **Hotel Anaco** has a drab color scheme, but offers 39 quiet, comfortable rooms in a central location (Sb-€69, Db-€84, tax not included, breakfast-€4.20, CC, air con, elevator, Tres Cruces 3, a few steps off Plaza del Carmen and its underground parking lot, tel. 915-22-4604, fax 91-531-6484, e-mail: info@anacohotel.com).

The huge **Hotel Liabeny** is a business-class hotel with 222 plush, spacious rooms and all the comforts (Sb-€99, Db-€132, Tb-€156, cheaper July–Aug, taxes not included, breakfast-€10.80, CC, air con, if one room is smoky ask for another, off Plaza Carmen at Salud 3, tel. 91-531-9000, fax 91-532-7421, www.apunte .es/liabeny, e-mail: liabeny@apunte.es).

Hotel Opera, a serious, modern hotel with 79 classy rooms, is located just off Plaza Isabel II, a four-block walk from Puerta del Sol toward the Royal Palace (Sb-€75, Db-€105, Db with terrace-€114, Tb-€137, tax not included, buffet breakfast-€8, CC, air con, elevator, ask for a higher floor—there are eight—to avoid street noise; consider their "singing dinners" offered nightly at 22:00—average price €42, Cuesta de Santo Domingo 2, Metro: Opera, tel. 91-541-2800, fax 91-541-6923, www.hotelopera.com, e-mail: reservas@hotelopera.com).

Sleeping at Gran Vía #44
(zip code: 28013)

The pulse (and noise) of today's Madrid is best felt along the Gran Vía. This main drag in the heart of the city stays awake all night. Despite the dreary pile of prostitutes just a block north, there's a certain urban decency about it. My choices (all at Gran Vía #44) are across from Plaza del Callao, which is four colorful blocks (of pedestrian malls) from Puerta del Sol. Although many rooms are high above the traffic noise, cooler and quieter rooms are on the back side. The Café & Te next door provides a classy way to breakfast. The Callão Metro stop is at your doorstep, and the handy Gran Vía stop (direct to Atocha) is two blocks away.

Hostal Residencia Miami is clean and quiet, with 11 well-lit rooms (3 with private bath), padded doors, and plastic-flower decor throughout. It's like staying at your eccentric aunt's in Miami Beach (Ss-€30, Ds-€36, Db-€42, T-€42, Tb-€51, Qb-€60, includes tax, CC, 8th floor, tel. & fax 91-521-1464). This *hostal* and the Alibel (see below), owned by the same family, might merge next year.

Across the hall, **Hostal Alibel,** like Miami with less sugar, rents eight big, airy, quiet rooms (D-€30, Ds-€33, Db-€36, no CC, tel. 91-521-0051, grandmotherly Terese NSE).

These next two are well-worn and suffer from street noise. **Hostal Residencia Valencia** is a tired old place with 32 big, stark rooms. The friendly manager, Antonio Ramirez, speaks English (Sb-€29.50, Ds-€39, Db-€42, Tb-€57, Qb-€63, includes tax, CC, 5th floor, tel. 91-522-1115, fax 91-522-1113, e-mail: hostalvalencia@wanadoo.es). **Hostal Residencia Continental,** with 29 older, basic but bright rooms, is downstairs and closer to the traffic (Sb-€29, Db-€42, includes tax, CC, 3rd floor, tel. 91-521-4640, fax 91-521-4649, www.hostalcontinental.com, e-mail: continental@mundivia.es, SE).

Sleeping on or near Plaza Santa Ana (zip code: 28012 unless otherwise noted)

The Plaza Santa Ana area has small, cheap places mixed in with fancy hotels. While the neighborhood is noisy at night, it has a rough but charming ambience, with colorful bars and a central location (3 min from Puerta del Sol's "Tío Pepe" sign; walk down Calle San Jerónimo and turn right on Príncipe; Metro: Sol). To locate hotels, see map on page 89.

Cheap: Because of the following three places, I list no Madrid youth hostels. At these cheap hotels, fluent Spanish is spoken, bathrooms are down the hall, and there's no heat during winter.

Hopeless romantics might enjoy playing corkscrew around the rickety cut-glass elevator to the very simple yet homey **Pensión La Valenciana**'s seven old and funky rooms with springy beds. All rooms have balconies; three of them overlook the square (S-€13, D-€24, includes tax, no CC, Príncipe 27, lots of stairs, 4th floor, right on Plaza Santa Ana next to the theater with flags, tel. 91-429-6317, Esperanza NSE).

For super-cheap beds in a dingy time warp, consider **Hostal Lucense** (13 rooms, S-€15-18, D-€18-21, Db-€30-36, €1.20 per shower, no CC, Nuñez de Arce 15, tel. 91-522-4888, run by Sr. and Sra. Muñoz, both interesting characters, Sr. SE) and **Casa Huéspedes Poza** (14 rooms, same prices, street noise, and owners—but Sr. does the cleaning, at Nuñez de Arce 9, tel. 91-522-4871).

Moderate: Hostal R. Veracruz II, between Plaza Santa Ana and Puerta del Sol, rents 22 decent, quiet rooms (Sb-€34, Db-€46, Tb-€65, no breakfast, CC, elevator, air con, Victoria 1, 3rd floor, tel. 91-522-7635, fax 91-522-6749, NSE).

Splurges: Suite Prado, two blocks toward the Prado from Plaza Santa Ana, is a good value, offering 18 sprawling, elegant, air-conditioned suites with a modern yet homey feel (Db suite-€150, sitting rooms and refrigerators, some have kitchens, extra adult-€24, extra kid free, breakfast at café next door-€3.60, CC, elevator, Manuel Fernandez y Gonzalez 10, at intersection with

Venture de la Vega, 28014 Madrid, tel. 91-420-2318, fax 91-420-0559, www.suiteprado.com, hotel@suiteprado.com, Anna SE). Across the street, **Residencia Hostal Lisboa** is also a good value (24 rooms, Sb-€39, Db-€50, Tb-€63, CC, air con, elevator, Ventura de la Vega 17, tel. 91-429-4676, fax 91-429-9894, e-mail: hostallisboa@inves.es).

To be on Plaza Santa Ana and spend in a day what others spend in a week, luxuriate in **Hotel Reina Victoria**. This is where out-of-town bullfighters stay before a fight (201 rooms, Sb-€180, Db-€220, prices generally discounted to "weekend rate" of Db-€120 on Fri, Sat, Sun in summer, and all of July, when this becomes a fine deal, prices don't include tax, breakfast-€18, CC, Plaza Santa Ana 14, tel. 91-531-4500, fax 91-522-0307, e-mail: reinavictoria@trypnet.com). For a royal, air-conditioned breather, spit out your gum, step into its lobby, grab a sofa, and watch the bellboys push the beggars back out the revolving doors.

Sleeping Near the Prado
(zip code: 28014)
Two fine places are at #34 Cervantes (Metro: Anton Martin). **Hostal Gonzalo**—with 15 spotless, comfortable rooms, well-run by friendly and helpful Javier—is deservedly in all the guidebooks. Reserve in advance (Sb-€33, Db-€39, Tb-€51, CC, elevator, 3rd floor, tel. 91-429-2714, fax 91-420-2007). Downstairs, the nearly-as-polished **Hostal Cervantes,** also with 15 rooms, is also good (Sb-€36, Db-€48, Tb-€60, CC, 2nd floor, tel. 91-429-8365, tel. & fax 91-429-2745, www.hostal-cervantes.com).

Eating in Madrid
In Spain, only Barcelona rivals Madrid for taste-bud thrills. You have three dining choices: an atmospheric sit-down meal in a well-chosen restaurant, an unmemorable basic sit-down meal, or a stand-up meal of tapas in a bar or (more likely) in several bars. Many restaurants are closed in August (especially through the last half).

Eating near Puerta del Sol
Restaurante Puerto Rico has good meals, great prices, and few tourists (Mon–Sat 13:00–16:30, 20:30–24:00, closed Sun, Chinchilla 2, between Puerta del Sol and Gran Vía, tel. 91-532-2040).

Hotel Europa Cafeteria is a fun, high-energy scene with a mile-long bar, traditionally clad waiters, great people-watching, local cuisine, and super prices (daily 7:30–24:00, next to Hotel Europa, 50 meters off Puerta del Sol at Calle del Carmen 4, tel. 91-521-2900). **Corte Inglés'** seventh-floor cafeteria is popular with locals (Mon–Sat 10:00–11:30, 13:00–16:15, 17:30–20:00, has nonsmoking section).

La Casa de las Torrijas, looking much like it did on opening day in 1907, serves cheap home-cooked lunch specials, tapas, and good wine. Avoid the *callos* (tripe). Their dessert specialty is *torrijas*, which is like cinammon French toast, Spanish-style. Try it with *mistela* (sweet wine). Many restaurants in Madrid serve *torrijas* around Easter as a traditional treat, but you can try it here any time of year (Mon–Sat 10:00–16:00, 18:00–23:30, closed Sun and Aug, good pictures of early-20th-century Madrid, a block off Puerta del Sol at Calle Paz 4, tel. 91-532-1473).

Vegetarian: Artemisia II is a hit with vegetarians who like good, healthy food in a smoke-free room (great €8.50 3-course lunch menu, daily 13:30–16:00, 21:00–24:00, CC, 2 blocks north of Puerta Sol at Tres Cruces 4, a few steps off Plaza Carmen, tel. 91-521-8721). **Artemisia I** is like its sister (same hours, 4 blocks east of Puerta Sol at Ventura de la Vega 4 off San Jerónimo, tel. 91-429-5092).

Eating on or near Plaza Mayor

Many Americans are drawn to Hemingway's favorite, **Sobrino del Botín** (daily 13:00–16:00, 20:00–24:00, CC, Cuchilleros 17, a block downhill from Plaza Mayor, tel. 91-366-4217). It's touristy, pricey (€24–30 average), and the last place he'd go now, but still, people love it and the food is excellent. If phoning to make a reservation, choose between the downstairs (for dark, medieval-cellar ambience) or upstairs (for a still-traditional but airier and lighter elegance). While this restaurant boasts it's the oldest in the world (dating from 1725), a nearby restaurant brags, "Hemingway never ate here."

Restaurante Los Galayos is less touristy and plenty *tipico* with good local cuisine (daily 9:30–24:00, lunch specials, lunch from 13:00, dinner from 20:30, arrive early or make a reservation, 30 meters off Plaza Mayor at Botoneras 5, tel. 91-366-3028). For many, dinner right on the square at a sidewalk café is worth the premium (consider Cerveceria Pulpito, southwest corner of the square at #10).

La Torre del Oro Bar Andalu on Plaza Mayor has soul. Die-hard bullfight aficionados hate the gimmicky Bull Bar listed under "Tapas," below. Here the walls are lined with grisly bull-fight photos from annual photo competitions. Read the gory description above in the Introductory Walk. Have a drink but be careful not to let the aggressive staff bully you into high-priced tapas you don't want (daily 11:00–16:00, 18:00–24:00, closed Jan, Plaza Mayor 26, tel. 91-366-5016).

Plaza Mayor is famous for its *bocadillos calamares*. For a cheap and tasty squid-ring sandwich, line up at **Casa Rua** at Plaza May-or's northwest corner, a few steps up Calle Ciudad Rodrigo (daily 9:00–23:00). Hanging up behind the bar is a photo/ad of Plaza Mayor from the 1950s, when the square contained a park.

Eating South of Plaza Mayor

Few tourists frequent this traditional neighborhood—Barrio de los Austrias—named after the Hapsburgs. It's five minutes south of Plaza Mayor, or a 10-minute walk from Puerta del Sol. For a more authentic Madrileño experience, come here.

El Madroño, a fun tapas bar, perserves chunks of old Madrid. A mosaic copy of Velázquez' famous *Drinkers* grins from its facade. Inside, look for the photo of laundry hanging by the river with the Royal Palace in the background, and plunk a few notes on the little 100-year-old organ. Study the coats of arms of Madrid through the centuries as you try a *vermut* on tap, *pisto* (mixed vegetables), and eggy *huevos rotos* (daily 10:00–24:00, Plaza Puerta Cerrada 7, tel. 91-364-5629). Two blocks farther down the street you'll find the atmospheric **Taberna los Austrias**, with tapas, salads, and light meals served on wood-barrel tables (daily 12:00–16:00, 20:00–24:00, Calle Nuncio 17). Next door is the **Taberna de los 100 Vinos** (Tavern of 100 Wines, Tue–Sat 20:00–24:00, closed Sun–Mon, Calle Nuncio 17).

On Calle Cava Baja: On this street is a string of fine restaurants, all within a stretch of two long blocks. Stroll up and down until you find a favorite. **Posada de la Ville** serves Castilian cuisine in a 17th-century posada. Take a look at the ovens (daily 13:00–16:00, 20:00–24:00, Calle Cava Baja 9, tel. 91-366-1860). **El Schotis** specializes in bull stew and fish dishes. Named after a popular local dance, the restaurant retains the traditional character of old Madrid (daily 12:00–17:00, 20:00–24:00, Calle Cava Baja 11, tel. 91-365-3230). **Julian de Tolosa** does Basque cuisine from T-bone steak to red *tolosa* beans (Mon–Sat 13:30–16:00, 21:00–24:00, Sun 13:30–16:00, Calle Cava Baja 18, tel. 91-365-8210). **Taberna los Lucio** has good tapas, salads, egg dishes, and wine (daily 13:00–16:00, 20:30–24:00, Calle Cava Baja 30, tel. 91-366-2984). For a splurge, dine at **Casa Lucio**, where the king and queen of Spain go (daily 13:00–17:00, 21:00–24:00, Calle Cava Baja 35; unless you're the king or queen, reserve several days in advance; tel. 91-365-3252). For wine-lovers, **Taberna Tempranillo** offers 250 kinds of wine, along with tapas. Arrive by 20:00 to avoid a wait (daily 13:00–15:30, 20:00–24:00, Cava Baja 38, tel. 91-364-1532).

Eating near the Sights

Near the Royal Palace: For a fine meal with no tourists and locals who appreciate good local-style cooking, try **Casa Ciriaco** (€18 meals, Thu–Tue 13:30–16:00, 20:30–24:00, closed Wed and Aug, halfway between Puerta del Sol and Royal Palace at Calle Mayor 84, tel. 91-548-0620). It was from this building in 1906 that an anarchist threw a bomb at the royal couple on their wedding day (for details, see "Introductory Walk," above). Photos of the carnage are on the wall in the dining room.

Near the Prado: Each of the big-three art museums has a decent cafeteria. The following two cafés are near the Prado. **La Plateria** is a hardworking little café/wine bar with a good menu for tapas, light meals, and hearty salads. Its tables spill onto the leafy little Plaza de Platarias de Matinez (daily 8:00–24:00, directly across busy boulevard Paseo del Prado from Atocha end of Prado, tel. 91-429-1722). Good-looking, young tour guides eat cheap and filling salads at **VIPS**, a bright, popular chain restaurant engulfed in a big bookstore (daily 9:00–24:00, across Paseo del Prado boulevard from northern end of Prado in Galeria del Prado under Palace Hotel).

Fast Food and Picnics

Fast Food: For an easy, light, cheap meal, try **Rodilla**—a popular sandwich chain on the northeast corner of Puerta del Sol at #13 (Mon–Fri 9:30–23:00, opens on Sat at 10:00, Sun at 11:00). **Pans & Company,** with shops throughout Madrid and Spain, offers healthy, tasty sandwiches and chef's salads (daily 9:00–24:00, on Puerta del Sol, Plaza Callão, Gran Vía 30, and many more).

Picnics: The department store **El Corte Inglés** has a well-stocked **deli** downstairs (Mon–Sat 10:00–22:00, closed Sun). A perfect place to assemble a cheap picnic is downtown Madrid's neighborhood market, **Mercado de San Miguel**. How about breakfast surrounded by early-morning shoppers in the market's café? (Mon–Fri 9:00–14:30, 17:15–20:15, Sat 9:00–14:30, closed Sun; to reach the market from Plaza Mayor, face the colorfully painted building and exit from the upper left-hand corner.)

Churros con Chocolate

If you like hash browns and eggs in American greasy-spoon joints, you must try the Spanish equivalent: Greasy *churros* dipped in thick, hot chocolate. **Bar Valladolid** is a good bet (daily 7:00–22:30, best in the morning, 2 blocks off Tío Pepe end of Puerta del Sol, south on Espoz y Mina, turn right on Calle de Cadiz). With luck, the *churros* machine in the back will be cooking. Notice the expressive WC signs.

The classy **Chocolatería San Ginés** is much loved by locals for its *churros* and chocolate (Tue–Sun 19:00–7:00, closed Mon). While empty before midnight, it's packed with the disco crowd in the wee hours; the popular Joy disco is next door. Dunk your *churros* into the pudding-like hot chocolate, as locals have done here for over 100 years (from Puerta del Sol, take Calle Arenal 2 blocks west, turn left on book-lined Pasadizo de San Ginés, you'll see the café—it's at #5, tel. 93-365-6546).

Tapas: The Madrid Pub-Crawl Dinner

For maximum fun, people, and atmosphere, go mobile and do the "tapa tango," a local tradition of going from one bar to the next,

Plaza Santa Ana Area

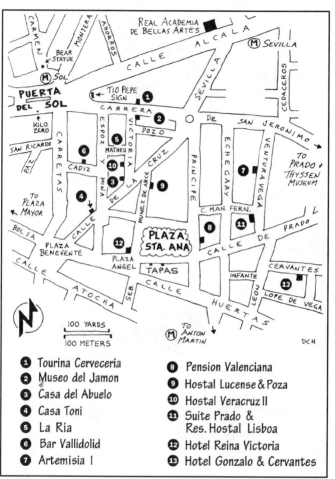

1 Tourina Cerveceria
2 Museo del Jamon
3 Casa del Abuelo
4 Casa Toni
5 La Ria
6 Bar Vallidolid
7 Artemisia I
8 Pension Valenciana
9 Hostal Lucense & Poza
10 Hostal Veracruz II
11 Suite Prado & Res. Hostal Lisboa
12 Hotel Reina Victoria
13 Hotel Gonzalo & Cervantes

munching, drinking, and socializing. Tapas are the toothpick appetizers, salads, and deep-fried foods served in most bars. Madrid is Spain's tapa capital—tapas just don't get any better. Grab a toothpick and stab something strange—but establish the prices first. Some items are very pricey, and most bars push larger *raciónes* rather than smaller tapas. *Un pincho* is a bite-sized serving (not always available), *una tapa* is a snack, and *una ración* is half a meal. *Un bocadillo* is a tapa on bread. A *caña* (can-yah) is a small glass of draft beer. A *chato* is a small glass of house wine.

Prowl the area between Puerta del Sol and Plaza Santa Ana. There's no ideal route, but the little streets (in this book's map) between Puerta del Sol, San Jerónimo, and Plaza Santa Ana hold tasty surprises. Nearby, the street Jesus de Medinaceli is also lined with popular tapas bars. Below is a five-stop tapa crawl. These places are good, but don't be blind to making discoveries on your own. The action is better after 20:00.

1. From Puerta del Sol, walk east a block down Carrera de San Jerónimo to the corner of Victoria Street. Across from Museo del Jamón, you'll find **La Tourina Cervecería**, a bullfighters' Planet Hollywood (daily 8:00–24:00). Wander among trophies and historic photographs. Each stuffed bull's head is named, along with its farm, awards, and who killed him. Among the photos study the first post: It's Che Guevara, Orson Welles, and Salvador Dalí all enjoying a good fight. Around the corner, the Babe Ruth of bullfighters, El Cordobes, lies wounded in bed. The photo below shows him in action. Kick off your pub crawl with a drink here. If inspired, you could go for the *rabo de toro* (bull-tail stew, €9.60). Across the street at San Jerónimo 5 is...

2. **Museo del Jamón (Museum of Ham),** tastefully decorated— unless you're a pig. This frenetic, cheap, stand-up bar is an assembly line of fast and simple *bocadillos* and *raciónes*. Options are shown in photographs with prices. For a small sandwich, ask for a *chiquito* (€0.60, unadvertised). The pricey Jamón Iberico—from pigs who led stress-free lives in acorn valley—is best. Just point and eat (daily 9:00–24:00, sit-down restaurant upstairs). Next, forage halfway up Calle Victoria (passing the Irish-type pub La Fontana de Oro) to the tiny...

3. **La Casa del Abuelo,** for seafood-lovers who savor sizzling plates of tasty little *gambas* (shrimp) and *langostinos* (prawns). Try *gambas a la plancha* (grilled shrimp, €3.60), *gambas al ajillo* (ahh-hheee-yoh, shrimp version of escargot, cooked in oil and garlic and ideal for bread dipping—€5), and a €1 glass of red wine (daily 11:30–15:30, 18:30–23:30, Calle Victoria 12). Continue uphill and around the corner to...

4. **Casa Toni,** for refreshing bowls of gazpacho—the popular cold tomato-and-garlic soup (€1.50). Their specialty is *berenjena*, deep-fried slices of eggplant (€3.60, daily 11:30–16:00, 18:00–23:30, closed July, Calle Cruz 14). Backtrack halfway down Calle Victoria and turn left, walking through an alley littered with tourist-filled dining tables to...

5. **La Ria,** a tapas bar that sells plates of 10 mussels (*mejillones*). Slurp out the meat, scoop the juice with the shells, and toss the shells on the floor as you smack your lips—don't look down (daily 11:30–15:30, 19:30–23:30, Pasaje Matheu 5). You can get your *mejillones* mild *con limone* or spicy—*picante* (€3). Wash them down with the crude, dry, white Ribeiro wine from Galicia—served in

a ceramic bowl to disguise its lack of clarity. The place is draped in mussels. Notice the photo showing the floor filled with litter—a reminder that mussel bars, while lonely these days, have seen better times. In the 1970s they sold 14 tons a month. Now—with other, more trendy evening activities entertaining the cruising youth—it takes a year to sell 14 tons. Next door, **Las Bravas** brags that its sauce (ladled on boiled potatoes) is so good it's patented (daily 12:00–16:00, 19:30–24:00).

If you're hungry for more, head for Plaza Santa Ana. The south side of the square is lined with trendy bars that offer good tapas, drinks, and a classic setting right on the square. Consider **Naturbeer** (brews its own beers—like our microbrews), **Cerveceria de Santa Ana** (tasty tapas with a beer-hall atmosphere), **La Moderna** (wine, pâté, and cheese plates), and others.

Transportation Connections—Madrid

By train to: Toledo (9/day, 1 hr, from Madrid's Atocha station, if daytripping there's a direct Madrid–Toledo express at 8:34 or 9:44 and a Toledo–Madrid express at 18:56), **Segovia** (9/day, 2 hrs, both Chamartin and Atocha stations), **Ávila** (6/day, 90 min, from Chamartin and Atocha), **Salamanca** (4/day, 2.5 hrs, from Chamartin), **Barcelona** (7/day, 8 hrs, mostly from Chamartin, 2 overnight), **Granada** (2/day, 6–9 hrs, including an overnight train, from Chamartin), **Sevilla** (15/day, 2.5 hrs by AVE, 3.5 hrs by Talgo, from Atocha), **Córdoba** (16 AVE trains/day, 2 hrs, from Atocha), **Málaga** (5/day, 4 hrs, from Atocha), **Lisbon** (1/day, 10 hrs, pricey overnight Hotel Train from Chamartin), **Paris** (4/day, 12–16 hrs, 1 direct overnight—a pricey Hotel Train, from Chamartin). Train info: tel. 90-224-0202.

Spain's AVE bullet train opens up some good itinerary options. Pick up the brochure at the station. Prices vary with times and class. The basic Madrid–Sevilla second-class fare is €61 (€6.50 less on the almost-as-fast Talgo). AVE is heavily discounted for Eurail passholders (the Madrid–Sevilla 2nd-class trip costs Eurailers about €14). So far AVE only covers Madrid–Córdoba–Sevilla, but within a couple of years it's slated to extend to Barcelona. Consider this exciting daytrip from Madrid: 7:00 depart, 8:45–12:40 in Córdoba, 13:30–21:00 in Sevilla, 23:30 back in Madrid. Reserve each AVE segment (tel. 90-224-0202, Atocha AVE info: tel. 91-534-0505).

By bus to: Segovia (2/hr, 1.25 hrs, first departure 6:30, last return at 21:30, La Sepulvedana buses, Paseo de la Florida 11, from Metro stop: Príncipe Pío go past Hotel Florida Norte and look for yellow mailbox—near it is the Larrea bus station, tel. 91-530-4800). For **Ávila** (7/day, 2 hrs) or **Toledo** (2/hr, 60–75 min), catch a bus from Estación sur Autobuses (which sits squarely atop of Metro: Méndez Alvaro, with eateries and a small TI—open daily 9:00–20:45, Avenida de Méndez Alvaro, tel. 91-468-4200).

By bus, train, and car to El Escorial: Buses leave from the basement of Madrid's Metro stop Moncloa and drop you in the El Escorial center (4/hr, 45 min, in Madrid take bus #664 or #661 from Intercambiador's bay #3, tel. 91-896-9028). One bus a day (except for Mon, when sights are closed) is designed to let travelers do the Valley of the Fallen as a side trip from El Escorial; the bus leaves El Escorial at 15:15 (15-min trip) and leaves Valley of the Fallen at 17:30. Trains run to El Escorial but let you off a 20-minute walk (or a shuttle-bus ride, 2/hr) from the monastery and city center. By car, visiting El Escorial and Valley of the Fallen on the way to Segovia is easy (except on Mon, when both sights are closed).

Drivers' note: Avoid driving in Madrid. Rent your car when you leave. It's cheapest to make car-rental arrangements before you leave home. In Madrid, consider **Europcar** (central reservations tel. 90-210-5030, San Leonardo 8 office: tel. 91-541-8892, Chamartin station: tel. 91-323-1721, airport: tel. 91-393-7235), **Hertz** (central reservations tel. 90-240-2405, Gran Vía 88: tel. 91-542-5803, Chamartin station: tel. 91-733-0400, airport: tel. 91-393-7228), **Avis** (Gran Vía 60: tel. 91-547-2048, airport: tel. 91-393-7222), **Alamo** (central reservations tel. 90-210-0515), and **Budget** (central reservations tel. 90-120-1212, www.budget .es). Ask about free delivery to your hotel. At the airport, most rental cars are returned at Terminal 1.

Madrid's Barajas Airport

Sixteen kilometers east of downtown, Madrid's modern airport has three terminals. You'll likely land at Terminal 1, which has a helpful English-speaking TI (marked "Oficina de Información Turistica," Mon–Fri 8:00–20:00, Sat 9:00–13:00, closed Sun, tel. 91-305-8656); an ATM (part of the BBVA bank) far busier than the lonely American Express window; a 24-hour exchange office (plus shorter-hour exchange offices); a flight info office (marked simply "Information" in airport lobby, open 24 hrs/day, tel. 902-353-570); a post office window; a pharmacy; lots of phones (buy a phone card from the machine near the phones); a few scattered Internet terminals (small fee); eateries; a RENFE office (where you can get train info and buy train tickets; daily 8:00–21:00, tel. 91-305-8544); and on-the-spot car-rental agencies (see above). The three terminals are connected by long indoor walkways; it's about an eight-minute walk between terminals (the Metro is in Terminal 2).

Iberia is Spain's airline, connecting many cities in Spain as well as international destinations (Velázquez 130, phone answered 24 hrs/day, tel. 90-240-0500, www.iberia.com).

Getting between the airport and downtown: By public transport, consider an affordable, efficient **airport bus/taxi combination**. Take the airport bus (#89, usually blue) from the airport to Madrid's Plaza Colón (€2.40, 4/hr, 20–30 min, leaves Madrid

4:30–24:00, leaves airport 5:15–02:00; stops at both Terminals 1 and 2; at the airport the bus stop is outside Terminal 1's arrivals door—cross the street filled with taxis to reach stop marked "Bus" on median strip; at Plaza Colón the stop is underground). Then, to reach your hotel from Plaza Colón, you can take a taxi (insist on meter, ride to hotel should be far less than €6, to avoid supplement charge for rides from a bus station, it's a little cheaper to go upstairs and flag down a taxi). Or from Plaza Colón, you can take the subway (to get to the subway from the underground bus stop, walk up the stairs and face the blue "URBIS" sign high on a building—the subway stop, M. Serrano, is 50 meters to your right; it takes two transfers to reach Puerta del Sol).

At the airport, ignore bus #101, a holdover from the time when the airport didn't have a Metro stop (it runs to Canillejas Metro stop on Madrid's outskirts).

You can take the **Metro** all the way between the airport and downtown. The airport's futuristic Aeropuerto Metro stop in Terminal 2 provides a cheap but time-consuming way into town (€1, or get a shareable 10-pack for €4.50; takes 45 min with 2 transfers; at airport, access Metro at check-in level; from Terminal 1 arrivals level, stand with your back to baggage claim, then go to your far right, up the stairs, and follow red-and-blue diamond-shaped Metro diamond signs to Metro station, 8-minute walk; to get to Puerta del Sol from the airport, transfer at Mar de Cristal to brown line #4—direction Arguelles, then transfer at Goya to red line #3—direction Cuatro Caminos).

For a taxi to or from the airport, allow €18 (€2.40 airport supplement is legal). Cabbies routinely try to get €30—a rip-off. At the airport, get a rough idea of the price before you hop in. Approach an idle cabbie (who's not in a hurry) who is waiting farther back in the taxi lineup. Ask "*¿Cuanto cuesta a Madrid, más o menos?*" ("How much is it to Madrid, more or less?")

NORTHWEST OF MADRID:
EL ESCORIAL, VALLEY OF THE FALLEN, SEGOVIA, SALAMANCA

Before slipping out of Madrid by train, consider several fine side trips northwest of Spain's capital city.

Spain has a lavish, brutal, and complicated history. An hour from Madrid, tour the imposing and fascinating palace of Monasterio de San Lorenzo de El Escorial, headquarters of the Spanish Inquisition. Nearby, at the awesome Valley of the Fallen, pay tribute to the countless victims of Spain's bloody civil war.

Segovia, with its remarkable Roman aqueduct and romantic castle, is also an easy side trip from Madrid. Farther out, you can walk the perfectly preserved medieval walls of Ávila. And at Salamanca, enjoy Spain's best town square, caffeinated with a frisky college-town ambience.

Planning Your Time

See El Escorial and the Valley of the Fallen together in less than a day (but not Mon, when sights are closed). By car, do them en route to Segovia; by bus, make it a daytrip from Madrid.

Segovia is worth a half day of sightseeing and is a joy at night. Ávila, while not without charm, merits only a quick stop to marvel at its medieval walls, if you're driving in the neighborhood.

Salamanca, with its art, university, and Spain's greatest Plaza Mayor, is worth a day and a night but is stuck out in the boonies. On a three-week Barcelona–Lisbon "open-jaw" itinerary, I'd hook south from Madrid and skip Salamanca. If you're doing a circular trip, Salamanca is a natural stop halfway between Portugal and Madrid.

In total, these sights are worth a maximum of three days if you're in Iberia for less than a month. If you're in Spain for just a week, I'd still squeeze in a look at El Escorial and the Valley of the Fallen.

Sights Near Madrid

EL ESCORIAL

The Monasterio de San Lorenzo de El Escorial is a symbol of power rather than elegance. This 16th-century palace, 50 kilometers northwest of Madrid, gives us a better feel for the Counter-Reformation and the Inquisition than any other building. Built at a time when Catholic Spain felt threatened by Protestant "heretics," its construction dominated the Spanish economy for 20 years (1563–1584). Because of this bully in the national budget, Spain has almost nothing else to show from this most powerful period of her history.

The giant, gloomy building looks more like a prison than a palace (gray-black stone, 200 meters long, 150 meters wide, over 160 kilometers of passages, 2,600 windows, 1,200 doors, 1,600 overwhelmed tourists). Four hundred years ago, the enigmatic, introverted, and extremely Catholic King Philip II ruled his bulky empire and directed the Inquisition from here. To 16th-century followers of Luther, this place epitomized the evil of Catholicism. Today it's a time capsule of Spain's "Golden Age," packed with history, art, and Inquisition ghosts.

The Monasterio looks confusing at first, but you simply follow

El Escorial

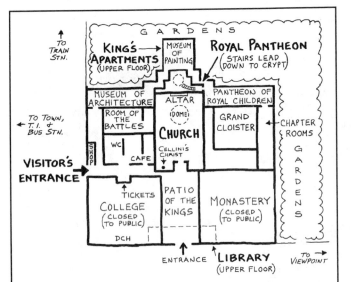

the arrows and signs in one continuous walk-through. Guides in
each room can answer basic questions. The entrance (off Grimaldi,
a minute's walk from TI) is the best place to start. This is the general order you'll follow (though some rooms are sure to be closed
for renovation). The small **Museum of Architecture** (*Museo de
Arquitectura*) has easy-to-appreciate models of the palace and the
machinery used to construct it. The **Museum of Painting** (*Museo
de Pintura*), packed with big paintings in small rooms, features works
by Titian, Veronese, Rubens, Bosch, van Dyck, and van der Wey-
den. The **King's Apartments** are notable for their austerity, with
a bed that's barely queen-size. The king made sure his quarters
came with a view ... of the church's high altar. Stairs take you down
into the **Royal Pantheon** (*Panteón Real*), the gilded resting place
of 26 kings and queens, four centuries' worth of Spanish monarchy.
The lazy Susan–like **Pantheon of Royal Children** (*Panteón de los
Infantes*) holds the remains of various royal children and relatives.
Paintings by Ribera, El Greco, Titian, and Velázquez elegantly
decorate the **Chapter Rooms** (*Salas Capitulares*). The **cloister**
glows with bright, newly restored paintings by Tibaldi. The vivid
frescoes in the newly-reopened **Room of the Battles** (*Sala de
Batallas*) depict important Spanish battles.

Follow the signs to the **church**. The altar is spectacular when
illuminated (put a coin in the small box near the church entrance,

just before the gated doors), but the highlight is Cellini's marble sculpture *The Crucifixion* (to the left as you enter).

Last comes the **Library** *(Biblioteca)*—have your ticket handy. Savor this room. The ceiling is a burst of color, and the meshed bookcases feature illustrated books. At the far end of the room, the elaborate model of the solar system looks like a giant gyroscope, revolving unmistakably around the earth. Notice the misshapen North America.

Admission to the palace is €6 (Tue–Sun 10:00–19:00, enter before ticket office closes at 18:00, closed Mon; Oct–March palace closes at 18:00; tel. 91-890-5904). To include a tour (available 10:00–18:00), pay €7 for admission, but the tour is limited to the apartments and mausoleum only, and English tours occur only if there is an English-speaking guide available. To visit the ornate, luxurious Bourbon apartments, call for a reservation a day in advance (€3 extra, mandatory guided tour in Spanish, tel. 91-890-5904).

You'll find scanty but sufficient captions in English within the palace. For more information, get the *Visitor's Guide: Monastery of San Lorenzo El Real de El Escorial*, which follows the general route you'll take (€6, available at any of several shops in the palace).

If you arrive by bus at the town of San Lorenzo de El Escorial, walk from the bus station to the TI. Exit the bus station from the back ramp and not by the street in front. This way leads you through the Duque de Leyra pedestrian street. Take a left at Duque de Medinaceli, go down the stairs at the park, and you'll see the palace at the end of the street Grimaldi. The **TI** (Mon–Thu 11:00–18:00, Fri–Sun 10:00–19:00, tel. 91-890-5313) is on the corner of Grimaldi in front of the entrance of the palace.

The town is worth a browse. Up the hill from the TI on Grimaldi are two pleasant, stair-stepped plazas (Jacinto Benavente and San Lorenzo).

Eating in El Escorial

To shop for a picnic, stop by the Mercado Publico on Calle del Rey 9, a four-minute walk from the palace (Mon–Fri 9:00–14:00, 17:00–20:00, Sat 10:00–14:00, closed Thu afternoon and Sun). For a change from Spanish fare, consider pizza at Tavolata Reale (Plaza de Las Animas, a block from Monasterio entrance, tel. 91-809-4591) or Restaurante China Hong Kong (Calle San Anton 6, tel. 91-896-1894).

Transportation Connections—El Escorial

From Madrid: Buses leave from the basement level of Madrid's Metro stop Moncloa and drop you in the town center of San Lorenzo de El Escorial, near the Monasterio (4/hr, 45 min, in Madrid take bus #664 or #661 from Intercambiador's bay #3, tel. 91-890-4100).

The **train** is less convenient. Although trains leave twice hourly from Madrid's Atocha and Chamartín stations, you're dropped a 20-minute walk (or shuttle-bus ride, 2/hr) from San Lorenzo de El Escorial town center and Monasterio.

To Valley of the Fallen: Without a car, the easiest way to get to the Valley of the Fallen from El Escorial is by bus (1/day except Mon when sights are closed, 15 min, leaves El Escorial at 15:15, leaves Valley of the Fallen at 17:30, €7 round-trip includes admission to the site). Buy your ticket in El Escorial at the bar on Calle del Rey, just around the corner from the bus stop (the bus driver will point the way).

VALLEY OF THE FALLEN (EL VALLE DE LOS CAÍDOS)

Eight kilometers from El Escorial, high in the Guadarrama Mountains, a 150-meter-tall granite cross marks an immense and powerful underground monument to the victims of Spain's 20th-century nightmare—its civil war (1936–1939).

The stairs that lead to the imposing monument are grouped in sets of tens, meant to symbolize the Ten Commandments (including "Thou shalt not kill"—hmm). The emotional pietà draped over the entrance was sculpted by Juan de Avalos, the same artist who created the dramatic figures of the four evangelists at the base of the cross.

A solemn silence and a stony chill fill the basilica—larger (265 meters long) than St. Peter's—as Spaniards pass under the huge, forbidding angels of fascism to visit the grave of General Franco. The term "basilica" normally designates a church built over the remains of a saint, not a fascist dictator. Franco's prisoners, the enemies of the right, dug this memorial out of solid rock.

The sides of the monument are lined with copies of 16th-century Brussels tapestries of the Apocalypse and side chapels containing alabaster copies of Spain's most famous statues of the Virgin Mary.

Interred behind the high altar and side chapels are the remains of the approximately 50,000 people, both Republicanos and Franco's Nacionalistas, who lost their lives in the war. Regrettably the urns are not visible, so it is Franco who takes center stage. His grave, strewn with flowers, lies behind the high altar. In front of the altar is the grave of José Antonio, the founder of Spanish fascism. Between these fascists' graves is the statue of a crucified Christ. The seeping stones seem to weep.

On your way out, stare into the eyes of those angels with swords and two right wings and think about all the "heroes" who keep dying "for God and country," at the request of the latter (€4.80, or €7 to include round-trip bus from El Escorial, Tue–Sun 10:00–19:00, ticket office closes at 18:00, closed Mon, tel. 91-890-7756).

The expansive view from the monument's terrace includes

the peaceful, forested valley and sometimes snow-streaked mountains. A funicular climbs to the base of the cross and a better view (€2.40 round-trip, Tue–Sun 10:30–19:00, tel. 91-890-5611). A small snack bar and picnic tables are near the parking lot (and bus stop). Overnight lodging is available at the monastery behind the cross (D-€40, includes meals, tel. 91-890-5494, NSE).

For information on how to reach Valley of the Fallen from El Escorial by bus, see "Transportation Connections— El Escorial," above.

SEGOVIA

Eighty kilometers from Madrid, this town of 55,000 boasts a great Roman aqueduct, a cathedral, and a castle. Segovia is a medieval "ship" ready for your inspection. Start at the stern—the aqueduct— and stroll up Calle de Cervantes to the prickly Gothic masts of the cathedral. Explore the tangle of narrow streets around Plaza Mayor and then descend to the Alcázar at the bow.

If you're visiting between mid-January and August, look for storks nesting atop church belltowers (such as the Church of San Justo's, near the base of the aqueduct). Off-season, most of the storks split for southern Spain or northern Africa, but some stay in Segovia year-round.

Orientation

Tourist Information: There are two TIs. The one on Plaza del Azoguejo, at the base of the aqueduct, is a city TI and charges €0.30 for Segovia maps (daily 10:00–20:00, tel. 92-146-2906 or 92-146-2914, e-mail: segoviaturism@interbook.net). The other TI, at the top of the old town at Plaza Mayor 10, covers the region, is probably better funded, and dispenses Segovia maps for free (daily 9:00–14:00, 17:00–19:00, tel. 92-146-0334).

Arrival in Segovia: The train station is a 30-minute walk from the center. Take a city bus from the station to get to Calle de Colón, about 100 meters from Plaza Mayor (catch bus at the same side of the street as the station—confirm by asking, "*¿Para Plaza Mayor?*; 2/hr, €0.60, pay driver). Taxis are a reasonable option (€4.20) if any are around. If you arrive by bus, it's a 15-minute walk to the center (turn left out of the bus station and continue straight across the street, jog right a couple meters around the building and you're on Avenida de Fernandez Ladreda—follow this to the aqueduct). Daytrippers can store luggage at the train station (buy €3 tokens at ticket window), but not at the bus station. Drivers can park for free during the day in the Alcázar's lot (in the old town), but must retrieve their cars by 19:00. Outside of the old city, there's an Acueducto Parking underground garage kitty-corner from the bus station, and free parking east of the aqueduct on the south side of Via Roma and the streets directly south of Via Roma.

Helpful Hint: If you buy handicrafts such as tablecloths from street vendors, make sure the item you're buying is the one you actually get; some unscrupulous vendors substitute inferior goods at the last minute.

Sights—Segovia

▲**Roman Aqueduct**—Built by the Romans, who ruled Spain for more than 500 years, this 2,000-year-old *acueducto Romano* is 770 meters (2,500 feet) long and 30 meters (100 feet) high, has 118 arches, was made without any mortar, and still works. It's considered Segovia's backup plumbing. On Plaza Azoguejo, a stairway (to right of TI) leads from the base of the aqueduct to the top—offering close-up looks at the imposing work. (If going *down* the steps next to the aqueduct has more appeal, tour Segovia like this: Take the charming Calle Juan Bravo up to Plaza Mayor, see the sights, then go down the stairs by the aqueduct to finish up your visit.)

Cathedral—Segovia's cathedral was Spain's last major Gothic building. Embellished to the hilt with pinnacles and flying buttresses, the exterior is a great example of the final overripe stage of Gothic, called Flamboyant. The dark, spacious, and elegantly simple interior provides a delightful contrast. In the chapel to the immediate left of the entry, notice the dramatic gilded, wheeled "Carroza de la Custadia." (If it's not here, look in the cathedral museum.) The Holy Communion is placed in the top of this temple-like cart and paraded through town each year during the Corpus Christi festival. The painting of *Tree of Life*, by Ignacio Ries, is also worth finding (as you enter, go right, to the last chapel—the painting is on the wall to the left of the altar). It shows hedonistic mortals dancing atop the tree of life. Look closely to see a skeletal Grim Reaper preparing to receive them into hell and Jesus ringing a bell imploring them to wake up before it's too late (€1.80, free only on Sun 9:00–14:00; open daily March–Oct 10:00–18:30, Nov–Feb 9:30–17:30). The peaceful cloister, opposite the cathdral entrance, contains a small but interesting museum (closed Sun 9:00–14:00).

▲**Alcázar**—This Disneyesque rebuild, an exaggeration of an old castle that burned down here in 1862, is fun to explore and worthwhile for the view of Segovia. While it's said that Isabel first met Ferdinand here and that Columbus came here to get his fantasy financed, the tower is of little importance historically. Only a portion of the keep, which you'll pass through as you enter, is from the original castle (€3, daily 10:00–19:00, off-season until 18:00, get the cheap English leaflet, tel. 92-146-0759).

Strolling—Roman and Romanesque Segovia was made for roamin'. Rub shoulders with Segovian yuppies parading up and down Calle Juan Bravo. For subtler charm, wander the back

Segovia

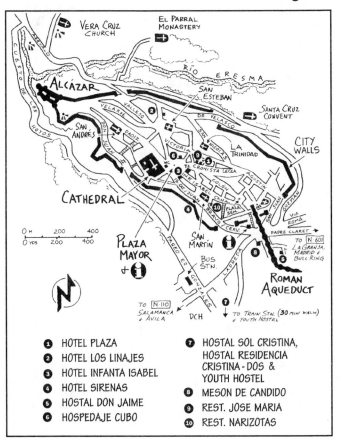

● HOTEL PLAZA
● HOTEL LOS LINAJES
● HOTEL INFANTA ISABEL
● HOTEL SIRENAS
● HOSTAL DON JAIME
● HOSPEDAJE CUBO

● HOSTAL SOL CRISTINA,
  HOSTAL RESIDENCIA
  CRISTINA - DOS &
  YOUTH HOSTEL
● MESON DE CANDIDO
● REST. JOSE MARIA
● REST. NARIZOTAS

streets, away from the trinket shops and ladies selling lace. Segovia
has a wealth of 12th- and 13th-century Romanesque churches
(usually open during Mass, often around 8:00 and 19:30, ask at
TI). Look Catholic and drop in. The **Church of San Justo** has
well-preserved 13th-century frescoes and a storks' nest atop its
tower (free, Tue–Sat 12:00–14:00, 17:00–19:00; in winter 11:00–
13:45, 16:00–19:00; closed Sun–Mon, near base of aqueduct, a
couple of blocks from Plaza Azoguejo, in the newer side of town).
The kind old caretaker, Rafael, will likely let you climb the bell
tower for "the best view of Segovia."

▲**Vera Cruz Church**—This 12-sided 13th-century Romanesque
church, built by the Knights Templar, used to house a piece of the

"true cross" (€1.20, Tue–Sun 10:30–13:30, 15:30–19:00, closed Mon and Nov, closes at 18:00 in winter, outside of town beyond the castle, a 20-min walk from main square, tel. 92-143-1475). There's a postcard view of the city from here, and more views follow as you continue around Segovia on the small road below the castle labeled *ruta turistica panoramica*.

▲La Granja Palace—This "Little Versailles," 10 kilometers south of Segovia, is much smaller and happier than El Escorial. The palace and gardens were built by the homesick French King Philip V, grandson of Louis XIV. It's a must for tapestry-lovers. Fountain displays send local crowds into a frenzy from 18:00 to 19:00 on most summer Wednesdays, Saturdays, Sundays, and holidays; July 25th and August 25th have the best shows of the year (confirm schedule at Segovia TI). Entry to the palace includes a required 45-minute guided tour, usually in Spanish (€4.80, June–Sept Tue–Sat 10:00–18:00, Sun 10:00–14:00, closed Mon; Oct–May Tue–Sat 10:00–13:30, 15:00–17:00, Sun 10:00–14:00; tel. 92-147-0019). Twelve buses a day (fewer on Sun) make the 30-minute trip from Segovia (catch at the bus station) to "San Idlefonso la Granja."

Sleeping in Segovia
(€1.10 = about $1, country code: 34, zip code 40001)
Sleep Code: **S** = Single, **D** = Double/Twin, **T** = Triple, **Q** = Quad, **b** = bathroom, **s** = shower only, **CC** = Credit Cards accepted, **no CC** = Credit Cards not accepted, **SE** = Speaks English, **NSE** = No English.

The best places are on or near the central Plaza Mayor. This is where the city action is: the cheapest and best bars, most touristic and *típico* eateries, and the TI. Segovia is crowded on weekends and in July and August, so arrive early or call ahead. The 7 percent IVA tax and breakfast aren't included.

Hostal Plaza is just off Plaza Mayor toward the aqueduct. You'll find *serioso* management, snaky corridors, and faded bedspreads, but the 26 rooms are clean and cozy (S-€19.75, 1 Sb-€32, D-€28.75, Db-€37, Tb-€50, CC, Cronista Lecea 11, tel. 92-146-0303, fax 92-146-0305, SE). If you're taking the bus from the train station, you'll get let off about 50 meters from this hotel.

Hotel Los Linajes is ultra-classy, with rusticity mixed into its newly poured concrete. This poor man's parador is a few blocks beyond the Plaza Mayor, with commanding views and modern, air-conditioned niceties (Sb-€49–59, Db-€76–99, depending on room size, Tb-€95, cheaper off-season, breakfast-€6, parking-€9, CC, air con, elevator, Dr. Velasco 9, tel. 92-146-0475, fax 92-146-0479, e-mail: hotelloslinages@terra.es). From Plaza Mayor, take Escuderos downhill; at the five-way intersection, angle right on Dr. Velasco. Drivers, follow brown signs from aqueduct.

Hotel Infanta Isabel, right on Plaza Mayor, is the ritziest hotel in the old town. Its 37 elegant rooms are pricey, but cheaper off-season (Sb-€53, Db-€75–87 depending on room size, some rooms with plaza views, CC, elevator, tel. 92-146-1300, fax 92-146-2217, e-mail: hinfanta@teleline.es, SE).

The big, stuffy hotelesque **Hotel Sirenas** has comfortable rooms in a central location (Sb-€35–41, Db-€47–59, CC, air con, elevator, 3 blocks down from Plaza Mayor at Calle Juan Bravo 30, tel. 92-146-2663, fax 92-146-2657, e-mail: hotelsirenas@terre.es, NSE).

The family-run **Hostal Don Jaime,** near the base of the aqueduct, is shiny-new, clean, well-maintained, and homey (S-€22, Db-€38, Tb-€48, Qb-€51, CC, Ochoa Ondategui 8; from TI at aqueduct, cross under the aqueduct, go right, angle left, then snake uphill for 2 blocks, tel. 92-144-4787, SE).

Right on Plaza Mayor at #4 is a tiny and dark but clean enough place (look hard for "Hospedaje Habitaciones" sign). The **Hospedaje Cubo** has five simple, sinkless but tidy rooms; request a room *con ventana* to avoid the windowless room (S-€10.80, D-€20.40, T-€30, ask at the ground-level La Oja Blanca Bar if rooms are available before climbing up, Plaza Mayor 4, tel. 92-146-0318, Maria Jesus Cubo NSE). **Pensión Ferri**, around the corner, is OK but a last resort (S-€10.75, D-€16.75, shower-€2.10, Escuderos 10, half block off Plaza Mayor, tel. 92-146-0957, NSE).

Across from the train station is **Hostal Sol Cristina** (17 fine rooms, S-€18, D-€30, Db-€39, Tb-€48, Calle Obispo Quesada 40, tel. 92-142-7513, NSE) and its nearby twin, **Hostal Residencia Sol Cristina-Dos** (11 rooms, same prices, same phone number).

The **Segovia Youth Hostel** is a great hostel—easygoing, comfortable, clean, friendly, and very cheap (€13 beds, open July–Aug only, Paseo Conde de Sepulveda 4, between the train and bus stations, tel. 92-144-1111).

Eating in Segovia

Look for Segovia's culinary claim to fame, roast suckling pig (*cochinillo asado*: 21 days of mother's milk, into the oven, and onto your plate—oh, Babe). It's worth a splurge here or in Toledo or Salamanca. While you're at it, try *sopa Castellana*—soup mixed with eggs, ham, and garlic bread.

Mesón de Candido, one of the top restaurants in Castile, is the place to spend €24 on a memorable dinner (daily 13:00–17:00, 20:00–23:00, Plaza Azoguejo 5, under aqueduct, tel. 92-142-8103 for reservations, gracious Alberto SE). In the old town, you can pig out at **Jose Maria**, a block off Plaza Mayor (daily 10:00–24:00, Cronista Lecea 11, tel. 92-146-6017).

Narizotas, a more modern place, attracts locals and tourists with €12 *platos combinados* (daily 13:00–16:00, 21:00–24:00, CC, Plaza de Medina del Campo 1, tel. 92-146-2679).

Rodilla, the popular chain, offers a great assortment of tasty half-sandwiches at cheap prices. Several make a meal (on Calle Juan Bravo, at intersection with Calle de la Herreria).

Inexpensive bars and eateries line Calle de Infanta Isabel, just off Plaza Mayor. For nightlife, the bars on Plaza Mayor, Calle de Infanta Isabel, and Calle Isabel la Católica are packed. And there are a number of discos along the aqueduct.

An **outdoor produce market** thrives on Plaza de los Huertos (Thu 8:00–14:00). Nearby, a few stalls are open Monday through Saturday on Calle del Croista Ildefonso Rodriguez.

Transportation Connections—Segovia

By train to: Madrid (9/day, 2 hrs, both Chamartin and Atocha stations). If day-tripping from Madrid, look for the *Cercanías* (commuter train) ticket window and departure board in either of Madrid's train stations and get a return schedule (or get these from either TI in Segovia). Train info: tel. 90-224-0202.

By bus to: La Granja Palace (12/day, 30 min), **Ávila** (3/day, 45 min), **Salamanca** (3/day, 3–4 hrs, transfer in Labajos; consider busing from Segovia to Ávila for a visit, then continuing to Salamanca by bus or train; tel. 92-142-7705), **Madrid** (hrly, 1.25 hrs, quicker than train, from Madrid's Larrea bus station, La Sepulvedana buses, Metro: Príncipe Pío, just past Hotel Florida Norte at Paseo de la Florida 11, tel. 92-142-7707). Bus schedules are always sparse on Sunday.

ÁVILA

A popular side trip from Madrid, the birthplace of St. Teresa is famous only for its perfectly preserved medieval walls. You can climb onto them through the gardens of the parador. Ávila's old town is charming, with several fine churches and monasteries. Pick up a box of the famous local sweets called *yemas*—like a soft-boiled egg yolk cooled and sugared. For an overnight trip, consider Hotel Continental, next to the TI (Db-€38, CC, Plaza de la Cathedral, tel. 92-021-1502, fax 92-025-1691).

Ávila is well connected to **Segovia** (3 buses/day, 45 min), **Madrid** (1 train/hr, 2 hrs, from Chamartin station, less frequent from Atocha; plus 8 buses/day from Madrid's Larrea bus station, Paseo de la Florida 11, Metro: Príncipe Pío, tel. 92-142-7707), and **Salamanca** (4 trains/day, 2 hrs; 4 buses/day, 2 hrs). While there are no lockers at the bus station, you can leave bags at the train station—a 10-minute walk away. Train info: tel. 92-224-0202. By car, Ávila is easy and worth a look if you're driving from Segovia or Madrid to Salamanca.

SALAMANCA

This sunny sandstone city boasts Spain's grandest plaza, its oldest university, and a fascinating history, all swaddled in a strolling, college-town ambience.

Salamanca is a youthful and untouristy Toledo. The city is a series of monuments and clusters of cloisters. The many students help keep prices down. Take a paseo with the local crowd down Rua Mayor and through Plaza Mayor. The young people congregate until late in the night, chanting and cheering, talking and singing. When I asked a local woman why young men all alone on the Plaza Mayor suddenly break into song, she said, "Doesn't it happen where you live?"

Along with Bruges in Belgium, Salamanca has been designated one of Europe's two Cultural Capitals for 2002. This means a busy slate of activities—such as theater, concerts, dance, and festivals—and possibly a new modern-art museum (for more information, see www.salamanca2002.org). Locals hope the temporary status will bring lasting results—attracting theaters that stick around, drawing conventions, and prompting better, more frequent transportation connections with Madrid and Portugal.

Orientation

Tourist Information: The more central Turismo is on Plaza Mayor (under the arch, on your right as you face the clock; Mon–Fri 9:00–14:00, 16:30–18:30, Sat–Sun from 10:00, tel. 92-321-8342). Pick up their free map, city brochure, and current list of museum hours. The other TI, covering Salamanca plus the Castile region, is in Casa de las Conchas on Rua Mayor (Mon–Fri 9:00–21:00, Sat–Sun 10:00–14:00, 16:00–19:00, tel. 92-326-9317). Ask for brochures on the Castile and Leon regions. Summertime-only TIs also spring up at the train and bus stations.

The little tourist tram you'll see about town does 20-minute loops through the city with a Spanish narration. For this Cultural Capital year, maybe they'll add English headphones—or maybe not (€2.40, daily 10:00–14:00, 16:00–20:00, leaves from new/old cathedrals). The daily walking tours at 11:00 are also in Spanish—maybe for this Cultural Capital year... (€4.20, 2 hrs, depart from TI at Casa de las Conchas).

Arrival in Salamanca: From Salamanca's train and bus stations to Plaza Mayor, it's a 20-minute walk, an easy bus ride (€0.60—pay driver), or a €3 trip by taxi. To walk to the center from the train station, exit left and walk down to the ring road, cross it at Plaza España, then angle slightly left up Calle Azafranal. Or you can take bus #1 from the train station, which lets you off at Plaza Mercado (the market), next to Plaza Mayor. Daytrippers can store bags in a train-station locker (€1.80–3.60).

To walk to the center from the bus station, exit right and

walk down Avenue Filiberto Villalobos; take a left on the ring
road and the first right on Ramon y Cajal. Or take bus #4 from
the station (exit station right, catch bus on same side of the street
as the station) to the city center; the closest stop is on Gran Vía,
about four blocks from Plaza Mayor (ask a fellow passenger,
"*¿Para Plaza Mayor?*").

Drivers will find a handy underground parking lot at Plaza
Santa Eulalia (€0.75/hr, €9/day); some hotels give you a discount
stamp on your parking receipt.

Helpful Hints

Internet Access: Cyberplace Internet is on Plaza Mayor (daily
11:00–24:00, near TI at Plaza Mayor 10, 1st floor, tel. 92-326-
4281). The Internet Café, down the alley under Plaza Mayor's
clock tower, is a little quieter.

Travel Agency: Viajes Salamanca, which books flights,
trains, and some buses, has two branches on Plaza Mayor (at
#11—next to TI, and #24, tel. 92-321-1414 or 92-321-5215,
www.viajessalamanca.com).

Local Guide: Maria Cruz is good (2-hr tour/€66 for small
group, tel. 92-319-3166, cellular 60-922-0757).

Sights—Salamanca

▲**Plaza Mayor**—Built in 1755, this ultimate Spanish plaza is a
fine place to nurse a cup of coffee and watch the world go by.
The town hall, with the clock, grandly overlooks the square. The
Arch of the Toro (built into the eastern wall) leads to the covered
market. Imagine the excitement of the days, just 100 years ago,
when bullfights were held in the square. How about coffee at
the town's oldest café, Café Novelty?

▲▲**Cathedrals, Old and New**—These cool-on-a-hot-day cathedrals share buttresses and are both richly ornamented. You get to
the old through the new. Before entering the new church, check
out the ornate Plateresque facade—Spain's version of Flamboyant
Gothic. At the side door of the facade (to the left as you face the
entrance), look for the astronaut added by a capricious restorer in
1993. This caused an outrage in town, but now locals shrug their
shoulders and say, "He's the person closest to God." I'll give you
a chance to find him on your own. Otherwise, look at the end of
this listing for help.

The "new" cathedral, built from 1513 to 1733, is a mix of
Gothic, Renaissance, and Baroque (free and lackluster). The
recorded music (sometimes live) helps. The *coro*, or choir, blocks
up half of the church, but its wood carving is sumptuous; look
up to see the elaborate organ.

The entrance to the old cathedral (12th-century Romanesque) is near the rear of the new one (€1.80, free English leaflet,

Salamanca

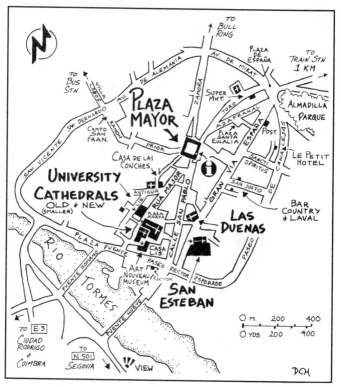

daily 10:00–13:30, 16:00–19:30, closes at 18:00 off-season; during Mass the old cathedral is free, but the cloister isn't). Sit in a front pew to study the 53 altarpiece scenes from Mary's life (by the Italian Florentino, 1445) and the dramatic Last Judgment fresco above it—Jesus is sending condemned souls into the literal jaws of hell.

Then head into the cloister (off the right transcept) and explore the chapels, notable for their unusual tombs, ornate altarpieces, and ceilings with leering faces. Capilla San Bartolome de Los Anajas, the farthest from the cloister entrance, has a gorgeously carved 16th-century alabaster tomb and wooden Mudejar organ. (Mudejar is the Gothic-Islamic style of the Moors in Spain after the Christian conquest.)

Find that astronaut: He's just a little guy, about the size of a Ken-does-Mars doll, entwined in the stone trim to the left of the door, roughly three meters up.

▲▲**University**—Salamanca University, the oldest in Spain (est. 1230), was one of Europe's leading centers of learning for 400 years. Columbus came here for travel tips. Today many Americans enjoy its excellent summer program. The old lecture halls around the cloister, where many of Spain's Golden Age heroes studied, are open to the public (€1.80, Mon–Sat 9:30–13:30, 16:00–18:30, Sun 10:00–13:00, enter from Calle Libreros, tel. 92-329-4400, ext. 1150). Some of the rooms are still used by the university for prestigious academic ceremonies.

The entrance portal of the university is a great example of Spain's Plateresque style—masonry so intricate it looks like silver work. The people studying the facade aren't art fans. They're trying to find a tiny frog on a skull that students looked to for good luck. (Its location appears at the end of this listing.)

After paying admission, you get a free English leaflet full of details; to follow it, go left (clockwise around the courtyard) upon entering. Note that a few rooms will be closed.

In the Hall of Fray Luis de León, the tables and benches are made of narrow wooden beams, whittled down by centuries of studious doodling. Professors spoke from the church-threatening *catedra*, or pulpit. It was here that free-thinking Fray Luis de León, after the Inquisition jailed and tortured him for five years because he translated part of the Bible into Castilian, returned to his place and started his first post-imprisonment lecture with, "As we were saying…"

The altarpiece in the chapel depicts professors swearing to Mary's virginity (how did they know?), and the only sight upstairs—the library—is definitely worth the climb. Check out the cloister's ceiling outside the library entrance for home-decorating ideas.

As you leave the university, you'll see the statue of Fray Luis de León. Behind him, to your left (his right), is the entrance to a peaceful courtyard containing the Museum of the University, notable for Gallego's fanciful 16th-century *Sky of Salamanca* (included in university admission, no photos allowed in museum).

Find that frog: On the right pillar of the facade, nearly halfway up, are three skulls. Ribet.

▲**Museo Art Nouveau y Art Deco**—Located in the Casa Lis, this museum—with its beautifully displayed collection of stained glass, jewelry, cancan statuettes, and toy dolls—is a refreshing change of pace (€1.80, Tue–Fri 11:00–14:00, 17:00–21:00, Sat–Sun 11:00–21:00, closed Mon, worthwhile English leaflet-€0.30, no photos—you must leave your camera at baggage check, Calle Gibraltar 14, between the new/old cathedrals and the river, tel. 92-312-1425, www.museocasalis.org).

Casa de las Conchas—The aptly named "House of Shells," dating from 1503, is a landmark on Rua Mayor (free, courtyard open Mon–Fri 9:00–21:00, Sat 9:00–14:00, 16:00–19:00, Sun 10:00–14:00, 16:00–19:00, tel. 92-326-9317). If you see shells broken off or missing, it's because long ago people believed there were pearls beneath each shell. The front of this building houses one of Salamanca's TIs. Go around to the left of the TI to enter the free courtyard. Head upstairs for a better view of the powerful towers of the 17th-century Clerecia church. The church, worth a look if you happen to be here at the right time, is open to tourists only one hour a day before services (free, open Mon–Fri 12:30–13:30, Sat 18:30–19:30, Sun 11:30–12:30—confirm hours at TI).

Church of San Esteban—Dedicated to St. Stephen (Esteban) the martyr, this complex contains a cloister, tombs, museum, sacristy, and church. Before you enter, notice the Plateresque facade and its bas-relief of the stoning of St. Stephen. The crucifixion above is by Cellini. Once inside, follow the free English pamphlet. Upstairs you'll find the museum (with illustrated 16th-century choir books at the far end) next to the entrance to the choir (this upper gallery overlooks the interior of the church and offers a rare opportunity to sit in wooden choir stalls). The church is overwhelmed by a Churriguera altarpiece, a textbook example of the style named after him. Quietly ponder the dusty gold-plated cottage cheese, as tourists retch and say "too much" in their mother tongue (€1.20, Mon–Fri 9:00–13:30, 16:00–20:00, Sat–Sun 9:30–13:30, 16:00–20:00).

Convento de las Dueñas—Next door, the much simpler *convento* is a joy. It consists of a double-decker cloister with a small museum of religious art. Check out the stone meanies exuberantly decorating the capitals on the cloister's upper deck (€1.20, daily 10:30–13:00, 16:30–19:00, no English info). The nuns sell sweets daily except Sunday (€2.40 for a box, €0.60 for small bag of cookies, no assortments possible even though their display box raises hopes). The nuns welcome the public to their 9:30 Sunday Mass (with singing). For the Mass, enter the door to the left of the cloister entry.

Honorable Mention—Romantics will enjoy the low-slung Roman bridge, much of it original, spanning the Rio Tormes. The ancient pre-Roman headless bull (or boar), blindly guarding the entrance to the bridge, is a symbol of the city. Nearby, at Parque Fluvial, you can rent rowboats.

Nightlife—Salamanca's high student population supports a vast array of trendy hangouts. Popular places include **Cum Laude** (nearly across from Bar Bambu at Calle Prior 7); **Country**, with great music, a student vibe, and dice-for-free-drinks games (Juan de Almeida 5, a 5-min walk southeast of Plaza Mayor, a half-block off Gran Vía); and the tacky **De Laval Genoves Sub-marino**, with its submarine-like interior (Calle San Justo 27–31, a block away from Country; see previous listing).

Sleeping in Salamanca
(€1.10 = about $1, country code: 34)

Sleep Code: **S** = Single, **D** = Double/Twin, **T** = Triple, **Q** = Quad, **b** = bathroom, **s** = shower only, **CC** = Credit Cards accepted, **no CC** = Credit Cards not accepted, **SE** = Speaks English, **NSE** = No English.

Salamanca, being a student town, has plenty of good eating and sleeping values, and now, even a self-service laundry. **Coin Laundry** is a five-minute walk from Plaza Mayor (Mon–Fri 8:30–14:00, 16:00–20:00, Sat 10:00–14:00, closed Sun, Paseje Azafranal 18, located in a passageway a half-block north of Plaza Santa Eulalia).

Most of my listings are on or within a three-minute walk of the Plaza Mayor. Directions are given from the Plaza Mayor, assuming you are facing the building with the clock (e.g., 3 o'clock is 90 degrees to your right as you face the clock). The 7 percent IVA tax is included only in the prices charged by the cheap hotels.

Hotels

Hotel Las Torres, on Plaza Mayor, has 44 modern, spacious rooms with all the amenities (Sb-€60–78, Db-€80–103, tax extra, CC, skip their restaurant, hotel entrance just off square at Consejo #4, Plaza Mayor 47, exit the plaza at 11:00, 37002 Salamanca, tel. 92-321-2100, fax 92-321-2101, www.mmteam.com/lastorres, e-mail: lastorres@mmteam.com, SE). Rooms with views cost the same as viewless rooms.

Hotel Don Juan, just off Plaza Mayor, has 16 classy, comfy rooms and an attached restaurant (Sb-€42, Db-€60, Tb-€81, cheap breakfast, CC, elevator, air con, double-paned windows; exit Plaza Mayor at about 5 o'clock and turn right to Quintana 6, 37001 Salamanca; tel. 92-326-1473, fax 92-326-2475, e-mail: hoteldonjuan@wanadoo.es, SE).

Hostal Plaza Mayor has 19 small but welcoming rooms and a good location just southwest of Plaza Mayor (Sb-€30, Db-€51, Tb-€60, CC, exit Plaza Mayor at 7 o'clock, Plaza del Corrillo 20, attached restaurant, tel. 92-326-2020, fax 92-321-7548).

Le Petit Hotel, with 16 comfortable rooms, overlooks a church on a fairly quiet side street two blocks east of Gran Vía. The rooms with views of the church are particularly bright; ask for a *vista de iglesias* (Sb-€25, Db-€40, Tb-€52, breakfast-€3, air con, elevator, no CC, Ronda Sancti-Spiritus 39, about 6 blocks east of Plaza Mayor; exit Plaza Mayor at 3 o'clock and continue east, turn left on Gran Vía, right on Sancti Spiritus, and left after the church; tel. 92-326-5567 or 92-326-1707, NSE).

Hotel Condal has 70 decent rooms, overlooks Plaza Santa Eulalia (parking underneath), and has an attached bar/café (Sb-€39, Db-€54, breakfast-€4.50, CC, air con, elevator, parking-€7.80/day,

Central Salamanca

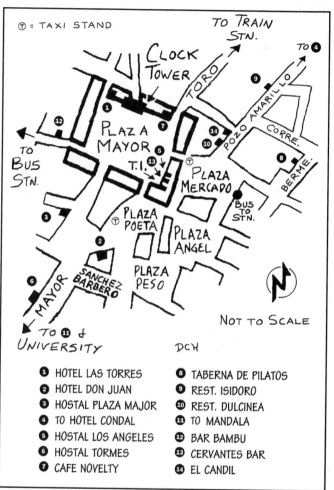

① = TAXI STAND

CLOCK TOWER

TO TRAIN STN.

TORO

TO ④

⑨

POZO AMARILLO

CORRE.

PLAZA MAYOR

⑫

①

⑦

⑭

⑩

BERME.

⑧

TO BUS STN.

T.I.

⑬

ⓣ

PLAZA MERCADO

③

ⓣ

PLAZA POETA

PLAZA ANGEL

BUS TO STN.

②

MAYOR

SANCHEZ BARBERO

PLAZA PESO

⑥

NOT TO SCALE

TO ⑪ & UNIVERSITY

DCH

❶ HOTEL LAS TORRES
❷ HOTEL DON JUAN
❸ HOSTAL PLAZA MAJOR
❹ TO HOTEL CONDAL
❺ HOSTAL LOS ANGELES
❻ HOSTAL TORMES
❼ CAFE NOVELTY

❽ TABERNA DE PILATOS
❾ REST. ISIDORO
❿ REST. DULCINEA
⓫ TO MANDALA
⓬ BAR BAMBU
⓭ CERVANTES BAR
⓮ EL CANDIL

laundry service; about a 5-min walk from Plaza Mayor, exit Plaza
Mayor at 3 o'clock and head north on Pozo Amarillo, Plaza Santa
Eulalia 3; tel. & fax 92-321-8400, www.algara.com/condal, e-mail:
condal@algara.com).

Splurge: Hotel Residencia Rector has 14 stately rooms, a
pleasant staff, and a mediocre location on a busy road (Sb-€75,
Db-€108, "superior" rooms €20 extra, breakfast-€7, CC, air con,
elevator, located south of new/old cathedrals, exit Plaza Mayor at

5 o'clock, take San Pablo for several blocks, then turn right on Rector Esperabe to #10, tel. 92-321-8482, fax 92-321-4008, www.teleline.es/personal/hrector, SE).

Cheaper Hotels

Hostal Los Angeles, at about three o'clock, has 11 simple but cared-for rooms, with four overlooking the square. Stand on the balcony and inhale the essence of Spain (S-€13.50, D-€21, Db-€28.50, T-€31, Tb-€37, view rooms have full bathrooms, includes tax, Plaza Mayor 10, 37002 Salamanca, tel. & fax 92-321-8166, Luis and Sabina NSE). To try for a view, request, "*Con vista, por favor.*" If that fails, avoid the one windowless room by requesting, "*Con ventana*" (window).

The handy **Hostal Tormes** is a student-type residence with 13 clean but spartan rooms on the pedestrian street connecting Plaza Mayor and the university (S-€20.50, D-€28.25, Db-€31, includes tax, CC, Rua Mayor 20, 37008 Salamanca, tel. & fax 92-321-9683, NSE).

Eating in Salamanca

There are plenty of good, inexpensive restaurants between Plaza Mayor and Gran Vía and as you leave the Plaza Mayor toward Rua Mayor. Just wander and eat at your own discovery or try **Café Novelty** (Plaza Mayor's oldest coffee shop—dating from 1905, daily 8:00–24:00). Consider any of several places on Calle Bermejeros, such as **Taberna de Pilatos** at #5 (Mon–Sat 13:00–15:00, 21:00–24:00, closed Sun, near covered market and Plaza Mayor).

Restaurante Isidro is touristy, but has a good assortment of seafood and meat dishes (menu of the day-€8.50, Mon–Sat 13:00–16:00, 20:00–24:00, Sun 13:00–16:00, CC, has seating in its *comedor*, Pozo Amarillo 19, about a block north of covered market, near Plaza Mayor, tel. 92-326-2848). **Restaurante Dulcinea** is a classier, pricier, less touristy version of the Isidro (menus of the day-€8.50 and €11.75, daily 13:00–16:00, 20:00–24:00, Pozo Amarillo 5, tel. 92-321-7843).

Mandala is popular for its tasty tapas and meals, attractive setting, and good prices (daily 8:00–24:00, Calle Serranos 9–11; from Casa de las Conchas follow Rua Antigua alongside Clerecia church for 2 short blocks—it's on your left, tel. 92-312-3342). Wash down your tapas or *plato combinado* with a *batido* (milkshake) or *zumo de sandia* (watermelon juice).

Bar Bambu offers a surprisingly large assortment of cheap, good tapas throughout the day (daily 9:00–01:30, Calle Prior 4, just off the southwest corner of Plaza Mayor, pass the Burger King and immediately head downstairs).

Cervantes Bar, overlooking Plaza Mayor, serves great tapas, salads, and meals to a mainly local crowd (daily 8:00–24:00, tapas served 9:00–16:30, 19:30–24:00, next door to TI, go up the stairs, also has tables on square).

Other centrally located tapas bars are **El Candil** (daily 10:00–20:00, Ventura Ruiz Aguilera 14, at intersection with Pozo Amarillo, between recommended Isidro and Dulcinea restaurants) and **La Covachuela**, where the older waiter, Antonio, is known for his coin tricks (in Portales de San Antonio; establish prices before ordering).

The **Rodilla** and **Pan & Company** sandwich chains are always fast and affordable. Pan & Company has a branch on Calle Prior across from Bar Bambu and another on Rua Mayor (daily 10:00–24:00). Rodilla is on Consejo, a few steps off Plaza Mayor, across from the entrance of the recommended Hotel Las Torres.

Picnics: The covered *mercado* (market) on Plaza Mercado has fresh fruits and veggies (Mon–Sat 8:00–14:30, closed Sun, on east side of Plaza Mayor). A small Consum grocery, three blocks east of Plaza Mayor, has just the basics (Mon–Sat 9:00–14:00, 17:00–20:00). For variety, the big Champion Supermercado is your best best, but it's a six-block walk north of Plaza Mayor on Toro (Mon–Sat 9:15–21:15, across from Plaza San Juan de Sahagun and its church). If you always wanted seconds at Communion, buy a bag of giant Communion wafers, a local specialty called *obleas*.

Transportation Connections—Salamanca

By train to: Madrid (3/day, 2.5 hrs, Chamartin station), **Ávila** (3/day, 1 hr; also 3 buses/day), **Barcelona** (1/day, 10 hrs), **Coimbra** (1/day, 5 hrs, departs Salamanca station at about 04:40, no kidding). Along with the locals, we hope the Cultural Capital designation brings Salamanca more liveable connections to Portugal. But if not, you can catch a taxi to the train station at any hour from Plaza Mercado (a few steps east of Plaza Mayor) and from Plaza Poeta Iglesias (across from the Gran Hotel, immediately south of Plaza Mayor, €3.50 during day, €4.50 at night.) Train info: tel. 90-224-0202.

By bus to: Madrid (hrly, 2.5 hrs), **Segovia** (3/day, 4 hrs, transfer in Labajos or Ávila; consider a brief visit to Ávila en route), **Ávila** (4/day, 1.5 hrs), **Ciudad Rodrigo** (nearly hrly, 1 hr), **Barcelona** (1/day, 12 hrs). Bus info: tel. 92-323-6717.

CIUDAD RODRIGO

(Worth a visit only if you're traveling from Salamanca to Coimbra.) This rough-and-tumble old town of 16,000 people caps a hill overlooking the Río Agueda. Spend an hour wandering among the Renaissance mansions that line its streets and exploring its cathedral and Plaza Mayor. Have lunch or a snack at El Sanatorio (Plaza Mayor 14). The tapas are cheap, the crowd is local, and the walls are a Ciudad Rodrigo scrapbook, including some bullfighting that makes the Three Stooges look demure.

Ciudad Rodrigo's cathedral—pockmarked with scars from Napoleonic cannon balls—has some entertaining carvings in the choir and some pretty racy work in its cloisters. Who said, "When you've seen one Gothic church, you've seen 'em all?"

The TI (tel. 92-346-0561) is just inside the old wall near the cathedral and can recommend a good hotel, such as Hotel Conde Rodrigo (Db-€47, tel. 92-346-1404). The Plaza Mayor is a two-block walk from the TI.

Ciudad Rodrigo is a convenient stop on the Salamanca-to-Coimbra drive. Buses connect Salamanca and Ciudad Rodrigo with surprising efficiency in about an hour.

Route Tips for Drivers

Madrid to El Escorial to the Valley of the Fallen to Segovia (80 km): Taxi to your car-rental office (or ask if they'll deliver the car to your hotel). Pick up the car by 8:30 and ask directions to highway A6. Follow "A6-Valladolid" signs to the clearly marked exit on M505 to El Escorial. Get to El Escorial by 9:30 to beat the crowds. The nearby **Silla de Felipe** (Philip's Seat) is a rocky viewpoint where the king would come to admire his palace being built.

From El Escorial, follow "C600-Valle de los Caídos" signs to the Valley of the Fallen. You'll see the huge cross marking it in the distance. After the tollbooth, follow "Basilica" signs to the parking place (tacky souvenirs, cafeteria, WCs). As you leave, turn left to Guadarrama on C600, go under the highway, and follow signs to Puerto de Navacerrada. From there, you climb past flocks of sheep, over a 1,850-meter-high (6,000 feet) mountain pass (Pto. de Navacerrada) into old Castile, and through La Granja to Segovia. (Segovia is much more important than La Granja, but garden-lovers enjoy a quick La Granja stop.)

At the Segovia aqueduct, turn into the old town (the side where the aqueduct adjoins the crenellated fortress walls). You can park for free on the south side of Via Roma and the neighborhood directly south of Via Roma. Free parking is also available in the Alcázar's lot, but you must move your car out by 19:00, when the gates close. Outside of the old city, there's an Acueducto Parking underground garage kitty-corner from the bus station. If you want to park near Plaza Mayor, be legal or risk an expensive ticket. Buy a ticket from the nearby machine to park in areas marked by blue stripes, and place the ticket on your dashboard (€0.25 for 30 min, 90-min maximum 9:00–20:00; free parking 20:00–9:00, Sat afternoon, and all day Sun).

Segovia to Salamanca (160 km): Leave Segovia by driving around the town's circular road, which offers good views from below the Alcázar. Then follow signs for Ávila (road N110).

Notice the fine Segovia view from the three crosses at the crest of the first hill. Just after the abandoned ghost church at Villacastin, turn onto N501 at the huge Puerta de San Vicente (cathedral and TI are just inside). The Salamanca road leads around the famous Ávila walls to the right. The best wall view is from the signposted Cuatro Postes, 1.5 kilometers northwest of town. Salamanca (N501) is clearly marked, about an hour's drive away.

A few kilometers before Salamanca, you might want to stop at the huge bull on the left of the road. There's a little dirt path leading right up to it. As you get closer, it becomes more and more obvious it isn't real. Bad boys climb it for a goofy photo, but I wouldn't. For a great photo op of Salamanca, complete with river reflection, stop at the edge of the city (at the light before the first bridge).

In Salamanca, the only safe parking is in a garage; try the underground lot at Plaza Santa Eulalia. Otherwise, parking is terrible. Gamblers park at their own risk over the river or in the city between Rua Palomino and Avenida de Portugal wherever there are blue parking lines (€0.60 for 90 min, 9:00–14:00, 16:00–20:00, free Sat afternoon and Sun). Leave nothing of value in your car.

TOLEDO

An hour south of Madrid, Toledo teems with tourists, souvenirs, and great art by day, delicious roast suckling pig, echoes of El Greco, and medieval magic by night. Incredibly well-preserved and full of cultural wonder, the entire city has been declared a national monument.

Spain's historic capital is 2,000 years of tangled history—Roman, Visigothic, Moorish, and Christian—crowded onto a high, rocky perch protected on three sides by the Tejo River. It's so well-preserved that the Spanish government has forbidden any modern exteriors. The rich mix of Jewish, Moorish, and Christian heritages makes it one of Europe's art capitals.

Toledo was a Visigothic capital back in 554 and—after a period of Moorish rule—Spain's political capital until 1561, when it reached its natural limits of growth as defined by the Tejo River Gorge. Though the king moved to more spacious Madrid, Toledo remains the historic, artistic, and spiritual center of Spain. In spite of tremendous tourist crowds, Toledo just sits on its history and remains much as it was when Europe's most powerful king and El Greco each called it home.

Planning Your Time
To properly see Toledo's museums (great El Greco), cathedral (best in Spain), and medieval atmosphere (best after dark), you'll need two nights and a day. Note that a few sights are closed Monday.

Toledo is just 60 minutes away from Madrid by bus (2/hr), train (9/day), or taxi (about €60 one-way from Puerto del Sol—negotiate the ride without a meter). A car is useless in Toledo. See the town outside of car-rental time (pick up or drop your car here).

Toledo

200 YARDS
200 METERS

TO MADRID & ❻

BISAGRA GATE

BUS STATION

RIO LLANO

CITY WALLS

TO RING ROAD & PARADOR

TO TRAIN STATION & ❼

❽ & ❾

ESCALATOR

SUBIDA LA GRANJA

❸

❶❻

PLAZA MERCED

MERCED

CUESTA

SANTA CRUZ MUSEUM

CALLE REAL

❷

CERVANTES

TO TRAIN STN.

POST

❶❸

SAN JUAN DE LOS REYES

❶❷

LA PLATA

❶❶

ALEX SABIO

NUNCIO

COMERCIO

TAXIS

SANTO TOMÉ

❶❺

ALFONSO XII

TRINIDAD

S. TOMÉ

ANGEL

SALVADOR

ALCÁZAR

MARKET

CATHEDRAL

SYNAGOGUE SANTA MARIA BLANCA

❶❹

MUSEO VICTORIO MACHO

SAN JUAN DIO

❶❼

❶❽

❶❽

❶❻

S. ISABEL

S. URSULA

RIO TEJO

SYNAGOGUE TRANSITO

❺

PARK

❹

PLAZA AYUNTAMIENTO & CITY HALL

DCH

EL GRECO'S HOUSE

NOTE: STREET WIDTH IS EXAGGERATED FOR CLARITY

❶ PLAZA ZOCODOVER
❷ HOTEL SOL
❸ HOSTAL DEL CARDENAL
❹ HOTEL SANTA ISABEL
❺ HOTEL PINTOR EL GRECO
❻ TO HOSTAL GAVILANES II, HOSTAL MADRID & HOTEL MARIA CRISTINA
❼ TO YOUTH HOSTEL SAN SERVANDO
❽ TO PARADOR
❾ TO HOTEL LA ALMARAZA
❿ CASA AURELIO I
⓫ CASA AURELIO II & III ON SINAGOGA STREET
⓬ REST. - MESON PALACIOS
⓭ REST. LOPEZ DE TOLEDO
⓮ REST. LA PERDIZ
⓯ BAR CERVECERIA GAMBRINUS
⓰ TAVERNA DE AMBOADES
⓱ ZAMORANO KNIVES
⓲ TICKETS & CATHEDRAL ENTRY

Orientation

Lassoed into a tight tangle of streets by the sharp bend of the Tejo River (called the Tagus where it hits the Atlantic, in Lisbon), Toledo has Spain's most confusing medieval street plan. But it's a small town of 65,000, major sights are well-signposted, and most locals will politely point you in the right direction.

El Greco's Art

Born on Crete and trained in Venice, Domenikos Theoto-copoulos (tongue-tied friends just called him "The Greek") came to Spain to get a job decorating El Escorial. He failed there but succeeded in Toledo, where he spent the last 37 years of his life. He mixed all three regional influences into his palette. From his Greek homeland, he absorbed the solemn, abstract style of icons. In Venice he learned the bold use of color and dramatic style of the later Renaissance. These styles were then fused in the fires of fanatic Spanish-Catholic devotion.

Not bound by the realism so important to his 16th-century contemporaries, El Greco painted dramatic visions of striking colors and figures—bodies unnatural and elongated as though stretched between heaven and earth. He painted souls, not faces. His work is on display at nearly every sight in Toledo. Thoroughly modern in its disregard of realism, it seems as fresh as contemporary art.

Look at the map and take a mental orientation walk past Toledo's main sights. Starting in the central Plaza Zocódover, go southwest along the Calle de Comércio. After passing the cathedral on your left, follow the signs to Santo Tomé and the cluster of other sights. The visitor's city lies basically along one small but central street—and most tourists never stray from this axis. Make a point to get lost. It's a small town, bounded on three sides by the river. When it's time to get somewhere, I pull out the map or ask, "*¿Dónde está Plaza Zocódover?*"

Tourist Information

Toledo has two TIs. The TI that covers Toledo as well as the region is in a small, free-standing brick building just outside the Bisagra Gate, where those arriving by train or bus enter the old town (Mon–Fri 9:00–18:00, Sat 9:00–19:00, Sun 9:00–15:00, tel. 92-522-0843). Historians: The Bisagra Gate is the last surviving gate of the 10th-century fortifications.

The second TI, which covers solely Toledo, is in front of the cathedral on Plaza Ayuntamiento (Mon 10:30–14:30, Tue–Sun 10:30–14:30, 16:30–19:00, tel. 92-525-4030). Consider the readable local guidebook, *Toledo, Its Art and Its History* (small version for €5.50, sold all over town). It explains all of the sights (which generally provide no on-site information) and gives you a photo to point at and say, "*¿Dónde está...?*"

Arrival in Toledo

"Arriving" in Toledo means getting uphill to Plaza Zocódover. From the train station, that's a 20-minute hike, taxi ride (€3), or easy bus ride (#5 or #6, €0.70, pay on bus, confirm by asking, "*Para Plaza Zocódover?*"). You can stow extra baggage in the station's lockers (buy tokens at ticket booth). Consider buying a city map at the kiosk; it's better than the free one at the TI. If you're walking, turn right as you leave the station, cross the bridge, pass the bus station, go straight through the roundabout, and continue uphill to the TI and Bisagra Gate.

If you arrive by bus, go upstairs to the station lobby. You'll find lockers and a small bus information office—near the lockers and opposite the cafeteria. Confirm your departure time (probably every half hour on the hour if you're returning to Madrid). When you buy your ticket—which you can do as late as a few minutes before you leave—specify you'd like a *directo* bus; the *ruta* trip takes longer (for Madrid, 60 vs. 75 min). From the bus station, Plaza Zocódover is a 15-minute walk (see directions from train station, above), a taxi ride (€2.40), or a short bus ride (catch #5 downstairs, underneath the lobby, €0.70, pay driver).

A new series of escalators runs near Bisagra Gate, giving you a free ride up, up, up into town. You'll end up far from Plaza Zocódover, but just start with the synagogues, continue to the cathedral, and end at Plaza Zocódover. It's great for drivers, who can park in the lot across the street from the base of the escalator (or park in Garage Alcázar lot opposite Alcázar in old town—€1.20/hr, €12/day).

Getting around Toledo

This small city is walkable, though surprisingly hilly. For great city views, consider hopping on the cheesy Tren Imperial Tourist Tram. Crass as it feels, you get a 50-minute putt-putt through Toledo and around the Tagus River Gorge. Warning: It's a bumpy ride and the windows aren't crystal clear (€3.60, daily from 11:00, leaves Plaza Zocódover on the hour, tape-recorded English/Spanish commentary, no photo stops but goes slow; for the best views of Toledo across the gorge, sit on right side, not behind driver; tel. 925-142-274).

Sights—Toledo

▲▲▲**Cathedral**—Holy Toledo! Spain's leading Catholic city has a magnificent cathedral. Shoehorned into the old center, its exterior is hard to appreciate. But the interior is so lofty, rich, and vast that it grabs you by the vocal cords, and all you can do is whisper, "Wow."

Cost and Hours: While the basic cathedral is free, seeing the great art—located in four separate places within the cathedral

Toledo Cathedral

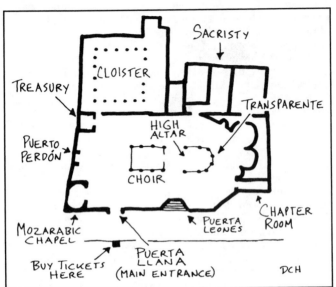

(the choir, chapter house, sacristy, and treasury)—requires an
€4.80 ticket (well worthwhile, sold in Tienda la Catedral shop
opposite church entrance, shop open Mon–Sat 10:30–18:30,
Sun 14:00–18:00; also rents audioguides for €2.70). The strict
dress-code sign covers even your attitude: no shorts, no tank
tops, no slouching.

The cathedral has shorter hours (daily 10:30–12:00, 16:00–
18:00) than the four sights (10:30–18:00). Even though the cathedral closes from 12:00 to 16:00, if you have a ticket you can get in
and tour the cathedral as well, with fewer crowds. (Note that the
cloister is closed to everyone from 13:00–15:30.)

Self-guided Tour: Holy redwood forest, Batman! Wander
among the pillars. Sit under one and imagine when the light
bulbs were candles and the tourists were pilgrims—before the "No
Photo" signs, when every window provided spiritual as well as physical light. The cathedral is primarily Gothic, but since it took more
than 200 years to build (1226–1493), you'll see a mix of styles—
Gothic, Renaissance, and Baroque. Enjoy the elaborate wrought-
iron work, lavish wood carvings, window after colorful window of
500-year-old stained glass, and a sacristy with a collection of paintings that would put any museum on the map.

This confusing collage of great Spanish art deserves a guided
tour. Hire a private guide, freeload on a tour (they come by every

few minutes during peak season), or follow this quick tour. Here's a framework for your visit:

First, walk to the high altar to marvel through the iron grill at one of the most stunning altars in Spain. Real gold on pine wood, by Flemish, French, and local artists, it's one of the country's best pieces of Gothic art. About-face...

The **choir**, facing the high altar, is famous for its fine carving and requires a piece of your four-part ticket. The lower wooden stalls are decorated with scenes from the Christian victory over the Muslims at Granada. The upper stalls feature Old Testament figures carved out of alabaster. The iron grill of the choir is notable for the dedication of the man who built it. Domingo de Cespedes, a Toledo ironworker, accepted the commission to build the grill for 6,000 ducats. The project, which took from 1541 to 1548, was far more costly than he anticipated. The medieval Church didn't accept cost overruns, so, to finish it, he sold everything he owned and went into debt. He died a poor—but honorable—man.

Face the altar and go around it to your right. The **chapter house** (*sala capitular*), which takes a chunk of your ticket, has a rich gilded ceiling, interesting Bible-storytelling frescoes, and a pictorial review of 1,900 years of Toledo archbishops. The upper row of portraits was not painted from life; the lower portraits were, and therefore hold more historic and artistic interest. Imagine sitting down to church business surrounded by all this tradition and theology. As you leave, notice the iron-pumping cupids carved into the panels lining the walls.

The *transparente*, behind the high altar, is a unique feature of the cathedral. In the 1700s a hole was cut into the ceiling to let a sunbeam brighten the Mass. Melding this big hole into the Gothic church presented a challenge that resulted in a Baroque masterpiece. Gape up at this riot of angels doing flip-flops, babies breathing thin air, bottoms of feet, and gilded sunbursts. I like it, as did, I guess, the long-dead cardinal whose faded red hat hangs from the edge of the hole. (A perk that only cardinals enjoy is choosing the place in the cathedral in which their hat will hang until it rots.)

The cathedral's **sacristy** has 20 El Grecos and masterpieces by Goya, Titian, Rubens, Velázquez, Caravaggio, and Bellini (there goes another part of your ticket). First, look at the fine perspective work on the ceiling. Then walk to the most important painting in the collection (end of room). El Greco's first masterpiece, from 1579, *The Spoiliation* (a.k.a. *The Denuding of Christ*) hangs above the marble altar. This was one of El Greco's first Toledo commissions after arriving from Venice. Notice the parallel contrasts: Jesus' delicate hand before a flaming red tunic and Jesus' noble face among the sinister mob. On the right is a rare religious painting by Goya, the *Betrayal of Christ*, which shows

Judas preparing to kiss Jesus, identifying him to the Roman
soldiers. Enjoy the many other El Grecos. Find the small but
lifelike 17th-century carving of St. Francis by Pedro de Mena
(to your right as you entered the door).

The **treasury** (*tesoro*) has plenty to see. The highlight is the
three-meter-high, 430-pound monstrance—the tower designed to
hold the Holy Communion bread (the Host) during the festival of
Corpus Christi (body of Christ) as it parades through the city.
Built in 1517 by a man named Arfe, it's made of 5,000 individual
pieces held together by 12,500 screws. There are diamonds, emer-
alds, rubies, and 400 pounds of gold-plated silver. The inner part
is 35 pounds of solid gold. Yeow. The base is a later addition from
the Baroque period. Traditionally, it's thought that much of this
gold and silver arrived on Columbus' first load home. To the right
of the monstrance find the fancy sword of Franco. To the right of
that is a gift from St. Louis, the king of France—a 700-year-old
Bible printed and beautifully illustrated by French monks. Imagine
the exquisite experience of reading this with its lavish illustrations
through medieval eyes. The finely painted small crucifix on the
opposite side—by the great Gothic Florentine painter Fra
Angelico—depicts Jesus alive on the back and dead on the front.
This was a gift from Mussolini to Franco. Hmmm. There's even a
gift in this room from Toledo's sister city, Toledo, Ohio.

If you're at the cathedral between 9:30 and 9:45, you can
peek into the otherwise-locked **Mozarabic Chapel** (Capilla Moz-
arabe). The Visigothic Mass, the oldest surviving Christian ritual
in Western Europe, starts at 9:45 (not sung on Sun). You're welcome to partake in this stirring example of peaceful coexistence of
faiths—but once the door closes, you're a Visigoth for 30 minutes.

▲▲**Santa Cruz Museum**—Most of this museum will be closed
for renovation much of 2002. During renovation, the museum's
cloister and staircase will be open and free. The building's Plateresque facade is worth seeing anytime.

This great Renaissance building was an orphanage, built from
money left by the humanist and diplomat Cardinal Mendoza when
he died in 1495. The cardinal, confirmed as Chancellor of Castile
by Queen Isabel, was so influential he was called the third king.
The building is in the form of a Greek cross under a Moorish
dome. The arms of the building—formerly wards—are filled with
16th-century art, tapestries, furniture, armor, and documents.
It's a stately, classical, music-filled setting with a cruel lack of
English information.

Fifteen El Grecos gather in one wing upstairs, including
the impressive *Assumption of Mary*—a spiritual poem on canvas
(notice old Toledo on the bottom). Painted one year before El
Greco's death in 1614, this is considered the culmination of his
artistic development.

An enormous blue banner hangs like a long, skinny tooth opposite the entry. This flew from the flagship of Don Juan of Austria and recalls the pivotal naval victory over the Muslims at the Battle of Lepanto in 1571. Lepanto was a key victory in the centuries-long Muslim threat to Christian Europe (when museum opens, cost will be €1.20, Mon 10:00–18:30, Tue–Sat 10:00–18:30, Sun 10:00–14:00, just off Plaza Zocódover, go through arch, Cervantes 3).

▲Alcázar—This huge former imperial residence—built on the site of Roman, Visagothic, and Moorish fortresses—dominates the Toledo skyline. The Alcázar became a kind of right-wing Alamo during Spain's civil war when a force of Franco's Nationalists (and hundreds of hostages) were besieged for two months. Finally, after many fierce but futile Republican attacks, Franco sent in an army that took Toledo and freed the Alcázar. The place was rebuilt and glorified under Franco. Today you can see its civil war exhibits, giving you an interesting—and right-wing—look at the horrors of Spain's recent past (€1.20, Tue–Sun 9:30–14:30, closed Mon).

Sights—Southwest Toledo
▲Santo Tomé—A simple chapel holds El Greco's most-loved painting. *The Burial of the Count of Orgaz* couples heaven and earth in a way only The Greek could. It feels so right to see a painting left where the artist put it 400 years ago. Take this slow. Stay a while—let it perform. It's 1323. You're at the burial of the good count. After a pious and generous life, he left his estate to the Church. Saints Augustine and Steven have even come down for the burial—to usher him directly to heaven. "Such is the reward for those who serve God and his saints."

More than 250 years later, in 1586, a priest hired El Greco to make a painting of the burial to hang over the count's tomb. The painting has two halves divided by a serene—but not sad—line of noble faces. The physical world ends with the line of nobles. Above them a spiritual wind blows as colors change and shapes stretch. Notice the angel, robe caught up in that wind, "birthing" the soul of the count through the neck of a celestial womb into Heaven—the soul abandoning the physical body to join Christ the Judge. Mary and John the Baptist both intervene on behalf of the arriving soul. Each face is a detailed portrait. El Greco himself (eyeballing you, 7th figure in from the left) is the only one not involved in the burial. The boy in the foreground is El Greco's son (€1.20, daily 10:00–18:45, until 17:45 off-season, tel. 92-525-6098).

▲Museo El Greco—You'll see about 20 El Greco paintings, including his masterful *View of Toledo* and portraits of the Apostles (€1.20, free Sat afternoon from 14:30 and all day Sun; Tue–Sat 10:00–14:00, 16:00–17:45, Sun 10:00–13:45, closed Mon,

Samuel Levi 3). Usually this museum costs twice as much and includes a look at the interior of a traditionally furnished Renaissance home, often wrongly called El Greco's House. The house is undergoing restoration, which may be completed in 2002. Once the house is ready, you'll have to pay more, but you'll see more. Without the house, the museum is not worth it for most, because overall, you'll see better El Grecos elsewhere in Toledo.

Sinagoga del Transito (Museo Sefardi)—Built in 1366, this is the best surviving slice of Toledo's Jewish past. The museum displays Jewish artifacts, including costumes, menorahs, and books, regrettably without a word of English description (€2.40, free Sat afternoon from 14:30 and all day Sun; Tue–Sat 10:00–14:00, 16:00–17:45, Sun 10:00–13:45, closed Mon, near Museo El Greco, with same price and hours, no photos allowed, on Calle de los Reyes Católicos).

Sinagoga de Santa Maria Blanca—This synagogue-turned-church with Moorish arches is an eclectic but harmonious gem (€1.20, daily 10:00–14:00, 15:30–19:00, closes off-season at 18:00, no photos allowed, Reyes Católicos 2-4).

Museo Victorio Macho—After *mucho* El Greco, try Macho. Overlooking the gorge, this small, attractive museum—once the home and workshop of the 20th-century sculptor, Victorio Macho—offers several rooms of his work interspersed with view terraces. The highlight is *La Madre*, Macho's lifesize sculpture of a older woman sitting in a chair. But the big draw for many is the air-conditioned theater featuring a good 29-minute video on Toledo's history. You can choose a shorter nine-minute version, but why rush? (€3, Mon–Sat 10:00–19:00, Sun 10:00–15:00, cheaper for young and old, request video showing in English, Plaza de Victorio Macho 2, between the two Sinagogas listed above, tel. 92-528-4225.)

Shopping

Toledo probably sells as many souvenirs as any city in Spain. This is the place to buy medieval-looking swords, armor, maces, three-legged stools, and other nouveau antiques. It's also Spain's damascene center, where, for centuries, craftspeople have inlaid black steel with gold, silver, and copper wire.

At the workshop of English-speaking Mariano Zamorano, you can see swords and knives being made, as well as the damascene process in action. Judging by what's left of Mariano's hand, his knives are among the best (Mon–Sat 9:00–14:00, 16:00–18:00, Calle Ciudad 19, near the cathedral and Plaza Ayuntamiento, tel. 92-522-2634).

El Martes, Toledo's colorful outdoor flea market, bustles on Paseo de Marchen (near TI at Bisagra Gate) on Tuesdays from 9:00 to 14:00.

Sleeping in Toledo
(€1.10 = about $1, country code: 34)

Sleep Code: **S** = Single, **D** = Double/Twin, **T** = Triple, **Q** = Quad, **b** = bathroom, **s** = shower only, **CC** = Credit Cards accepted, **no CC** = Credit Cards not accepted, **SE** = Speaks English, **NSE** = No English. Breakfast and the 7 percent IVA tax aren't included unless noted. Toledo's zip code is 45001, unless otherwise noted.

Madrid daytrippers darken the sunlit cobbles, but few stay to see Toledo's medieval moonrise. Spend the night. Spring and fall are high season; November through March and July and August are low. There are no private rooms for rent.

Sleeping near Plaza Zocódover

Hotel Residencia Imperio is well-run, offering 21 rooms with solid air-conditioned comfort in a handy old-town location (Sb-€26.50, Db-€39, Tb-€52, includes tax, 5 percent discount with this book, CC, elevator, cheery café, from Calle Comercio at #38 go a block uphill to Calle Cadenas 5, tel. 92-522-7650, fax 92-525-3183, www.terra.es/personal/himperio, e-mail: himperio@teleline.es).

Hostal Centro rents 23 modern, clean, and comfy rooms just around the corner (Sb-€27, Db-€39, Tb- €54, no CC, 50 meters off Plaza Zocódover, first right off Calle Comercio at Calle Nueva 13, roof garden, tel. 92-525-7091, fax 925-257-848).

The quiet, modern **Hostal Nuevo Labrador**, with 12 clean, shiny, and spacious rooms, is a good value (Sb-€25.75, Db-€39, Tb-€52, Qb-€60, includes tax, no breakfast, CC, elevator, Juan Labrador 10, 45001 Toledo, tel. 92-522-2620, fax 92-522-9399, NSE).

Hotel Maravilla is wonderfully central and convenient with narrow halls and simple rooms (Sb-€25, Db-€40, Tb-€55, Qb-€65, includes tax, CC, back rooms are quieter, air con, a block behind Plaza Zocódover at Plaza de Barrio Rey 7, tel. 92-522-8317, fax 92-522-8155, Felisa Maria SE).

Splurges: Hotel Las Conchas, a new three-star hotel, gleams with marble and sheer pride. It's beautiful, with 35 sleek rooms—even three ground-floor rooms for disabled travelers (Sb-€51, Db-€69, Db with terrace-€75, breakfast-€4.50, includes tax, CC, cool elevator with phone keypad, same owners as recommended Imperio, Juan Labrador 8, tel. 92-521-0760, fax 92-522-4271, www.lasconchas.com, e-mail: lasconchas@ctv.es).

Hotel Carlos V overlooks the cathedral midway between the Alcázar and Plaza Zocódover. While suffering from the obligatory stuffiness of a correct hotel, it has 69 bright, pleasant rooms (Sb-€71, Db-€104, Tb-€140, plus tax, breakfast-€8, less off-season, CC, air con, elevator, Plaza Horno Magdalena 3, tel. 92-522-2100, fax 92-522-2105, SE). Ask for a room with a view of the cathedral.

Across from the Alcázar is **Hotel Alfonso VI**, a big, touristy

Toledo's Plaza Zocódover

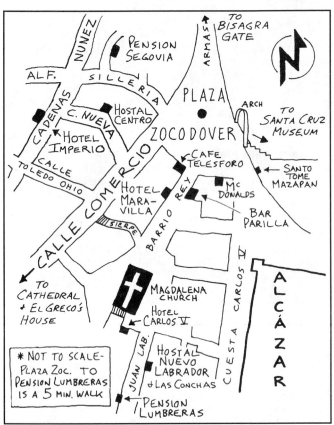

establishment with large, airy rooms, tour groups, and souvenirs for sale all over the lobby (Sb-€74, Db-€118, Tb-€157, breakfast-€8.50, plus tax, CC, air con, General Moscardo 2, 45001 Toledo, tel. 92-522-2600, fax 92-521-4458, www.hotelalfonsoVI.com, e-mail: info@hotelalfonsoVI.com). Ask for a room with a view.

Sleeping near Bisagra Gate
Hotel Sol, which has 25 plain, modern, and clean rooms, isn't exactly glamorous but is a great value on a quiet street halfway between the Bisagra Gate and Plaza Zocódover (Sb-€32.50, Db-€43.50, Tb-€56, includes tax, breakfast-€3.30, CC, air con, parking-€6.70/day, 50 meters down lane off busy main drag at Hotel Real, Azacanes 8, 45003 Toledo, tel. 92-521-3650,

fax 92-521-6159, www.fedeto.et/hotelsol). Their "Hostal Sol"
annex across the street is just as comfortable and a bit cheaper.

Splurge: Hostal del Cardenal, a 17th-century cardinal's
palace built into Toledo's wall, is quiet and elegant with a cool
garden and a stuffy restaurant. This poor man's parador, at the
dusty old gate of Toledo, is closest to the station but below all the
old-town action—however, the new escalator can levitate you into
town (Sb-€45–56, Db-€72–90, Tb-€94–117, cheaper in winter,
breakfast-€6.50, CC, air con, nearby parking-€11.50/day, no-fun
staff likely because of the management, enter through town wall
100 meters below Puerta Bisagra, Paseo de Recaredo 24, 45004
Toledo, tel. 92-522-4900, fax 92-522-2991, www.cardenal.aser-
net.es, e-mail: cardenal@asernet.es).

Sleeping beyond the Cathedral, Deep in Toledo
Hotel Santa Isabel, in a 15th-century building two blocks from
the cathedral, has 23 clean, modern, and comfortable rooms and
squeaky tile hallways. Avoid the few *atico* rooms that have only a
skylight (Sb-€25, Db-€39, Tb-€48, includes tax, breakfast-€3.60,
parking-€5.40, CC, air con, elevator; buried deep in old town so
take a taxi, not the bus; drivers enter from Calle Pozo Amargo,
Calle Santa Isabel 24, 45002 Toledo, tel. 92-525-3120, fax 92-525-
3136, www.santa-isabel.com, e-mail: santa-isabel@arrakis.es).

Hotel Pintor El Greco, at the far end of the old town,
has 33 plush and modern-feeling rooms with all the comforts,
yet it's in a historic 17th-century building. A block from Santo
Tomé in a Jewish Quarter garden, it's very quiet (Sb-€80, Db-
€104, plus tax, includes breakfast, CC, air con, elevator, Ala-
millos del Transito 13, tel. 92-528-5191, fax 92-521-5819, www.
hotelpintorelgreco.com).

Sleeping Cheap near Plaza Zocódover
The very central **Pensión Segovia** has eight old, rickety, and
dingy rooms, with questionable beds, head-banger doorways, and
memorable balconies (D-€18, T-€27, includes tax, no CC; from
Plaza Zocódover go down Calle de la Sillería, take 2nd right and
another right to Calle de Recoletos 2, tel. 92-521-1124).

Pension Castilla, just around the corner, is another family-
run cheapie, but has six modern and more comfortable rooms
(S-€13.25, Db-€24, fans, no CC, Calle Recoletos 6, tel. 925-
256-318, José SE).

Pensión Lumbreras has a tranquil courtyard and 12 simple
rooms, some with views—such as room #6. Bought by the people
who own the fancy Carlos V and Alfonso VI, the pension lacks the
hominess and cheaper prices it used to have—the reception is now
at the Carlo V around the corner. Prices may increase (S-€17.25,
D-€31, Juan Labrador 9, 45001 Toledo, tel. 92-522-1571).

Sleeping Outside of Town

On the road to Madrid (near bullring): There's a conspiracy of clean, modern, and hard-working little hotels with comfy rooms a five-minute walk beyond Puerta Bisagra near the bullring (Plaza de Toros, bullfights only on holidays), bus station, and TI. Drivers will enjoy easy parking here. The downside: It's a 15-minute uphill hike to the old-town action. Two good bets are **Hostal Gavilánes II** (19 rooms, Sb-€33, Db-€42, Db suite-€84, Tb-€56, Qb-€69, includes breakfast and taxes, CC, air con, parking-€5.50/day, Marqués de Mendigorría 14, 45003 Toledo, tel. & fax 92-521-1628, NSE) and **Hostal Madrid** (9 rooms, Sb-€29, Db-€33, Tb-€51, includes tax, breakfast-€2.40, CC, air con, parking-€6.50/day, Calle Marqués de Mendigorría 7, 45003 Toledo, tel. 92-522-1114, fax 925-228-113, NSE). This *hostal* rents lesser rooms from an annex across the street (Db-€36 without air-con).

Splurge: Hotel Maria Cristina, also next to the bullring, is part 15th-century and all modern. This sprawling 73-room hotel has all the comforts under a thin layer of prefab tradition (Sb-€57, Db-€89, extra bed-€27, suites available, breakfast-€5.50, plus tax, CC, air con, elevator, attached restaurant, parking-€7.20/day, Marques de Mendigorria 1, tel. 92-521-3202, fax 92-521-2650, www.hotelesmayoral.com, SE).

Hostel: The **Albergue Juvenil San Servando** youth hostel is lavish but cheap, with small rooms, a swimming pool, views, and good management (€8.50 per bed if under age 26, €11 if age 26 or older, hostel membership required, no CC, in San Servando castle 10-min walk from train station, over Puente Viejo outside town, tel. 92-522-4554, reservations tel. 92-526-7729, NSE).

Sleeping Outside of Town with the Grand Toledo View

Toledo's **Parador Nacional Conde de Orgaz** is one of Spain's most well-known inns, enjoying the same Toledo view El Greco made famous from across the Tejo Canyon (76 rooms, Sb-€90, Db-€112, Db with view-€127, breakfast-€8.50, CC, 3 windy kilometers from town at Cerro del Emperador, 45002 Toledo, tel. 92-522-1850, fax 92-522-5166, www.parador.es, e-mail: toledo@parador.es, SE). Take a cab here just to see the sunset from the terrace (€4.80 one-way).

Hotel Residencia La Almazara was the summer residence of a 16th-century archbishop of Toledo. Fond of its classic Toledo view, El Greco hung out here for inspiration. A lumbering old place with cushy public rooms, 28 simple bedrooms, and a sprawling garden, it's truly in the country but just three kilometers out of Toledo (Sb-€26, Db-€36, Db with view-€42, Tb-€48, 10 of 24 rooms have view, fans, CC, Ctra. de Piedrabuena 47, between the 3-km and 4-km markers on the Toledo-Arges road, set back off road, marked with small sign, P.O. Box 6, Toledo 45080, tel. 92-522-3866, fax 92-525-0562, www.hotelalmazara.com, e-mail: hotelalmazara@ribernet.es).

Eating in Toledo

A day full of El Greco and the romance of Toledo after dark puts me in the mood for partridge (*perdiz*), roasted suckling pigs (*cochinillo asado*), or baby lamb (*cordero*), similarly roasted after a few weeks of mother's milk.

Toledo's three **Casa Aurelio** restaurants each offer traditional cooking, reasonable prices, and classy atmosphere (€15 menu, 13:00–16:30, 20:00–23:00, all closed Sun, each closed either Mon, Tue, or Wed, CC). All are within three blocks of the cathedral: Plaza Ayuntamiento 4 (tel. 92-522-7716), Sinagoga 6 (tel. 92-522-2097), and Sinagoga 1 (popular with Toledo's political class, has newly-opened wine cave, tel. 92-522-1392).

Restaurante-Meson Palacios serves good food at cheap prices (lunch from 13:00, dinner from 19:30, on Alfonso X, near Plaza de San Vicente). **Rincón de Eloy** is more elegant (€9 *menu*, Juan Labrador 16, near the Alcázar, tel. 92-522-9399).

Restaurante Lopez de Toledo, a fancy restaurant located in an old nobility palace, specializes in Castilian food, particularly venison and partridge (€18 meals, daily 13:30–16:00, 20:30–23:30, Calle Silleria 3, near Plaza Zocódover, tel. 92-525-4774).

For a splurge near the Santa Tomé sights, consider the classy **La Perdiz**, which offers partridge (as the restaurant's name suggests), venison, suckling pig, fish, and more (Tue–Sat 12:00–23:00, closes Sun about 16:00, closed Mon and first half of Aug, Calle Reyes Católicos 7, tel. 92-521-4658). **Bar Cerveceria Gambrinus** is a good tapas bar in the Santa Tomé area (daily 9:00–24:00, Santa Tomé 10, tel. 92-521-4440).

Restaurants Plaza and **La Parrilla** share a tiny square behind Plaza Zocódover (facing the Casa Telesforo on Plaza Zocódover, go left down alley 30 meters to Plaza de Barrio Rey). The bars and cafés on Plaza Zocódover are reasonable, seasoned with some fine people-watching.

At **Taverna de Amboades**, a wine-and-tapas bar near the Bisagra Gate, expert Miguel Angel explains the differences among Spanish wines (Tue–Sat 19:30–24:00, also Thu–Sun 12:30–16:00, Alfonso VI 5, cellular 67-848-3749).

Picnics are best assembled at the **Mercado Municipal** on Plaza Mayor (on the Alcázar side of cathedral, open until 14:00, closed Sun). This is a fun market to prowl, even if you don't need food. If you feel like munching a paper plate–size Communion wafer, one of the stalls sells crispy bags of *obleas* (a great gift for your favorite pastor).

Toledo's famous almond-fruity-sweet *mazapan* is sold all

over town. On Plaza Zocódover try the modern **Santo Tomé** (daily 9:00–22:22) or the bar-like **Casa Telesforo** (daily 9:00–23:00, go inside to the far right counter). Each has a great window display and sells single *mazapan* goodies (€0.80 each) or small mixed boxes.

For a sweet and romantic evening moment, get a pastry and head down to the cathedral. Sit on the Plaza del Ayuntamiento (on stone wall to right of TI). The fountain is on your right, Spain's best-looking city hall is behind you, and her top cathedral, built back when Toledo was Spain's capital, shines brightly against the black night sky before you.

Transportation Connections—Toledo

Far more buses than trains connect Toledo with Madrid. Consider taking the train to Madrid and the bus back. (To get to Granada from Toledo, it's easiest to transfer in Madrid.)

To Madrid by bus (2/hr, 60–75 min, *directo* is faster than *ruta*, Madrid's Estación sur Autobuses, Metro: Méndez Alvaro, Continental bus company, tel. 92-522-3641), **by train** (9/day, 50–75 min, Madrid's Atocha station), **by car** (65 kilometers, 1 hr). Toledo bus info: tel. 92-521-5850; train info: tel. 90-224-0202.

LA MANCHA

(Visit only if you're driving between Toledo and Granada.) Nowhere else is Spain so vast, flat, and radically monotonous. La Mancha, Arabic for "parched earth," makes you feel small—lost in rough seas of olive-green polka dots. Random buildings look like houses and hotels hurled off some heavenly Monopoly board. It's a rough land where roadkill is left to rot, where bugs ricochet off the windshield and keep on flying, and where hitchhikers wear red dresses and aim to take you for the ride.

This is the setting of Cervantes' *Don Quixote*, published in the 17th century, after England sank the Armada and the Spanish Empire began its decline. Cervantes' star character fought doggedly for good, for justice, and against the fall of Spain and its traditional old-regime empire. Ignoring reality, Don Quixote was a hero fighting a hopeless battle. Stark La Mancha was the perfect stage.

The epitome of Don Quixote country, the town of **Consuegra** must be the La Mancha Cervantes had in mind. Drive up to the ruined 12th-century castle and joust with a windmill. It's hot and buggy here, but the powerful view overlooking the village, with its sun-bleached, light-red roofs; modern concrete reality; and harsh, windy silence makes for a profound picnic (a 1-hr drive south of Toledo). The castle belonged to the Knights of St. John (12th and 13th centuries) and is associated with their trip to Jerusalem during the Crusades. Originally built from the ruins of a nearby Roman circus, it has been newly restored (€1.20). Sorry, the windmills are post-Cervantes, only 200 to 300 years old.

If you've seen windmills, the next castle north (above Almon-acid, 12 kilometers from Toledo) is free and more interesting than the Consuegra castle. Follow the ruined lane past the ruined church up to the ruined castle. The jovial locals hike up with kids and kites.

Route Tips for Drivers

Granada to Toledo (400 km, 5 hrs): The Granada–Toledo drive is long, hot, and boring (see "La Mancha," above). Start early to minimize the heat and make the best time you can. Follow signs for Madrid/Jaen/N323 into what some call the Spanish Nebraska—La Mancha. After Puerto Lapice, you'll see the Toledo exit.

View the city from many angles along the Circumvalación road across the Tejo Gorge. Drive to Parador Conde de Orgaz just south of town for the view (from the balcony) El Greco made famous in his portrait of Toledo.

You can park at the lot outside the old town, near the Bisagra Gate (opposite recommended Hostal del Cardenal; take escalator up to town from here), or in the old town across the street from the Alcázar (€1.20/hr, €12/day). You can usually park free in the lot just down the street from the garage or in the huge dirt lot below and behind the Santa Cruz Museum.

Toledo to Madrid (65 km, 1 hr): It's a speedy *autovía* north, past one last bullboard, to Madrid. The highways converge into M30, which circles Madrid. Follow it to the left ("Nor y Oeste") and take the Plaza de España exit to get back to Gran Vía. If you're airport-bound, keep heading into Madrid until you see the airplane symbol (N-II). Turn in your rental car at terminal T-1.

GRANADA

For a time, Granada was the grandest city in Spain; but in the end, it was left in the historic dust. Today it's a provincial town with more than its share of history and bumper stickers reading, "Life is short. Don't run." We'll keep things fun and simple, settling down in the old center and exploring monuments of the Moorish civilization and monuments of its conquest. And we'll taste the treats of an African-flavored culture that survives today.

Granada's magnificent Alhambra fortress was the last stronghold of the Moorish kingdom in Spain. The city's exotically tangled Moorish quarter bustles under the grand Alhambra, which glows red in the evening while locals stroll, enjoying the city's cool late-night charms.

There is an old saying: "Give him a coin, woman, for there is nothing worse in this life than to be blind in Granada." This city has much to see, yet it reveals itself in unpredictable ways. It takes a poet to sort through the jigsaw-puzzle pieces of Granada. Peer through the intricate lattice of a Moorish window. Hear water burbling, sight unseen, among the labyrinthine hedges of the Generalife garden. Listen to a flute trilling deep in the swirl of alleys around the cathedral. Don't be blind in Granada—open your senses.

Planning Your Time

Granada is worth one day and two nights. Consider the night train connection with Madrid (or Barcelona), giving the city a night and a day. The Costa del Sol's best beach town, Nerja, is just two quick hours away (by bus), white hill towns such as Ronda are three hours away (bus or train), and Sevilla is an easy three-hour train ride. To use your time efficiently in Granada, reserve in advance for the Alhambra (see "Sights—The Alhambra," below).

In the morning, tour the cathedral and Royal Chapel (both closed roughly 13:00–16:00) and stroll the pedestrian-zone shopping scene. Do the Alhambra in the late afternoon. Be at the Albayzín viewpoint—in the Moorish Quarter—for sunset and then find the right place in this neighborhood for a suitably late dinner.

Orientation

While modern Granada sprawls (300,000 people), its sights are all within a 20-minute walk of Plaza Nueva, where dogs wag their tails to the rhythm of the street musicians. Nearly all my recommended hotels are within a few blocks of Plaza Nueva. Make this the hub of your Granada visit.

Plaza Nueva was a main square back when kings called Granada home. This historic center is in the Darro River Valley, which separates two hills (the river now flows under the square). On one hill is the great Moorish palace, the Alhambra; and on the other is the best-preserved Moorish quarter in Spain, the Albayzín. To the southeast are the cathedral, Royal Chapel, and Alcaicería (Moorish market), where the city's two main drags, Gran Vía de Colón and Calle Reyes Católicos, lead away into the modern city.

Tourist Information

There are three TIs. The handiest—in the courtyard of what was a Moorish hotel 500 years ago—is at Corral del Carbon. It covers Granada as well as all Andalucía (Mon–Sat 9:00–19:00, Sun 10:00–14:00; from Plaza Isabel la Católica, take Reyes Católicos in the opposite direction from Alhambra, take first left, walk through keyhole arch, tel. 95-822-5990; festival office in the same courtyard—see "Helpful Hints," below). Another TI, with its focus solely on Granada, is on Plaza de Mariana Pineda (Mon–Fri 9:30–19:00, Sat 10:00–14:00, closed Sun, 3 blocks south of Plaza Carmen and Puerta Real, tel. 95-824-7128). The third TI is at the Alhambra entrance, across from the ticket windows (Mon–Fri 10:00–14:00 only). Get the free Granada map and verify your Alhambra plans. Bus and train schedules are posted in a small room next to the TI at Corral del Carbon.

Arrival in Granada

By Train: Granada's train station is connected to the center by frequent buses, a €3.60 taxi ride, or a 20-minute walk down Avenida Constitución and Gran Vía de Colón. The train station has lockers. Reserve your train out upon arrival.

Exiting the train station, walk straight ahead down the tree-lined road. At the first major intersection (Avenida de la Constitución), you'll see the bus stop on your right. Take buses #9 or #11 and confirm by asking the driver, "*¿Catedral?*" (kat-ay-dral; the nearest stop to Plaza Nueva, ticket-€0.75, pay driver). Get off

Granada

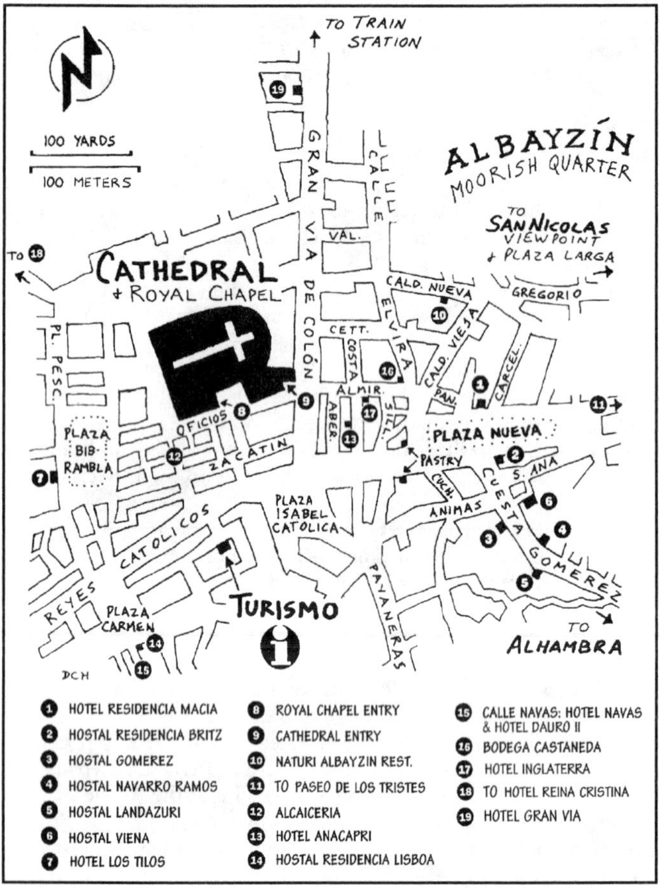
TO TRAIN STATION
100 YARDS
100 METERS
ALBAYZÍN
MOORISH QUARTER
TO SAN NICOLAS VIEWPOINT & PLAZA LARGA
TO 18
CATHEDRAL & ROYAL CHAPEL
GRAN VIA DE COLÓN
CALLE ELVIRA
VAL.
CALD. NUEVA
GREGORIO
CETT.
COSTA
ALMIR.
CALD. VIEJA
PAN.
CARCEL
PL. PESC.
PLAZA BIB-RAMBLA
OFICIOS
ZACATIN
ABER.
PLAZA NUEVA
PASTRY
S. ANA
CUCH.
ANIMAS
CUESTA GOMEREZ
PLAZA ISABEL CATOLICA
CATOLICOS
REYES
PLAZA CARMEN
TURISMO
PAVANERAS
TO ALHAMBRA
DCH
1 HOTEL RESIDENCIA MACIA
2 HOSTAL RESIDENCIA BRITZ
3 HOSTAL GOMEREZ
4 HOSTAL NAVARRO RAMOS
5 HOSTAL LANDAZURI
6 HOSTAL VIENA
7 HOTEL LOS TILOS
8 ROYAL CHAPEL ENTRY
9 CATHEDRAL ENTRY
10 NATURI ALBAYZIN REST.
11 TO PASEO DE LOS TRISTES
12 ALCAICERIA
13 HOTEL ANACAPRI
14 HOSTAL RESIDENCIA LISBOA
15 CALLE NAVAS: HOTEL NAVAS & HOTEL DAURO II
16 BODEGA CASTANEDA
17 HOTEL INGLATERRA
18 TO HOTEL REINA CRISTINA
19 HOTEL GRAN VIA

when you see the fountain of Plaza Isabel la Católica in front of the bus at the stop near the cathedral; cross the busy Gran Vía and walk three short blocks to Plaza Nueva.

By Bus: Granada's bus station (with a café, ATMs, lockers, and a don't-bother-me-with-questions info office, tel. 95-818-5480) is located on the outskirts of the city. To get to the center, either take a taxi (€4.20) or bus #3 (€0.75, pay driver). It's about a 15-minute ride by bus; nearing the center, the bus goes up Gran Vía de Colón. For Plaza Nueva, get off at the stop for the cathedral (cathedral not visible from bus), a half-block before the grand square Plaza Isabel la Católica—from the bus you'll see the big

Banco Santander building across the square. From this stop, you're a three-block walk from Plaza Nueva (facing Banco Santander, go left up Reyes Católicos).

By Car: Driving in Granada's historic center is restricted to buses, taxis, and tourists with hotel reservations (tell the police officer). The *autovía* (freeway) circles the city with a *circumvalación* road. To reach Plaza Nueva, take exit #129, direction "*Centro, Recogidas.*" Calle Recogidas leads directly into the heart of town. There will probably be a police block at Puerta Real (Victoria Hotel). You can pull into Plaza Nueva if you have a hotel reservation: There are posts with hotel buzzers on Reyes Católicos and on Calle Elvira on the approach to Plaza Nueva. You press a button on the pillar for your hotel; the hotel buzzes back, releasing the road block to allow you through. Of Granada's many parking garages, one is at Puerta Real and another is Parking San Agustin, near the cathedral, just off Gran Vía (€12/24 hrs, on Gran Vía as you approach Plaza Isabel la Católica, turn right on Carcel Baja to reach garage).

By Plane: To get between the airport and downtown, you can take a taxi (€17.50) or, much cheaper, the airport bus, timed to leave when flights arrive/depart (6/day, 30 min, €2.70). Hop on (or get off) at Gran Vía del Colón, nearly across from the cathedral. Airport info: tel. 95-824-5223.

Getting around Granada

With such cheap taxis, efficient minibuses, and nearly all points of interest an easy walk from Plaza Nueva, you may not even need the regular city buses. Three handy little red minibuses depart frequently (roughly every 10 min until late in eve) from Plaza Nueva: bus #30 goes up to the Alhambra and back; bus #31 does the Albayzín loop (a few go through Sacromonte); and bus #32 connects the Alhambra and Albayzín (from Plaza Nueva, the bus goes up to the Alhambra, returns to Plaza Nueva, then loops through the Albayzín and ends at Plaza Nueva). You buy bus tickets (€0.75) from the driver. Sharable *bonobus* tickets for five trips (€3) or 13 trips (€6) save you money if you'll be taking a lot of trips, or if you're part of a group (buy from driver, valid on minibuses and city buses).

Helpful Hints

When you see women wanting to give you leaves or flowers, avoid them like the plague. They may even grab at you. Firmly say no, and walk away (for more information see Alcaicería under "Sights—Central Granada," below).

City Pass: The new Bono Turístico city pass covers the Alhambra, Cathedral, Royal Chapel, Caruja Monastery, and 10 free bus trips, plus other lesser sights and discounts on more

(€15, valid for a week). When you buy your pass, the vendor schedules a time for your Alhambra visit. Passes are sold at the Royal Chapel, Alhambra, and Caja General de Ahorros bank on Plaza Isabel la Católica. This pass works best for people who are staying two or more days, ideally off-season (because in peak-season there's a risk you might not get in the Alhambra within 2 days).

Long-Distance Buses, Trains, and Flights: To save yourself a trip to the train or bus stations, get information from the TI (schedules posted next to TI at Corral del Carbon) or a travel agency. All travel agencies book flights, and many also sell long-distance bus and train tickets (generally open Mon–Fri 9:00–13:30, 17:00–20:00, Sat 10:00–13:30, closed Sun; Viajes Bonanza is convenient at Reyes Católicos 30, near main TI, tel. 95-822-3578).

Post Office: The P.O. is on Puerta Real (Mon–Fri 8:30–20:30, Sat 9:30–14:00, tel. 95-822-1138).

American Express: It's across from the main TI (Mon–Fri 9:00–20:00, Sat 10:00–14:00, 15:00–19:00, Reyes Católicos 31, tel. 95-822-4512).

Internet Access: Madar Internet, one of many Internet points scattered throughout Granada, is in the midst of tea shops at Calderia Nueva 12 (Mon–Sat 10:00–24:00, Sun 12:00–24:00, 2 long blocks off Plaza Nueva).

Festivals: From late June to early July the International Festival of Music and Dance offers some of the world's top classical music and art (ballet, flamenco, and zarzuela) nightly in the Alhambra at reasonable prices. The ticket office is open from mid-April through the festival (in Corral del Carbon, in same courtyard as TI, tel. 95-822-1844). Tickets can also be booked online at www.granadafestival.org from February on. During the festival, flamenco is free every night at midnight; ask the ticket office or TI for the venue.

Local Guide: Margarita Landazuri, a local English-speaking guide, knows how to teach and has good rates (tel. 95-822-1406); if she's busy, her partner, Miguel Angel, is also good.

Walking Tours: Run by locals, Granada Romántic's two-hour walking tour of the Albayzín ends with a drink and tapa (€17, 2/day year-round, tel. 95-821-0127, cellular 63-026-2840).

Sights—The Alhambra

A ▲▲▲ sight, this last and greatest Moorish palace is one of Europe's top attractions. Attracting up to 8,000 visitors a day, it's the reason most tourists come to Granada. Nowhere else does the splendor of Moorish civilization shine so brightly.

The last Moorish stronghold in Europe is, with all due respect, really a symbol of retreat. Granada was only a regional capital for centuries. Gradually the Christian Reconquista moved south, taking Córdoba (1236) and Sevilla (1248). The Moors held

Alhambra

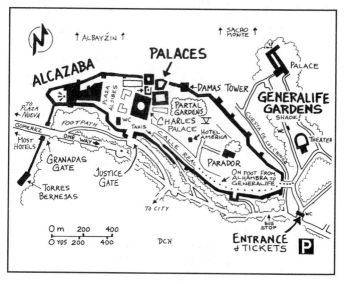

Granada until 1492. As you tour their grand palace, remember that while Europe slumbered through the Dark Ages, Moorish magnificence blossomed—busy stucco, plaster "stalactites," colors galore, scalloped windows framing Granada views, exuberant gardens, and water, water everywhere. Water—so rare and precious in most of the Islamic world—was the purest symbol of life to the Moors. The Alhambra is decorated with water: standing still, cascading, masking secret conversations, and drip-dropping playfully.

The Alhambra—not nearly as confusing as it seems—consists of four sights: Charles V's Palace (free, Christian Renaissance palace plopped on top of the Alhambra after the reconquest), Alcazaba (empty old fort with tower and views), Palacios Nazaries (exquisite Moorish palace), and Generalife Gardens (fancy gardens); for descriptions of these sites, see "The Alhambra in Four Parts," below. Note that some rooms or portions of the Alhambra may be closed for restoration.

Cost: The Alcazaba fort, Moorish palace (Palacios Nazaries), and Generalife Gardens require a €6 combo ticket. (Only Charles V's Palace is free.) Audioguides are €3, available at the entrance and at Charles V's Palace. No map is included with your ticket, but a simple map comes with the audioguide. The bookshop adjacent to the ticket office sells guidebooks (see "Guidebooks," below; books are also sold at shops throughout the Alhambra) and the dismal Official Map of the Alhambra, which looks great but doesn't mark sights clearly (€1.10, open it up to check it before you buy, the back is more detailed than the front).

Hours: The Alhambra is open daily from 8:30 to 20:00 (closes Nov–Feb at 18:00); ticket office closes an hour earlier (Alhambra closed on Dec 25 and Jan 1).

Alhambra by Moonlight: Late-night visits include only the Moorish palace and not the fort or gardens—but hey, the palace is 80 percent of the Alhambra thrills (March–Oct Tue–Sat 22:00–23:30, reserve ahead during peak season, ticket office open 21:45–22:45; Nov–Feb only Fri–Sat 20:00–21:30, ticket office open 19:45–20:15).

Getting a Reservation for the Alhambra: The Alhambra is the main reason most tourists visit Granada, yet some never see the sight because the tickets can sell out fast. It's smart to make a reservation for the Alhambra in advance, especially if you know the dates you'll be in Granada—and if you'll be visiting during peak season (April–June and Sept–Oct). Off-season, you might be able to just walk right into the Alhambra. Still, it can be worth the peace of mind and your valuable time to reserve ahead. The Alhambra's top sight is the Moorish palace—Palacios Nazaries. Only 400 visitors per half hour are allowed inside. Your 30-minute time span is printed on your ticket (you can request a particular half hour). While you must enter Palacios Nazaries within this time, once inside you may linger as long as you like.

The Alhambra is trying out some crowd-control techniques, but only for visitors scheduled from 14:00 on. If your entry time to Palacios Nazaries is before 14:00, you can enter the grounds anytime in the morning, see the palace at your appointed time, and then stay all day at the Alhambra if you choose. But if your ticket is stamped for 14:00 or later, you can enter the site no earlier than 14:00. For instance, if you have a reservation to visit Palacios Nazaries between 16:30 and 17:00, you can enter the Alhambra grounds as early as 14:00 and see the fort and Generalife Gardens before the palace. (Because of the time restriction on afternoon visits, morning times sell out the quickest, but for most travelers, an afternoon allows ample time to see the site.) Here's the scoop on how to make a reservation for the Alhambra.

Reserving in Advance: There are three possibilites, each costing a worthwhile €0.75 surcharge. With any of these options, you might be required to show your passport (as an identity card) when you pick up your ticket at the Alhambra, but in reality this rarely happens.

1. You can drop by any BBVA bank in Spain and make a reservation (Banco Bilbao Vizcaya Argentaria, Mon–Fri 8:30–14:15, closed Sat–Sun); you'll pay in advance and get a piece of paper that you take to the ticket window at the Alhambra (a minimum of 15 min before your allotted appointment time) to

exchange for a ticket. The BBVA bank personnel usually speak just enough English to make this transaction (which takes about 10 min). If you know when you'll be in Granada, it's simplest to reserve a ticket soon after you arrive in Spain. BBVA banks are easy to find in virtually every Spanish town.

2. You can order by phone. If you're calling within Spain, dial 90-222-4460. If calling internationally, dial the international access code first (00 for a European country, 011 for the U.S. or Canada), then 34-91-346-5936 (daily 8:00–18:00, can reserve between 1 day and a year in advance, use credit-card number to pay and you'll get a reference number to tell the ticket window at the Alhambra to get your ticket, you'll be advised to pick up your ticket an hour before your palace entry time).

3. Or order online at www.alhambratickets.com (currently this Web site is in Spanish, but an English version will likely be added eventually).

If you're in Granada without a reservation: You have a number of alternatives, the first of which involves getting up unnaturally early.

1. Stand in line at the Alhambra. The Alhambra admits 8,000 visitors a day. Six thousand tickets are sold in advance (see above). Two thousand are sold each day at the Alhambra ticket window (near Generalife Gardens and parking lot). On busy days, tickets can sell out as early as 10:00.

The ticket office opens at 8:00. People start lining up about 7:30, but generally if you're in line by 8:15, you'll get an entry time. On a slow day you'll get in right away. During busy times you'll have an appointment for later that day. However, you're on vacation, and it's a pain to get up this early and miss breakfast to stand in line. It's more efficient to reserve in advance.

2. Consider getting Granada's new Bono Turístico city pass if you'll be staying at least two days in the city. It costs €15, covers admission to the Alhambra and the city's other top sights, and includes a reservation for the Alhambra (scheduled when you buy the pass). The pass is valid for seven days. Usually you can get into the Alhambra on the second day (possibly even the first). If you have only a day in Granada, this is risky. Even with two days, though it's probable you'll get in, there are no guarantees (especially during peak season: April–June and Sept–Oct). This pass is easiest to buy at the Royal Chapel (for details, see "Helpful Hints," above).

3. Make a reservation at a BBVA bank in Granada (for a following day, not the same day). People wait in line at the most visible BBVA bank in Granada—on Plaza Isabel la Católica—but any of the many BBVA branches in Granada (or anywhere in Spain) can make a reservation for you at a minimal €0.75 surcharge (bank hours Mon–Fri 8:30–14:15).

4. Your hotel (particularly if it's a 3- or 4-star) may be willing to book a reservation for you; ask when you reserve your room.

5. Take a tour of the Alhambra. The pricier hotels can book you on a €30 tour that includes Palacios Nazeries.

Getting to the Alhambra: There are three ways to get to the Alhambra.

1. From Plaza Nueva, hike 20 minutes up the street Cuesta de Gomerez. Keep going straight, with the Alhambra high on your left, and follow the street to the ticket pavilion at the far side of the Alhambra, near the Generalife Gardens.

2. From Plaza Nueva, catch a red minibus #30 or #32, marked "Alhambra" (€0.75, runs every 10 min).

3. Take a taxi (€3, taxi stand on Plaza Nueva).

Don't drive. If you do, you'll park on the far, far side of the Alhambra, and when you leave, one-way streets will send you into the traffic-clogged center of New Granada.

Planning Your Visit: It's a 10-minute walk to Palace Nazaries from the entry. Be sure to arrive at the Alhambra with enough time to make it to the palace before your allotted half-hour appointment ends. The ticket-checkers at Palacios Nazaries are strict.

To minimize walking, see the Alcazaba fort and Charles V's Palace before your visit to Palacios Nazaries. Because the Alhambra is long (about a 10-min walk from end to end), you don't want to do a lot of backtracking, especially if it's hot. When you exit Palacios Nazaries, leave through the Partal Gardens (don't duck out early to visit the fort). This is your only chance to see these gardens and their great views of the Albayzín. You'll exit the gardens near the Alhambra entrance, and if you haven't seen the fort and Charles V's Palace yet, you'd need to backtrack to do so. (Note that, because of crowd-control restrictions, if you have a 14:00 appointment for Palacios Nazaries, you can't be admitted to the Alhambra any earlier than this.)

Depending on your time, you can visit the Generalife Gardens before or after your visit to Palacios Nazaries. If you've got any time to kill before your palace appointment, do it luxuriously at the parador bar (actually within the Alhambra walls). While you can find drinks, WCs, and guidebooks near the entrance of Palacios Nazaries, you'll find none inside the actual palace.

Cuisine: There are only three places to eat within the Alhambra walls: the restaurants at the parador and Hotel America, and a small bar/café kiosk in front of the Alcazaba fort (near entrance of Palacios Nazaries). You're welcome to bring in a picnic.

Guidebooks: Consider getting a guidebook in town and reading it the night before to understand the layout and history of this remarkable sight before entering. The classic is *The Alhambra and the Generalife* (€6, includes great map, available in town and at shops throughout the Alhambra), but even better is the slick new

The Alhambra and Generalife in Focus, which combines vibrant color photos and more readable text (€7.25, sold at Libreria next to TI in Corral del Carbon).

The Alhambra in Four Parts

1. Charles V's Palace—It's only natural for a conquering king to build his own palace over his foe's palace—and that's exactly what the Christian King Charles V did. The Alhambra palace wasn't good enough for Charles, so he built this one—destroying the dramatic Alhambra facade and financing his new palace with a salt-on-the-wound tax on Granada's defeated Moorish population. This palace—a unique circle within a square—is Spain's most impressive Renaissance building. It was designed by Pedro Machuca, a devotee of Michelangelo and Raphael. Stand in the circular courtyard, then climb the stairs. Imagine being here for one of Charles' bullfights. Charles' palace was never finished because his son Philip II moved the royal building focus to El Escorial. Inside the palace are two boring museums: Museo de Bellas Artes (€1.50, Tue 14:30–20:00, Wed–Sat 9:00–20:00, Sun 9:00–14:30, closed Mon, shorter hours off-season, located upstairs) and Museo de Alhambra, showing off some of the Alhambra's best Moorish art (free, Tue–Sat 9:00–14:30, on ground floor). The palace itself is free; to see only this, you can enter the Alhambra at either of the two gates located midway along the length of the grounds (between the fort and official entrance).

2. Alcazaba Fort—The fort—the oldest and most ruined part of the Alhambra—offers exercise and fine city views. What you see is mid-13th century, but there was probably a fort here in Roman times. Once upon a time this tower defended a town (or medina) of 2,000 Arabs living within the Alhambra walls. From the top find Plaza Nueva, the Albayzín viewpoint, and the mountains. Is anybody skiing today? Look to the south and think of that day in 1492 when the cross and flags of Aragon and Castille were raised on this tower and the fleeing Moorish King Boabdil looked back and wept. His mom chewed him out, saying, "Don't weep like a woman for what you couldn't defend like a man." Much later, Napoleon stationed his troops here, contributing substantially to its ruin when he left. Follow the signs down and around to the Palacios Nazaries (WCs to right of entry); if you're early, duck into the exhibit across from the palace entry. It's in Spanish, but the models of the Alhambra upstairs are easy to appreciate.

3. Palacios Nazaries—During the 30-minute window of time stamped on your ticket, enter the jewel of the Alhambra: The Moorish royal palace. You'll walk through three basic sections: royal offices, ceremonial rooms, and private quarters. Built mostly in the 14th century, this palace offers your best possible look at the refined, elegant Moorish civilization of Al-Andalus. If you can

Alhambra's Palacios Nazaries

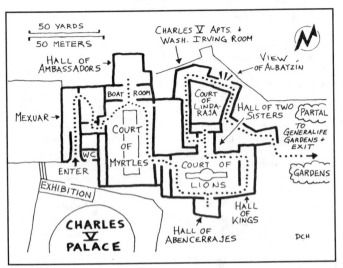

imagine a few tapestries, carpets, pillows, ivory-studded wooden furniture, and painted stucco, the place is much as it was for the Moorish kings. Rather then hire an interior decorator, the Moors just read the Koran: Recommended color scheme—red (blood), blue (heaven), green (oasis), and gold (wealth). As you tour the palace, keep the palace themes in mind: water, no images, "stalactite" ceilings throughout—and few signs telling you where you are. Even today, the route constantly changes. Use the map to locate these essential stops:

Court of Myrtles: Walk through a few administrative rooms (the *mexuar*) and a small courtyard until you hit the big rectangular courtyard with a fish pond lined by a myrtle bush hedge—the Court of Myrtles (Patio de los Arrayanes). Moors loved their patios—with a garden, water, and under the sky. Women, who rarely went out, stayed in touch with nature here. The living quarters for the wives (the Koran allowed a man "all the women you can maintain with dignity") were upstairs. Notice the wooden "jealousies"—screens (erected by jealous husbands) allowing the cloistered women to look out without clearly being seen.

Boat Room: Head left (north) from the entry into the long, narrow antechamber to the throne room, called the "Boat Room." While it's understandable that many think this is named for the upside-down hull shape of its fine cedar ceiling, the name is actually a corruption of the Arab word *baraka*, meaning "divine blessing and luck." This was the waiting room for meetings with the sultan, and blessings and luck are exactly what you'd need if you had business in the next room. Oh, it's your turn now...

The Hall of the Ambassadors (Grand Salon de Embajadores) functioned like a throne room. It was here that the sultan received foreign emissaries. The king's throne stood opposite the entrance. The ceiling, made of cedar of Lebanon—8,000 inlaid pieces—is original. The walls, even without their original paint and gilding, are still glorious. Note the finely carved Arabic script. Muslims couldn't make images of living things—that was God's work. But they could carve decorative religious messages. One phrase—"only Allah is victorious"—is repeated 9,000 times throughout the palace. Find the character for Allah—it looks like a cursive W with a nose on its left side. The swoopy toboggan blades underneath are a kind of artistic punctuation marking off one phrase.

In 1492 two historic events took place in this room. Culminating a 700-year-long battle, the Reconquista was completed here as the last Moorish king, Boabdil, signed the terms of his surrender before packing light and fleeing to Africa. For four years Isabel had put off Columbus as she focused on the Reconquista. That accomplished, Isabel and Ferdinand finally received Columbus in this room. Imagine the scene: The king, queen, and the greatest minds from the University of Salamanca gathered here to hear Columbus make his case that the world was round—then a still-loony notion that got people burned a few years earlier. Ferdinand and the professors laughed, calling Columbus mad. But Isabel said "*Sí, señor.*" Columbus fell to his knees (promising to wear a moneybelt and use the most current guidebooks available) and she gave him an ATM card with a wad of traveler's checks as a backup.

Continue deeper into the palace to a court where, 600 years ago, only the royal family and their servants could enter. It's the much-photographed...

Court of the Lions: The Patio de los Leones features a fountain with 12 lions. Why 12? Since the fountain was a gift from a Jewish leader celebrating good relations with the sultan (Granada had a big Jewish community), the lions probably represent the 12 tribes of Israel. During Moorish times, the fountain functioned as a clock, with a different lion spouting water each hour. (Conquering Christians disassembled the fountain to see how it worked and it's never worked since.) From the center, four streams went out—figuratively to the corners of the earth and literally to various apartments of the royal family. Notice how the court resembles, with its 124 columns, the cloister of a Catholic monastery. Six hundred years ago the Muslim Moors could read the Koranic poetry that ornaments this court, and they could understand the symbolism of this lush, enclosed garden (considered the embodiment of paradise or truth). Imagine—they appreciated this part of the palace even more than we do today.

On the right, off the courtyard, is a square room called the **Hall of the Abencerrajes (Sala de los Abencerrajes)**. According to legend, the father of Boabdil took a new wife and wanted to disinherit the children of his first marriage—one of whom was Boabdil. In order to deny power to Boabdil and his siblings, he killed nearly the entire pro-Boabdil Abencerrage family. The sultan thought this would pave the way for the son of his new wife to be the next sultan. Happily, he stacked 36 Abencerrage heads in the pool under this sumptuous honeycombed stucco ceiling. But his scheme failed, and Boabdil ultimately assumed the throne. Bloody power struggles like this were the norm here in the Alhambra.

The Hall of the Kings (Sala de los Reyes) is at the end of the court opposite where you entered. Notice the ceilings of the three chambers branching off this gallery. Breaking from the tradition of imageless art, paintings on the goat-leather ceiling depict scenes of the sultan and his family. The center room shows a portrait of the first 10 of the Alhambra's 22 sultans. The scene is a fantasy, since these people lived over a span of many generations. The two end rooms show scenes of princely pastimes, such as hunting and shooting skeet. In a palace otherwise devoid of figures, these offer a rare look at royal life in the palace.

The next room, the **Hall of the Two Sisters**, has another oh-wow stucco ceiling but no figures—only geometric patterns and stylized Arabic script quoting verses from the Koran.

Washington Irving Room: That's about it for the palace. From here you wander through a few more rooms including one (marked with a large plaque) where Washington Irving wrote *Tales of the Alhambra*. While serving as the U.S. ambassador to Spain in 1829, Irving lived in the Alhambra. It was a romantic time when the place was home to Gypsies and donkeys. His "tales" kindled interest in the place, causing it to become recognized as a national treasure.

Hallway with a view: Stop at the open-air hallway for the best-in-the-palace view of the labyrinthine Albayzín—the old Moorish town on the opposite hillside. Find the famous viewpoint at the base of the white St. Nicolás church tower breaking the horizon. Creeping into the mountains on the right are the Gypsy neighborhoods of Sacromonte. Still circling old Granada is the Moorish wall (built by the Moors in the 1200s to protect the city's population, swollen by Muslim refugees driven south by the Reconquista).

Leaving the Palacios Nazaries, follow signs to the Partal Gardens, go through the gardens, then follow signs directing you left to the Generalife Gardens or right to the exit.

4. Generalife Gardens—On the hillside to the east, the garden with carefully pruned hedges is Generalife (henneraw-LEEF-ay). This most perfect Arabian garden in Andalucía was the summer home of the Moorish kings, the closest thing on earth to the Koran's description of heaven. If you have a long wait before your entry to the Palacios, tour these gardens first, then the Alcazaba fort and Charles V's Palace.

Sights—Central Granada

▲▲**Royal Chapel (Capilla Real)**—Without a doubt Granada's top Christian sight, this lavish chapel holds the dreams—and bodies—of Queen Isabel and King Ferdinand (€2.10, April–Sept Mon–Sat 10:30–13:00, 16:00–19:00, Sun 11:00–13:00, 16:00–19:00; Oct–March Mon–Sat 10:30–13:00, 15:30–18:30, closed Sun, no photos, entrance on Calle Oficios, just off Gran Vía de Colón; go through iron gate, tel. 95-822-9239).

In the lobby, before you enter the chapel, notice the painting of Boabdil (on the black horse) giving the key of Granada to the conquering King Ferdinand. Boabdil wanted to fall to his knees, but the Spanish king, who had great respect for his Moorish foe, embraced him instead. They fought a long and noble war (for instance, respectfully returning the bodies of dead soldiers). Ferdinand is in red, and Isabel is behind him wearing a crown. Next to her (under a black hood) is their daughter Juana. And next to Juana is her husband, Philip the Fair, wearing a crown. Philip died young, and for two years Juana kept his casket at her bedside, kissing his embalmed body good night. These four people are buried in this chapel. The painting is flanked by two large portraits of Ferdinand and Isabel.

Isabel decided to make Granada the capital of Spain (and burial place for Spanish royalty) for three reasons: 1) With the conquest of Granada, Christianity had overcome Islam in Europe; 2) her marriage with Ferdinand, followed by the conquest of Granada, had marked the beginning of a united Spain; and 3) in Granada, she agreed to sponsor Columbus' fateful voyage.

Step into the **chapel**. It's Plateresque Gothic—light and lacy, named for and inspired by the fine silverwork of the Moors. This was the most lavish interior money could buy 500 years ago. Because of its speedy completion, the chapel is an unusually harmonious piece of architecture.

The four **royal tombs** are Renaissance-style. Carved in Italy in 1521 out of Carrara marble, they were sent by ship to Spain. The faces—based on death masks—are considered accurate. If you're facing the altar, Ferdinand and Isabel are on the right. (Isabel fans attribute the bigger dent she puts in the pillow to brains.) Philip the Fair and Juana are on the left. Philip was a Hapsburg. Their son, Charles V (known as Carlos I in Spain), was a key character in European history, as his coronation merged the Holy Roman Empire (Hapsburg domain) with the Spanish empire. Europe's top king, he ruled a vast empire stretching from Budapest to Bolivia (1519–1556).

When Phillip II, the son of Charles V, decided to build El Escorial and establish Madrid as the single capital of a single Spain, Granada lost power and importance.

More important, Spain declined. After Charles V, Spain squandered her awesome wealth trying to maintain this impossible empire—not for material riches but to defend the romantic Quixote-esque dream of a Catholic empire ruled by one divinely ordained Catholic monarch against an irrepressible tide of nationalism and Protestantism. Spain's relatively poor modern history can be blamed, in part, by her stubborn unwillingness to accept the end of this "old regime" notion.

Look at the fine carving on the tombs (unfortunately vandalized by Napoleon's troops). It's a humanistic statement with healthy, organic, realistic figures rising above the strict and heavy Gothic past.

From the feet of the marble tombs, step downstairs to see the actual coffins. They are plain. Isabel was originally buried as simply as a monk at the Franciscan monastery (in what is today the parador at the Alhambra). The fifth coffin (with PM on it) is that of a young Prince Michael, who would have been king of a united Spain and Portugal. A sad—but too long—story...

The **high altar** is one of the finest Renaissance works in Spain. It's dedicated to John the Baptist and John the Evangelist. In the center, you can see the Baptist and the Evangelist chatting as if over tapas (an appropriately humanist scene). Scenes from the Baptist's life are on the left: John beheaded after Salome's fine dancing and (below) John baptizing Jesus. Scenes from the Evangelist's life are on the right: John's martyrdom (a failed attempt to boil him alive in oil) and John on Patmos (where he wrote the last book of the Bible, Revelation). John is talking to the eagle that, according to legend, flew him to Heaven.

Anyone who paid for church art got his mug in it. Find Ferdinand and Isabel kneeling in prayer in opposite corners. The eagle banners around the room are not the aggressive, two-headed, claws-exposed Hapsburg eagles but eagles with halos (and crowns for bras). These are symbolic of the eagle that inspired John on Patmos.

The Plateresque (silver-filigree-style) arch leads to a small glass pyramid in the **treasury**. This holds the silver crown of Queen Isabel, ringed by pomegranates (symbolizing Granada), and the sword of Ferdinand. Beside the entry arch you'll see the devout Isabel's prayer book, in which she followed the Mass. The book and its sturdy box date from 1496. The fancy box on the other side of the door is the one that Isabel (cash-poor because of her military expenses) filled with jewels and gave Columbus. Columbus sold these to finance his journey. Next, in the corner (and also behind glass), is the cross Cardinal Mendoza, staunch supporter of Queen Isabel, carried into the Alhambra on that historic day in 1492. Next, the big silk, silver, and gold tapestry is the altar banner for the mobile campaign chapel of Ferdinand and Isabel, who always traveled with their army. In the next case you'll see the original Christian army flags raised over the Alhambra in 1492.

The room holds the first great art collection ever established by a woman. Queen Isabel amassed more than 200 great paintings. After Napoleon's visit, only 30 remained. Even so, this is a fine collection, all on wood, featuring works by Botticelli, Perugino, the Flemish master Memling, and less-famous Spanish masters.

Finally, at the end of the room, the two carved sculptures of Ferdinand and Isabel were the originals from the high altar. Charles V considered them primitive and replaced these with the ones you saw earlier.

Cathedral—One of only two Renaissance churches in Spain (the other is in Córdoba), Granada's cathedral is the second-largest in Spain after Sevilla's. Its spacious and bright interior is a refreshing break from the dark Gothic and gilded-lily Baroque of so many Spanish churches. In a modern move back in the 18th century, the choir walls were taken out so that people could be involved in the worship. To make matters even better, an 18th-century bishop ordered the interior painted with lime (for hygienic reasons, during a time of disease). The people liked it, and it stayed white. Most of the side chapels are decorated in Baroque style. On the far wall (to the right of the high altar) is St. James the Moorslayer, with his sword raised high and an armored Moor under his horse's hooves. The Renaissance facade and paintings of the Virgin in the rotunda are by Granada's own Alonso Cano (1601–1661) and can be lit by dropping a coin in the box (entry: €1.80, April–Sept Mon–Sat 10:30–13:30, 16:00–19:00, Sun 16:00–19:00; Oct–March Mon–Sat 10:30–13:30, closed Sun, audioguide-€2.70, entrance off Gran Vía de Colón through iron gateway, tel. 95-822-2959).

Alcaicería—Originally an Arab silk market, this neighborhood (around the cathedral) still functions as a silk and jewelry market. Ignore the aggressive, obnoxious Gypsy women giving tourists sprigs of rosemary for good luck. (The flowers they used to give became too expensive. After somehow rerouting the magic power, they now use rosemary, which comes from the parks—for free.) By accepting the sprig you start a relationship. This, while free, leads to palm reading, which isn't.

Explore the mesh of tiny shopping lanes between the cathedral and Calle Reyes Católicos. Go on a photo and sound safari: popcorn machines popping, men selling balloons, leather goods spread out on streets, kids playing soccer, barking dogs, dogged shoeshine boys, and the whirring grind of bicycle-powered knife sharpeners.

The exuberant square behind the cathedral is **Bib-Rambla.**
While today it's fine for a coffee or meal amidst the color and
fragrance of flower stalls, in Moorish times this was a place of
public execution. A block away, the square Pescaderia is a smaller,
similarly lively version of Bib-Rambla.

Plaza Isabel la Católica—Granada's two grand boulevards,
Gran Vía and Reyes Católicos, meet a block off Plaza Nueva
at Plaza Isabel la Católica. Here you'll see a fine statue of Columbus unfurling a long contract with Isabel. It lists the terms of
Columbus' MCDXCII voyage.

Isabel was driven by her desire to spread Catholicism.
Columbus was driven by his desire for money. For adding territory to Spain's Catholic empire, Isabel promised Columbus the
ranks of Admiral of the Oceans and Governor of the New World.
To sweeten the pie, she tossed in 10 percent of all the riches
he brought home. Isabel died thinking Columbus had found
India or China. Columbus died poor and disillusioned.

From here, Reyes Católicos leads to Puerta Real. There
Acera de Darro takes you through modern Granada to the river
via the huge El Corte Inglés department store and lots of modern
commerce.

Paseo de los Tristes—In the cool of the evening—with dinner
as a popular destination—consider strolling the Paseo de los
Tristes (if you're tired, note that bus #31 and #32 stop here).
This "walk of the sad ones" is the route of funeral processions
to the cemetery at the edge of town.

Start at Plaza Nueva. The Church of Santa Anna, which
stands at the far end of the square, was originally a mosque, its
tower a minaret. Notice the ceramic brickwork. This is Mudejar art,
the technique of the Moors used by Christians. Inside you'll see a
fine Alhambra-style cedar ceiling. Follow Carrera del Darro along
the River Darro under the Alhambra. (Nine kilometers upstream,
part of the Darro is diverted to provide water for the Alhambra's
many fountains.) Past the church, on your right is the turn-off for
the Arab Baths (described below) and on the left, the Convent of
Santa Catalina de Zafra, a home of cloistered nuns (they worship
behind a screen that divides the church's rich interior in half). Farther ahead, on the right, across from the Archaeological Museum,
is the Church of San Pedro, the parish church of Sacromonte's
Gypsy community. Within its rich interior is an ornate oxcart used
to carry the Holy Host on the annual pilgrimage to Rocio near
Portugal. Finally, you reach the Paseo de los Tristes. Covered with
happy diners, this is a great spot at night, under the floodlit Alhambra. From here the road arcs up (past a rank of "burro taxis" for
those into adventure sports) into Sacromonte. And from here a
lane (called Cuesta de los Chinos or Carretera del Rey Chico)
leads up to the Alhambra "through the back door."

Arab Baths—Consider a visit to the Arab baths at Hammam Baños Arabes Al Andaluz. The soak and a 15-minute massage cost €18 (daily 9:00–24:00, appointment times scheduled in 2-hr blocks, co-ed with mandatory swimsuits, quiet atmosphere encouraged, lockers available, just off Plaza Nueva at Santa Ana 16; from Plaza Nueva, it's the first right—over a bridge—past the church; reservation necessary, some hoteliers are happy to call for you, tel. 95-822-9978).

Sights—Albayzín

Explore Spain's best old Moorish quarter, with countless colorful corners, flowery patios, and shady lanes to soothe the 21st-century-mangled visitor. Climb high to the San Nicolás church for the best view of the Alhambra. Then wander through the mysterious backstreets.

Getting to the Albayzín: A handy city minibus threads its way around the Albayzín from Plaza Nueva (see Bus Tour, below), getting you scenically and sweatlessly to the St. Nicolás viewpoint. You can also taxi to the St. Nicolás church and explore from there. Consider having your cabbie take you on a Sacromonte detour en route.

If walking up, leave the west end of Plaza Nueva on Calle Elvira. After about 200 meters, turn right on Calderería Nueva. Follow this stepped street past tapas bars and *teterías* (see "Eating," below) as it goes left around the church, slants, winds, and zigzags up the hill, heading basically straight. Pass the peach-colored building on your left (resisting the temptation to turn left on Muladar Sancha). When you reach a T-intersection, go left on Calle del Almirante. Near the crest, turn right on Camino Nuevo de San Nicolás, then walk several blocks to the street that curves up left (look for brown sign: "Mirador de San Nicolás" where a street sign would normally be). Soon you'll see steps leading up to the church's viewpoint.

▲▲San Nicolás Viewpoint—For one of Europe's most romantic viewpoints, be here at sunset when the Alhambra turns red and the Albayzín widows share the benches with local lovers and tourists. In 1997 President Clinton made a point to bring his family here—a favorite spot from a trip he made as a student.

Exploring the Albayzín: From the San Nicolás viewpoint you're at the edge of a neighborhood even people of Granada recognize as a world apart. From the viewpoint turn your back to the Alhambra and walk north (passing the church on your right and the Biblioteca Municipal on your left). A lane leads past a cream-colored stone arch (on your right)—now a chapel built into the old Moorish wall. At the end of the lane, step down to the right through the 11th-century "New Gate" (Puerta Nueva—older than the Alhambra) and into **Plaza Larga**. In medieval times this tiny square (called "long," because back then it was) was the local

Albayzín Neighborhood

NOTE:
NOT TO SCALE
PLAZA NUEVA TO
SAN NICOLAS IS
A 20 MIN WALK
UPHILL

① BUS STOP FOR ALBAYZIN LOOP
② CALDERERIA NUEVA
   (TAPAS BARS, TETERIAS)
③ PLAZA DE CARVAJALES
④ RESTAURANT LADRILLO I
⑤ RESTAURANT LADRILLO II
⑥ CASA TORCUATO
⑦ EL AGUA CASA DE VINOS
⑧ MIRADOR DE MORAYMA
⑨ NATURI ALBAYZIN
⑩ BODEGA CASTANEDA
⑪ BUS TO ALHAMBRA
⑫ ARAB BATHS

marketplace. It still is a busy market each morning, with locals blaring their cheap, pirated cassettes as if to prove there is actually music on them. Casa Pasteles, at the near end of the square, serves good coffee and cakes.

Leave Plaza Larga on Calle Agua de Albayzín (as you face Casa Pasteles, it's to your right). The street, named for the public baths that used to line it, shows evidence of the Moorish plumbing system—gutters. Back when Europe's streets were filled with muck, Granada actually had Roman Empire–style gutters with drains leading to clay and lead pipes.

This road leads to a T-intersection. You can turn left for the recommended restaurant Casa Torcuato (a block away, see "Eating," below) or right for the recommended El Ladrillo (2 blocks away). Or just explore. You're in the heart of the Albayzín. Poke into an old church. They're plain by design—to go easy on the Muslim converts who weren't used to being surrounded by images as they worshiped. You'll see lots of real Muslim culture living in the streets, including many recent Spanish converts. Those aren't

the Spice Girls, just Gypsy teenagers—as influenced as any teenagers these days by TV.

Albayzín Circular Bus Tour—The handy Albayzín bus #31
makes the 15-minute loop, departing from Plaza Nueva about
every 10 minutes (pay driver €0.75, better views on the right,
bus #32 also works but—depending on where you catch it—goes
to Alhambra first). While good for a lift to the top of the Albayzín,
I'd stay on for an entire circle (and return to the Albayzín later for
dinner—either on foot or by bus). While a few #31 buses detour
up Sacromonte, all pass its entrance (you'll see the humble brown
statue of the Gypsy king on the right). Two stops later the driver
announces the San Nicolás mirador (viewpoint). The next stop
is San Miguel el Bajo (a fun square with several fine little restaurants). Just after that you get a commanding view of modern
Granada on the left. Hitting the city's main drag, Gran Vía,
you make a U-turn at the Garden of the Triumph, celebrating
the Immaculate Conception of the Virgin Mary (notice her statue
atop a column). Behind Mary stands the old Royal Hospital—
built in the 16th century for Granada's poor by the Catholic
kings after the Reconquista in hopes of winning the favor of
Granada's conquered residents. From here you zip past the
cathedral and home to Plaza Nueva.

Sights—Sacromonte and Granada's Gypsies

Spain's Gypsies came from India via Egypt. The Spanish word
for Gypsy, *Gitano*, means "Egyptian." They settled mostly in the
south, where they found people less racist and more tolerant.
Ages ago a Spanish king, exasperated by Gypsy problems, actually
declared that these nomads must stay in one place and get a
religion—any religion. In most of Spain, Gypsies are more assimi-
lated into the general community, but Granada's Sacromonte
district is a large and distinct Gypsy community. Granada's
Gypsies arrived in the 16th century and have stuck together
ever since. Today 50,000 Gypsies call Granada home.

Spaniards, who consider themselves accepting and not racist,
claim that in maintaining such a tight community, the Gypsies
segregate themselves. The Gypsies call Spaniards *Payo* ("whites").

Sacromonte has one main street. Camino del Sacromonte is
lined with caves primed for tourists and restaurants ready to fight
over the bill. Intriguing lanes run above and below this main drag.
Notice the statue of a Gypsy "king"—actually a wise community
elder—in traditional attire marking the start of Sacromonte.

Formerly Europe's most disgusting tourist trap, famous for
its cave-dwelling, foot-stomping, flamenco-dancing Gypsies,
Sacromonte is not quite as bad as it used to be. Still, don't go
here expecting to get a good value for anything. Flamenco is
better in Sevilla.

Sights—Near Granada

Carthusian Monastery (La Cartuja)—A church with an interior that looks as if it squirted out of a can of whipped cream, La Cartuja is nicknamed the "Christian Alhambra" for its elaborate white Baroque stucco work. In the rooms just off the cloister, notice the gruesome paintings of martyrs placidly meeting their grisly fate. It's located 1.5 kilometers north of town on the way to Madrid. Drive north on Gran Vía de Colón and follow the signs or take bus #8 from Gran Vía de Colón (entry: €2.10, April–Sept Mon–Sat 10:00–13:00, 16:00–20:00, Sun 10:00–12:00, 16:00–20:00, Oct–March Mon–Sat 10:00–13:00, 15:30–18:00, Sun 10:00–12:00, 15:30–18:00, tel. 95-816-1932).

Sleeping in Granada
(€1.10 = about $1, country code: 34)

Sleep Code: **S** = Single, **D** = Double/Twin, **T** = Triple, **Q** = Quad, **b** = bathroom, **s** = shower only, **CC** = Credit Cards accepted, **no CC** = Credit Cards not accepted, **SE** = Speaks English, **NSE** = No English. Breakfast and the 7 percent IVA tax are usually not included.

In July and August, when the streets are littered with sunstroke victims, rooms are plentiful. Crowded months are April, May, June, September, and October. Except for the Alhambra and near-train-station listings, all recommended hotels are within a five-minute walk of Plaza Nueva. While almost none of the hotels have their own parking facilities, all can direct you to a garage (such as Parking San Agustin, just off Gran Vía de Colón, €12/24 hrs.)

Hotels on or near Plaza Nueva
(zip code: 18009 unless otherwise noted)

Each of these is big, professional, plenty comfortable, and perfectly located. Prices vary with the demand.

Hotel Residencia Macia, right on the colorful Plaza Nueva, is a hotelesque place with 44 clean, modern, and classy rooms. Choose between an on-the-square view or a quieter interior room (Sb-€42–50, Db-€63, Tb-€84, show this book upon arrival to get a 10 percent discount, good buffet breakfast-€5, tax extra, CC, elevator, air con, Plaza Nueva 4, tel. 95-822-7536, fax 95-822-7533, e-mail: maciaplaza@maciahoteles.com, SE).

Hotel Anacapri is a bright, cool, marble oasis with 49 modern rooms and a quiet lounge (Sb-€54–60, Db-€72–84, extra bed-€18, CC, elevator, air con, 2 blocks toward Gran Vía from Plaza Nueva at Calle Joaquin Costa 7, just a block from cathedral bus stop, tel. 95-822-7477, fax 95-822-8909, www.hotelanacapri.com, e-mail: reservas@hotelanacapri.com, helpful Kathy speaks Iowan).

Hotel Inglaterra, a chain hotel, is modern and peaceful, with 36 rooms offering all the comforts (Sb-€84–88, Db-€84–101, breakfast-€7.75, tax extra, CC, elevator to 3rd floor only, air con, Cettie Meriem 4, 18010 Granada, tel. 95-822-1559, fax 95-822-7100, e-mail: nhinglaterra@nh-hoteles.es).

Hotel Gran Vía, right on Granada's main drag, has a stately lobby with Euro-modern business-class rooms (Sb-€42–48, Db-€66–75, Tb-€88–101, show this book for a 10 percent discount, CC, elevator, air con, 5-min walk from Plaza Nueva, Gran Vía de Colón 25, tel. 95-828-5464, fax 95-828-5591, e-mail: granvia @maciahoteles.com, SE).

Cheaper Places on Cuesta de Gomerez
(zip code: 18009)

These are cheap and ramshackle lodgings on the street leading from Plaza Nueva up to the Alhambra.

Hostal Landazuri is run by friendly, English-speaking Matilda Landazuri and her son, Manolo. While most of its 18 rooms are well worn, a few are newly renovated, and all are lovingly decorated and homey. It has a great roof garden with an Alhambra view and a hardworking, helpful management (Sb-€27, D-€22.75, Db-€33, Tb-€45, simple €1.80 breakfast or their hearty €2.30 eggs-and-bacon breakfast, includes tax, no CC, Cuesta de Gomerez 24, tel. & fax 95-822-1406). The Landazuris also run a good, cheap café.

Hostal Residencia Britz is a simple, no-nonsense place overlooking Plaza Nueva. All of its 24 basic rooms—with single-paned windows—are streetside. Bring earplugs (S-€15, D-€25.75, Db-€36, includes tax, no breakfast, CC, coin-op washing machine, elevator, Plaza Nueva y Gomerez 1, tel. & fax 95-822-3652).

Hostal Navarro Ramos has 15 rooms that are comfortable enough (S-€10.25, D-€16.25, Db-€27, Tb-€36, no breakfast, no CC, Cuesta de Gomerez 21, 1st floor, tel. 95-825-0555, NSE).

Hostal Viena, run by English-speaking Austrian Irene ("ee-RAY-nay"), is on a quieter side street with basic backpacker-type rooms (S-€24, D-€33, Db-€39, Tb-€51, family rooms, includes tax, no breakfast, CC, air con, Hospital de Santa Ana 2, 10 meters off Cuesta de Gomerez, tel. & fax 95-822-1859, e-mail: viena@arrakis.es). Irene also manages the similar **Hotel Austria** nearby.

Hostal Gomerez is run by English-speaking Sigfrido Sanchez de León de Torres (who will explain to you how Spanish surnames work if you've got the time). Clean and basic and listed in nearly every country's student-travel guidebook, this is another fine cheapie. Sigfrido is adding double-paned windows to the rooms. Quieter rooms are in the back (S-€13.75, D-€19.25, T-€25.25, Q-€30, includes tax, no breakfast, no CC, laundry service-€6, Cuesta de Gomerez 10, 1 floor up, tel. 95-822-4437).

Sleeping near Plaza Carmen
Two blocks from the TI is the pleasant Plaza Carmen and the beginning of Calle Navas, a pedestrian street offering a couple of good values.

Hotel Residencia Lisboa, which overlooks Plaza Carmen opposite Granada's city hall, offers 28 simple but well-maintained rooms with friendly owners (S-€16.75, Sb-€25.75, D-€25.75, Db-€36, T-€34, Tb-€48, includes tax, no breakfast, CC, elevator, no public rooms, Plaza de Carmen 27, tel. 95-822-1413, fax 95-822-1487).

Hotel Navas, a block down Calle Navas, is a modern, well-run, tour-friendly, and business-class hotel with 49 spacious rooms (Sb-€54, Db-€78, Tb-€105, breakfast buffet-€5.50, tax extra, CC, air con, attached restaurant, Calle Navas 24, tel. 95-822-5959, fax 95-822-7523, e-mail: alixares@jet.es, SE).

Hotel Dauro II has 53 fine but darkly-decorated rooms, with double-paned windows that at least minimize the noise of the pedestrian street below (Sb-€66, Db-€90, tax extra, breakfast-€5.50, CC, air con, Acera del Darro 19, tel. 95-822-1581, fax 95-822-2732, www.hoteles-dauro.com).

Sleeping near the Cathedral
Hotel Los Tilos offers 30 comfortable rooms, some with balconies, on the charming, traffic-free Bib-Rambla square behind the cathedral. All clients are welcome to use the fourth-floor view terrace overlooking a great café, shopping, and people-watching neighborhood (Sb-€35, Db-€50, Tb-€69, tax extra, 20 percent discount with this book and cash, breakfast buffet-€4.80, CC, air con, elevator, Plaza Bib-Rambla 4, tel. 95-826-6712, fax 95-826-6801, friendly Jose-Maria SE).

Reina Cristina has 43 quiet, elegant rooms a few steps off a park-like square, near the lively Pescaderia and Bib-Rambla squares (Sb-€60–81, Db-€81-138, tax extra, CC, tel. 95-825-3211, fax 95-825-5728, www.hotelreinacristina.com).

Sleeping near the Train Station
Hotel Condor, with 104 modern rooms in a high-rise, has more four-star comfort than character. It's an eight-minute walk from the station, and 15 minutes—or a bus ride—to the center of town (Sb-€59–72, Db-€79–110, breakfast-€7.20, CC, laundry service, non-smoking floor, attached restaurant, Avenida de la Constitución 6, tel. 95-828-3711, fax 95-828-3850, e-mail: condor@maciahoteles.com).

Sleeping in or near the Alhambra
(zip code: 18009)
If you want to stay on or bordering the Alhambra grounds, three popular options are a kilometer up the hill from Plaza Nueva.

The first two—famous, overpriced, and often booked up—are actually within the Alhambra grounds.

Parador Nacional San Francisco, offering 36 air-conditioned rooms in a converted 15th-century convent, is called Spain's premier parador (Sb-€148–165, Db-€183–204, breakfast-€10.75, free parking, CC, Real de la Alhambra, tel. 95-822-1440, fax 95-822-2264, e-mail: granada@parador.es, SE). You must book ahead several months to spend the night in this lavishly located, stodgy, classy, and historic place. Any peasant, however, can drop in for a coffee, drink, snack, or meal (daily 8:00–11:00, 13:00–16:00, 20:30–23:00).

Next to the parador, the elegant and cozy **Hotel America** rents 15 rooms (Sb-€66, Db-€102, breakfast-€6, includes tax, CC, closed Nov–Feb, tel. 95-822-7471, fax 95-822-7470, e-mail: hamerica@moebius.es, SE). Book months in advance.

The ramshackle old **Hotel Washington Irving** is pleasant, spacious, and charmingly rundown. Not quite as romantically located, it offers the best reasonable beds in this prestigious neighborhood (Sb-€60, Db-€96, Tb-€114, Qb-€132, buffet breakfast-€8, CC, elevator, Paseo del Generalife 2, tel. 95-822-7550, fax 95-822-7559, e-mail: hwirving@arrakis.es, SE).

Eating in Granada

Traditionally, Granada bars serve a small tapa plate free with any beer or wine ordered. Two well-chosen beers can actually end up being a light meal. In search of an edible memory? A local specialty, *tortilla Sacromonte*, is a spicy omelet with pig's brain and other organs.

These places are peppered with lively eateries and tapas bars: Albayzín, Calle Elvira (near Plaza Nueva), Calle Navas (off Plaza Carmen), and Bib-Rambla and Pescaderia (a block apart from each other, just west of the cathedral).

In the Albayzín: The most interesting meals hide out deep in the Albayzín quarter. Two good squares are near the San Nicolás viewpoint. Plaza San Miguel el Bajo has some charming restaurants and kids playing soccer (look for the view over the modern city a block away). Plaza Larga, within two blocks of the first three listings below, also has good eateries (to find the square, ask any local, take bus #31 or #32 from Plaza Nueva, or follow directions and map above, in "Sights—Albayzín").

For fish, consider **El Ladrillo**, with outdoor tables on a peaceful square (Plaza Fatima, just off Calle Pages), or **El Ladrillo II**, with indoor dining only and a more extensive menu (Calle Panaderos 35, off Plaza Larga, tel. 95-829-2651). They each serve a popular *barca* (€7.25 "boatload" of mixed fried fish), a fishy feast that stuffs two to the gills. The smaller *medio-barca*, for €4.80, fills one adequately. (A *medio-barca* and a salad feed 2.) Each restaurant is open daily (13:00–16:00, 20:00–24:00). For fewer tourists, more locals and village atmosphere, and great inexpensive food, eat at **Casa Torcuato** (Mon–Sat 13:00–16:00, 20:00–24:00, closed Sun, 2 blocks beyond Plaza Larga on Placeta de Carniceros, Calle Carniceros 4, tel. 95-820-2039).

For a more romantic, candlelit setting with Alhambra views, splurge at **El Agua Casa de Vinos** (€15 3-course meals—most with cheese fondue, Tue 20:00–23:00, Wed–Mon 13:30–16:00, 20:00–23:00, CC, Placeta Aljibe de Trillo 7, halfway up Albayzín hill, below San Nicolás viewpoint, reservations necessary, tel. 95-822-4356).

Mirador de Morayma, with a similarly intimate, garden-view-mansion ambience, also requires reservations (€24 meals, Mon–Sat 13:30–15:30, 20:30–23:00, closed Sun, CC, Calle Pianista Garcia Carrillo 2, tel. 95-822-8290).

Hippie Options on Calle Calderería Nueva: From Plaza Nueva walk two long blocks down Calle Elvira and turn right onto the wonderfully hip and Arabic-feeling Calderería Nueva, which leads uphill into the Albayzín. The street is lined with trendy *teterías*. These small tea shops, open all day, are good places to linger, chat, and imagine an America where marijuana was legal. Some are conservative and unmemorable, and others are achingly romantic, filled with incense, beaded cushions, live African music, and effervescent young hippies. They sell light meals and a worldwide range of teas. The plush **Kasbah** has good (canned) music.

Naturi Albayzín is a vegetarian place with €7.75 three-course meals featuring classy couscous (daily 13:00–16:00, 19:00–23:00, Calle Calderería Nueva 10, tel. 95-822-0627). Wafting up to the end of the teahouse street you'll find **Bar Restaurant Las Cuevas**—its rickety tables spilling onto the street—serving salads, pizzas, tapas, and wine to a fun family/bohemian crowd.

A half-block off Plaza Nueva, the cheap and easy **Bodega Castaneda** serves fine *ensaladas* and baked potatoes with a fun variety of toppings (on Calle Elvira, just 20 meters off Plaza Nueva, not the other bodega a block away with the same name—which doesn't serve baked potatoes). For people-watching ambience, consider the many restaurants on Plaza Nueva, Bib-Rambla, or Paseo de los Tristes.

Markets: The Mercado San Augustin, while heavy on meat, also sells fruits and veggies. If nothing else, it's as refreshingly cool as a meat locker (Mon–Sat 8:00–15:00, has small café/bar, Calle Cristo San Augustin, a block north of cathdral, half-block off Gran Vía de Colón). Pescadaria, a block from Bib-Rambla, usually has some fruit stalls on its northern end, along with inviting restaurants in the square itself.

Transportation Connections—Granada

By train to: Barcelona (3/day, 12 hrs, handy night train), **Madrid** (3/day, 6–9 hrs, 1 night-train; or go via Córdoba and catch the AVE train), **Toledo** (3/day, 1/night, 9 hrs, transfer in Aranjuez), **Algeciras** (3/day, 4 hrs; also 6 buses/day, 3.5–5 hrs), **Ronda** (4/day, 3 hrs), **Sevilla** (4/day, 3 hrs, transfer in Bobadilla; also 10 buses/day, 3 hrs), **Córdoba** (1/day, 4 hrs, transfer in Bobadilla; also 6 buses/day, 3 hrs), **Málaga** (2/day, 3.5 hrs, transfer in Bobadilla; also 16 buses/day, 2 hrs). Train info: tel. 90-224-0202.

By bus to: Nerja (3/day, 2 hrs, more frequent with transfer in Motril), **Sevilla** (10/day, 3 hrs; plus trains, above), **Córdoba** (6 buses/day, 3 hrs; plus trains, above), **Málaga** (16/day, 2 hrs; plus trains, above), **Algeciras** (6/day, 3.5-5 hrs, some are *directo*, some are *ruta*), **Linea/Gibraltar** (2/day, 5 hrs). Bus info: tel. 95-818-5480.

SEVILLA

This is the flamboyant city of Carmen and Don Juan, where bull-fighting is still politically correct and where little girls still dream of growing up to become flamenco dancers. While Granada has the great Alhambra, and Córdoba the remarkable Mezquita, Sevilla has a soul. It's a great-to-be-alive-in kind of place.

Sevilla, the gateway to the New World in the 16th century, boomed when Spain did. Explorers such as Amerigo Vespucci and Ferdinand Magellan sailed from its great river harbor. In the 17th century, local artists such as Velázquez, Murillo, and Zurbarán made it a cultural center. Sevilla's Golden Age, with its New World riches, ended when the harbor silted up and the Spanish empire crumbled.

In the 19th century, Sevilla was a big stop on the Romantic grand tour of Europe. To build on this tourism, Sevilla planned the World Exposition of 1929. Bad year. The Expo crashed with the stock market. In 1992 Sevilla got a second chance at a World's Fair. This Expo was a success, leaving the city with an impressive infrastructure: new airport, train station, seven bridges, and the super AVE bullet train to Madrid.

Today Spain's fourth-largest city (pop. 700,000) is Anda-lucía's leading city, buzzing with festivals, life, color, and casta-nets. James Michener wrote, "Sevilla doesn't *have* ambience, it *is* ambience." Sevilla has its share of impressive sights, but the real magic is the city itself, with its tangled Jewish Quarter, riveting flamenco shows, thriving bars, and teeming evening paseo.

Planning Your Time

If ever there was a big Spanish city to linger in, it's Sevilla. With three weeks in Iberia, spend two nights and a day in Sevilla. On a shorter trip, at least zip down here via the slick AVE train for a daytrip from Madrid.

The sights—the cathedral and the Alcázar (about 3 hrs) and a wander through the Santa Cruz district (1 hr)—are few and simple for a city of this size. You could spend half a day touring its other sights (described below). Stroll along the bank of the Guadalquivir River and cross the Bridge of Triana for a view of Torre del Oro and the cathedral. An evening is essential for the paseo and a flamenco show. Bullfights are on most Sundays, April through October. Sevilla's Alcázar is closed on Monday.

Córdoba (described at the end of this chapter) is worth a stopover if you're taking the AVE.

Orientation

For the tourist, this big city is small. Sevilla's major sights, including the lively Santa Cruz district and the Alcázar, surround the cathedral. The central boulevard, Avenida de la Constitución (with TI, banks, and a post office), zips right past the cathedral to Plaza Nueva (the shopping district). Nearly everything is within easy walking distance. Taxis are reasonable (€2.40 minimum), friendly, and easy. The horse-and-buggy rides are popular (around €30 for a 60-min clip-clop).

Tourist Information

Handy TIs are in the center and at the train station. The central TI is a block toward the river from the cathedral (Mon–Fri 9:00–19:00, Sat 10:00–14:00, 15:00–19:00, Sun and festivals 10:00–14:00, Avenida de la Constitución 21, tel. 95-422-1404). The train station TI (Mon–Fri 9:00–20:00, Sat–Sun 10:00–14:00, tel. 95-453-7626) offers the same services. Ask for the city map (far better than the one in the promo city magazine); the English-language magazines *Welcome Olé* and *The Tourist;* a current listing of sights, hours, and prices; and a schedule of bullfights. The free monthly events guide, *El Giraldillo,* in nearly readable Spanish, covers cultural events in all of Andalucía with a focus on Sevilla. If heading south, ask for the "Route of the White Towns" brochure and a Jerez map (€0.60 each). If arriving by bus or train, you'll find helpful TIs in or near your station (see "Arrival," below).

Arrival in Sevilla

By Train: Trains arrive at the sublime Santa Justa station (banks, ATMs, TI, luggage storage). The town center, marked by the ornate Giralda Cathedral bell tower (visible from the front of the station), is a 30-minute walk, €3 taxi ride, or short bus ride away (take bus #70 to the cathedral; pay the driver €0.80 as you board).

By Bus: Sevilla's two major bus stations have information offices, cafés, and luggage storage. The Prado de San Sebastian

station covers Andalucía, Barcelona, and points east. To get downtown from the station, turn right on the major street Carlos V,
then right again on Avenida de la Constitución (10-min walk).

The Plaza de Armas station (near the river, opposite EXPO
'92 site) serves southwest Spain, Madrid, Salamanca, and Portugal.
To get downtown from this station, head toward the angled brick
apartment building and cross the busy Boulevard Expiración. Go
a half-block up Calle Arjona to the stop for bus #C4, which goes
into town (€0.80, pay driver; get off at Puerta de Jerez, near main
TI), or, even better, continue walking a couple more blocks to the
helpful, uncrowded TI at Calle Arjona #28 (near Isabel II Bridge,
daily 8:00–20:45, tel. 95-450-5600). From here you can catch bus
#C4 or walk 15 minutes into the center (following map from TI).

By Car: Driving in Sevilla is difficult and many cars are broken into. I'd pay to park in a garage. To enter Sevilla, follow signs
to Centro Ciudad (city center) and drive along the river. If you
need a brief place to park (to get set up), find a place near the
cathedral and tower (leave your partner in the car). Paseo de
Cristobal Colón has free street parking but is particularly theft-
prone in the summer.

Helpful Hints
Sevilla Festivals: Sevilla's peak season is April and May. And it
has two festival periods when the city is packed. All over Spain,
Holy Week (Semana Santa—the week between Palm Sunday and
Easter Sunday) is big, but it's biggest in Sevilla. The most crowded
days are Thursday and Friday; to minimize crowds, visit earlier in
the week. Then, after taking enough time off to catch its communal breath, the city holds its **April Fair.** This is a celebration of
all that's Andalusian, with plenty of eating, drinking, singing,
and having fun. Book rooms well in advance for festival times.
Warning: Prices can go sky-high.

Telephone: A telephone office, Locutorio Público, has
metered phone booths. Calls are slightly more expensive than calls
made with Spanish phone cards, but you get a quiet setting with
a seat (Mon–Fri 10:00–14:00, 17:00–21:00, Sat 10:00–14:00, in
the passage at Sierpes 11, near intersection with Calle de Rafael
Padura, tel. 95-422-6800).

Post Office: The post office is on Avenida de la Constitución
32, across from the cathedral (Mon–Fri 8:30–20:30, Sat 9:30–14:00).

Train Tickets: The downtown RENFE office gives out train
schedules and sells train tickets (Mon–Fri 9:00–13:15, 16:00–
19:00, CC, Calle Zaragoza 29, tel. 95-421-7998, you can't work
here if you speak English). Many travel agencies sell train tickets
for the same price as the train station (look for train sticker in
agency window). USIT Student Travel is at Mateos Gago 2, just
off the cathedral square.

Internet Access: Cibercenter is central (Mon–Sat 9:00–22:00, closed Sun, just off Reyes Católicos at Julio Cesar 8, tel. 95-422-8899).

Laundromat: Lavanderia Roma offers quick and economical drop-off service (Mon–Sat 9:30–13:30, 17:00–20:30, Sun 9:00–14:00, Castela 2, tel. 95-421-0535).

Tours of Sevilla

Guided City Walks—Concepción Delgado, an enthusiastic teacher and a joy to listen to, takes small groups on English-language-only walks. Concepción has designed a fine two-hour introduction to the city sharing important insights the average visitor misses. This is two hours well-spent, even on a one-day visit (€10, daily except Sun at 9:30 and 11:30, starting from Plaza Nueva, call to reserve a place, cellular 61-650-1100, tel. 90-215-8226, www.sevi-ruta.com, e-mail: sevi-ruta@sevi-ruta.com).

For other guides, contact the **Guides Association of Sevilla** (tel. 95-421-0037, e-mail: apitsevilla@alehop.com).

Hop-on Hop-off Bus Tours—Two competing city bus tours leave from the curb near the golden tower, Torre del Oro (on the river). You'll see the buses parked with a salesperson handing out fliers. Each does about an hour-long swing through the city with a tape-recorded narration (green route slightly better because it includes María Luisa Park). The tours are heavy on Expo '29 and Expo '92 neighborhoods of little interest in '02. While the narration does its best, Sevilla is most interesting where buses can't go (€9, departures daily 10:00–20:00).

Sights—Sevilla

▲▲**Cathedral and Giralda Tower**—This is the third-largest church in Europe (after the Vatican's St. Peter's and London's St. Paul's) and the largest Gothic church anywhere. When they ripped down a mosque on the site in 1401, the Reconquista Christians bragged, "We'll build a cathedral so huge that anyone who sees it will take us for madmen." They built for 120 years. Even today, the descendants of those madmen proudly display an enlarged photocopy of their *Guinness Book of Records* letter certifying, "The cathedral with the largest area is: Santa Maria de la Sede in Sevilla, 126 meters long, 82 meters wide, and 30 meters high" (€4.80, Mon–Sat 11:00–18:00, free on Sun 14:00–19:00, last entry 1 hr before closing). There's only one way in for tourists, on the south end. Here's a six-stop tour:

1. Giralda Tower exterior: Before going in, step across the street from the entry and look at the bell tower. Formerly a Moorish minaret from which Muslims were called to prayer, it became the cathedral's bell tower after the Reconquista. It's named for the 4,500-pound bronze statue symbolizing the Triumph of Faith that caps it and serves as a weathervane. In fact, the name of the tower comes from the Spanish word for turning (*girando*). In 1356 the original top of the tower fell. You're looking at a 16th-century Christian-built top with a ribbon of letters proclaiming, "This is stronger now, made in the name of God." Needing more strength than their bricks could provide for the lowest section of the tower, the Moors used Roman-cut stones. (At the end of your visit, when you leave the cathedral, look at the corner of the tower at ground level; you can actually read the Latin on one of the stones.)

Notice also the fine Moorish-style arch (it's actually 16th-century Christian—the banners are a give-away). Like so much other Moorish-looking art in town, it's done by Moorish artists under Christian rule. The relief above the door shows the Bible story of Jesus ridding the temple of the merchants...just a reminder to contemporary merchants that there will be no retail activity in the church. The plaque on the right is one of many scattered throughout town showing a place Cervantes—the great 16th-century Spanish writer—mentioned in his books. (In this case, the topic was pickpockets.) Crossing the chains that ring the church you have entered the protective sanctuary of this house of God (handy if you were a medieval criminal). The huge green doors are a bit of the surviving pre-1248 mosque—wood covered with bronze. As you go in, knock on wood.

2. Cloister: The cloister used to be the mosque's Court of the Naranjos (Oranges). Twelfth-century Muslims stopped at the fountain in the middle to wash their hands, face, and feet before praying. The lanes between the bricks were once irrigation streams—a reminder that the Moors introduced irrigation to Iberia. The mosque was made of bricks; the church was made of stone.

3. Giralda Tower climb: From inside the church you can enter and climb the bell tower. Notice the beautiful Moorish simplicity as you climb to its top, 100 meters up, for a grand city view. The spiraling ramp is designed to accommodate riders on horseback, so find the entrance (just inside the church on the left, same hours and ticket as cathedral) and gallop up the 34 ramps for a Pegasus'-eye view of Sevilla.

4. Sanctuary: Hike through the sanctuary. Then sit down in front of the main chapel (*capilla mayor*) in the center. The incredible main altarpiece (*retablo mayor*) has 4,000 pounds of gold (imported in Spain's post-1492 "free trade" era). Twenty meters tall, with 36 scenes from the life of Jesus, it's composed of 1,500 figures.

5. Tomb of Columbus: Opposite the entry you'll see four kings carrying the tomb of Christopher Columbus. His pallbearers are the kings of Castile, Aragon, Leon, and Navarra (identify them by their team shirts). Columbus even traveled a lot posthumously. He was buried in Santo Domingo, then Cuba, and—when Cuba gained independence from Spain, around 1900—he sailed home to Sevilla. Are the remains actually his? Sevilla likes to think so.

6. Treasury: The treasury (*tesoro*) is scattered in several rooms at the exit. Find the Corona de la Virgen de los Reyes, Spain's most valuable crown, with 11,000 precious stones and the world's largest pearl, made into the torso of an angel. Also on display: relics (thorns, chunks of the cross, splinters from the Last Supper table) and some of the lavish Corpus Christi festival parade regalia.

The cathedral is wonderfully floodlit at night. A good place to view it is from the rooftop bar of the huge Hotel Dona Maria across the square (open in the summer, just step in and ride the elevator).

▲**Alcázar**—Originally a 10th-century palace built for the governors of the local Moorish state, this still functions as a royal palace...the oldest still in use in Europe. What you see today is an extensive 14th-century remodel job, done by Moorish workmen (Mudejar) for the Christian King Pedro I. Pedro was nicknamed either "the Cruel" or "the Just," depending on which end of his sword you were on.

The Alcázar is a thought-provoking glimpse of a graceful Al-Andalus (Moorish) world that might have survived its Castilian conquerors—but didn't. But I have a tough time hanging any specific history on it. The throne room (#7, Salon de Embajadores) is most impressive. Sit here for a while and freeload off passing tours. The floor plan is intentionally confusing, part of the style designed to make experiencing the place more exciting and surprising.

With a grand collection of royal courts, halls, patios, and apartments, it's been a Spanish royal residence for 600 years (and maintains that function today). The upper floors are more European-style palatial. Seek out the Grand Hall, with its fine tapestries celebrating Emperor Charles V's 1535 victory in Tunis over the Turks. Trace your itinerary on the south-up tapestry map of Iberia and Northern Africa.

The garden is full of tropical flowers, wild cats, cool fountains, and hot tourists (€4.20, Tue–Sat 9:30–19:00, Sun 9:00–17:00, off-season Tue–Sat 9:30–17:00, Sun 10:30–13:00, closed Mon, tel. 95-450-2323). The €2.40 audio guide is tempting and tries hard. But sorry, there's no way to make this palace worth a flowery hour of hard-to-follow commentary.

Archivo de Indias, the archive of the documents of the discovery and conquest of the New World, could be fascinating, but little of importance is on display (old maps of Havana) and there's not a word of English (free, Mon–Fri 10:00–13:00, closed Sat–Sun, in Lonja Palace, across street from Alcázar).

▲▲**Barrio de Santa Cruz**—Only the tangled street plan survives from the days this was Sevilla's Jewish Quarter. The narrow streets—some with buildings so close they're called "kissing lanes"—were actually designed to maximize shade. Even today, locals claim the Barrio de Santa Cruz is three degrees cooler than the rest of the city. While its charm is trampled by tour groups in the mornings, this classy maze of lanes too narrow for cars, white-washed houses with wrought-iron latticework, and *azulejo* tile–covered patios is a great refuge from the summer heat and bustle of Sevilla. The TI map has a helpful Barrio de Santa Cruz inset, but it's best to just get lost.

Forget about eating any of the oranges. They're bitter and used only to export to Britain where they're made into that awful marmalade you can't avoid in England's B&Bs.

Hospital de la Caridad—Between the river and the cathedral is the charity hospital, founded by a nobleman in the 17th century. Peek into the fine courtyard. On the left, the chapel has some gruesome art (above both doors) illustrating that death is the great equalizer, and an altar sweet as only a Spaniard could enjoy. The Dutch tiles depicting scenes of the Old and New Testament are a reminder of the time when the Netherlands were under Spanish rule in the late 16th century (€2.40, Mon–Sat 9:00–13:30, 15:30–18:30, Sun 9:00–13:00, tel. 95-422-3232).

Torre del Oro/Naval Museum—Sevilla's historic riverside "golden tower" was the starting point and ending point for all shipping to the New World. It's named for the golden tiles that once covered it—not for all the New World booty that landed here. Since the 13th century it has been part of the city's fortifications, with a heavy chain draped across the river to protect the harbor. Today it houses a dreadful little naval museum, featuring dried fish, charts of knots, and a few highlights. Look for the mural showing the world-spanning journeys of Vasco da Gama and Juan Sebastian Elcano; the model of the Santa Maria (the first boat to have landed in America); and an interesting mural of Sevilla in 1740. Enjoy the view of the belltower of Santa Ana Church from the balconies of the second floor (€0.60, free Tue, Tue–Fri 10:00–14:00, Sat–Sun 11:00–14:00, closed Mon, tel. 95-422-2419).

Plaza Nueva/Calle Sierpes—While many tourists never get beyond the cathedral and Santa Cruz, it's important to wander west into the lively shopping center of town, which also happens to be the oldest part of town. Plaza Nueva—a 19th-century square facing the ornate city hall and serving as the starting point of half of Sevilla's city buses—features a statue of Ferdinand III, a local favorite because he freed Sevilla from the Moors in 1248. Wander down Calle Tetuan into Sevilla's pedestrian-zone shopping center—a delightful alternative to the suburban mall.

Take a right on Jovellanos street and notice the tiles. The Moors gave this region its characteristic glazed tiles…but without any figures. In later centuries, Christians decorated their tiles with social scenes. Either way, the tiles made sense because they kept buildings cooler in the summer heat.

Calle Sierpes has been a commercial center for 500 years. It's also the main street of the Holy Week processions when the street is packed and the balconies bulge with spectators.

Find Sagasta street and notice it has two names—the modern version and a medieval one: "Antiqua Calle de Gallegos" ("Ancient Street of the Galicia"). With the Christian victory in 1248, the Muslims were given one month to evacuate. To consolidate Christian control here, settlers from the north were planted. This street was home to the Galicians.

Continue down Sagasta street to Plaza del Salvador and Sevilla's #2 church. This is the high ground where Phoenicians established the town. The Romans built their Forum here. Today it's lined with shops (wedding dresses fill the lane behind the church).

University—Today's university was yesterday's *fabrica de tabacos* (tobacco factory), which employed 10,000 young female *cigareras*—including Bizet's Carmen. In the 18th century, it was the second-largest building in Spain, after El Escorial. Wander through its halls as you walk to the Plaza de España. The university's bustling café is a good place for cheap tapas, beer, wine, and conversation (Mon–Fri 8:00–21:00, Sat 9:00–13:00, closed Sun).

▲**Plaza de España**—The square, the surrounding buildings, and the nearby María Luisa Park are the remains of the 1929 fair that crashed with the U.S. stock market. This delightful area, the epitome of World's Fair–style building, is great for people-watching (especially at early-evening paseo time). Stroll through the park and along the canal. The highlight is what was the Spanish Pavilion. Its *azulejo* tiles (a trademark of Sevilla) show historic scenes and maps from every province of Spain (arranged in alphabetical order from Alava to Zaragoza). Climb to one of the balconies for a fine view.

▲**Museo de Bellas Artes**—Spain's second-best collection of paintings (after Madrid's Prado) has 50 Murillos and works by Zurbarán, El Greco, and Velázquez. Rather than exhausting, the museum—which fills a former convent—is pleasantly enjoyable (€1.50, Tue 15:00–20:00, Wed–Sat 9:00–20:00, Sun 9:00–14:00, closed Mon, Plaza Museo 9, tel. 95-422-0790).

▲▲**Basilica Macarena**—Sevilla's Holy Week celebrations are Spain's grandest. During the week leading up to Easter, the city's packed with pilgrims witnessing 50 processions carrying about 100 religious floats. Get a feel for this event by visiting Basilica Macarena (built in 1947) to see the two most impressive floats and the darling of Semana Santa, the Weeping Virgin (Virgen de la Macarena or La Esperanza, church free, museum-€2.40, daily 9:30–13:00, 17:00–20:00, taxi to Puerta Macarena or bus #C4 from Puerta Jerez).

Grab a pew and study Mary, complete with crystal teardrops. She's like a 17th-century doll—with human hair and articulated arms, and even dressed with underclothes. Her beautiful expression—halfway between smiling and crying—is moving, in a Baroque way. Her weeping can be contagious—look around you. La Macarena is considered the protector of bullfighters (she's big in bullring chapels). In 1912 the bullfighter José Ortega—hoping for protection—gave her the five emerald brooches she wears. It worked for eight years...until he was gored to death in the ring. Filling a side chapel (on left) is "Christ of the Sentence" showing Jesus the day he was condemned (from 1654).

To see the floats that Mary and Jesus ride every Good Friday, head for the museum (through door, left of altar).

The three-ton float, slathered in gold leaf, shows a commotion of figures acting out the sentencing of Christ (who's placed in the front of this crowd). Pontius Pilate is about to wash his hands. Pilate's mother cries as a man reads the death sentence. Relays of 50 men carry this—only their feet showing under the drapes—as they shuffle through the streets from midnight to 14:00 each Good Friday. Shuffle upstairs for another perspective.

The weeping Mary—called La Esperanza—follows the Sentencing of Christ in the procession. Her smaller (1.5-ton) float, in the next room, seems all silver and candles—"strong enough to support the roof but slender enough to quiver in the soft night breeze." Mary has a wardrobe of three huge mantels (each displayed here) worn in successive years. The big green one is from 1900. Her six-pound gold crown/halo is from 1913. This float has a mesmerizing effect on the local crowds. They line up for hours, clapping, weeping, and throwing roses as it slowly works its way through Sevilla.

Before leaving, find the case of matador outfits (also upstairs) given to the church over the years by bullfighters in thanks for the protection they feel they received from La Macarena.

Outside, notice the best surviving bit of Sevilla's old walls. Originally Roman, what remains today is 12th-century Moorish, a reminder that for centuries, Sevilla was the capital of the Moorish kingdom in Iberia.

▲Bullfights—Spain's most artistic and traditional bullfighting is done in Sevilla's Plaza de Toros, with fights on most Sundays, Easter through October. Serious fights with adult matadors—called *corrida de toros*—are in April and October. Summer fights are usually *novillada*, with teenage novices doing the killing. (*Corrida de toros* seats range from €18–78; *novillada* seats are half that; get information at TI, your hotel, or tel. 95-422-8229.)

▲▲Bullfight Museum—Follow a two-language, 20-minute guided tour through the Plaza de Toros' strangely quiet and empty arena, its museum, and the chapel where the matador prays before the fight (€3, daily 9:30–14:00, 15:00–19:00; or 9:30–15:00 on fight days though the chapel and horseroom are closed). See the appendix for more on the dubious "art" of bullfighting.

Across Paseo de Cristobal Colón from the bullring, note the statue of **Carmen.** This beautiful girl from the cigar factory was the inspiration for Bizet's famous opera.

Nightlife

▲▲**Evening Paseo**—Sevilla is meant for strolling. The areas along either side of the river between the San Telmo and Isabel II bridges (Paseo de Cristobal Colón and Triana district; see "Eating," below), around Plaza Nueva, at Plaza de España, and throughout Barrio de Santa Cruz thrive every non-winter evening. Spend some time rafting through this sea of humanity. Savor the view of floodlit Sevilla by night from the far side of the river—perhaps over dinner.

▲▲▲**Flamenco**—This music-and-dance art form has its roots in the Gypsy and Moorish cultures. Even at a packaged "Flamenco Evening," sparks fly. The men do most of the flamboyant machine-gun footwork. The women concentrate on graceful turns and a smooth, shuffling step. Watch the musicians. Flamenco guitarists, with their lightning finger-roll strums, are among the best in the world. The intricate rhythms are set by castanets or the hand-clapping (called *palmas*) of those who aren't dancing at the moment. In the raspy-voiced wails of the singers you'll hear echoes of the Muslim call to prayer.

Like jazz, flamenco thrives on improvisation. Also like jazz, good flamenco is more than just technical proficiency. A singer or dancer with "soul" is said to have *duende*. Flamenco is a happening, with bystanders clapping along and egging on the dancers with whoops and shouts. Get into it.

For a tourist-oriented flamenco show, your hotel can get you nightclub show tickets. **Los Gallos** gives nightly two-hour shows at 21:00 and 23:30 (€18 ticket plus a €3 drink, manager Nuria promises goose bumps and a 10 percent discount to those who book directly with Los Gallos and show this book—maximum 2 per book, arrive 30 min early for better seats without obstructed views, Plaza de Santa Cruz 11, tel. 95-421-6981, reservations by fax: 95-421-3436). **El Arenal** also does a good show (€26, shows at 21:30 and 23:30, near bullring at Calle Rodo 7, tel. 95-421-6492). **El Patio Sevillano** is more of a variety show (€25.50, shows at 19:30 and 22:00, next to bullring at Paseo de Cristobal Colón, tel. 95-421-4120). These prepackaged shows can be a bit sterile, and an audience of tourists doesn't help. But I find both Los Gallos and El Arenal professional and riveting. El Arenal may have a slight edge on talent, but Los Gallos has a more intimate setting, with cushy rather than hard chairs—and it's cheaper.

The best flamenco erupts spontaneously in bars throughout

Restaurants and Flamenco in Sevilla

❶ TO PLAZUELA SANTA ANA:
    BAR SANTA ANA, TABERNA
    PLAZUELA & REST. BISTEC

❷ RIO GRANDE REST. &
    REST. LA PRIMERA

❸ TO REST. MARIA ANGELES

❹ BAR BALADO

❺ CERVECERIA GIRALDA

❻ BAR LA TERESAS

❼ REST. MESON DON RAIMUNDO

❽ HORNO SAN BUENAVENTURA

❾ BODEGA MORALES

❿ FRIED-FISH JOINT

⓫ BODEGAS DIAZ SALAZAR

⓬ MERCADO DEL ARENAL

⓭ LOS GALLOS

⓮ EL ARENAL

⓯ EL PATIO SEVILLANO

⓰ LO NUESTRO & REJONEO

⓱ LA CARBONERIA

⓲ CASA PARA LA MEMORIA
    DEL ALANDALUS

the old town after midnight. Just follow your ears as you wander down Calle Betis, leading off Plaza de Cuba across the bridge. The **Lo Nuestro** and **Rejoneo** bars are local favorites for impromptu flamenco (at Calle Betis 30 and 32).

In the Barrio Santa Cruz, a mix of students and tourists gathers in **La Carboneria** to hear free flamenco—usually Thursdays after 23:00 (Levies 10, unsigned door, music only, no dancing).

For an alcohol-free atmosphere and authentic shows featuring flamenco, Sephardic, or other Andalusian music, consider **Casa para la Memoria de Alandalus**—House for the Memory of Alandalus, the Moorish name for Andalucía (€9–10.80, shows

vary, usually start at 21:30, Ximenez Enciso 28, also in Barrio
Santa Cruz, tel. 95-456-0670).

Shopping

The popular pedestrian streets Sierpes, Tetuan, and Velázquez,
as well as the surrounding lanes near Plaza Nueva, are packed with
people and shops. Nearby is Sevilla's top department store, El
Corte Inglés. While small shops close between 13:30 and 16:00
or 17:00, big ones like El Corte Inglés stay open (and air-conditioned) right through the siesta. It has a supermarket downstairs
and a good but expensive restaurant (Mon–Sat 10:00–21:30, closed
Sun). **Flea markets** hop on Sunday (stamps and coins at Cabildo
Square near cathedral; antiques and furniture at Alameda de Hércules; animals at Alfalfa Square) and Thursday (books at Alameda
de Hércules).

Sleeping in Sevilla
(€1.10 = about $1, country code: 34, zip code: 41004)

Sleep Code: **S** = Single, **D** = Double/Twin, **T** = Triple, **Q** = Quad,
b = bathroom, **s** = shower only, **CC** = Credit Cards accepted, **no
CC** = Credit Cards not accepted, **SE** = Speaks English, **NSE** =
No English.

All of my listings are centrally located and within a five-
minute walk of the cathedral. The first ones are near the charming
but touristy Santa Cruz neighborhood. The last group is just as
central but closer to the river, across the boulevard in a more
workaday, less touristy zone. See map on next page.

Room rates as much as double during the two Sevilla fiestas
(roughly the week before Easter and a week or so after Easter).
In general, the busiest and most expensive months are April, May,
September, and October. Hotels put rooms on the discounted
push list in July and August. Prices rarely include the 7 percent
IVA tax. A price range indicates low- to high-season prices (but
I have not listed festival prices). Hoteliers speak enough English.
Skip ground-floor rooms (because of noise) and ask for upper
floors (*piso alto*). Many of these hotels are reportedly unreliable
for reservations, particularly the small, family *pensiónes* (as opposed
to normal big hotels). Always telephone to reconfirm what you
think is a reservation.

Sleeping near the Santa Cruz Neighborhood

Off Calle Santa Maria la Blanca: The **Hostal Córdoba** has
12 tidy, quiet, air-conditioned rooms, solid modern furniture,
and a showpiece plant-filled courtyard (S-€18–36, Sb-€24–39,
D-€39–51, Db-€45–60, includes tax, no CC, a tiny lane off Calle
Santa Maria la Blanca, Farnesio 12, tel. 95-422-7498).

Hostal Good Sleep is a homey, backpacker-type place filled

Sevilla Hotels

❶ HOSTAL CORDOBA & GOOD SLEEP
❷ HOTEL LAS CASAS DE LA JUDERIA
❸ HOTEL FERNANDO III
❹ HOSTAL SIERPES
❺ HOSTAL SANCHEZ SABARIEGO
❻ HOTEL ALCAZAR
❼ PENSION ALCAZAR & HOSTAL ARIAS
❽ HOSTAL PICASSO
❾ HOTEL RESIDENCIA DONA MARIA
❿ HOTEL SEISES
⓫ HOTEL LAS CASAS DE LOS MERCADORES
⓬ HOTEL INGLATERRA
⓭ HOTEL SIMON
⓮ HOTEL LA RABIDA

with cheery tiles, caged birds, family ambience, and 20 neon-lit and cheaply furnished rooms (S-€15, D-€24, Ds-€27, Db-€30, T-€36, Tb-€45, tax included, CC, laundry service €6/load, fans in rooms, birds wake at 8:00, welcoming rooftop terrace for picnicking and socializing, next to Hostal Córdoba at Farnesio 8, tel. 95-421-7492, friendly Rene and Myriam speak English).

Off Plaza Santa Maria: The **Hotel Las Casas de la Juderia** has quiet, elegant rooms and suites tastefully decorated with hardwood floors and a Spanish flair. The rooms surround a series of peaceful courtyards. This is a romantic splurge and a fine value (Sb-€66–78, Db-€96–117, Db suite-€111–132, Qb suite-€168–192, extra bed-€30; low-season prices—July, Aug, late-Nov–Feb—are discounted a further 10 percent to those with this book who ask; CC, great buffet breakfast-€9.75, parking-€12, air con, elevator, on small traffic-free lane off Plaza Santa Maria, Callejon de Dos Hermanas 7, tel. 95-441-5150, fax 95-442-2170, www.casasypalacios.com, e-mail: juderia@zoom.es, SE).

Hotel Fernando III, popular with groups, is cavernous with 155 comfortable, modern rooms (Sb-€95–131, Db-€119–149, Tb-€162–222, CC, mostly twin beds—all with plastic sheets, breakfast-€8.75, air con, rooftop pool, garage with parking-€11.40, elevator, San Jose 21, just off Plaza Santa Maria, tel. 95-421-7307, fax 95-422-0246, www.altur.com/fernandoiii, e-mail: fernando3@altur.com).

On Corral del Rey: Walking from the cathedral square straight up Argote de Molina (200 meters) you come to **Hostal Sierpes,** a sprawling, 40-room place with fine lounges and a big, cool, airy courtyard. Rooms are small and basic but air-conditioned, with shiny new bathrooms (Sb-€27–33, Db-€36–48, Tb-€45–63, Qb-€54–75, breakfast-€5.10, CC, parking-€9/day, some air con, noisy downstairs, quieter rooms upstairs, reconfirm reservations, Corral del Rey 22, tapas bar next door, tel. 95-422-4948, fax 95-421-2107, e-mail: hsierpes@infonegocio.com, run by the serious and hard-working Melquiades).

Across the street, **Hostal Sanchez Sabariego** is a homier, 10-room place with a folksy garden courtyard. The higher floors are most peaceful and air-conditioned (S-€21, Db-€36–48, no CC, laundry-€9/load, nearby parking-€12/day, Corral del Rey 23, tel. 95-421-4470, friendly Macu speaks English and does everything).

Near Old Bus Station: The **Hotel Alcázar,** on the big and busy Menendez y Pelayo boulevard, has 93 air-conditioned rooms, lavish public areas, and everything you'd find in a modern, big-city American hotel (Sb-€77–107, Db-€106–136, Tb-€124–154, includes breakfast, CC, elevator, Menendez y Pelayo 10, tel. 95-441-2011, fax 95-442-1659, SE). Ask for a quiet room off the street.

Sleeping near the Alcázar

The first three places are in a quiet eddy of lanes on the side of the Alcázar nearest the river.

Pensión Alcázar rents eight pleasant rooms. The lower rooms have ceiling fans, the three top rooms are air-conditioned with terraces (Db-€35–45, extra bed-€12, Qb-€60–72, no CC, Dean Miranda 12, tel. 95-422-8457, owners Micky and Liliane SE).

Around the corner, the less friendly **Hostal Arias** is cool, clean, and no-nonsense. Its 14 basic rooms are air-conditioned and come equipped with medieval disco-balls (Sb-€29–41, Db-€37–43, Tb-€50–57, Qb-€56–64, Quint/b-€65–74, CC, nearby parking-€13.50/day, Calle Mariana de Pineda 9, tel. 95-422-6840, fax 95-421-8389, www.hostalarias.com, e-mail: reina@arrakis.es, manager Manuel Reina SE, but rest of staff doesn't).

Hostal Picasso has 17 smallish rooms (D-€40, Db-€51, extra bed-€19.25, 10 percent off with this book, confirm your bill, CC, Calle San Gregorio 1, tel. & fax 95-421-0864, e-mail: hpicasso@arrakis.es, Rocio SE).

Hotel Residencia Doña María tries to be elegant but is just big and stuffy. Facing the cathedral on Plaza Vírgen de los Reyes, it brags that its 68 rooms are "very modern but furnished in an ancient style," with four-poster beds and armoires. The rooftop swimming pool has a view of Giralda Tower (Sb-€51–72, Db-€90–117, breakfast-€9.50, CC, parking-€12, elevator, Don Remondo 19, tel. 95-422-4990, fax 95-421-9546, www .hdmaria.com, e-mail: reservas@hdmaria.com).

Hotel Seises—a modern business-class place spliced into the tangled old town—offers a fresh and spacious reprieve for anyone ready for good old contemporary luxury. Ask to see the Roman ruins inside this elegant hotel. Its rooftop garden comes with a pool and a great cathedral view (Sb-€90–126, Db-€120–174, extra bed-€27, lower prices in July, Aug, and winter, CC, elevator, air con, 2 blocks northwest of the cathedral at Segovias 6, tel. 95-422-9495, fax 95-422-4334, www.hotellosseises.com, e-mail: seises@jet.es).

Hotel Las Casas de los Mercaderes feels like the Hotel Casas de la Juderia because it's run by the same people. Traditionally Andalusian in a modern way with all the comforts, it's beautifully located between the cathedral and the best shopping streets; though like any central hotel, it can be noisy at night (48 rooms, Sb-€63–89, Db-€90–111, extra bed-€19.25–22.25, breakfast-€9, parking-€12, CC, air con, elevator, Calle Alvarez Quintero 9, tel. 95-422-5858, fax 95-422-9884, www.casasypalcios.com, e-mail: mercaderes@zoom.es).

Hotel Inglaterra, a big four-star place on the no-nonsense Plaza Nueva, is big and modern, with 109 rooms and all the professional comforts (high season April–May, low season rest of year, Sb-€72–106, Db-€117–141, extra bed-€24–36, breakfast-€9, CC, air con, nonsmoking floor, elevator, attached restaurant and Irish pub, American Express office, Plaza Nueva 7, tel. 95-422-4970, fax 95-456-1336, www.hotelinglaterra.es, e-mail: hotelinglaterra@ svq.servicom.es).

Sleeping West of Avenida de la Constitución

Hotel Simón is a classic 18th-century mansion with a faded-elegant courtyard. Room quality varies; many of its 30 rooms are decorated with period furniture under high ceilings. On weekends, avoid rooms on the noisy street (Sb-€39–48, Db-€57–75, extra person-€18, high prices are only for April–May, continental breakfast-€3.60, CC, air con, a block west of the cathedral at Calle García de Vinuesa 19, tel. 95-422-6660, fax 95-456-2241, www.hotelsimonsevilla.com, e-mail: info@hotelsimonsevilla.com).

Hotel La Rabida has 100 business-class rooms surrounding a spacious lobby, a delightful garden courtyard, and a classy breakfast room. Prices will increase when the hotel reopens in April 2002 after remodeling (Sb-€45, Db-€65, Tb-€80, CC, air con, elevators, Castelar 24, tel. 95-422-0960, fax 95-422-4375, www .hotellarabida.com, e-mail: info@hotellarabida.com, SE). From the cathedral, go down Calle García de Vinuesa and turn right on Calle Castelar.

Eating in Sevilla

A popular Andalusian meal is fried fish, particularly marinated *adobo*. The soups, such as *salmorejo* (Córdoba-style super-thick gazpacho) and *ajo blanco* (almond-based), are light and refreshing. If you're hungry for dinner before the Spaniards are, do the tapa tango, using the "Tapa Tips" from this book's introduction. Wash down your tapas with *fino* (dry sherry) or, more refreshing, *tinto de Verano* (literally "summer" red), an Andalusian red wine with soda, like a light sangria. A good light white wine is *barbadillo*.

Eating in Triana across the River

South of the river between the San Telmo and Isabel II bridges is the colorful Triana District—filled with fine and fun eateries.

Tapas: The riverside street, Calle Betis (the Roman name for the Guadalquivir River), is classier than Calle Pureza, a block inland, and best for tapas bars. Before sitting down, walk to the Santa Ana church (midway between the bridges) to check out two great tapas bars. Each has tables spilling into the street and square in the shadow of the floodlit church spire. It feels like the whole neighborhood is out celebrating. **Taberna la Plazuela**, on the square, is bigger with more of a menu (daily, Plazuela de Santa Ana, tel. 95-427-0471) and **Bar Santa Ana** is draped in bullfighting memorabilia with a fun list of tapas (Pureza 82, tel. 95-427-2102). The Pena Sevillista de Triana (at Pureza 61) is Triana's soccer fans' clubhouse (satellite TV for all the best matches and bullfights—wild on weekend soccer nights).

Dinners: For a riverside restaurant dinner (with properly attired waiters and full menus as opposed to tapas), consider these three (each are neighbors on Calle Betis, next to the San Telmo bridge): **Río Grande** is the place for a candlelight-fancy meal (€24 dinners, daily 13:00–16:00, 20:00–24:00, tel. 95-427-8371). Its terrace is less expensive and more casual. Next door, **Restaurante La Primera del Puente** serves about the same thing with about the same view for half the price (Thu–Tue 11:30–17:00, 19:30–24:00, closed Wed and the last half of Aug, tel. 95-427-6918).

At the Isabel II bridge, in the yellow bridge tower, **Restaurante Maria Angeles** offers romantic dining atop the tower (daily 3-course menus from around €12) and cheaper, more casual tables filling the sidewalk along the riverside (fried fish *raciónes*, daily 13:00–17:00, 19:30–24:00, Puente de Isabel II, tel. 95-433-7498).

Bar Balado, a home-cooking kind of restaurant, has good gazpacho and filling *caldereta de cerdo*—pork stew (Wed–Mon 12:00–17:00, 20:00–24:00, closed Tue and Aug 20–Sept 5, dining room in back, Pureza 64, tel. 95-433-3010).

Restaurante Bistec specializes in pigeon, snails, and "tigers" (deep-fried, stuffed mussels) along with tamer fame (Thu–Tue 11:30–16:00, 20:00–1:00, closed Wed, Plazuela de Santa Ana, tel. 95-427-4759).

Eating in the Santa Cruz Area

Plenty of atmospheric-but-touristy restaurants fill the old quarter near the cathedral and along Calle Santa Maria la Blanca.

For tapas, the Barrio de Santa Cruz is trendy, touristic, and *romántico*. From the cathedral, walk up Mateos Gago where several classic old bars now keep tourists and locals well-fed and watered. **Cerveceria Giralda** (Mateos Gago 1), a standard meeting place for locals, is famous for its fine tapas (see the award it won at the Spanish tapas convention posted on the wall). Turn right off Mateos Gago at Meson del Moro, which leads to **La Teresas**, a fine and characteristic little bar draped in fun photos (including one of Ted Kennedy sandwiched between matadors and local intellectuals) and serving good tapas from a user-friendly menu (Santa Teresa 2, tel. 95-421-3069). Just past La Teresas is the artist Murillo's house (free when open and a good example of a local courtyard). The lane continues past a convent of cloistered nuns (notice the spiked window) to the most romantic little square in Santa Cruz (where you'll find the Las Gallos flamenco club).

Restaurante Meson Don Raimundo, proudly serving traditional Andalusian cuisine drenched in Andalusian ambience in a museum-like building, is a good choice for a full meal in a fancy indoor restaurant (€17 3-course menu, CC, daily 12:30–17:00, 19:30–24:00, air con, 2 blocks northwest of cathedral at Argote de Molina 26, tel. 95-422-3355).

Eating along Calle García de Vinuesa

This street (across from the cathedral) has several colorful and cheap tapas places. On the corner, the slick and chrome **Horno San Buenaventura** is handy for coffee and dessert (tapas are posted on the pillar). Farther down the street you'll find **Bodega Morales** (#11, closed Sun, tel. 95-422-1242). Go in the back section to munch tiny sandwiches (*montaditos*) and tapas and sip wine among huge kegs. Farther along is a **fried-fish joint** (*pescado frito*) that also sells homemade potato chips, and the lonely but potent **Bodegas Diaz Salazar.** More restaurants, tapas bars, and a recommended flamenco bar (**El Arenal** at Calle Rodo 7) are in the streets just beyond.

Picnickers forage at the covered fish-and-produce **Mercado del Arenal** (with a small café/bar for breakfast inside, Mon–Sat 9:00–13:00, closed Sun, on Calle Pastor y Landero at Calle Arenal, just beyond bullring).

Transportation Connections—Sevilla

To: Madrid (2.5 hrs by AVE express train, from 7:00–23:00 departures are on the hour—except 13:00, €9 reservation fee with railpass; 10 buses/day, €16.25), **Córdoba** (15 trains/day, 1.5 hrs; 50 min by speedy AVE; 10 buses/day, 2 hrs), **Málaga** (5 trains/day, 2.5 hrs; 11 buses/day, 3 hrs), **Ronda** (3 trains/day, 3 hrs, change at Bobadilla; 5 buses/day, 3 hrs), **Tarifa** (4 buses/day, 3 hrs), **La Línea/Gibraltar** (4 buses/day, 4 hrs), **Granada** (3 trains/day, 3 hrs; 8 buses/day, 4 hrs), **Arcos** (2 buses/day, 2 hrs), **Jerez** (hrly, 1.25 hrs), **Barcelona** (3 trains/day, 10–12 hrs), **Algeciras** (3 trains/day, 5 hrs, change at Bobadilla; 10 buses/day, 4 hrs), **Lisbon** (2 buses most days, 1 is direct, 10 hrs, €27; or AVE to Madrid and night train). Train info: tel. 90-224-0202. Bus info: tel. 95-490-8040.

For driving ideas south into Andalucía and west into Portugal's Algarve, see those chapters.

From Sevilla to Portugal's Algarve

Note that Portuguese time is one hour earlier than Spanish time.

To Lagos/Salema: You have three possibilities: the direct bus (best, but only offered in peak season); several buses (best choice for off-season weekdays); or a bus/ferry/train combination (best option for off-season weekends).

The direct bus between Lagos and Sevilla is a godsend (€15, 2/day, 5 hrs, daily May-Sept, sometimes starting in April and continuing into Oct, doesn't run in winter, tel. 95-490-8040 or 95-490-1160). The bus departs from Sevilla's Plaza de Armas bus station and arrives at the Lagos bus station. From Lagos take a 30-minute bus ride to Salema.

Off-season, it'll take you longer (8 to 10 hrs) to get from Sevilla to Lagos. The all-bus option is best on weekdays because bus frequency drops on weekends. On weekdays, you can catch a bus from Sevilla to Faro (2/day, allow 4 hrs with transfer in Huelva), then a bus from Faro to Lagos (7/day, 2 hrs), and a bus to Salema (nearly hrly, 30 min).

The bus/ferry/train combination takes the longest (about 10 hrs total). Get an early start: Sevilla–Ayamonte bus (4/day from Plaza de Armas station, fewer on weekends, 2.5 hrs; also see train option below) to Ayamonte at the border, ferry to Vila Real in Portugal (17/day, 26/day July-Sept, 15 min), train to Lagos (4/day, allow 4.5 hrs with transfer in Tunes or Faro). In Vila Real, you'll find ATMs near the dock (indoor ATM next to Hotel Guadiana, the big hotel kitty-corner from the dock; outdoor ATM to the left of hotel, up Rua do Dr. Teofilo Braga). The bus station is at the dock (Vila Real by bus to: Lagos—7/day, 4 hrs, transfer in Faro; to Tavira—8/day, 40 min; to Évora—3/day, 4-6 hrs, transfer in Faro; to Lisbon—5/day, 5.25 hrs; frequency drops on weekends; buy tickets at bus kiosk at dock). Vila Real's train station is a kilometer away from the ferry dock/bus station. To get to the train station from the dock, exit the dock straight on Rua Ayamonte, then take a right on Rua Eça de Queiroz.

Taking the train from Sevilla to the Algarve is slower and requires a transfer to a bus at Huelva (Sevilla–Huelva: 4 trains/day, 90 min; Huelva–Ayamonte: 10 buses/day, 1 hr, Huelva bus station tel. 95-925-6900). The Sevilla–Ayamonte bus (4/day, fewer on weekends, 2.5 hrs) is preferable, cheap, direct, and less hassle.

CÓRDOBA

Córdoba is one of Spain's three big Moorish cities. Even though it was the center of Moorish civilization in Spain for 300 years (and an important Roman city), Sevilla and Granada are far more interesting. Córdoba has a famous mosque surrounded by the colorful Jewish Quarter, and that's it.

The **Mezquita** (meh-SKEET-ah) was the largest Islamic mosque in its day. Today you can wander past its ramshackle "patio of oranges" and into the cavernous 1,200-year-old building. Grab the English pamphlet at the door (which predictably describes the church history much better than the mosque's). The interior is a moody world of 800 rose- and blue-marble columns and as many Moorish arches. If a guide told me I was in the basement of something important, I'd believe him. The center was gutted to make room for an also-huge Renaissance cathedral (€6, Mon–Sat 10:00–19:00, Sun 14:00–19:00, tel. 95-747-0512). The mosque is near the TI (Mon–Fri 9:30–20:00, Sat 10:00–20:00, Sun 10:00–14:00, closes early in winter, tel. 95-747-1235). The TI also has a handy kiosk at the train station (with a room-finding service).

From the station to the mosque it's a €2.40 taxi ride or a pleasant 30-minute walk (left on Avenida de America, right on Avenida del Gran Capitan, which becomes a pedestrian zone; when it ends ask someone "¿Dónde está la mezquita?" and you'll be directed downhill through the whitewashed old Jewish Quarter).

Sleeping and Eating in Córdoba: Two comfortable, air-conditioned, and expensive hotels are located within a five-minute walk of the station. **Hotel Gran Capitan** is closer (Db-€117, breakfast-€9, parking-€12.50, CC, 96 rooms, Avenida de America

5, tel. 95-747-0250, fax 95-747-4643, www.occidental-hoteles
.com, e-mail: pina@ch-es.com). **Hotel Sol los Gallos** is cheaper
and has a pool (Db-€86, breakfast-€7, CC, 115 rooms, Avenida
de Medina Azahara 7, tel. 95-723-5500, fax 95-723-1636, www
.solmelia.com, e-mail: sol.in.gallo@solmelia.es). For food, try
Taverna Salinas (Tendidores 3, near mosque, tel. 95-748-0135).

Transportation Connections—Córdoba

Now that Córdoba is on the slick AVE train line, it's an easy
stopover between **Madrid** and **Sevilla** (15 trains/day, about 1.5
hours from each city, reservations required on all AVE trains).

By bus to: Granada (9/day, 3 hrs), **Málaga** (5/day, 3 hrs),
Algeciras (4/day, 4.5–5 hrs; 2 direct, 2 with transfers in Bobadilla).
The bus station is at Medina Azahara 29 (tel. 95-723-6474).

ANDALUCÍA'S
WHITE HILL TOWNS

Just as the American image of Germany is Bavaria, the Yankee dream of Spain is Andalucía. This is the home of bullfights, flamenco, gazpacho, pristine-if-dusty whitewashed hill towns, and glamorous Mediterranean resorts. The big cities of Andalucía (Granada, Sevilla, and Córdoba) and the Costa del Sol are covered in separate chapters. This chapter explores its hill-town highlights.

The Route of the White Towns, Andalucía's charm bracelet of cute towns, gives you wonderfully untouched Spanish culture. Spend a night in the romantic queen of the white towns, Arcos de la Frontera. Towns with "de la Frontera" in their names were established on the front line of the centuries-long fight to recapture Spain from the Muslims, who were slowly pushed back into Africa. The hill towns, no longer strategic, no longer on any frontier, are now just passing time peacefully. Join them. Nearby, the city of Jerez is worth a peek to see its famous horses in action and for a sherry bodega tour.

Before you go, visit www.andalucia.com for information on hotels, festivals, museums, nightlife, and sports in the region.

Planning Your Time

While the towns can be (and often are) accessed from the Costa del Sol resorts via Ronda, Arcos makes the best home base. Arcos, near Jerez and close to interesting smaller towns, is conveniently situated halfway between Sevilla and Tarifa.

On a three-week Iberian vacation, the region is worth two nights and two days sandwiched between Sevilla and Tarifa. Spend both those nights in Arcos. See Jerez (horses and sherry) on your way in or out, spend a day hopping from town to town (Grazalema and Zahara, at a minimum) in the more remote interior, and enjoy Arcos early and late in the day.

Andalucía

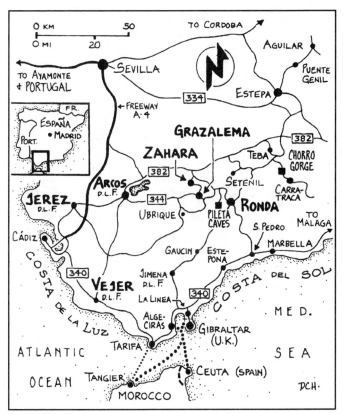

Without a car you might keep things simple and focus only on Arcos and Jerez (both well-served by public buses). Spring and fall are high season throughout this area. In summer you'll find empty hotels and no crowds.

ARCOS DE LA FRONTERA

Arcos, smothering its hilltop and tumbling down all sides like an oversized blanket, is larger than the other Andalusian hill towns but equally atmospheric. The old center is a labyrinthine wonderland, a photographer's feast. Viewpoint-hop through town. Feel the wind funnel through the narrow streets as cars inch around tight corners. Join the kids' soccer game on the churchyard patio.

There are two towns: The fairy-tale old town and the fun-loving lower or new town. Check out the pleasant evening paseo and café scene, best at Plaza España and the adjacent Paseo Andalucía, the base of the hill where the new and old towns meet. Enjoy the moonlit view from the main square in the old town.

Though it tries, Arcos doesn't have much to offer other than its basic whitewashed self. The locally produced English guidebook on Arcos waxes poetic and at length about very little. Since the church is open until early evening and the town market is open in the morning, you can arrive late and leave early.

Orientation

Tourist Information: The TI, on the main square across from the parador, is helpful and loaded with information, including bus schedules (Mon–Sat 10:00–15:00, 16:00–20:30, Sun 10:30–15:00, Oct–Feb Mon–Sat 10:00–13:00, 15:00–19:30, Sun 10:30–15:00, Plaza del Cabildo, tel. 95-670-2264, fax 95-670-2226).

Walking Tours: Year-round the TI organizes two different one-hour walking tours: "Old Town" and "Patios of Arcos." They leave from the main square, are given in Spanish and/or English, and cost €3. Old-town walks include the church and general history (Mon–Fri 10:30 and 17:00, Sat 10:30 only, 1.5 hrs). Patio walks get you into private courtyards and cover lifestyles and Moorish influences (Mon–Fri 12:00 and 18:30, Sat 12:00, 2 hrs). Groups can hire a private guide for any walk any time (€36).

Arrival in Arcos: The bus station is on Calle Corregidores. To get to the old town, catch a bus marked "Centro" (2/hr, €0.70), hop a taxi (€3.60), or take a 15-minute uphill walk. As you leave the station, turn left on Corregidores, angle left uphill, cross the four-way intersection, angle right uphill, and take Muñoz Vazquez up into town. Go up the stairs by the church to the main square and TI. Parking is also available in the main square (Plaza del Cabildo).

Helpful Hints: Arcos' little post office is a few doors away from Hotel Los Olivos (Mon–Fri 8:30–14:30, Sat 9:30–13:00, Paseo Boliches 26). Parking is available in Arcos' main square (ticket from machine €0.70/hr, only necessary 9:30–14:00 and 18:00–21:00, can get half-price ticket from old-town hotels, free Sat afternoon and all day Sun).

Self-Guided Tour of the Old Town

Avoid this walk during the hot midday siesta.

1. Plaza del Cabildo: Stand at the viewpoint opposite the church on the town's main square. Survey the square, which in the old days doubled as a bullring: On your right is the parador, a former palace of the governor. On your left is the **city hall** (with the TI), below the 11th-century Moorish **castle** where Ferdinand and Isabel met to plan the Reconquista (closed to the public). Directly in front is the Church of Santa Maria. Notice the fine but unfinished **church bell tower**. The old one fell in the earthquake of

Arcos de la Frontera

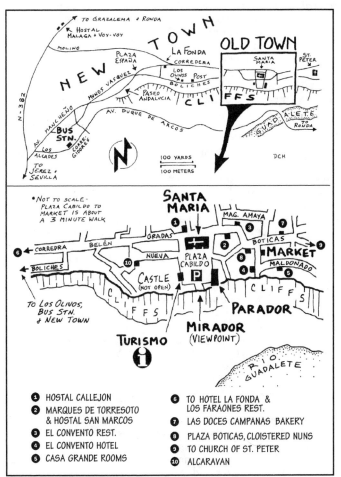

- ❶ HOSTAL CALLEJON
- ❷ MARQUES DE TORRESOTO & HOSTAL SAN MARCOS
- ❸ EL CONVENTO REST.
- ❹ EL CONVENTO HOTEL
- ❺ CASA GRANDE ROOMS
- ❻ TO HOTEL LA FONDA & LOS FARAONES REST.
- ❼ LAS DOCES CAMPANAS BAKERY
- ❽ PLAZA BOTICAS, CLOISTERED NUNS
- ❾ TO CHURCH OF ST. PETER
- ❿ ALCARAVAN

1755 (famous for destroying Lisbon). The new Baroque replacement was intended to be the tallest in Andalucía after Sevilla's—but money ran out. It looks like someone lives on an upper floor. They do. You can go through the brown door on the right and climb up to a living room hung with bell-ringing ropes and ask the church guardian if you can go to the top of the tower. He may give you the key (tip €0.60 per person), or he may say "scram."

Enjoy the square's viewpoint. The people of Arcos boast that only they see the backs of the birds as they fly. Ponder the parador's erosion concerns, orderly orange groves, flower-filled greenhouses, and fine views toward Morocco. Belly up to the railing and look down—the town's suicide departure point.

2. Inside the Church of Santa Maria: After Arcos was retaken from the Moors in the 13th century, this church was built—atop a mosque. The fine Renaissance **high altar** covers up a Muslim prayer niche surviving from the older mosque. The altar shows God with a globe in his hand on top and scenes from the life of Jesus on the right and from Mary's on the left. While most of the architecture is Gothic, the elaborate **chapels** are decorated Baroque and rococo. The ornate statues are used in the Holy Week processions. In the choir notice the historic **organ** (1,500 pipes, from 1789). Sniff out the "incorruptible body" of St. Felix (a third-century martyr). Rome sent it in 1764 after recognizing this church as the most important in Arcos. Study the finely carved stalls and, if you're tired, flip up a seat to see how priests used to rest and "stand" at the same time. In the back of the church, under a huge fresco of St. Christopher (carrying his staff and baby Jesus), is a giant votive candle from 1767 (€0.90, Mon–Fri 10:00–13:00, 15:30–18:30, Sat 10:00–13:00, closed Sun).

3. Church Exterior: Circle clockwise around the church. Down four steps find the third-century **Roman votive altar** with a carving of the palm tree of life. While the Romans didn't build this high, they did have a town and temple below Arcos. This was found in the foundation of the old Moorish mosque that stood here before the first church was built.

Down a few more steps you come to the **main entrance** (west portal) of the church—open for worship on Sundays and every evening at 19:00. This is a fine example of Plateresque Gothic (Spain's last and most ornate kind of Gothic), not counting the minaret incorporated into the wall. In the pavement notice the 15th-century **magic circle:** 12 red and 12 white stones—the white ones with various constellations marked. When a child came to the church to be baptized, the parents would stop here first for a good Christian exorcism. The exorcist would stand inside the protective circle and cleanse the baby of any evil spirits. While locals no longer use this (and a modern rain drain now marks the center), Sufis from a sect of Islam still come here in a kind of magical pilgrimage.

Continue around the church to the intersection below the **flying buttresses**. These buttresses were built to shore up the church when it was wounded by an earthquake in 1699. Thanks to this, the church survived the bigger earthquake of 1755. Look at the arches supporting the houses downhill on the left. All over town, arches support earthquake-damaged structures. The spiky security grill over the window above protected cloistered nuns when this building was a convent. Sr. Gonzalez Oca's tiny barbershop at the corner has some exciting posters of bulls running

Pamplona-style through the streets of Arcos during Holy Week—
an American from the nearby Navy base at Rota was killed here by
a bull in 1994. (Sr. Gonzalez Oca is happy to show off his posters;
drop in and say, "*Hola.*" Need a haircut? €4.80.) Continuing along
under the buttresses, notice the scratches of innumerable car mirrors on each wall (and be glad you're walking).

4. From the Church to the Market: Completing your circle
around the church, turn left under more earthquake-damaged
arches and walk down the bright white Calle Escribanos. From
now until the end of this walk you're going basically straight until
you come to the town's second big church (St. Peter's). After a
block you hit Plaza Boticas. At the end of the street on your left is
the finest restaurant in town (El Convento—see "Eating," below).
On your right is the last remaining **convent** in Arcos. Notice the
no-nunsense window grills above, with tiny peepholes for the cloistered nuns. Step into the lobby under the fine portico to find a one-
way mirror and a blind spinning cupboard. Push the buzzer and
one of the eight sisters inside will spin some boxes of freshly baked
cookies for you to consider buying (€4.20). If you ask for *magda-
lenas*, bags of cupcakes will swing around (€1.50). These are traditional goodies made from completely natural ingredients (daily
8:30–14:30, 17:00–19:00). Buy some cupcakes to support their
church work and give them to kids as you complete your walk.

The covered **market** (*mercado*) at the bottom of the plaza
resides in an unfinished church. Notice the half-a-church wall at
the entry. This was being built for the Jesuits, but construction
stopped in 1767 when King Charles III, tired of the Jesuit appetite
for politics, expelled the order from Spain. (Jesuits encountered no
such tough treatment in South America.) The market is closed on
Sunday and on Monday—when you rest on Sunday there's no produce, fish, or meat ready for Monday. Poke inside (public WC).

5. From the Market to the Church of St. Peter: Continue
straight (passing the market on your right) down Calle Boticas.
Peek into private **patios**. These wonderful, cool-tiled courtyards
filled with plants, pools, furniture, and happy family activities are
typical of Arcos (and featured on the TI's "Patios" walks).

Look for Las Doce Campanas bakery, which sells traditional
sultana cookies. These big, dry macaroons (named for sultans) go
back to Moorish times. At the next corner, squint back above the
bakery to the corner of the tiled rooftop. The tiny mask was placed
here to scare evil spirits from the house. This is Arcos' last surviving
mask from a tradition that lasted until the mid-19th century.

At the next intersection notice the **ancient columns** on each
corner. All over town these columns, many actually Roman
(appropriated from their ancient settlement at the foot of the hill),
were put up to protect buildings from reckless donkey carts.

As you walk down the next block, notice that the walls are

scooped out on either side of the windows—a reminder of the days when women stayed inside but wanted the best possible view of any people action in the streets.

At the old facade of San Miguel, duck right into the first of two **courtyards**. Retired men hang out here and play poker and dominoes. See the historic photos on the walls of the second courtyard.

Just beyond is Arcos' second church, **St. Peter's**. It really is the second church, having had an extended battle with Santa Maria for papal recognition as the leading church in Arcos. When the pope finally recognized Santa Maria, parishioners from St. Peter's even changed their prayers. Rather than say "Maria," they prayed "Saint Peter, mother of God."

In the cool of the evening, the tiny **square** in front of the church—about the only flat piece of pavement around—serves as the old-town soccer field for neighborhood kids. Until a few years ago this church also had a resident bellman—notice the cozy balcony halfway up. He was a basket-maker and a colorful character—famous for bringing a donkey into his quarters that grew too big to get back out. Finally, he had no choice but to kill and eat the donkey.

Twenty meters beyond the church is a fine **gallery**, Galería de Arte San Pedro, featuring painting, pottery, and artisans in action.

From St. Peter's church, circle down and around back to the main square, wandering the tiny neighborhood lanes, peeking into patios, kicking a few soccer balls, and enjoying the views.

Nightlife

New-Town Evening Action—The newer part of Arcos has a modern charm, as all the generations are out enjoying life in the cool of the evening around Plaza España (a 10-min walk from the old town). Several fine tapas bars border the square along with a good Egyptian restaurant (see "Eating," below). The big park below the square (Recinto Ferial) is the late-night fun zone in the summer (June–Sept)—the *carpas* (tents) fill with merrymakers, especially on weekends, when the scene includes open-air tapas bars, disco music, and dancing. There are free live concerts on Friday evenings throughout the summer.

Flamenco—On Plaza Cananeo in the old town, amateur flamenco sizzles on Thursday evening (free, from 22:00 July–Aug).

Sleeping in Arcos

(€1.10 = about $1, country code: 34, zip code: 11630)
Sleep Code: **S** = Single, **D** = Double/Twin, **T** = Triple, **Q** = Quad, **b** = bathroom, **s** = shower only, **CC** = Credit Cards accepted, **no CC** = Credit Cards not accepted, **SE** = Speaks English, **NSE** = No English. A price range reflects off-season to peak-season prices.

Breakfast is not included; nor is the 7 percent IVA tax (unless noted below).

Hotel El Convento, deep in the old town just beyond the parador, is the best value in town. Run by a hardworking family, this cozy hotel offers 11 fine rooms—all with great views, half with view balconies. In 1998 I enjoyed a big party with most of Arcos' big shots present as they dedicated a fine room with a grand-view balcony to "Rick Steves Periodista Turistico" (Sb-€48, Db-€60, third person or balcony-€12 extra, tax extra, CC, parking on the Plaza del Cabildo-€3, Maldonado 2, tel. 95-670-2333, fax 95-670-4128, www.webdearcos.com/elconvento, e-mail: elconvento@viautil.com, Estefania SE). Enjoy a bird-watching breakfast on their view terrace with all of Andalucía spreading beyond your *café con leche*. The family also runs a good restaurant (see "Eating," below).

Parador de Arcos de la Frontera is royally located, recently refurbished, and, for all its elegance, reasonably priced. If you're going to experience a parador (and you can't get into El Convento), this might be the one (Sb-€78–84, Db-€111, €6 more with a terrace—well worthwhile if you're into relaxing, breakfast-€8.50, CC, elevator, air con, 24 rooms—8 with balconies, minibars, free parking, Plaza del Cabildo, tel. 95-670-0500, fax 95-670-1116, www.parador.es, e-mail: arcos@parador.es, SE).

Hotel Los Olivos is a bright, cool, and airy place with a fine courtyard, roof garden, bar, view, friendly English-speaking folks, and easy €4.20/day parking. This is a poor man's parador (Sb-€30–35, Db-€45–57, Tb-€57–70, extra bed-€17, breakfast-€6, tax extra, 10 percent discount for readers of this book, CC, San Miguel 2, tel. 95-670-0811, fax 95-670-2018, www.losolivos.profesionales.org, e-mail: mmoreno0237@viautil.com, Raquel SE).

Hotel La Fonda is a great traditional Spanish inn with all 19 rooms off one grand hall (Sb-€27, Db-€45, third person-€12, no breakfast, CC, attached restaurant has good garlic soup and €7.25 meals, Calle Corredera 83, tel. 95-670-0057, fax 95-670-3661, e-mail: lafonda@pobladores.com, SE).

Hotel Marques de Torresoto is a restored 17th-century palace with 15 classy rooms (few views), a peaceful courtyard, and a view terrace. Once the home of a former Philippine governor, the hotel sports decorations with an Asian flair (Sb-€41, Db-€55, Db with salon-€67, breakfast-€3.20, CC, air con, across from Restaurante El Convento, Marques de Torresoto 4, tel. 95-670-0717, fax 95-670-4205, www.tugasa.com, e-mail: marques-torresoto@tugasa.com, SE).

Hostal San Marcos offers four air-conditioned rooms and a great sun terrace above a neat little bar in the heart of the old town (Sb-€15–18, Db-€24–30, Tb-€36, includes tax, CC, Marques de Torresoto 6, tel. 95-670-0721, e-mail: sanmarcosarcos@mixmail.com, Loli NSE).

La Casa Grande has four shipshape rooms with porthole windows and Moroccan-tiled bathrooms, plus a terrace with fine views (Db-€54–66, Db suite-€78–84, Tb-€102–108, Qb suite with kitchen-€114–120, Maldonado 10, tel. & fax 95-670-3930, www.lacasagrande.net, e-mail: lacasagrande@lacasagrande.net, friendly owners Helena and Ferran).

Hostal Callejon de las Monjas offers the closest thing to budget beds in the old town but is on a noisy street behind the Church of Santa Maria. Its nine simple, decent, clean rooms have fans (Sb-€18, D-€21, Db-€30, tax included, CC, air con, Dean Espinosa 4, tel. 95-670-2302, NSE). Friendly Sr. Gonzalez Oca runs a tiny barbershop in the foyer and a rest-aurant in the cellar.

If for some reason you want to sleep on the big, noisy road at the Jerez edge of town, two fine hotels nestle between truck stops on A-382: **Hostal Málaga** is surprisingly nice, with 15 clean, attrac-tive rooms and a breezy two-level roof garden (Sb-€18–21, Db-€30–33, Qb apartment-€48, CC, air con, TV, parking-€3/ day, Ponce de Leon 5, tel. & fax 95-670-2010, e-mail: hostalmalaga @teleline.es, NSE); they also rent two apartments in the center of Arcos (Db/Qb-€48). **Hostal Voy-Voy** is clean and next door to Hostel Málaga, but can be noisy (Sb-€15–18, Db-€30–36, tax included, attached restaurant, CC, Ponce de Leon 9, tel. 95-670-1412, NSE).

Eating in Arcos

The parador is very expensive, though a costly drink on its million-dollar-view terrace can be a good value. **Restaurante El Convento** has a wonderful atmosphere and is graciously run by Señora María Moreno-Moreno and her husband, Señor Roldan (daily 13:00–16:00, 19:00–22:30, near parador at Marques Torresoto 7, reserva-tions necessary, tel. 95-670-3222). The food is the best of traditional local cuisine and well worth the splurge. The hearty €24 menu of the day includes a fine red house wine and circular bread sticks (*picos de Arcos*), a local specialty. Many readers report this to be the best meal of their trip.

The *típico* **Alcaravan** is two blocks off Plaza Cabildo under the castle. You can enjoy your tapas on its classy patio or inside what was actually the dungeon of the castle (closed Mon, Calle Nueva 1).

Los Faraones serves good Egyptian cuisine in the new town near the paseo zone of Plaza España (€9, Tue–Sun from 20:00, closed Mon, Debajo del Corral 8, tel. 95-670-0612, Hussein SE).

Restaurante Marques de Torresoto offers good €18 à la carte meals (closed Tue, across from Restaurante El Convento, Marques de Torresoto 4).

Transportation Connections—Arcos

By bus to: Jerez (hrly, 30 min), **Ronda** (4/day, 2 hrs), **Cadiz** (9/day, 1 hr), **Sevilla** (2/day, 2 hrs). From Jerez there are hourly connections to Sevilla. Two bus companies share the Arcos bus station. Their Jerez offices keep longer hours and know the Arcos schedules (Jerez tel. 95-634-2174 or 95-634-1063—make it clear you're in Arcos).

RONDA

With 40,000 people, Ronda is one of the largest white towns; and with its gorge-straddling setting, it's also one of the most spectacular. While it can be crowded with daytrippers, nights are peaceful. And since it's served by train and bus, Ronda makes a relaxing break for nondrivers traveling between Granada, Sevilla, and Córdoba.

Ronda's main attractions are its gorge-spanning bridges, the oldest bullring in Spain, and an interesting old town. Spaniards know it as the cradle of modern bullfighting and the romantic home of old-time banditos. Its cliffside setting is as dramatic today as it was practical yesterday. For the Moors it provided a tough bastion, taken by the Spaniards only in 1485, seven years before Granada fell. To 19th-century bandits it was a Bolivia without the boat ride.

Ronda's breathtaking ravine divides the town's labyrinthine old Moorish quarter and its new, noisier, and more sprawling Mercadillo quarter. A massive-yet-graceful 18th-century bridge connects these two neighborhoods. Most things of touristic importance (TI, post office, hotels, and bullring) are clustered within a few blocks of the bridge. While daytrippers from the touristy Costa del Sol clog the streets during the day, locals retake the town in the early evening. The paseo scene happens in the new town, on Ronda's major pedestrian street, Carrera Espinel.

Orientation

Tourist Information: The main TI is on the main square, Plaza España, opposite the bridge (Mon–Fri 9:00–19:00, Sat–Sun 10:00–14:00, tel. 95-287-1272). Get the free Ronda map, excellent Andalusian road map, and a listing of the latest museum hours; consider buying maps of Granada, Sevilla, or the "Route of the White Towns" (€0.60 each). A second TI is located at Paseo Blas Infante, opposite the bullring (tel. 95-218-7119).

While the town has precious little organized for tourism, you may see the tiny Tajotur bus parked in front of the TI gathering tourists for a drive outside of town to the most scenic places from which to view the gorge and bridge (€9, 45 min, English narration, runs erratically, up to 8/day).

Arrival in Ronda: The train station is a 15-minute walk from the center. Turn right out of the station on Avenida Andalucía, turn left at the roundabout (the bus station is on your right), and then walk four blocks and you'll cross Calle Almendra (where several recommended hotels are located). At the pedestrian street (Carrera Espinel, a few blocks farther), turn right to reach the TI. From the bus station, cross the roundabout and follow directions above. A taxi to the center costs around €3.

Drivers coming up from the coast catch A376 at San Pedro de Alcantara and wind 50 kilometers into the mountains. The handiest place to park is the underground lot at Plaza del Socorro (1 block from bullring, €0.90/hr, €10.75/24 hrs).

Excursions: Helena Wirtanen, a personable Finnish guide, will take you to nearby Roman ruins and hill towns (starting at €30 per person, 4 hrs, tel. 95-287-5556, cellular 65-693-2820).

Sights—Ronda

▲▲▲**The Gorge and New Bridge**—Ronda's main bridge, called Puente Nuevo (New Bridge), mightily spans the gorge. A bridge was built here in 1735 but fell after six years. This one was built from 1751 to 1793. The ravine, called El Tajo—110 meters (360 feet) down and 60 meters (200 feet) wide—divides Ronda into the whitewashed old Moorish town (called La Cuidad) and the new town (El Mercadillo), which was built after the Christian reconquest in 1485. Look down...carefully. The architect fell to his death while inspecting it, and hundreds from both sides were thrown off this bridge during Spain's brutal civil war.

You can see the foundations of the original bridge (and a great view of the New Bridge) from the park named Vista Panoramica Jardines Ciudad de Cuenca. From Plaza España walk down Calle Villanueva and turn right on Calle Los Remedios at the sign for the park.

▲▲**Bullfighting Ring**—Ronda is the birthplace of modern bullfighting, and this ring is the first great Spanish bullring. In the early 1700s Francisco Romero established the rules of modern bullfighting and introduced the scarlet cape, held unfurled with a stick. His son Juan further developed the ritual or sport, and his grandson Pedro was one of the first great matadors (killing nearly 6,000 bulls in his career).

To see the **museum**, buy tickets from the booth at the main entrance (which is at the back of the bullring, the farthest point from the main drag). The museum is located right before the entry into the arena.

This tiny museum—which has translations in English—is a shrine to bullfighting and the historic Romero family. You'll see stuffed heads (of bulls), photos, artwork, posters, and costumes.

Take advantage of the opportunity to walk in the actual arena, with plenty of time to play "*toro*" surrounded by 5,000 empty seats. The arena was built in 1784. Notice the 176 classy

Ronda

200 YARDS
200 METERS

SOUTH

TO COSTA DEL SOL, MALAGA

SANTA MARIA LA MAYOR

MONDRAGON PALACE

CITY WALL

MOORISH QUARTER

ARAB BRIDGE

PUENTE NUEVO

GUADALEVIN RIVER

PARA-DOR

PLAZA ESPAÑA

INFO

PLAZA C. ABELA

MERCA-DILLO QUARTER

PLAZA DE TOROS

ALAMEDA

PLAZA MERCED

TO TRAIN STATION

BUS STATION

TO SEVILLA, ARCOS & PILETA CAVES

1 ROYAL
2 RONDA SOL
3 BIARRITZ
5 EL TAJO
6 LA ESPANOLA
7 REST. SANTA POLA

8 DON MIGUEL
9 REINA VICTORIA
10 MUSEO DEL BANDOLERO
11 CASA DEL REY MORO
12 CASA DEL MARQUES DE SALVATIERRA

13 PUENTE VIEJO
14 HOSTAL SAN FRANCISCO
15 HOTEL REST. ALAVERA DE LOS BANOS
16 HOTEL SAN GABRIEL
17 HOSTAL ANDALUCIA

Tuscan columns. With your back to the entry, look left and you can see the ornamental columns and painted doorway where the dignitaries sit (near the gate where the bull enters). On the right is the place for the band—in the case of a small town like Ronda, a high-school band. *Sol* means "sun" (cheap seats) and *sombra* means "shade." (€3.60, daily 10:00–20:00, Oct–April 10:00–19:00, on the main drag in the new town, 2 blocks up and on left from the New Bridge and TI, tel. 95-287-4132).

Bullfights are scheduled for the first weekend of September and occur only rarely in the spring. For September bullfights, tickets go on sale the preceding July (tel. 95-287-6967). The Alameda del Tajo park, a block away, is a fine place for people-watching or a snooze in the shade.

Santa Maria la Mayor Cathedral—This 15th-century church shares a fine park-like square with orange trees and the city hall. Its Renaissance bell tower still has parts of the old minaret. It was built on and around the remains of Moorish Ronda's main mosque (which was itself built on the site of a temple to Julius Caesar). Partially destroyed by an earthquake, the reconstruction of the church resulted in the Moorish/Gothic/Renaissance/Baroque fusion (or confusion) you see today. Enjoy the bright frescoes, elaborately carved choir and altar, and the new bronze sculpture depicting the life of the Virgin Mary. The treasury displays vestments that look curiously like matadors' brocaded outfits (€1.50, daily 10:00–20:00, Oct–April 10:00–19:00, in the old town).

Mondragon Palace (Palacio de Mondragon)—This beautiful Moorish building was built in the 14th century, possibly as the residence of Moorish kings, and lovingly restored in the 16th century. It houses an enjoyable prehistory museum, with exhibits on Neolithic toolmaking and early metallurgy (many captions in English). Even if you have no interest in your ancestors, this is worth it for the architecture alone (€1.80, Mon–Fri 10:00–19:00, Sat–Sun 10:00–15:00, Oct–April 10:00–18:00, on Plaza Mondragon in the old town, tel. 95-287-8450). Linger in the two small gardens, especially the shady one. Wander out to the nearby Plaza de Maria Auxiliadora for more views.

Museo del Bandolero—This tiny museum, while not as intriguing as it sounds, is an interesting assembly of *bandito* photos, guns, clothing, and knickknacks. The Jesse Jameses of Andalucía called this remote area home, and brief but helpful English descriptions make this a fun detour. One brand of romantic bandits were those who fought Napoleon's army—often more effectively than the regular Spanish troops (€2.40, daily 10:00–20:00, Oct–April 10:00–18:00, across the main street below the Church of Santa Maria at Calle Armiñan 65, tel. 95-287-7785).

Parador National de Ronda—Walk around and through this

newest of Spain's fabled paradors. The views from the walkway just below the outdoor terrace are magnificent. Anyone is welcome at the cafés, but you have to be a guest to use the pool.

Hot-Air Balloon Ride—For a bird's-eye view of Ronda, consider a balloon ride with Graham Elson (starting at €120, half day, Aviacon Del Sol, tel. 95-287-7249, www.andalucia.com/balloons, e-mail: balloonsspain@mercuryin.es).

Walk through Old Town—From the New Bridge you can descend into a world of whitewashed houses, tiny grilled balconies, and winding lanes—the old town.

The **Casa del Rey Moro** garden may be in jeopardy if a five-star hotel opens on this site as planned. They may or may not offer access to the "the Mine," an exhausting series of 365 stairs (like climbing down and then up a 20-story building) leading to the floor of the gorge. The Moors cut this zigzag staircase into the wall of the gorge in the 14th century. They used Spanish slaves to haul water to the thirsty town.

Fifty meters downhill from the garden is **Casa del Marques de Salvatierra** (closed to public, but may reopen). With the "distribution" following the Reconquista here in 1485, the Spanish king gave this fine house to the Salvatierra family. The façade is rich in colonial symbolism from Spanish America. Note the pre-Columbian-looking characters flanking the balcony above the door and below the family coat of arms.

Continuing downhill you come to **Puente Viejo** (Old Bridge), built in 1616 upon the ruins of a Roman bridge. From here look down to see the old Puente Arabe, originally built by the Moors. Far to the right you can glimpse some of the surviving highly fortified old Moorish city walls. Crossing the bridge you see stairs on the right leading scenically along the gorge back to the New Bridge via a fine viewpoint. Straight ahead bubbles the welcoming "Eight Springs" fountain.

Near Ronda: Pileta Caves

The Pileta Caves (Cuevas de la Pileta) are the best look a tourist can get at prehistoric cave painting in Spain. The caves, complete with stalagmites, bones, and 20,000-year-old paintings, are 22 kilometers from Ronda, past the town of Benoajan, at the end of the road.

Farmer Jose Pullon and his family live down the hill from the caves. He offers tours on the hour, leading up to 25 people through the caves, which were discovered by his grandfather (€5.50, daily 10:00–13:00, 16:00–18:00, closes off-season at 17:00, closing times indicate last entrance, no reservations taken—just join the line, minimum of 12 people required for tour, bring flashlight, sweater, and good shoes, it's slippery inside, tel. 95-216-7343). Sr. Pullon is a master at hurdling the language barrier. As you walk the cool kilometer, he'll spend over an hour pointing out lots of black, ochre, and red drawings (five times as old as the Egyptian pyramids), and some weirdly recognizable natural formations such as the Michelin man and a Christmas tree. The famous caves at Altamira are closed, so if you want to see Neolithic paintings in Spain, this is it.

While possible without wheels (taking the Ronda–Benoajan bus—2/day, 30 min—then a 2-hr, 5-km uphill hike), I wouldn't bother. By car, it's easy: Leave Ronda on the highway to Sevilla—C339, exit after a few kilometers left toward Benoajan, then follow the signs, bearing right just before Benoajan, up to the dramatic deadend. Leave nothing of value in your car. Nearby Montejaque has a great outdoor restaurant, La Casita.

Sleeping in Ronda
(€1.10 = about $1, country code: 34, zip code: 29400)
Ronda has plenty of reasonably priced, decent-value accommodations. It's crowded only during Holy Week (the week before Easter) and through September. My recommendations are in the new town, a short walk from the New Bridge and a 10-minute walk from the train station. (The exceptions are Hostal Andalucía, across from the station, and Reina Victoria, at the edge of town—and the gorge.) In the cheaper places, ask for a room with a *ventana* (window) to avoid the few interior rooms. Breakfast and the 7 percent IVA tax are usually not included.

Hotel La Española is perfectly located on a pedestrian street just off Plaza España around the corner from the TI. Each of its 18 rooms is newly remodeled and comfy, with air-conditioning and modern bathrooms (Sb-€36–39, Db-€66–78, big Db suite-€78–90, includes breakfast buffet but not tax, CC, José Aparicio 3, tel. 95-287-1052, fax 95-287-8001, www.ronda.net/usuar/laespanola/, e-mail: laespanola@ronda.net, NSE). The newly-remodeled Hotel San Javier, across from Hotel La Española, is run by the same family, who give a 10 percent discount at either hotel if you show this book (Sb-€49-61, Db-€81-102, extra bed-€15, same contact info as above).

Hotel Royal has 29 clean, boring rooms—many on a busy street. Ask for a *tranquilo* room in the back (Sb-€24, Db-€39, Tb-€48, CC, air con, 42 Virgen de la Paz 42, 3 blocks off Plaza España, tel. 95-287-1141, fax 95-287-8132, www.ronda.net/usuar /hotelroyal/, e-mail: hroyal@ronda.net, some English spoken).

The friendly **Hostal Ronda Sol** has a homey atmosphere with 15 cheap but monkish rooms (S-€10.50, D-€17, no CC, Almendra 11, tel. 95-287-4497, NSE). Next door, and run by the same man, **Hostal Biarritz** offers 21 similar rooms, some with private baths (Sb-€10.50, D-€17, Db-€21, T-€24, Tb-€31, includes tax, no CC, Almendra 7, tel. 95-287-2910, NSE).

The 65-room **Hotel El Tajo** has pleasant, quiet rooms once you get past the tacky Moorish decoration in the foyer (Sb-€27, Db-€45, includes tax, parking-€6/day, CC, air con, Calle Cruz Verde 7, a half-block off the pedestrian street, tel. 95-287-4040, fax 95-287-5099, helpful Puri and Beli SE).

Hostal San Francisco offers 15 small, humble rooms a block off the main pedestrian street in the town center (Sb-€15, Db-€27, Tb-€42, includes tax, CC, Maria Cabrera 18, tel. & fax 95-287-3299).

Hostal Andalucía, a plain but clean place with 11 comfortable rooms, is immediately across the street from the train station (Sb-€18, Db-€30, includes tax, no CC, air con, easy street parking, Martinez Astein 19, tel. & fax 95-287-5450, Sra. Campos Garcia NSE).

Hotel San Gabriel has 16 pleasant rooms, a friendly staff, and a fine garden terrace (Sb-€60, Db-€72, Db suite-€78, CC, air con, Calle Jose M. Holgado 19, just off Plaza Poeta Abul-Beca, tel. 95-219-0392, fax 95-219-0117, www.hotelsangabriel.com, e-mail: info@sangabriel.com, SE). If you are a cinema-lover, settle into one of the seats from the old Ronda theater that now grace the charming TV room. Ask to see the Don Quixote movie that was partially filmed in the hotel.

Alavera de Los Baños, located next to ancient Moorish baths, has 10 clean and colorful rooms (Sb-€42, Db-€54–66, includes tax and breakfast, CC, Calle San Miguel, tel. & fax 95-287-9143, www.andalucia.com/alavera, e-mail: alavera @ctv.es, Christian SE). This hotel offers a rural setting within the city, a swimming pool, and wonderful restaurant (see "Eating," below).

Splurges: Ronda offers three tempting splurges. The gorge-facing **Don Miguel** is just left of the bridge. Many of its 30 red-tiled, comfortable rooms have balconies and gorgeous views at no extra cost, but street rooms come with a little noise (Sb-€39, Db-€57, cheaper off-season, breakfast-€3, CC, parking garage a block away-€5.75/day, air con, elevator, Plaza de España 4, tel. 95-287-7722, fax 95-287-8377, www.donmiguel.com, e-mail: reservas @donmiguel.com, SE).

You can't miss the striking **Parador de Ronda** on Plaza España. It's an impressive integration of stone, glass, and marble. All 78 rooms have hardwood floors and most have fantastic view balconies (ask about family-friendly duplexes) and are surprisingly reasonable. There's also a pool overlooking the bridge (Sb-€76–94, Db-€95–111, breakfast-€7.80, garage-€7.20, CC, Plaza España, tel. 95-287-7500, fax 95-287-8188, e-mail: ronda@parador.es, SE). Consider at least a drink on the terrace.

The royal **Reina Victoria**, hanging over the gorge at the edge of town, has a great view—Hemingway loved it—but you'll pay for it (Sb-€66–73, Db-€90–111, breakfast-€9, CC, air con, elevator, pool, 10-min walk from city center and easy to miss, look for intersection of Avenida Victoria and Calle Jerez, Jerez 25, tel. 95-287-1240, fax 95-287-1075, www.ronda.net/usuar/reinavictoria, e-mail: e-mail: reinavictoriaronda@husa.es, SE).

Hotel La Casona is a beautiful splurge in the old town close to the Minarete de San Sebastian. The hotel features nine thoughtfully-decorated rooms, several suites, a swimming pool, and garden (Db-€90, suites-€120–150, breakfast-€9, CC, parking-€9, Marques de Salvatierra 5, tel. 95-287-9595, fax 95-216-1095, www.lacasonadelaciudad.com, e-mail: reservas @lacasonadelaciudad.com).

Eating in Ronda

Dodge the tourist traps. They say the best meal in Ronda is at the **parador** (*muy* elegant, figure €21). **Plaza del Socorro**, a block in front of the bullring, is a wonderful local scene, where families enjoy the square and its restaurants. Take a paseo with the locals down pedestrian-only Carrera Espinel and choose a place with tables spilling out into the action. The best drinks and views in town are sipped on the terraces of the **Don Miguel Hotel** or the parador.

Restaurante Pedro Romero, assuming a shrine to bullfighting draped in *el toro* memorabilia doesn't ruin your appetite, gets good reviews (€11 menus, lunch from 12:30, dinner from 20:00, air con, across the street from bullring at Calle Virgen de la Paz 18, tel. 95-287-1110). Rub elbows with the local bullfighters or dine with the likes (or photographic likenesses) of Orson Welles, Hemingway, and Franco.

Restaurante Asador Santa Pola serves cheap *típico* food with friendly service, gorge views, and a great Moorish cliffside ambience (3-course dinners €11, good *rabo de toro*—bull-tail stew, lunch from 12:30, dinner 19:00–23:30; crossing New Bridge, take the first left downhill and you'll see the sign, Calle Santo Domingo, tel. 95-287-9208).

Located in the hotel of the same name, **Alavera de los Baños** serves tasty Moorish specialties such as lamb and chicken *tajine*, along with vegetarian dishes (Calle San Miguel, tel. 95-287-9143.)

The no-frills **Café & Bar Faustina** offers the cheapest tapas in town mixed with a lively crowd of locals and internationals (Tue–Sun 12:00–01:00, closed Mon, just off Plaza Carmen Abela, Santa Cecilia 4, tel. 95-287-6746).

Transportation Connections—Ronda

By bus to: Algeciras (1/day, Mon–Fri only), **Arcos** (4/day, 2 hrs), **Benoajan** (2/day, 30 min), **Jerez** (4/day, 3 hrs), **Grazalema** (2/day, 1 hr), **Zahara** (2/day, Mon–Fri only, 1 hr), **Sevilla** (5/day, 2.5 hrs; also see trains below), **Málaga** (10/day, 1.75 hrs; access other Costa del Sol points from Málaga), **Marbella** (5/day, 75 min), **Fuengirola** (5/day, 2 hrs), **Nerja** (4 hrs, transfer in Málaga; can

take train or bus from Ronda to Málaga). There's no efficient way
to call "the bus company" because there are four sharing the same
station; it's best to just drop by and compare schedules (on Plaza
Concepción García Redondo, several blocks from train station).

 By train to: Algeciras (6/day, 2 hrs), **Bobadilla** (4/day, 1 hr),
Málaga (3/day, 2.5 hrs, transfer in Bobadilla), **Sevilla** (3/day,
3.5 hrs, transfer in Bobadilla), **Granada** (3/day, 2.5 hrs, transfer
in Bobadilla), **Córdoba** (2/day, 3.5 hrs, transfer in Bobadilla),
Madrid (5/day, 5 hrs, 1 direct night train—23:20–8:40). It's a
sleepy station serving only 11 trains a day. Transfers are a snap
and time-coordinated in Bobadilla; with four trains arriving and
departing simultaneously, double-check that you've jumped on
the right one. Train info: tel. 90-224-0202.

MORE ANDALUSIAN HILL TOWNS: THE ROUTE OF THE PUEBLOS BLANCOS

There are plenty of undiscovered and interesting hill towns to
explore. About half the towns I visited were memorable. Unfortunately, public transportation is frustrating; I'd do these towns
only by car. Good information on the area is rare. Fortunately,
a good map, the tourist brochure (pick it up in Sevilla or Ronda),
and a spirit of adventure work fine. Along with Arcos, here are
my favorite white villages.

▲▲**Zahara**—This tiny town with a tingly setting under a Moorish
castle (worth the climb) has a spectacular view. While the big
church, facing the town square, is considered one of the richest in
the area, the smaller church has the most-loved statue. The Virgin
of Dolores is Zahara's answer to Sevilla's Virgin of Marcarena
(and is similarly paraded through town during Holy Week).
Zahara is a fine overnight stop for those who want to hear only
the sounds of wind, birds, and elderly footsteps on ancient cobbles.
(TI open Mon–Sat 9:00–14:00, 16:00–19:00, Sun 10:00–14:00,
tel. 95-612-3114.)

▲**Zahara Castle**—During Moorish times Zahara lay within the
fortified castle walls above today's town. It was considered the
gateway to Granada and a strategic stronghold for the Moors by
the Christian forces of the Reconquista. Locals tell of the Spanish
conquest of the Moors' castle as if it happened yesterday: After the
Spanish failed several times to seize the castle, a clever Spanish
soldier noticed that the Moorish sentinel would check to see if any
attackers were hiding behind a particular section of the wall by
tossing a rock to set the pigeons to flight. If they flew, the sentinel
figured there was no danger. One night a Spaniard hid there with
a bag of pigeons and let them fly when the sentinel tossed his rock.
Seeing the birds fly, the guard assumed he was clear to enjoy a
snooze. The clever Spaniard then scaled the wall and opened the
door to let his troops in, and the castle was conquered. That was

Route of the White Hill Towns

in 1482. Ten years later Granada fell, the Muslims were back in Africa, and the Reconquista was completed. Today the castle is little more than an evocative ruin (always open, free) offering a commanding view. The lake is actually a reservoir. Before 1991 the valley had only a tiny stream.

Sleeping and Eating in Zahara: The **Hostal Marques de Zahara** is the best central hotel and a good value, with 10 comfortable rooms gathered around a cool, quiet courtyard and mother cooking traditional specialties in the restaurant (Sb-€24–27, Db-€34–39, breakfast-€3, CC, San Juan 3, 11688 Zahara, tel. & fax 95-612-3061, www.turismorural-cadiz.org, Santiago SE). **Pensión Los Tadeos** is a simple, blocky place just outside of town by the municipal swimming pool (*piscina*) offering basic rooms with great views (S-€12, D-€21, basic breakfast-€1.40, Paseo de la Fuente, tel. 95-612-3086, family Ruiz NSE). Sr. Manolo Tardio runs **Meson Los Estribos**, a fine little restaurant across from the church, and rents an apartment (Db-€24, CC, tel. 95-612-3145).

▲**Grazalema**—Another postcard-pretty hill town, Grazalema offers a royal balcony for a memorable picnic, a square where you can watch old-timers playing cards, and plenty of quiet, white-washed streets to explore. Plaza de Andalucía, a block off the view terrace, has several decent little bars and restaurants and a popular candy store. Grazalema, situated on a west-facing slope of the mountains, catches clouds and is famous as the rainiest place in Spain—but I've had only blue skies on every visit (TI open Tue–Sun 10:00–14:00, 18:00–20:00, Oct–Feb 10:00–14:00, 17:00–19:00, closed Mon, tel. 95-613-2225).

Sleeping in Grazalema: The **Casa de las Piedras** has

30 comfortable rooms just a block up from the town center—ask for a room in their new wing (S-€9, Sb-€22.75, D-€18, Db-€33, T-€24, Tb-€42, tax included, breakfast-€1.50, CC, Calle Las Piedras 32, 11610 Grazalema, tel. & fax 95-613-2014, NSE).

Villa Turistica Grazalema is a big, popular, happy place for locals enjoying their national park. It has apartments and regular hotel rooms, with balconies on the first floor or opening onto the swimming-pool garden on the ground floor (Db-€45 plus tax, extra person-€9.60, apartments-€60, CC, game rooms, restaurant, 1 km outside town, tel. 95-613-2136, fax 95-613-2213).

JEREZ

Jerez, with nearly 200,000 people, is your typical big-city mix of industry, garbage, car bandits, and dusty concrete suburbs, but it has two claims to touristic fame: horses and sherry.

Jerez is ideal for a noontime (or midday) visit on a weekday. See the famous horses, sip some sherry, wander through the old quarter, and swagger out.

Orientation

Tourist Information: The helpful TI gives out free maps and info on the sights (Mon–Fri 9:00–19:00, Sat 10:00–14:00, 17:00–19:00, Sun 10:00–14:00, 16:00–19:00, Oct–March 9:00–14:00, 17:00–20:00, closed Sun, Calle Larga 39, tel. 95-633-1150).

Arrival in Jerez: The bus station (at Calle Cartuja and Madre de Dios) has a simple baggage checkroom open weekdays (€0.40/piece, if it looks closed, knock on the window; it's open until 22:00). *Consigna* is the Spanish word for "baggage check." The train station, a block away, has 30 lockers; buy a €2.40 locker token (*ficha*) at the ticket window.

Exit the bus station farthest from the WCs and turn left. The center of town and the TI are a 20-minute walk away. At the five-way intersection angle right on Honda; then, at the fountain, make a sharp left on the pedestrian street, Calle Larga, to reach the TI.

If you're arriving by train, angle right as you leave the station. Cross the intersection. The bus station is on your left. Continue straight, following directions from the bus station (above). Taxis from the station to the horses cost about €3.

Sights—Jerez

▲▲**Royal Andalusian School of Equestrian Art**—If you're into horses, this is a must. Even if you're not, this is horse art like you've never seen. The school does its Horse Symphony show at noon every Thursday, and from March through October on Tuesday as well (€12–18, CC, reservations tel. 95-631-9635 or 95-631-8008, fax 95-631-8015, call for current schedule). This is an equestrian ballet with choreography, purely Spanish music, and costumes from the 19th century. The stern horsemen and their talented and obedient steeds prance, jump, and do-si-do in time to the music, to the delight of an arena filled with mostly local horse aficionados. Training sessions, open to the public on Monday, Wednesday, and Friday from 11:00 to 13:00, and from March through October 10:00 to 13:00, offer a €6 sneak preview. Practice sessions can be exciting or dull, depending on what the trainers are working on. Amble along (Mon and Wed only) during a one-hour guided tour of the stables, horses, tack room, and horse health center. Sip sherry in the arena's bar to complete this Jerez experience. If you're driving, follow signs from the center of Jerez to Real Escuela Andaluza de Arte Ecuestre (street parking). Otherwise it's a 30-minute walk from the train station, a 10-minute walk from the TI, or a short taxi ride.

▲▲**Sherry Bodega Tours**—Spain produces more than 10 million gallons per year of this fortified wine, ranging in taste from fino (dry) to amontillado (medium) to oloroso (sweet). The name sherry comes from English attempts to pronounce Jerez. While traditionally the drink of England's aristocracy, today it's more popular with Germans. Your tourist map of Jerez is speckled with wine barrels. Each of these barrels is a sherry bodega that offers tours and tasting.

Sandeman Sherry Tour: Just over a fence from the horse school is the venerable Sandeman Bodega (which has been producing sherry since 1790 and is the longtime choice of English royalty). This tour is the aficionado's choice for its knowledgeable guides and their quality explanations of the process (€3, tours Mon, Wed, and Fri 10:00–13:30 on the hour, Tue and Thu 10:00–15:00 every 90 minutes, Sat 11:30 and 13:30, bottling finishes at 14:00, finale is a chance to taste 3 varieties, tel. 95-630-1100 for English tour times and to reserve a place, fax 95-630-2626). During the high season, flamenco dancers perform just after the Horse Symphony concludes next door (March–Oct, some Tue and every Thu at 14:00, €1.80).

Harvey's Bristol Creme: Their English/German tours (Mon–Fri 10:00–13:00 (or by arrangement) aren't substantial but include a 10-minute video and all the sherry you like in the tasting room (€2.70–4.50, Calle Pintor Munoz Cebrian, reservations recommended, tel. 95-634-6004, fax 95-634-9427).

Gonzalez Byas: The makers of the famous Tío Pepe offer a tourist-friendly tour with more pretense and less actual sherry-making on display (it's done in a new, enormous plant outside of town), but it's the only bodega that offers daily tours (€6, open year-round, Manuel Maria Gonzalez 12, tel. 95-635-7000, fax 95-635-7046). Gonzales Byas is Disneyfying their tours, and schedules change frequently—call for the latest.

Alcazar—This gutted castle looks tempting, but don't bother.

Jerez

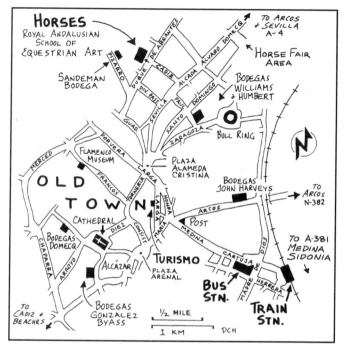

The €1.20 entry fee doesn't even include the ramparts. Its underground parking is convenient for those touring Gonzalez Byas Bodega (€0.90/hr).

Transportation Connections—Jerez

Jerez's bus station is shared by three bus companies, each with its own schedules, some specializing in certain destinations, others sharing popular destinations such as Sevilla and Algeciras. Shop around for the best departure time. By car it's a zippy 30 minutes from Jerez to Arcos.

By bus to: Tarifa (3/day, 2 hrs), **Algeciras** (8/day, 2.5 hrs), **Arcos** (hrly, 30 min), **Ronda** (5/day, 2.5 hrs), **Sevilla** (10/day, 90 min), **Málaga** (2/day, 5 hrs), **Córdoba** (1/day, 3.5 hrs), **Madrid** (6/day, 7 hrs).

By train to: Sevilla (12/day, 1 hr), **Madrid** (2/day, 4 hrs), **Barcelona** (2/day, 12 hrs). Train info: tel. 90-224-0202.

Drivers' note: In Jerez, blue-line zones require prepaid parking tickets on your dashboard on weekdays from 9:00 to 13:30 and 17:00 to 20:00 and on Saturday from 9:00 to 14:00; Sundays and July and August afternoons are free. Otherwise there's the handy underground parking lot near the Alcazar.

Easy Stops for Drivers

If you're driving between Arcos and Tarifa, here are several sights to explore.

Yeguada de la Cartuja—This breeding farm, which raises Hispanic Arab horses according to traditions dating back to the 15th century, offers shows on Saturday at 11:00 (€9, Finca Fuente del Suero, Ctra. Medina-El Portal, km 6.5, Jerez de la Frontera, tel. 95-616-2809, www.yeguadacartuja.com). From Jerez take the road to Medina Sidonia, then take a right in direction of El Portal— you will see a cement factory on your right. Drive for five minutes until you see the Yeguada de la Cartuja. A taxi from Jerez will charge around €12 one-way.

Medina Sidonia—This place has no TI (read "no tourists"). It is whitewashed as can be surrounding its church and castle ruins–topped hill. Give it a quick look. Signs to Vejer and then Centro Urbano route you through the middle to Plaza de España—great for a coffee stop. Or, if it's lunchtime, consider buying a picnic, as all the necessary shops are nearby and the plaza benches afford a fine workaday view of a perfectly untouristy Andalusian town at play. You can drive from here up to the church (Plazuela de la Yglesia Mayor), where, for a tip, the man will show you around. Even without a tip you can climb yet another belfry for yet another vast Andalusian view. The castle ruins just aren't worth the trouble.

Vejer de la Frontera—Vejer, south of Jerez and just 35 kilometers north of Tarifa, will lure all but the very jaded off the highway. Vejer's strong Moorish roots give it a distinct Moroccan (or Greek island) flavor—you know, black-clad women whitewashing their homes and lanes that can't decide if they're roads or stairways. Only a few years ago women wore veils. The town has no real sights (other than its women's faces) and very little tourism, but it makes for a pleasant stop. (TI open Mon–Sat 10:00–14:00, 17:00–20:00, closed Sun, tel. 95-645-0191.)

The coast near Vejer is lonely, with fine but windswept beaches. It's popular with windsurfers and sand flies. The Battle of Trafalgar was fought just off Cabo de Trafalgar (a nondescript lighthouse today). I drove the circle so that you need not.

Sleeping in Vejer: A newcomer on Andalucía's tourist map, the old town of Vejer has only two hotels. **Convento de San Francisco** is a poor man's parador in a classy refurbished convent (Sb-€41, Db-€55, breakfast-€3.20, prices negotiable in off-season, CC, La Plazuela, 11150 Vejer, tel. 95-645-1001, fax 95-645-1004, e-mail: convento-san-francisco.tugasa@cadiz.org, Ines SE). They have the rare but unnecessary Vejer town map.

A much better value is the clean and charming **Hostal La Posada** (S-€18, Db-€30, cheaper off-season, Los Remedios 21, tel. 95-645-0258, NSE). Both are at the entrance to the old town, at the top of the switchbacks past the town's lone traffic cop.

Route Tips for Drivers—Andalucía

Arcos to Tarifa (130 km): Drive from Arcos to Jerez in 30 minutes. If you're going to Tarifa, take the tiny C343 road at the Jerez edge of Arcos toward Paterna and Vejer. Later you'll pick up signs to Medina Sidonia and then to Vejer and Tarifa.

Sevilla to Arcos: The remote hill towns of Andalucía are a joy to tour by car with Michelin map #446 or any other good map. Drivers can zip south on N-IV from Sevilla along the river, following signs to Cádiz. Take the fast toll freeway (blue signs, E5, A4). The toll-free N-IV is curvy and dangerous. About halfway to Jerez, at Las Cabezas, take CA403 to Villamartin. From there, circle scenically (and clockwise) through the thick of the Pueblos Blancos—Zahara and Grazalema—to Arcos.

It's about two hours from Sevilla to Zahara. You'll find decent but winding roads and sparse traffic. It gets worse if you take the tortuous series of switchbacks over the 1,385-meter (4,500-foot) summit of Puerto de Las Palomas on the direct but difficult road from Zahara to Grazalema. Remember to refer to your "Ruta de Pueblos Blancos" pamphlet.

Traffic flows through old Arcos only from west to east (coming from the east, circle south under town). The TI, my recommended hotels, and parking (Paseo Andalucía) are all in the west. Driving in Arcos is like threading needles. But if your car is small and the town seems quiet enough, follow signs to the parador, where you'll find the only old-town car park.

COSTA DEL SOL:
SPAIN'S SOUTH COAST

It's so bad, it's interesting. To northern Europeans the sun is a drug, and this is their needle. Anything resembling a quaint fishing village has been bikini-strangled and Nivea-creamed. Oblivious to the concrete, pollution, ridiculous prices, and traffic jams, tourists lie on the beach like game hens on skewers—cooking, rolling, and sweating under the sun.

Where Europe's most popular beach isn't crowded by highrise hotels, most of it's in a freeway choke hold. Wonderfully undeveloped beaches between Tarifa and Cádiz and east of Alveria are ignored, while lemmings make the scene where the coastal waters are so polluted that hotels are required to provide swimming pools. It's a fascinating study in human nature.

Laugh with Ronald McDonald at the car-jammed resorts. But if you want a place to stay and play in the sun, unroll your beach towel at Nerja.

You're surprisingly close to jolly olde England. The land of tea and scones, fish and chips, pubs and bobbies awaits you—in Gibraltar. And beyond "The Rock" is the whitewashed port of Tarifa, the least developed piece of Spain's generally overdeveloped south coast and a good place to rest up for a visit to Morocco (see next chapter).

Planning Your Time
My opinions on the "Costa del Turismo" are valid for peak season. If you're there during a quieter time and you like the ambience of a beach resort, it can be a pleasant stop. Off-season it can be neutron-bomb quiet.

The whole 240 kilometers (150 miles) of coastline takes four hours to drive or six hours by bus. You can resort-hop by bus

Costa del Sol

across the entire Costa del Sol and reach Nerja for dinner. If you want to party on the beach, it can take as much time as Mazatlán.

If you want to fit in a daytrip to Tangier, Morocco, you can take a tour from Gibraltar or Algeciras (near Tarifa).

NERJA

Somehow Nerja, while cashing in on the fun-in-the-sun culture, has actually kept much of its quiet, old-world charm. It has good beaches, a fun evening paseo (strolling scene) that culminates in the proud Balcony of Europe terrace, enough pastry shops and nightlife, and locals who get more excited about their many festivals than the tourists do. For a taste of the British expatriate scene, pick up the monthly *Street Wise* magazine or tune in to Coastline Radio at 97.7 FM.

Orientation

Tourist Information: The helpful, English-speaking TI has bus schedules, tips on beaches and side trips, and brochures for nearby destinations such as Málaga and Gibraltar (Mon–Fri 10:00–14:00, 17:30–20:30, Sat 10:00–13:00, closed Sun, Puerta del March 2, just off Balcony of Europe, tel. 95-252-1531, www.nerja.net, e-mail: turismo@nerja.net). Ask for a free city map (or buy the more detailed version for €0.60). Pick up the free "Villa de Nerja Cultural Center" flyer with the latest theater and musical events, and the "Leisure Guide" with a comprehensive listing of activities. Their booklet on hiking is suitable only for drivers; you need a car to reach the trailheads. Another TI is located at the Caves of

Nerja

* NOT TO SCALE -
BUS INFO KIOSK TO
BALCON DE EUROPA
IS A 10 MIN WALK

1 DON PEQUE	**5** BALCON DE EUROPA	**9** BAR EL PULGUILLA
2 ATEMBENI	**6** HOSTAL LORCA	**10** BAR EL CHISPA
3 MENA	**7** PENSION EL PATIO	**11** HOSTAL MARISSAL
4 PLAZA CAVANA	**8** LOS CUNAOS BAR	

Nerja (Mon–Fri 10:30–14:00, 16:00–18:30, Sat 10:00–13:00, closed Thu afternoon and Sun, tel. 95-252-9024).

Internet Access: The most scenically situated of Nerja's few Internet cafés is Med Web C@fé, at the end of Calle Castilla Perez, on a square overlooking the beach (daily 10:00–24:00, 10 computers, tel. 95-252-7202).

Market: The lively open-air market is colorful and fun (Tue 9:30–14:00 and Sun 9:30–14:00, along Calle Almirante Ferrándiz, in the west end of town).

Getting Around Nerja

You can easily walk anywhere you need to go. A goofy little tourist **train** does a 30-minute loop through town every 45 minutes (€2.40, daily 10:30–22:00, until 24:00 in Aug, departs from Plaza Cavana, you can get off and catch a later bus using same ticket, route posted on door of train). Nerja **taxis** charge set fees (e.g., €6 to Burriana beach, taxi tel. 95-252-4519). To clip-clop on a **horse-and-buggy** through town, it's €18 for about 30 minutes (hop on at Balcony of Europe).

Sights—Nerja

▲▲**Balcony of Europe (Balcón de Europa)**—This bluff over the beach is the center of the town's paseo and a magnet for street performers. The mimes, music, and puppets can draw bigger crowds than the balcony, which overlooks the Mediterranean, kilometers of coastline, and little coves and caves below.

Promenades—Pleasant sea-view promenades lead in opposite directions from the Balcony of Europe, going east to Burriana beach and west to Torrecilla beach (10-min walks). Even if you're not a beach person, you're likely to enjoy the views. At Torrecilla beach, the promenade ends at the delightful Plaza Los Congrejos, with cascading terraces of cafés and greenery spilling into an overlook of the beach (at the end of Avenida Castilla Pérez).

Beaches—Nerja has several good beaches. The sandiest (and most crowded) is Playa del Salon, down the walkway to the right of the Restaurante Marissal, just off the Balcony of Europe. The pebblier beach—Playa Calahonda, is full of fun pathways, crags, and crannies (head down through the arch to the right of the TI office) with a fine promenade (mentioned above) leading east to a bigger beach, Playa de Burriana. This is Nerja's leading beach, with paddleboats and entertainment options. Another beach, Playa de la Torrecilla, is a 10-minute walk west of the Balcony of Europe. All of the beaches have showers, bars, restaurants, and—in season—beach chairs (about €4.80/day). Beware of red flags on the beach, which indicate when seas are too rough for safe swimming.

▲**Caves of Nerja (Cuevas de Nerja)**—These caves, four kilometers east of Nerja, have the most impressive array of stalactites and stalagmites I've seen anywhere in Europe, with huge caverns filled with expertly backlit formations and appropriate music. The visit is a 30-minute unguided ramble deep into the mountain, up and down lots of dark stairs congested with Spanish families. At the end you reach the Hall of the Cataclysm, where you'll circle what, according to Guinness, is the world's largest stalactite-made column. Then you hike out. Someone figured that it took one trillion drops to make the column (€4.80, daily 10:00–14:00, 16:00–18:30, until 20:00 July–Aug, tel. 95-252-9520). To get to the caves, catch a bus from the Nerja bus stop on Avenida de Pescia (€0.70, 14/day, 15 min). During the festival held here the last week of July, the caves provide a cool venue for hot flamenco and classical concerts.

Frigiliana—This picture-perfect whitewashed village, only six kilometers from Nerja, is easy by car or bus (7/day, 15 min, €0.70). It's a worthwhile detour from the beach, particularly if you don't have time for the Pueblos Blancos hill towns.

Sleeping in Nerja
(€1.10 = about $1, country code: 34, zip code: 29780)
Sleep Code: **S** = Single, **D** = Double/Twin, **T** = Triple, **Q** = Quad, **b** = bathroom, **s** = shower only, **CC** = Credit Cards accepted, **no CC** = Credit Cards not accepted, **SE** = Speaks English, **NSE** = No English spoken.

The entire Costa del Sol is crowded during August and Holy Week (when prices are at their highest). Reserve in advance for peak season, basically mid-July through mid-September, prime time for Spanish workers to hit the beaches. Any other time of year you'll find Nerja has plenty of comfy, low-rise, easygoing, resort-type hotels and rooms. Room rates are three-tiered, from low season (Nov–March) to high season (July–Sept). Compared to the pricier hotels, the better hostals (Marissal and Lorca) are an excellent value.

Sleeping in Hotels
Hotel Plaza Cavana overlooks a plaza lily-padded with cafés. If you like a central location, marble floors, modern furnishings, an elevator, and a small rooftop swimming pool, dive in (35 rooms, Sb-€52, €62, or €72, Db-€70, €85, or €100, Tb-€90, €105, or €120, some view rooms, includes breakfast, tax extra, CC, air con, a second small pool in basement, your car can ride an elevator down into the garage for €6/day, 2 blocks from Balcony of Europe at Plaza Cavana 10, tel. 95-252-4000, fax 95-252-4008, e-mail: hotelplazacavana@infonegocio.com, SE).

The most central place in town is **Balcón de Europa**, right on the water and on the square, with the prestigious address Balcón de Europa 1. It has 110 rooms with all the modern comforts, including a pool and an elevator down to the beach. All the suites have a sea-view balcony and most regular rooms come with a sea view (Sb-€60, €70 or €90, standard Db-€80, €95, or €115, add about €20 extra for sea view and balcony, Db suite with Jacuzzi-€145, €165, or €190, breakfast-€8, CC, air con, elevator, parking-€7.25/day, tel. 95-252-0800, fax 95-252-4490, www.hotel-balcon-europa.com, e-mail: balconeuropa@spa.es, SE).

Nerja's **parador**, housed in a new office-type building rather than a castle, lacks character but has spacious, suite-like rooms and overlooks Burriana beach (Sb-€75, €90, or €110, Db-€100, €120, or €130, CC, air con, free parking, large-for-Nerja swimming pool, 10-min walk from town center, Almuñecar 8, tel. 95-252-0050, fax 95-252-1997, e-mail: nerja@parador.es, SE).

Hotel Paraiso del Mar, next to the parador, is a destination place, with 12 attractive rooms, a great setting on the bluff, and a pool and two terraces en route to a private stairway to Burriana beach. You might not feel the need to make the 10-minute walk to the town center (Sb-€50, €65, or €75, Db-€55, €77, or €87, about €20 extra for sea view and Jacuzzi, suites available, includes breakfast, tax extra, CC, quiet, air con, friendly dog Ringo, Calle Prolongación de Carabeo 22, tel. 95-252-1621, fax 95-252-2309, www.hotelparaisodelmar.com, e-mail: info@hispanica-colint.es, SE).

Sleeping in Cheaper Hostals

These are listed in order of value.

Hostal Marissal, just next door to the fancy Balcón de Europa hotel, has an unbeatable location and 14 modern, spacious rooms, four with small view balconies overlooking the action on the Balcony of Europe (Db-€33, €42, or €51, CC, air con, Balcón de Europa 3, reception at Marissal café, tel. & fax 95-252-0199, e-mail: marissal@terra.es, SE).

A quiet residential section five minutes from the center (and 3 blocks from the bus stop) offers two good options (near a small, handy grocery store):

Hostal Lorca—run by a friendly young Dutch couple, Femma and Rick—has nine modern, comfortable rooms and an inviting, compact backyard that contains a terrace, palm tree, singing bird, and small pool. You can use the microwave and take drinks—on the honor system—from the well-stocked fridge. This quiet, homey place is a winner (Sb-€18–33, Db-€27–39, extra bed-€9, includes tax, breakfast-€3.30, no CC, Mendez Nunez 20, look for yellow house, near bus stop, tel. 95-252-3426, www.hostallorca.com, e-mail: hostallorca@teleline.es, SE).

Pensión El Patio has five clean, simple rooms. If you want to go local, this is worth the communication struggles (Sb-€18–36, Db-€24–36, Tb-€30–48, no CC, Mendez Nuñez 12, near bus stop, tel. 95-252-2930, NSE). If no one answers, ask at the nearby grocery shop.

The following three places are central—within three blocks of the Balcony of Europe, but none will stun you with warmth. **Hostal Residencia Mena** is erratically run but has fine rooms and a breezy garden (Sb-€18–24, Db-€27–39, includes tax, street noise, no CC, El Barrio 15, tel. & fax 95-252-0541, Maria speaks some English). The family-run **Hostal Atembeni** has 19 basic rooms (Sb-€18, €24, or €30, Db-€27, €33, or €39, includes tax, no breakfast, CC, ceiling fans, Diputación 12, tel. 95-252-1341, some English spoken). **Hostal Residencia Don Peque**, across from Hostal Atembeni, has 10 simple rooms (with older bathrooms), eight with balconies, and an indifferent manager. Front rooms over the noisy street have air-conditioning (Db-€30–39, includes tax, breakfast-€2.70, CC, Diputación 13, tel. & fax 95-252-1318, some English spoken).

Your cheapest and often most interesting bet may be a room in a private home (*casa particular*). Walk around with your rucksack on the residential streets within about a six-block radius of Calle La Parra or Calle Nueva. Ask around.

Eating in Nerja

There are three Nerjas: the private domain of the giant beachside hotels; the central zone packed with fun-loving expatriates and tourists enjoying great food with trilingual menus; and the back streets, where local life goes on as if there were no tomorrow (or tourists). The whole old town around the Balcony of Europe sizzles with decent restaurants. It makes no sense for me to recommend one over the others. Wander around and see who's eating best.

Farther inland, prices go down and locals fill the bars and tables. A 10-minute hike uphill takes you into the residential thick of things, where the sea views come thumbtacked to the walls. These three great places cluster within two blocks of each other around Herrera Oria (see map). Each specializes in seafood and is fine for a sit-down meal or a stop on a tapas crawl. Remember that tapas are snack-size portions. To turn tapas into more of a meal, ask for a *ración*—or a menu.

El Pulguilla specializes in seafood, with clams so fresh they squirt (daily 13:00–15:00, 19:30–24:00, Bolivia 1, tel. 95-252-1384). **El Chispa** is similarly big on seafood, with an informal restaurant terrace on the side (San Pedro 12, tel. 95-252-3697). **Los Cuñaos** is most fun late in the evening, when families munch tapas, men watch soccer on TV, women chat, and stray kids wander around like it's home (daily 12:00–16:00, 19:00–23:00, good seafood and prices, Herrera Oria 19, tel. 95-252-1107). These places are generally open all day for tapas and drinks; I've included just their serving hours in case you're hungry for a meal.

If you're out late, consider **Bar El Molino** for folk singing after 23:00; it's touristy but fun (Calle San Jose 4).

Transportation Connections—Nerja

The Nerja bus station is actually just a bus stop on Avenida de Pescia with an info booth (daily 8:00–20:00, helpful schedules posted on booth, tel. 95-252-1504).

By bus to: Nerja Caves (14/day, 15 min), **Frigiliana** (7/day, 15 min), **Málaga** (17/day, 70–90 min), **Granada** (3/day, more frequent with Motril transfer, 2 hrs), **Córdoba** (1–2/day, 4 hrs), **Sevilla** (3/day, 4 hrs).

Transportation Connections—Málaga

The train station nearest Nerja is an hourly 90-minute bus ride away in Málaga.

From Málaga by train to: Ronda (3/day, 2 hrs, transfer in Bobadilla), **Madrid** (5/day, 4.25 hrs on Talgo train), **Córdoba** (11/day, 2–2.75 hrs, fastest on Talgo), **Granada** (2/day, 2.5–3.25 hrs, transfer in Bobadilla), **Sevilla** (3/day, 3 hrs), **Barcelona** (2/day, 13.5 hrs). Train info: tel. 90-224-0202.

Buses: Málaga's bus station, a block from the train station, has a helpful information office with bus schedules (daily 9:00–14:30, 15:30–19:00, on Paseo de los Tilos, tel. 95-235-0061).

By bus to: Algeciras (7/day, 1.75 hrs), **Nerja** (17/day, 70–90 min), **Ronda** (4/day, 2 hrs), **La Línea/Gibraltar** (4/day, 3 hrs), **Sevilla** (11/day, 3 hrs), **Jerez** (1/day, 5 hrs), **Granada** (16/day, 2 hrs), **Córdoba** (5/day, 3 hrs), **Madrid** (12/day, 7 hrs).

Sights—From Nerja to Gibraltar

Buses take five hours to make the Nerja-to-Gibraltar trip. They leave nearly hourly and stop at each town mentioned.

Fuengirola/Torremolinos—The most built-up part of the region, where those most determined to be envied settle down, is a bizarre world of Scandinavian package tours, flashing lights, pink flamenco, multilingual menus, and all-night happiness. Fuengirola is like a Spanish Mazatlán with a few less-pretentious, older, budget hotels between the main drag and the beach. The water here is clean and the nightlife fun and easy. James Michener's idyllic Torremolinos has been strip-mauled and parking-metered.

Marbella—This is the most polished and posh town on the Costa del Sol. High-priced boutiques, immaculate streets, and beautifully landscaped squares are testimony to Marbella's arrival on the world-class-resort scene. Have a *café con leche* on the beautiful Plaza de Naranjas in the old city's pedestrian section. Wander down to new Marbella and the high-rise beachfront apartment buildings to check out the beach scene. Marbella is an easy stop on the Algeciras–Málaga bus route (as you exit the bus station, take a left to reach the center of town).

San Pedro de Alcántara—This town's relatively undeveloped sandy beach is popular with young travelers. San Pedro's neighbor,

Puerto Banus, is "where the world casts anchor." This luxurious jet-set port, complete with casino, is a strange mix of Rolls-Royces, yuppies, boutiques, rich Arabs, and budget browsers.

GIBRALTAR

One of the last bits of the empire upon which the sun never sat, Gibraltar is a fun mix of Anglican propriety, "God Save the Queen" tattoos, English bookstores, military memories, and tourist shops. The few British soldiers you'll see are enjoying this cushy assignment in the Mediterranean sun as a reward for enduring and surviving an assignment in another remnant of the British Empire: Northern Ireland. While things are cheaper in pounds, your Spanish money works as well as your English words here.

The 30,000 Gibraltarians have a mixed and interesting heritage. The Llanitos (yah-nee-tohs), as the Spanish call them, speak a Creole-like Spanglish. They are a fun-loving and tolerant mix of British, Spanish, and Moroccan.

You'll need your passport to cross the border (and you may still be able to charm an official into stamping it—ask or you'll get just a wave-through). Make Gibraltar a daytrip (or just an overnight); rooms are expensive compared to Spain.

Planning Your Time

For the best daytrip to Gibraltar, consider this plan: Walk across the border, catch bus #3, and ride it to the end, following the self-guided tour (see below). Catch bus #3 back to the cable-car station, ride to the top, and then walk down via St. Michael's Cave and the Apes' Den. From there catch the cable car back into town. Spend your remaining free time in town before returning to Spain.

Tourist who stay overnight find Gibraltar a peaceful place in the evening, when the town can just be itself. No one is in a hurry. Families stroll, kids play, seniors window-shop, and everyone chats.

If you won't make it to Tarifa or Algeciras, but want to carve out a day for Morocco, see "Daytrip to Tangier, Morocco," below.

Orientation

(tel. code: 9567 from Spain, 350 from other countries)
Tourist Information: Gibraltar's main TI is at Casemates Square, the grand new square at the entry of town (Mon–Fri 9:00–17:30, Sat–Sun 10:00–16:00, tel. 74982, www.gibraltar.gi). Another TI is in the Duke of Kent House on Cathedral Square, nearer the town center (Mon–Fri 8:45–17:30, closed Sat–Sun, bus #3 stops here, just after NatWest House, tel. 74950). More TIs are at Customs where you cross the border and at the Coach Park (bus terminal). The TIs give out free maps and can arrange tours of caves and the WWII tunnels that crisscross the island (€8.25/£5 per tour, 3 hrs).

Gibraltar

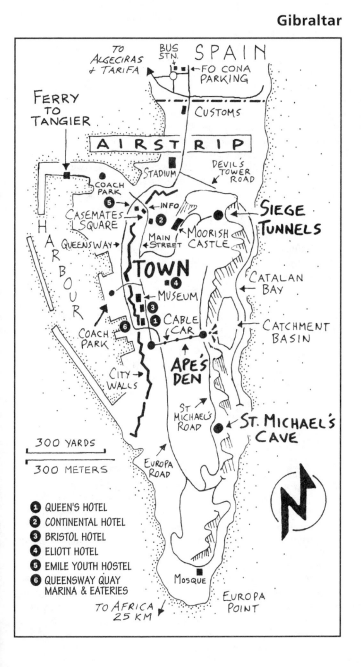

SPAIN

TO ALGECIRAS + TARIFA

BUS STN.

FO CONA PARKING

CUSTOMS

FERRY TO TANGIER

AIRSTRIP

STADIUM

DEVIL'S TOWER ROAD

COACH PARK

5 CASEMATES SQUARE

INFO

2

SIEGE TUNNELS

HARBOUR

QUEENSWAY

MOORISH CASTLE

MAIN STREET

TOWN

4

MUSEUM

CATALAN BAY

3

6 COACH PARK

1 CABLE CAR

CATCHMENT BASIN

CITY WALLS

APE'S DEN

ST MICHAEL'S ROAD

ST. MICHAEL'S CAVE

300 YARDS

300 METERS

EUROPA ROAD

1 QUEEN'S HOTEL
2 CONTINENTAL HOTEL
3 BRISTOL HOTEL
4 ELIOTT HOTEL
5 EMILE YOUTH HOSTEL
6 QUEENSWAY QUAY MARINA & EATERIES

MOSQUE

EUROPA POINT

TO AFRICA 25 KM

N

Helpful Hints

Telephone: To telephone Gibraltar from Spain, dial 9567 followed by the five-digit local number. To call the Rock from European countries other than Spain, dial 00-350-local number. To call from America or Canada, dial 011-350-local number. If you plan to make calls from Gibraltar, note that phone booths take English coins or Gibraltar phone cards (available at kiosks).

Electricity: If you have electrical gadgets, note that Gibraltar, like Britain, uses three-prong plugs. Your hotel may have an adapter (which plugs onto a European plug) to loan you.

Internet Access: Café Cyberworld has pricey Internet access (daily 12:00–24:00, Queensway 14, in Ocean Heights Gallery, near Casemates end of town, tel. 51416).

Arrival in Gibraltar

By Bus: Spain's La Línea bus station is a five-minute walk from the Gibraltar border. If you're daytripping to Gibraltar it's easy to store luggage in the lockers at the La Línea bus station (15 lockers, €2.40/£1.50 each) or the Algeciras train station.

From the La Línea bus station walk to the border (flash your passport) and then take a quick bus ride into town: Catch either the #3 minibus to the TI at Cathedral Square (or continue on the self-guided tour, below) or the double-decker bus #9 to Casemates Square—which also has a TI (€0.60/40 pence, every 15 min). Otherwise it's a 30-minute walk between the border and the center: From the "frontier" (as it's called), walk straight across the runway (look left, right, and up), then head down Winston Churchill Avenue, angling right at the Shell station on Smith Dorrien Avenue.

Avoid taking an expensive taxi ride into town. Compare the cost of a taxi from the border to the cable-car lift (€7.25/£4.50) with the cost of bus #3 (€0.60/40 pence).

By Car: After taking the La Línea-Gibraltar exit off the main Costa del Sol road, continue as the road curves left with the Rock to your right. The traffic light with the Aduana (customs) sign is just at the border; a right turn will take you into Gibraltar, or a left turn will take you immediately to La Línea (the Gibraltarians call this street Winston Churchill Avenue, the Spanish call it the 20th of April). Avoid long lines of cars going into Gibraltar by turning left and parking in La Línea. From here you make the five-minute walk across the border on foot. The handiest place to park is at Fo Cona underground parking lot (€0.90/hr, €6/day, left on 20th of April, 100 meters on your left). You will also find blue-lined parking spots in this area (€0.90/hr from meter, bring coins, leave ticket on dashboard, Sun free). The days of con artists dressed as cops taking bogus entrance fees from hapless tourists are gone. Today you will only find blue-uniformed Spanish police making sure all goes smoothly.

If you insist on driving into Gibraltar, there are plenty of parking lots (like the huge one near the cable car), but be prepared for up to a 90-minute wait both ways at the border.

Tours of Gibraltar

It's easy to visit the Rock's uppermost sights on your own at your own pace (e.g., take bus #3 to the cable-car lift, take the lift up and hike down to the sights). Those with more money than time take a tour (covers admission to the Upper Rock Nature Reserve sights included on tour). There are two types of tours: by minibus and by taxi. For the minibus tours, book at a travel agency. You can catch a taxi tour at the border (or cheaper at taxi stands at squares in the center).

By Minibus: Travel agencies offer approximately 90-minute tours for a set fee (around €18–21.25/£11–13). Stops include St. Michael's Cave, the Apes' Den, and Siege Tunnels. Consider Thomas Cook Exchange Travel (tours on Mon, Wed, Fri; 241 Main Street, near Marks & Spencers, tel. 76151), Bland Travel (tours also on Mon, Wed, Fri; 220 Main Street, tel. 79068), or Parodytur (priciest but offers tours daily; Cathedral Square, tel. 76070). If you call ahead to reserve a seat, you pay when you arrive in Gibraltar. Or just drop by any agency when you're in town (usually open Mon–Fri 9:30–18:00, to use CC you'll likely pay about €5.75/£3.50 extra). Nearly every travel agency in town offers the tour, with only minor variations.

By Taxi: Lots of aggressive cabbies at the border would love to take you for a ride—about €23/£14 per person if the taxi is packed. More people in a taxi means a lower cost per person; try to buddy up with other travelers. Cabbies at taxi stands in the center of Gibraltar are more low-key and charge a bit less (though it's harder to gather a group). The basic tour consists of four stops: an overlook over the Straits, St. Michael's Cave (for a 15–20 minute visit), near the top of the Rock, and the Siege Tunnels (for 15–20 minutes). A fifth stop—the ATM machine at NatWest House— is added for people who mistakenly thought they could pay for this tour with a credit card.

The Quick, Cheap, Bus #3 Self-Guided Orientation Tour

At the border, pick up a map at the customs TI. Then walk straight ahead for 200 meters to the bus stop on the right. Catch minibus #3 (4/hr, pay driver €0.60/40 pence) and enjoy the ride.

You enter Gibraltar by crossing an **airstrip**. Forty times a week, the entry road into Gibraltar is closed to allow airplanes to land or take off. (You can fly to London for as little as $180.) The airstrip, originally a sports stadium, was filled in with stones excavated from the 50 kilometers of military tunnels in the Rock.

This airstrip was a vital lifeline in the days when Spain and Britain were quarreling over Gibraltar and the border was closed.

Just after the airstrip, the bus passes a road leading left (which heads clockwise around the Rock to the town of Catalan Bay, peaceful beaches, and the huge mountainside rainwater "catchment" wall). As you pass apartments on the left, find the **Moorish castle** above (now a prison; only the tower is open to the public).

Over the bridge and on the right after the next stop you'll see **World War memorials**. The first is the American War Memorial (a building-like structure with a gold plaque and arch), built in 1932 to commemorate American sailors based here in World War I. Farther along you'll see 18th-century cannons and a memorial to Gibraltarians who died in World War II.

These following sights occur in rapid succession: Passing the NatWest House office tower on the left, you'll immediately see a **synagogue** (only the top peeks out above a wall; the wooden doors in the wall bear the Star of David). In the 19th century half of Gibraltar was Jewish. The Jewish community now numbers 600.

Just after the synagogue is little **Cathedral Square**, with a playground, TI, and the Moorish-looking Anglican church (behind the playground).

Now you'll pass a loooong wall; most of it is the back of the Governor's Residence (also called the Convent). At the front of the Residence (not visible from the bus), a miniature Changing of the Guard occurs midday.

The bus stops before the old **Charles V wall**, built in response to a 1552 raid in which the pirate Barbarossa stole 70 Gibraltarians into slavery.

Immediately after you pass under the wall, you'll see—on your left—a green park that contains the **Trafalgar cemetery** (free, daily 9:00–19:00). Buried here are the British sailors who died defeating the French off the coast of Portugal's Cape Trafalgar in 1805.

The next stop is at the big parking lot for the **cable car** to the top of the Rock, as well as the **botanical gardens** (free, daily 8:00–sunset) at the base of the lift. You can get off now or later, on the ride back into town.

Heading uphill out of town you pass the big ugly casino and the path leading up the Rock (a 2.5-hour hike). Reaching the end of the Rock you pass modern apartments and the new mosque. The lighthouse marks the windy Europa Point—end of the line. Buses retrace the route you just traveled, departing about every 15 minutes (check schedule before exploring farther).

The **Europa Point**, up the mound from the bus stop and tourist shop (on right), is an observation post. A plaque here identifies the mountains of Morocco 25 kilometers across the straits. The light of the lighthouse (from 1841, closed to visitors) can be seen from Morocco.

The **King Fahad Mosque**, a gift from the Saudi Sultan, was completed in 1997. Gibraltar's 300 Muslims worship here each Friday. Here—as across the straits in Morocco—five times a day the *imam* sings the call to prayer. Visitors (without shoes) are welcome outside of prayer time.

Sights—Gibraltar's Upper Rock Nature Reserve

▲▲▲**The Rock**—The real highlight of Gibraltar is the spectacular Rock itself. From the south end of Main Street, catch the cable car to the top (€6.50/£4 one-way, €8.50/£5 round-trip, or €12/£7 to include admission to all of the Upper Rock Nature Reserve sights, Mon–Sat 9:30–17:15, last cable car down at 17:45, 6/hr, closed Sun and when it's windy, brochure with necessary map included with ticket). The lift, usually closed on Sunday, may open on Sunday during peak season, June through September.

The cable car drops you at a slick **restaurant/view terrace** at the very top of the Rock, from which you can explore old ramparts and drool at the 360-degree view of Morocco, the Straits of Gibraltar, the bay stretching west toward Algeciras, and the twinkling Costa del Sol arcing eastward. Below you stretches the giant water-catchment system that the British built to catch rainwater in the not-so-distant past, when Spain allowed neither water nor tourists to cross its disputed border. The views are especially crisp on brisk off-season days.

Buying a one-way ticket up saves a little money and gives you a chance to hike down to all of the sites. Allow 90 minutes to hike down—or as much as 2.5 hours if you stop at the following listed sights in the Upper Rock Nature Reserve, which you'll see in order as you descend from the top of the Rock.

With a round-trip ticket, your best strategy is to take the cable car up, hike downhill to St. Michael's Cave and the Apes' Den, and then take the cable car down into town from the Apes' Den, skipping the other sights. Why hike at all, you ask? Because you'd miss St. Michael's Cave if you relied solely on the cable car.

The entire Upper Rock Nature Reserve is open daily from 9:30 to 19:00. Only the Apes' Den is free with your cable-car ticket. A pass for admission to the other sites is €12/£7 (better value if purchased with cable-car ticket—the same price includes the lift).

Approximate hiking times: From the top of cable-car lift to St. Michael's Cave—15 min, from the Cave to Apes' Den—10 min, from the Apes to Siege Tunnels—25 min, from the Tunnels to City Under Siege exhibit—5 min, from exhibit to Moorish Castle—5 min, and down to town—10 min.

▲▲**O'Hara's Battery**—If the Battery is still closed for renovation in 2002, it's not worth the 20-minute hike from the top of the cable-car lift (confirm status at cable-car lift or local TI).

At 426 meters, this is the highest point on the Rock. A 28-ton, 9-inch gun sits on the summit where a Moorish lookout post once stood. It was built after World War I, and the last test was fired in 1974. Locals are glad it's been mothballed. During test firings, if locals didn't open their windows to allow air to move freely after the concussion, their windows would shatter. Fifty kilometers of tunnels, like the tiny bit you see here, honeycomb this strategic rock. During World War II an entire garrison could have survived six months with the provisions stored in this underground base (Mon–Sat 10:00–17:30, closed Sun; from top of cable-car lift, walk 10 min down and then 10 min up). The iron rings you might see are anchored pulleys used to haul up guns such as the huge one at O'Hara's Battery.

▲**St. Michael's Cave**—Studded with stalagmites and stalactites, eerily lit and echoing with classical music, this cave is dramatic, corny, and slippery when wet. Considered a one-star sight since Neolithic times, these were alluded to in ancient Greek legends—when the Rock was one of the Pillars of Hercules, marking the end of the world, and the caves were believed to be the Gates of Hades. In the last century they were prepared (but never used) as a World War II hospital and are now just another tourist site with an auditorium for musical events. Notice the polished cross section of a stalagmite showing weirdly beautiful rings similar to a tree's. Spelunkers who'd enjoy a three-hour subterranean hike through the lower cave can make arrangements in advance at the TI (€8.25/£5 per person). To continue to the Apes' Den, refer to your map (free with lift ticket) and take the left fork.

Apes' Den—This small zoo without bars gives you a chance for a close encounter with some of the famous (and very jaded) apes of Gibraltar. Keep your distance from the apes and beware of their kleptomaniac tendencies. The man at the little booth posts a record of the names of all the apes. If there's no ape action, wait for a banana-toting taxi tour to stop by and stir some up. (The cable car stops here; you can catch the car down to town from here or continue on foot to see the following sights.)

▲**Siege Tunnels**—Also called the Upper Galleries, these chilly tunnels were blasted out of the rock by the Brits during the Spanish and French siege of 1779 to 1783. Hokey but fun dioramas help recapture a time when Brits were known more for conquests than for crumpets. The tunnels are at the northern end of the Rock, about 1.5 kilometers from the Apes' Den.

Gibraltar, A City Under Siege **Exhibition**—A spin-off of the Siege Tunnels, this excuse for a museum gives you a look at life during the siege. It's worth a stop only if you already have a combo ticket (just downhill from Siege Tunnels).

Moorish Castle—Actually more tower than castle, this building offers a tiny museum of Moorish remnants and carpets. The original castle was built by the Moorish Tarik-ibn-Zeyad in 711, but his name lasted longer than the castle; Gibel-Tarik (or Tarik's Hill) became Gibraltar. The tower marks the end of the Upper Rock Nature Reserve. Head downhill to reach the lower town and Main Street.

Sights—Lower Gibraltar

Gibraltar Museum—Built atop a Moorish bath, this museum in Gibraltar's lower town tells the story of a rock that has been fought over for centuries. Highlights are the history film and the prehistoric remains discovered here.

On the ground floor, you can see the 15-minute film, a "teaser" skull display, and the empty rooms of the 14th-century Moorish baths. The first floor contains military memorabilia, a model of the Rock, paintings by local artists, and, in a cave-like room off the art gallery, a collection of prehistoric remains and artifacts. The famous skull of a Neanderthal woman found in Forbes' Quarry is a copy (original in British Museum in London). This first Neanderthal skull was found in Gibraltar in 1848, though no one realized its significance until a similar skull found years later in Germany's Neanderthal Valley was correctly identified—stealing the name, claim, and fame from Gibraltar (€3.40/£2, Mon–Fri 10:00–18:00, Sat 10:00–14:00, closed Sun, no photos, on Bomb House Lane off Main Street).

▲**Catalan Bay**—Gibraltar's tiny second town originated as a settlement of Italian shipwrights whose responsibility was keeping the royal ships in good shape. Today it's just a huddle of apartments around a cute little Catholic church and the best beach on the Rock (fully equipped). Catch bus #4A from opposite the Governor's Residence or the roundabout near the airport.

Dolphin-Watching Cruises—Numerous companies take you on two-hour cruises of the bay to look for dolphins (€24.50–33/£15–20). The newest, Nautilus, runs boats with glass fronts and sides (€33/£20, 4/day, Admirals Walk 4, tel. 73400) and Dolphin World refunds your money if dolphins aren't sighted (€24.50/£15, 3/day, Admirals Walk, Marina Bay Pier, cellular 5448-1000).

Daytrip to Tangier, Morocco

Virtually any travel agency in Gibraltar offers daytrips to Tangier (ask at the TI for their "Tangier Day Trips" list, stop by any travel agency in Gibraltar, or check with Thomas Cook Exchange Travel and Parodytur (listed in "Tours of Gibraltar," above). Depending on the company, you'll pay about €57–74/£35–45 for the tour, which covers the ferry crossing, a tour of Tangier, lunch, a shopping stop at the market, and the return by ferry. Some tours leave from Gibraltar, others from Algeciras. But because Gibraltar is pricey compared to Spain, it makes sense to use your time here just to see

the Rock, and daytrip to Morocco from a cheaper homebase such
as Tarifa (a 30-min bus ride from port of Algeciras).

Sleeping in Gibraltar
**(€1 = about $1.60, tel. code: 9567 from Spain
or 350 international, zip code: 29780)**
Sleep Code: **S** = Single, **D** = Double/Twin, **T** = Triple, **Q** = Quad,
b = bathroom, **s** = shower only, **CC** = Credit Cards accepted,
no CC = Credit Cards not accepted. For instructions on calling
Gibraltar, see "Helpful Hints," above. Exterior rooms (with views
and traffic noise) often cost more than interior rooms (quiet, without a view).

Queen's Hotel, near the cable-car lift, has 62 comfortable
rooms in a noisy location (S-€33/£20, Sb-€66/£40, D-€49/
£30, Db-€69–90/£42–55, Db with sea view-€108/£66, Tb-€98
/£60, Qb-€115/£70, includes breakfast, 20 percent discount
for students with ISIC, CC, free parking, elevator, at #3 bus
stop, Boyd Street 1, tel. 74000, fax 40030, e-mail: queenshotel
@gibnynex.gi).

Continental Hotel isn't fancy but has a friendly feel. Its 18
high-ceilinged, air-conditioned rooms border an unusual ellipical
atrium (Sb-€69/£42, Db-€90/£55, Tb-€115/£70, Qb-€139/£85,
includes small breakfast, elevator, CC, in pedestrian area just off
Main Street, a couple of blocks from Casemates TI, tel. 76900,
fax 41702). The hotel runs an inexpensive café downstairs.

Bristol Hotel offers drab, overpriced rooms in the heart
of Gibraltar (Sb-€80–87/£49–53, Db-€105–113/£64–69, Tb-
€121–133/£74–81, breakfast-€8.25/£5, air con, elevator, has
swimming pool oddly located off breakfast room, CC, Cathedral
Square 10, tel. 76800, fax 77613, e-mail: bristhtl@gibnet.gi).

Splurge: Eliott Hotel is four stars and then some, with a
roof-top pool with a view, bar, and terrace; fine sit-a-bit public
spaces; and 114 modern, settle-in rooms (Db-€156–270/£95–165,
breakfast-€13–20/£8–12, laundry service, air con, elevator, nonsmoking floor, free parking, CC, centrally located at Governor's
Parade, tel. 70500, fax 70243, www.gibraltar.gi/eliotthotel, e-mail:
eliott@gibnet.gi).

Hostel: The cheapest place in town is **Emile Youth Hostel
Gibraltar** (37 beds, D-€43/£26, dorm bed-€19.75/£12, includes
breakfast, lockout 10:00–17:00, just outside Casemates Square
entry on Montagu Bastion, tel. & fax 51106).

Eating in Gibraltar
Casemates Square, newly refurbished, makes a grand entry to
Gibraltar. This big square contains a variety of restaurants, rang-
ing from fast food (fish-'n'-chips joint, Burger King, and Pizza
Hut) to pubs spilling out into the square. Consider the **All's Well**

pub, near the TI, with €8.25/£5 meals and pleasant, umbrellaed tables under leafy trees (daily 9:30–24:00, CC).

Queensway Quay Marina is the place to be when a misty sun sets over the colorful marina and rugged mountains of Spain. The string of restaurants that line the promenade have indoor and outdoor seating, offer seafood and other dishes, and are usually open daily for lunch and dinner. Next door to each other, **Raffles Restaurant** (daily, tel. 40362) and **Laus on the Rock Bistro** (closed Sun, tel. 48686) are popular; **Waterfront** (farther on) is less expensive; and the **Jolly Parrot** (just tapas and drinks) offers the cheapest seat on the promenade. Queensway Quay is at the cable-car end of town (walk through Ragged Staff Gate toward the water).

Main Street is dotted with sidewalk cafés perfect for people-watching. Tourists hang out at **Roy's** fish 'n' chips outside the Governor's House (a.k.a. the Convent) to watch the miniature Changing of the Guard ceremony around midday (exact time not announced for security reasons).

For good-value meals, consider **The Little Chef**, an adventure when the one English-speaking guy is off-duty. They have tasty, cheap €5.80/£3.50 meals but no menu. You just ask—in Spanish if necessary—what's cooking (daily 8:00–15:00, no dinner, Cornwalls Parade 7, a few blocks from Casemates Square). **The Clipper** is known for its filling €8.25/£5 pub meals (on Irish Town, at intersection with tiny Irish Place). The **Carpenter's Arms** at the Methodist Church does a cheap €5/£3 lunch special, open to anyone. Their tea and apple pie for €1.60/£1 is a local favorite, particularly at "elevens," as the British say, when hunger pangs strike before lunch (Mon–Fri 9:30–14:00, no smoking, Main Street 297, across from the Convent).

Grocery: A Checkout supermarket is on Main Street, off Cathedral Square, next to Marks & Spencer (Mon–Sat 8:30–20:00, Sun 10:00–15:00, has a take-away window with roast chicken to go). Fruit stands bustle at the Market Place (Mon–Sat 9:00–15:00, outside entry to Casemates Square).

Transportation Connections—Gibraltar

If you're leaving Gibraltar without a car, you must walk five minutes from Gibraltar's border into Spain to reach La Línea, the nearest bus station. The region's main transportation hub is Algeciras, with lots of train and bus connections, and ferries to Tangier and Ceuta. (For Algeciras connections, see "Tarifa," below.) If you're traveling between La Línea and Algeciras, buy tickets on the bus. Otherwise buy tickets inside the station.

La Línea by bus to: Algeciras (2/hr, 45 min), **Tarifa** (9/day, 1 hr), **Málaga** (4/day, 3 hrs), **Granada** (2/day, 5 hrs), **Sevilla** (3/day, 4 hrs), **Jerez** (2/day, 3.25 hrs), **Huelva** (1/day, 6.5 hrs), **Madrid** (2/day, 8 hrs).

TARIFA

Europe's most southerly town is a pleasant alternative to gritty, noisy Algeciras. It's an Arabic-looking town with a lovely beach, an old castle, restaurants swimming in fresh seafood, inexpensive places to sleep, and enough windsurfers to sink a ship. If you're going to Morocco, Tarifa is a far quieter and more liveable homebase than Algeciras.

As I stood on Tarifa's town promenade under the castle, looking out at almost-touchable Morocco across the Straits of Gibraltar, I regretted only that I didn't have this book to steer me clear of Algeciras on earlier trips. Tarifa has no blockbuster sights (and is pretty dead off-season), but it's a town where you just feel good to be on vacation.

Orientation

Tourist Information: The TI is on Paseo Alameda (Mon–Fri 11:00–13:00, 16:00–20:00, Oct–May 11:00–13:00, 17:00–19:00, tel. 95-668-0993).

Arrival in Tarifa: The bus station (really just a ticket office) is at Batalla de Salado 19 (Mon–Fri 7:15–11:00, 14:00–19:00, Sat–Sun 14:00–20:00, tel. 95-668-4038). When you get off the bus, orient yourself by facing the old-town gate. The recommended hotels in the old town are through the gate; the hotels in the newer part of town are a couple of blocks behind you.

Internet Access: Try Pandora, in the heart of the old town, across from Café Central and near the church (cheap prices, long hours).

Ferry to Morocco

Boats to Tangier, Morocco, sail from both Algeciras and Tarifa. Anyone can sail from Algeciras to Tangier, whether solo or with a tour. But currently the boats leaving Tarifa for Tangier are open only to people from countries that are members of the European Union. This may change. Even if it doesn't, I'd still homebase in Tarifa for a trip to Tangier (taking the 30-min bus ride to Algeciras, then the boat to Tangier and back, returning by bus in the evening to Tarifa). Certainly it'd be more convenient to sail directly from Tarifa to Tangier. For the latest on whether non-Europeans can make this crossing, call the Tarifa TI (tel. 95-668-4038) or the Marruecotur travel agency in Tarifa (tel. 95-668-1821 or 95-668-1242). Note that the Spanish refer to Tangier as Tanger, with a guttural "g" (sounding like tahn-hair, said at the back of the throat).

Tours: Marruecotur in Tarifa offers a daytrip that takes you by bus from Tarifa, by fast ferry to Ceuta (a Spanish possession in Morocco), with three-hour (basically shopping) stops in both Tetuan and Tangier (€51, leave Tarifa at 8:00, return by 19:45,

Tarifa

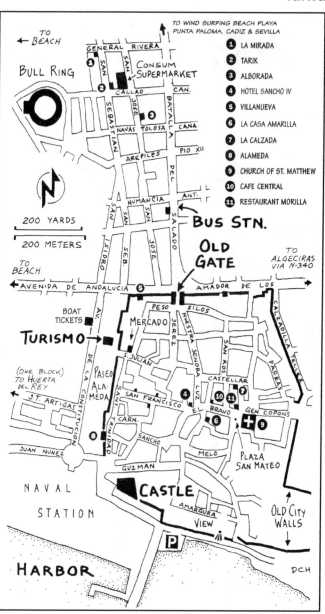

offered daily year-round, guide joins you in Algeciras, includes lunch at Tetuan; 2-day tour option available with overnight in Tangier for €110 for 1 person, €87 apiece for 2 people). Marruecotur's office is across the street from the Tarifa TI (daily 7:40–21:00, also books flights, trains, and some long-distance buses to destinations in Spain and Portugal, Avenida Constitución 5, tel. 95-668-1821 or 95-668-1242, fax 95-668-0256, e-mail: mcotur1 @e-savia.net). **Speedlines Tours**, across from the bus station, also books tours to Tangier (and books flights, trains, car and bike rentals, and so on, Batalla del Salado 10, tel. 95-662-7048, www.speedlines-tours.com).

If and when non-Europeans are allowed to sail directly from Tarifa to Tangier, tours offered from Tarifa will concentrate on Tangier (without Tetuan), and **FRS Maroc** will be another travel agency for you to consider, either for tours or ferry tickets (tel. 95-668-1830, at the Tarifa dock; currently they work only with people from the European Union).

Sights—Tarifa

Castle of Guzman El Bueno—This castle was named after a 13th-century Christian general who gained fame in a sad show of courage while fighting the Moors. Holding Guzman's son hostage, the Moors demanded he surrender the castle or they'd kill the boy. Guzman refused, even throwing his own knife down from the ramparts. It was used on his son's throat. Ultimately, the Moors withdrew to Africa, and Guzman was a hero. *Bueno.* The castle itself is a concrete hulk in a vacant lot, interesting only for the harbor views from the ramparts (€1.20, Tue–Sun 11:00–14:00, 16:00–18:00, closed Mon).

Church of St. Matthew—Tarifa's main church faces its main drag. Most nights it seems life squirts from the church out the front door and into the fun-loving Calle El Bravo. Wander inside (daily 8:45–13:00, 17:30–20:30, English leaflets—unless they're out—are inside on the right).

   1. Find the tiny square (about the size of a piece of copier paper) of **ancient tombstone** in the wall just before the transept on the right side. Probably the most important historic item in town, it proves there was a functioning church here during Visigothic times, before the Moorish conquest. The tombstone reads, in a kind of Latin Spanish, "Flaviano lived as a Christian for 50 years, a little more or less. In death he received forgiveness as a servant of God on March 30, 674. May he rest in peace." If that gets you in the mood to light a candle, switch on an electronic "candle" for a coin.

   2. Step into the transept beyond the candles. The centerpiece of the **altar** is a boy Jesus. By Andalusian tradition he used to be naked, but these days he's clothed with outfits that vary with the

Church calendar. On the left is a fine 17th-century statue of the "Virgin [protector] of the Fishermen."

3. A statue of **St. James the Moorslayer** (missing his sword) is on the right wall of the main central altar. Since the days of the Reconquista, James has been Spain's patron saint.

4. The chapel to the left of the main altar harbors several **statues** that go on parade through town during Holy Week. The **Captive Christ** (with hands bound) goes back to the days when Christians were held captive by Moors.

5. Circling around to the left side you'll find a side door, the **"door of pardons."** For a long time, Tarifa was a dangerous place—on the edge of the Reconquista. To encourage people to live here, the Church offered a huge amount of forgiveness to anyone who lived in Tarifa for a year. One year and one day after moving to Tarifa, they would have the privilege of passing through this special "door of pardons," and a Mass of thanksgiving would be held in that person's honor.

Bullfighting—Tarifa has a third-rate bullring where novices botch fights most Saturdays through the summer. Professional bullfights takes place the first week of September. The ring is a short walk from the town. You'll see posters everywhere.

▲**Whale-Watching**—Daily whale- and dolphin-watching excursions are offered by five companies in Tarifa. For any of the tours, it's wise to reserve one to three days in advance, though same-day bookings are possible. You'll get a multilingual tour and a two-hour trip (usually no WC on board). Sightings occur over 90 percent of the time. Dophins and pilot whales frolic here any time of year, while sperm whales visit May through June and orcas stay July through August. Depending on the wind and weather, boats may leave from Algeciras instead (drivers follow in a convoy, people without cars usually get rides from staff).

The best company is the Swiss nonprofit **FIRMM** (Foundation for Information and Research on Marine Mammals), which gives a 15-minute educational talk prior to departure—and if you don't see any dolphins or whales, you can go on another trip for free (€27 per person, no CC, runs 1–5 trips/day April–Oct, Pedro Cortés 3, next to Café Central—one door inland, also offers courses, details on their Web site, tel. 95-662-7008, fax 95-668-1424, cellular 61-945-9441, www.firmm.de, e-mail: firmm98 @aol.com, SE). Another company is **Whale Watch España**, across from the TI (€24 per person, CC, runs 1–4/day Jan–Oct, Avenida de la Constitución, tel. 63-947-6544, www .whalewatchtarifa.com, SE).

▲**Windsurfing**—**Playa Punta Paloma** is a vast, sandy beach about eight kilometers northwest of town. On windy summer days the sea is littered with sprinting windsurfers while the beach holds a couple hundred vans and fun-mobiles from northern Europe.

Under mountain ridges lined with modern energy-generating windmills, it's a fascinating scene. Drive down the sandy road and stroll along the beach. You'll find a cabana-type hamlet with rental gear, beachwear shops, a bar, and a hip, healthy restaurant with great lunch salads.

For drivers, it's a cinch to reach. Without a car, you're in luck July through August, when Speedlines Tours runs a cheap bus that does a circuit of nearby campgrounds, all on the waterfront (€0.60, every 90 min, the last stop—Dunas—is best; Speedlines Tours, across from the bus station, is at Batalla del Salado 10, tel. 95-662-7048).

Sleeping in Tarifa
(€1.10 = about $1, country code: 34, zip code: 11380)
Sleep Code: **S** = Single, **D** = Double/Twin, **T** = Triple, **Q** = Quad, **b** = bathroom, **s** = shower only, **CC** = Credit Cards accepted, **no CC** = Credit Cards not accepted, **SE** = Speaks English, **NSE** = No English spoken.

Room rates vary with the season (3 tiers vary but are, roughly: high—mid-June–Sept; medium—spring and fall; and low—winter). Breakfast is usually extra.

Sleeping Outside the City Wall
These hotels are right off the main drag—Batalla del Salado— with easy parking, in the modern, plain part of town. To get oriented if arriving by bus, face the old-town gate. These hotels are several blocks behind you.

Hotel La Mirada is shiny new, with 25 modern rooms, some of which come with sea views at no extra cost (Sb-€33, €39, or €45, Db-€45, €48, or €57, extra bed-€9, breakfast-€3.30, extra for American-type breakfast, includes tax, CC, elevator, great views from large terrace, attached restaurant, Calle San Sebastián 41, tel. 95-668-4427, fax 95-668-1162, www.hotel-lamirada.com, some English spoken). It's two blocks off the main drag and about five blocks away from the old town.

Hostal Alborada is a squeaky-clean place with an attractive courtyard. It's a couple of blocks closer to the old town on a plain street (Sb-€18, €24, or €30, Db-€27, €33, or €42, Tb-€36, €45, or €54, get your price and then show this book for a 10 percent discount any time of year *except* high season—mid-June–Sept, tax extra, CC, laundry and Internet services, Calle San José 52, tel. 95-668-1140, fax 95-668-1935, www.hotelalborada.com, fun-loving Rafael Mesa Rodriguez and his wife Juaquina speak only a little English).

The 22-room motel-style **Hostal Tarik** is clean but noisy, a bit tattered, and short on windows on the ground floor. Ask for a room upstairs (Db-€24, €36, or €48, Tb-€36, €54, or

€72, tax extra, CC, Calle San Sebastián 32, tel. 95-668-0648, some English spoken). Surrounded by warehouses, it's one block toward the town center from Hotel La Mirada.

Sleeping On or Inside the City Wall

Hostal Villanueva is your best budget bet. It's simple, clean, and friendly, and includes a great terrace overlooking the old town. It's on a busy street, and the quiet rooms in the back come with the best views (Sb-€15–18, Db-€33–51, includes tax, breakfast-€1.80, CC, attached restaurant, Avenida de Andalucía 11, just west of the old-town gate, with access outside the wall, tel. 95-668-4149, NSE).

Hostal La Calzada has eight airy, well-appointed rooms right in the noisy-at-night, old-town thick of things (Db-€42, €48, or €54, Tb-€48, €54, and €60, includes tax, closed Oct–March, CC, Calle Justino Pertinez 3, veer left and down from the old-town gate, tel. 95-668-0366 or 95-668-1492, NSE).

Hostal Alameda glistens with pristine marble floors and pastels. It overlooks a square where the local children play (Db-€39, €45, or €57, Tb-€45, €57, or €69, breakfast–€2.70, includes tax, CC, Paseo Alameda 4, tel. & fax 95-668-1181, some English spoken). Its 11 bright rooms are above its restaurant (great gazpacho).

La Casa Amarilla (the Yellow House) offers posh apartments with modern décor and miniature kitchens (Db-€37–55, Tb-€49–73, Qb-€60–91, tax extra, 20 percent deposit requested, CC, across street from Café Central, Calle Sancho IV El Bravo 9, entrance on alley, tel. 95-668-1993, fax 95-668-0590, www.tarifa.net/lacasaamarilla, e-mail: lacasaamarilla@lite.eunet.es).

Hotel Sancho IV has 12 comfortable, spacious, well-maintained rooms. The top-floor suite is grand, with private elevator access, a Jacuzzi, great views, and a big terrace—worth the splurge (Sb-€39, €57, or €66, Db-€48, €66, or €84, top-floor Db suite-€96, €132, or €168, tax extra, no breakfast, CC, double-paned windows, elevator, restaurant on ground floor, a block from Café Central, Sancho IV Bravo 18, tel. 95-662-7083, fax 95-662-7055, e-mail: hotelsancho4@terra.com).

Eating in Tarifa

You'll find good tapas throughout the old town. **Café Central** is the happening place nearly any time of day. The tapas are priced at €0.90 at the bar (€1.10 if you sit at a table); go to the bar and point. They also offer great, ingenious €4.80 salads (study the menu) and impressively therapeutic, healthy fruit drinks (off Plaza San Mateo, near church, tel. 95-668-0560). Across the street, the popular **El Barrilito** makes cheap, interesting sandwiches with a tapa option and indoor/outdoor seating. Next door, the tiny **La Calzada Panaderia** makes sandwiches-to-go and also has a few outdoor tables. A few doors down, in front of the church,

Restaurant Morilla serves good local-style food and paella on the town's prime piece of people-watching real estate (long hours, every day, Calle Sancho IV El Bravo, tel. 95-668-1757).

From Café Central follow the cars 100 meters to the first corner on the left to reach the simple, untouristy **Bar El Frances** for its fine tapas (generally €0.80), especially snails (*caracoles*, June–mid-July only, bar has no sign, it's at #21A). The nearby **Café Bar los Melli** is family-friendly and serves a good chorizo sandwich (from Bar El Frances, cross parking lot and take Calle del Legionario Rios Moya up 1 block). **Bar El Pasillo**, next to Melli, has tapas.

From Melli you can circle around toward the church past some very gritty and colorful tapas bars. Just to the seaside of the church you'll see the mysterious **Casino Tarifeño**. This is an old-boys' social club "for members only," but it offers a big, musty Andalusian welcome to visiting tourists, including women. Wander through. There's a low-key bar with tapas, a TV room, a card room, and a lounge.

From the town center, walk the narrow Calle San Francisco to survey a number of good restaurants, such as the classy, quiet **Guzman El Bueno** (indoor seating and outdoor seating in a courtyard, CC), the cheap and popular **Pizzeria La Capricciosa** (indoor seating only, also does take-out), and the only place offering outdoor seating on the street, **El Rincon de Juan** (indoor seating as well, CC).

The street Huerta del Rey is a family scene at night. Stop by the produce shop for fruit and veggies, the *heladeria* for ice cream, or **El Tuti** for a drink (outside the old city walls, 2 blocks west; a clothing market is held here Tue 9:00–14:00).

Confiteria la Tarifeña serves super pastries and flan (at the top of Calle Nuestra Sra. de la Luz, near the main old-town gate).

Picnics: Try the *mercado municipal* (Mon–Sat 8:00–14:00, closed Sun, in old town, inside gate nearest TI), any grocery, or the **Consum supermarket** (Mon–Sat 9:00–21:00, closed Sun, simple cafeteria, at Callao and San José, near the hotels in the new town).

Transportation Connections—Tarifa
By bus to: La Línea/Gibraltar (7/day, 1 hr, first departure at 9:40, last return at 20:00), **Algeciras** (12/day, 30 min, first departure from Tarifa weekdays at 6:30, on Sat 8:00, on Sun 10:00; return from Algeciras as late as 22:15), **Jerez** (3/day, 2 hrs), **Sevilla** (4/day, 3 hrs), **Huelva** (1/day, 5 hrs), and **Málaga** (2/day, 3.5 hrs). Bus info: tel. 95-668-4038.

Transportation Connections—Algeciras
Algeciras is only worth leaving. It's useful to the traveler mainly

as a transportation hub, offering ferries to Tangier (see next chapter) and trains and buses to destinations in southern and central Spain. The **TI** is on Juan de la Cierva, a block inland from the port, and on the same street as the train station and the Comes bus station which runs buses to Tarifa (Mon–Fri 9:00–14:00, tel. 95-657-2636).

Trains: The train station is four blocks inland on the far side of Hotel Octavio (up Juan de la Cierva, lockers on platform for €3—buy token at ticket window, tel. 95-663-0202). If arriving by train, head down Juan de la Cierva toward the sea for the TI and port.

By train to: Madrid (2/day, 6 hrs during day, 11 hrs overnight), **Ronda** (4/day, 2 hrs), **Granada** (3/day, 4.5 hrs), **Sevilla** (3/day, 5 hrs, transfer in Bobadilla), **Córdoba** (4/day, 4.5–5 hrs; 2 direct, 2 with transfers in Bobadilla), **Málaga** (3/day, 4 hrs, transfer in Bobadilla). With the exception of the route to Madrid, these are particularly scenic trips; the best is the mountainous journey to Málaga via Bobadilla.

Buses: Algeciras has three bus stations.

The **Comes bus station** (half-block away from train station, next to Hotel Octavio, tel. 95-665-3456) runs buses to **La Línea** (2/hr, 45 min, from 7:00–21:30), **Tarifa** (11/day, 7/day on Sun), **Sevilla** (5/day, 3.5 hrs), **Jerez** (3/day, 2.5 hrs), **Huelva** (1/day, 6 hrs), and **Madrid** (4/day, 8 hrs).

The **Portillo bus station** (on waterfront, kitty-corner from the port, Calle Virgen Carmen, next door to Restaurant Portillo, tel. 95-665-4304) offers frequent, direct buses to **Málaga** (7/day, 2 hrs) and **Granada** (4/day, 2 hrs).

The **Linesur bus station** (also on waterfront, 1 long block past Portillo station, Calle Virgen Carmen 31, tel. 95-666-7649) offers the most frequent direct buses to **Sevilla** (8/day, 3.25 hrs) and **Jerez** (13/day, 1.25 hrs).

Route Tips for Drivers

Tarifa to Gibraltar (45 min): It's a short drive, passing a silvery-white forest of windmills, from peaceful Tarifa past Algeciras to La Línea (the Spanish town bordering Gibraltar). Passing Algeciras, continue in the direction of Estepona. At San Roque take the La Línea-Gibraltar exit.

Gibraltar to Nerja (210 km): Barring traffic problems, the trip along the Costa del Sol is smooth and easy by car—much of it on new highways. Just follow the coastal highway east. After Málaga follow signs to Almería and Motril.

Nerja to Granada (130 km, 90 min, 100 views): Drive along the coast to Salobreña, catching N323 north for about 65 kilometers to Granada. While scenic side trips may beckon, don't arrive late in Granada without a firm reservation.

MOROCCO

Go to Africa. As you step off the boat you realize that the crossing (1–2.5 hrs, depending on the port you choose) has taken you farther culturally than did the trip from the United States to Iberia. Morocco needs no museums; its sights are living in the streets. Offered daily and year-round, the one-day excursions from Algeciras and Gibraltar (and Tarifa, once this port is opened to non-Europeans) are well-organized and reliable. Given that tours from Spain (rather than pricier Gibraltar) are virtually the cost of the boat passage alone, the tour package is a good value for those who can spare only a day for Morocco. For an extended tour of Morocco, see below.

Morocco in a Day?

There are many ways to experience Morocco, and a day in Tangier is probably the worst. But all you need is a passport (no visa or shots required), and if all you have is a day, this is a real and worthwhile adventure. Tangier is the Tijuana of Morocco, and everyone there seems to be expecting you.

You can use ATM machines in Tangier to get Moroccan dirhams, but for a short one-day trip, there's no need to change money. Everyone you meet will be happy to take your euros, dollars, or pounds. For more tips on Morocco, see "Helpful Hints," below.

Whether on tour or on your own, carefully confirm the time your return boat departs from Tangier. The time difference between the countries can be up to two hours. (I'd keep my watch on Spanish time and get my departure time clear in Spanish time.) Plan on spending one hour of your day in lines (passport control, etc.).

On Your Own: Just buy a ferry ticket at the port or from a local travel agency. Both ports, Algeciras and Gibraltar, have fine

Morocco

ferry terminals (for a look at Gibraltar's, see www.gibraltar.gi).
I'd go right to the port to buy a ticket, especially in Algeciras,
which is littered with divey-looking travel agencies. In Algeciras,
go to the very farthest building on the port, which is labeled in
large letters: Estación Maritima Terminal de Pasajeros (lockers
available here and at train station; easy parking at port). Inside
this main port building, directly behind the helpful little info
kiosk (daily 6:45–21:45, tel. 95-658-5463, SE), are the official
offices of the boat companies. Buy your ticket here. There are 8
to 12 crossings daily to Tangier. If the Tarifa port opens up to
non-Europeans, crossing there will be the best option for most
(more pleasant than Algeciras, cheaper than Gibraltar).

By Tour: You rarely need to book a tour more than a day in
advance, even during peak season. Tours generally cost about
€52/$45 from Spain or £40/$65 from Gibraltar. This includes a
round-trip crossing and a guide who meets you at a pre-arranged
point and hustles you through the hustlers and onto your bus.
Excursions vary, but usually offer a city tour, possibly a trip to the
desolate Atlantic Coast for some rugged African scenery and the
famous ride-a-camel stop, a walk through the medina (old town)
with a too-thorough look at a sales-starved carpet shop, and lunch

in a palatial Moroccan setting with live music.

Sound cheesy? It is. But no amount of packaging can gloss over how exotic and different this culture really is. This kind of cultural voyeurism is almost embarrassing, but it's nonstop action and more memorable than another day in Spain. The shopping is—Moroccan. Bargain hard!

The daytrip is so tightly organized you'll have hardly any time alone

Arabic Numerals

0	•	SIFR
1	١	WAAHID
2	٢	ITNEEN
3	٣	TALAATA
4	٤	ARBA´A
5	٥	KHAMSA
6	٦	SITTA
7	٧	SAB´A
8	٨	TAMANYA
9	٩	TIS´A
10	١٠	´ASHRA

in Tangier. For many people, that's just fine. Some, however, spend a night there and return the next day. If you're interested, ask travel agencies about the two-day tour (sample cost: one-day tour—€52, two-day tour including single room at hotel—€110, double room—€88 apiece). The first day of a two-day tour is the same as the one-day tour; you just go to a fancy hotel (with dinner) rather than to the afternoon boat and catch the same boat 24 unstructured hours later.

Tour tips: If you get a voucher when you pay for your tour at a travel agency, exchange it at the boat office to get your ticket prior to boarding. Confirm where you will meet the guide. You may need to relinquish your passport for the day; you will get it back. Note that there are variations on the tour; for instance, Marruecotur in Tarifa offers a tour that includes a crossing from Ceuta and a stop in Tetuan (for details, see "Tarifa" in Costa del Sol chapter).

Travel Agencies Offering Tours

There are dozens, particularly in Algeciras. Here are several.

In Algeciras: Marruecotur is at the port (€52 for one-day tour, Estación Maritima C-6, tel. 95-665-6185, e-mail: mcotur @e-savia.net).

In Tarifa: Marruecotur is across from the TI (€52, daily 7:40–21:00, Avenida Constitución 5, tel. 95-668-1821 or 95-668-1242, fax 95-668-0256, e-mail: mcotur1@e-savia.net). Another is **Speedlines Tours**, across from Tarifa's bus station (Batalla del Salado 10, tel. 95-662-7048, www.speedlines-tours.com).

In Gibraltar: Consider Thomas Cook Exchange Travel (£45 for one-day tour, 241 Main Street, tel. 76151) and Parodytur (£40, Cathedral Square, tel. 76070). Agencies are open Monday through Friday from 9:30 to 18:00.

Ferries to Morocco

Ferries have mediocre cafeteria bars, plenty of WCs, stuffy indoor chairs, and grand views. Boats are most crowded in August, when the Costa del Sol groups come en masse. Only a few crossings a year are canceled because of storms (mostly in winter.

The following information is for people going to Tangier on their own. If you're taking a tour, you wouldn't need to know these details.

From Algeciras to: Tangier (12/day in summer, 8/day in winter, 2.5 hrs via slow boat—no faster option at this time, €22.50 one-way, €46 round-trip; to bring a car: €70 one-way, €140 round-trip), **Ceuta** (hrly in summer, 7 ferries/day in winter, 35 min via Fast Ferry, €20.50 one-way, €37 round-trip; to bring a car: €60 one-way, €108 round-trip). Ceuta, an uninteresting Spanish possession in North Africa, is the best car-entry point (for info on the crossing, see "Extended Tour of Morocco," below) but is not for those relying on public transport.

From Tarifa to Tangier: 1/day, 1 hr (currently this crossing is open only to residents of the European Union).

From Gibraltar to Tangier: 2/day, 1 hr (£18 one-way, £30 round-trip, the morning boat returns from Tangier later the same day; the afternoon sailing forces an overnight in Tangier, returning the next day).

TANGIER

Tangier is split into two. The new town has the TI and fancy hotels. The medina (old town) has the markets, the Kasbah (with its palace), cheap hotels, decrepit homes, and 2,000 wanna-be guides. The twisty, hilly streets of the old town are caged within a wall accessible by keyhole gates. The big square, Grand Socco, is the link between the old and new parts of town.

Orientation (area code: 39)

Many assume they'll be lost in Tangier—because it's in Africa. This makes no sense. The town is laid out very simply. From the boat dock you'll see the old town—circled by its medieval wall—on the right (behind Hotel Continental). The new town sprawls past the industrial port zone to the left. Nothing mentioned in this chapter is more than a 15-minute walk from the port. Petit Taxis are a godsend for the hot and tired tourist. Use them generously and go ahead and just pay double the meter for any ride.

Tourist Information: Get a free map and advice at the TI (Mon–Sat 8:30–12:00, 14:30–18:30, Boulevard Pasteur 29, in newer section of town, tel. 94-80-50, fax 94-86-61).

Exchange rate: 12 dirhams = about $1.

Telephone: To call Tangier from Spain, dial 00 (international access code), 212 (Morocco's country code), 39 (Tangier's city code), then the local six-digit number.

Arrival in Tangier

If you're taking a tour, follow the leader.

Independent travelers will take a five-minute walk from the boat, through customs, and out of the port. Consider hiring a guide (see "Guides," below). Taxis at the port are more expensive. Ask the cost before taking one. The big yellow Port de Tanger gateway defines the end of the port area and the start of the city. Leave mental bread crumbs so you can find your way back to your boat. It will just stay put all day. Just outside the port gate on the busy traffic circle you'll find plenty of fair, metered Petit Taxis along with a line of decent fish restaurants, the boulevard arcing along the beach into the new town, and stairs leading up into the old town and the market (on the right).

Planning Your Time

Catch a Petit Taxi to the TI. From there you can walk to the Grand Socco and market. Or, to minimize uphill walking, catch a taxi to the Place de la Kasbah at the top of the old town and work your way downhill to the port.

In the old town, start at the Museum of the Kasbah, then wander through the fortress (Dar el-Makhzem) and the Old American Legation Museum. Then shop through the Petit Socco. Walk out of the old town into the noisy Grand Socco. From there, catch a taxi to the beach (Place el Cano) and sight-see along the beach and then along Avenue d'Espagne back to the port.

Guides

If you're on your own, you'll be fighting off "guides" all day. In order to have your own translator and a shield from less scrupulous touts that hit up tourists constantly throughout the old town, I recommend hiring a guide. Stress your interest in the people and culture rather than shopping. Guides, hoping to get a huge commission from your purchases, can cleverly turn your Tangier day into a Marco Polo equivalent of the Shopping Channel.

I've had good luck with the private guides who meet the boat. These hardworking, English-speaking, and licensed guides offer their services for the day for €18. Aziz Begdouri is good ($12 or €18 for 5 hrs, easier to reach him from Spain on his Spanish cellular, tel. 60-789-7967, than his Moroccan cellular, tel. 00-212-6163-9332, e-mail: aziztour@hotmail.com). The TI also has official guides (half-day for $12, €18, or 150 dirhams, tel. 94-80-50, or call guides' association directly at tel. 31372).

If you don't want a guide, ask directions of people who can't

Tangier

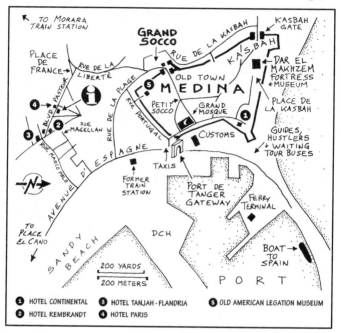

① HOTEL CONTINENTAL **③** HOTEL TANJAH - FLANDRIA **⑤** OLD AMERICAN LEGATION MUSEUM
② HOTEL REMBRANDT **④** HOTEL PARIS

leave what they're doing (such as the only clerk in a shop) or of women who aren't near men. Ask "Kasbah?" or wherever you want to go, and you'll get pointed in the right direction. Fewer hustlers are in the new (but less interesting) part of town.

Sights—Tangier

Kasbah—This is the fortress atop old Tangier. You'll find a history museum in a former palace on Place de la Kasbah (10 dirhams, Wed–Mon 9:00–12:30, 15:00–17:00, closed Tue) and a colorful gauntlet of Kodak moments waiting to ambush tour groups as they wander through: snake charmers, squawky dance troupes, and colorful water vendors. Before descending out of the Kasbah, don't miss the ocean viewpoint, the Mosque de la Kasbah, and Dar el-Makhzen, the fortress of the pasha of Tangier.
The *Medina* and Petit Socco—From the Kasbah, a maze of winding lanes and tiny alleys weave through the old-town market area. Petit Socco, a little square in the old town, is lined with tea shops. A casual first-time visitor cannot stay oriented. I just wander, knowing that if I keep going downhill, I'll eventually pop out at the port; if I veer to the right while going downhill, I'll

come to a gate leading into the modern town probably via
the Grand Socco, the big and noisy market square. The market
is filthy and reportedly dangerous after dark. Plain-clothed
tourist police are stationed throughout, making sure you are
safe as you wander.

Tangier American Legation Museum—Morocco was the
first country to recognize the United States as an independent
country. This building, given to the United States by the sultan
of Morocco, became the American government's first foreign
possession. It served as our embassy or consulate from 1821 to
1956, is still owned by the United States, and is the only U.S.
national historic landmark overseas. Today this 19th-century
mansion is a strangely peaceful oasis within Tangier's intense
old town. It offers a warm welcome, lots of interesting paintings,
and a reminder of how long the United States and Morocco
have had good relations (free, donations accepted, Mon–Fri
10:00–13:00, 15:00–17:00, Rue America 8, tel. 93-53-17).

Grand Socco—This big square is a transportation hub. From
here, a gate leads into the old-town market; Rue de la Kasbah
leads uphill along the old wall to Port de la Kasbah (a gate leading
into the Kasbah); Rue de la Liberte leads to Place de France and
Boulevard Pasteur (TI and recommended hotels); and Rue de la
Plage leads to the train station, the port, and the beach.

Tangier Beach—This fine, white-sand crescent beach, stretching eastward from the port, is lined by fun eateries and packed
with locals doing what people around the world do at the beach—
with a few variations: You'll see lazy camels and people, young
and old, covered in hot sand to combat rheumatism.

Sleeping in Tangier
(12 dirhams = about $1, country code: 212, area code: 39)
Sleep Code: **S** = Single, **D** = Double/Twin, **T** = Triple, **Q** = Quad,
b = bathroom, **s** = shower only, **CC** = Credit Cards accepted,
no CC = Credit Cards not accepted, **SE** = Speaks English, **NSE** =
No English.

These hotels are centrally located, near the TI and American
Express (Boulevard Pasteur 54), and within walking distance of
the market. The first two are four-star hotels. To reserve from
Europe, dial 00 (Europe's international access code), 212 (Morocco's country code), 39 (Tangier's city code), then the local
number. July through mid-September is high season, when
rooms may be a bit more expensive and a reservation is wise.

Hotel Rembrandt, with a restaurant, bar, and swimming
pool surrounded by a great grassy garden, has 75 clean, comfortable rooms, some with views (Sb-400 dirhams, Db-500 dirhams,
breakfast-52 dirhams, CC, elevator, Boulevard Pasteur, tel. 93-
78-70 or 33-33-14, fax 93-04-43, SE). Across the street, **Hotel**

Tanjah-Flandria is more formal, stuffy, and comfortable but a lesser value (Sb-425 dirhams, Db-530 dirhams, breakfast-65 dirhams, CC, restaurant, elevator, air con, rooftop terrace, small pool, Boulevard Pasteur, tel. 93-32-79, fax 93-43-47, SE).

Hotel Continental, the Humphrey Bogart option, is a grand old place sprawling along the old town. It overlooks the port, with lavish, evocative public spaces, a chandeliered breakfast room, and 70 spacious bedrooms with rough hardwood floors. Jimmy, who runs the place with a Moroccan flair, says he offers everything but Viagra. When I said, "I'm from Seattle," he said, "206." Test him. He knows your area code (Db-360 dirhams, includes tax and breakfast, Dar Baroud 36, tel. 93-10-24, fax 93-11-43, e-mail: hcontinental@iam.net.ma, SE).

Hotel Paris, across from the TI, is noisy, dingy, and friendly. Ask for a room in the back—and a mop. (Sb-150–210 dirhams, Db-250–310 dirhams, price varies according to size, no CC, Boulevard Pasteur 42, tel. 93-18-77; the helpful and informative manager, Abdullatif, SE.)

Extended Tour of Morocco

Morocco gets much better as you go deeper into the interior. The country is incredibly rich in cultural thrills—but you'll pay a price in hassles and headaches. It's a package deal, and if adventure's your business, it's a great option.

To get a fair look at Morocco, you must get past the hustlers and con artists of the north coast (Tangier, Tétouan). It takes a minimum of four or five days to make a worthwhile visit—ideally seven or eight. Plan at least two nights in either Fès or Marrakech. A trip over the Atlas Mountains gives you an exciting look at Saharan Morocco. If you need a vacation from your vacation, check into one of the idyllic Atlantic beach resorts on the south coast. Above all, get past the northern day-trip-from-Spain, take-a-snapshot-on-a-camel fringe. Oops, that's us. Oh, well.

If you're relying on public transportation for your extended tour, sail to Tangier, blast your way through customs, listen to no hustler who tells you there's no way out until tomorrow, and hop into a Petit Taxi for the Morora train station four kilometers away (24 dirhams, or $2). From there, set your sights on Rabat, a dignified, European-type town with fewer hustlers, and make it your get-acquainted stop in Morocco. Trains go farther south from Rabat.

If you're driving a car, sail from Algeciras to Ceuta, a Spanish possession. Crossing the border is a bit unnerving, since you'll be jumped through several bureaucratic hoops. You'll go through customs at both borders, buy Moroccan insurance for your car (cheap and easy), and feel at the mercy of a bristly bunch of shady-looking people you'd rather not be at the mercy of. Don't pay anyone on the Spanish side. Consider tipping a guy on the Morrocan

side if you feel he'll shepherd you through. Relax and let him
grease those customs wheels. He's worth it. As soon as possible,
hit the road and drive to Chefchaouen, the best first stop for
those with their own wheels.

Orientation (Mental)

Thrills: Morocco is culture shock—both bad and good. It makes
Spain and Portugal look meek and mild. You'll encounter oppres-
sive friendliness, the Arabic language, squiggly writing, the Islamic
faith, and ancient cities. It is a photographer's delight, very cheap,
and comes with plenty of hotels, surprisingly easy transportation,
and a variety of terrain, from Swiss-like mountain resorts to
fairy-tale mud-brick oasis towns to luxuriously natural beaches
to bustling desert markets.

Spills: Many travelers are overwhelmed by its intensity,
poverty, aggressive beggars, brutal heat, and slick con men.
Most of the English-speaking Moroccans that the tourist meets
are hustlers. Most visitors have some intestinal problems. Most
women are harassed on the streets by horny but generally harm-
less men. Things don't work smoothly. In fact, compared to
Morocco, Spain resembles Sweden for efficiency. People don't
see the world through the same filters we do, and good parents
name their sons Saddam. This is Islam.

Leave busy itineraries and split-second timing in Europe.
Morocco must be taken on its own terms. In Morocco things
go smoothly only "*Inshallah*"—if God so wills.

Helpful Hints

Friday: Friday is the Muslim day of rest, when most of the country (except Tangier) closes down.

Money: Change money only at banks, or even easier, at
ATMs (available at most major banks), all of which have uniform
rates. The black market is dangerous. Change only what you
need and keep the bank receipt to reconvert if necessary. Don't
leave the country with Moroccan money. (If you do, the Bank
of Morocco branch in Algeciras may buy it back from you.)

Health: Morocco is much more hazardous to your health
than Spain or Portugal. Eat in clean—not cheap—places. Peel
fruit, eat only cooked vegetables, and drink reliably bottled water
(Sidi Harazem or Sidi Ali). When you do get diarrhea, and you
should plan on it, adjust your diet (small and bland meals, no
milk or grease) or fast for a day but make sure you replenish lost
fluids. Relax; most diarrhea is not serious, just an adjustment that
will run its course.

Information: For an extended trip, bring travel information
from home or Spain. The guides published by Lonely Planet,
Rough Guide, and Let's Go (*Let's Go: Spain and Portugal* includes

Morocco) are good. The green *Michelin Morocco* guidebook is worthwhile (if you read French). Buy the best map you can find locally—names are always changing, and it's helpful to have towns, roads, and place-names written in Arabic.

Language: The Arabic squiggle-script, its many difficult sounds, and the fact that French is Morocco's second language make communication tricky for English-speaking travelers. A little French goes a long way, but learn a few words in Arabic. Have your first local friend help you pronounce *min fadlik* ("please"; meen FAD-leek), *shókran* ("thank you"; SHOW-kron), *ismahli* ("excuse me"; ees-MAY-lee), *yeh* ("yes"; EE-yuh), *lah* ("no"; lah), and *maa salama* ("good-bye"; mah sah-LEM-ah). In markets, I sing "la la la la la" to my opponents. *Lah shókran* means, "No, thank you." Listen carefully and write new words phonetically. Bring an Arabic phrase book. Make a point of learning the local number symbols; they are not like ours (which we call "Arabic").

Keeping your bearings: Navigate the labyrinthine medinas (old towns) by altitude, gates, and famous mosques or buildings. Write down what gate you came in so you can enjoy being lost—temporarily. *Souk* is Arabic for a particular market (such as leather, yarn, or metalwork).

Hustlers: While Moroccans are some of Africa's wealthiest people, you are still incredibly rich to them. This imbalance causes predictable problems. Wear your money belt. Assume con artists are more clever than you. Haggle when appropriate (prices sky-rocket for tourists). You'll attract hustlers like flies at every famous tourist sight. They'll lie to you, get you lost, blackmail you, and pester the heck out of you. Never leave your car or baggage where you can't get back to it without your "guide." Anything you buy in their company gets them a 20 percent commission. Normally locals, shopkeepers, and police will come to your rescue when the hustlers' heat becomes unbearable. I usually hire a guide, since it's helpful to have a translator, and once you're "taken," the rest seem to leave you alone.

Marijuana: In Morocco marijuana (*kif*) is as illegal as it is popular, as many Westerners in local jails would love to remind you. Some dealers who sell it cheap make their profit after you get arrested. Cars and buses are stopped and checked by police routinely throughout Morocco—especially in the north and in the Chefchaouen region, which is Morocco's *kif* capital.

Getting around Morocco: Moroccan trains are quite good. Second class is cheap and comfortable. Buses connect all smaller towns quite well. By car, Morocco is easy, but drive defensively and never rely on the oncoming driver's skill. Night driving is dangerous. Pay a guard to watch your car overnight.

Sights—Moroccan Towns

▲▲**Chefchaouen**—Just two hours by bus or car from Tétouan, this is the first pleasant town beyond the Tijuana-type north coast. Monday and Thursday are colorful market days. Stay in the classy old Hotel Chaouen on Plaza el-Makhzen. This former Spanish parador faces the old town and offers fine meals and a refuge from hustlers. Wander deep into the whitewashed old town from here.

▲▲**Rabat**—Morocco's capital and most European city, Rabat is the most comfortable and least stressful place to start your North African trip. You'll find a colorful market (in the old neighboring town of Salé), bits of Islamic architecture (Mausoleum of Mohammed V), the king's palace, mellow hustlers, and fine hotels.

▲▲▲**Fès**—More than just a funny hat that tipsy Shriners wear, Fès is Morocco's religious and artistic center, bustling with craftsmen, pilgrims, shoppers, and shops. Like most large Moroccan cities, it has a distinct new town from the French colonial period and an exotic—and stressful—old Arabic town, where you'll find the market. The Fès marketplace is Morocco's best.

▲▲▲**Marrakech**—Morocco's gateway to the south, this market city is a constant folk festival bustling with djellaba-clad Berber tribespeople and a colorful center where the desert, mountain, and coastal regions merge. The new city has the train station, and the main boulevard (Mohammed V) is lined with banks, airline offices, a post office, a tourist office, and comfortable hotels. The old city features the mazelike market and the huge Djemaa el-Fna, a square seething with people—a 43-ring Moroccan circus.

▲▲▲**Over the Atlas Mountains**—Extend your Moroccan trip several days by heading south over the Atlas Mountains. Take a bus from Marrakech to Ouarzazate (short stop) and then to Tinerhir (great oasis town, comfy hotel, overnight stop). The next day go to Er Rachidia and take the overnight bus to Fès.

By car, drive from Fès south, staying in the small mountain town of Ifrane, and then continue deep into the desert country past Er Rachidia and on to Rissani (market days: Sun, Tue, and Thu). Explore nearby mud-brick towns still living in the Middle Ages. Hire a guide to drive you past where the road stops and head cross-country to an oasis village (Merzouga) where you can climb a sand dune and watch the sun rise over the vastness of Africa. Only a sea of sand separates you from Timbuktu.

Transportation Connections—Morocco

In Tangier, all train traffic comes and goes from the suburban Morora train station, four kilometers from the city center and a short Petit Taxi ride away (24 dirhams, $2). Upon your return, take a taxi or catch the bus, which meets every train arrival and takes passengers all the way to the port for three dirhams. The bus also goes from downtown one hour before each departure but is not worth the trouble.

From Tangier by train to: Rabat (4/day, 6 hrs), **Casablanca** (5/day, 6 hrs), **Marrakech** (5/day, 10 hrs), **Fès** (2/day, 6 hrs), **Ceuta** and **Tétouan** (hrly buses, 1 hr).

From Fès to: Casablanca (8/day, 5 hrs), **Marrakech** (4/day, 9 hrs), **Rabat** (7/day, 4 hrs), **Meknes** (10/day, 1 hr), **Tangier** (5/day, 5 hrs).

From Rabat to: Casablanca (12/day, 90 min), **Fès** (6 buses/day, 5.5 hrs), **Tétouan** (2 buses/day, 4 hrs).

From Casablanca to: Marrakech (6/day, 5 hrs).

From Marrakech to: Meknes (4/day, 10 hrs), **Ouarzazate** (4 buses/day, 4 hrs).

By Plane: Flights within Morocco are convenient and cheap (around $80 to Casablanca).

LISBON

Lisbon is a ramshackle but charming mix of now and then. Old wooden trolleys shiver up and down its hills, bird-stained statues mark grand squares, taxis rattle and screech through cobbled lanes, and well-worn people sip coffee in Art Nouveau cafés.

Lisbon, like Portugal in general, is underrated. The country seems somewhere just beyond Europe. The pace of life is noticeably slower than in Spain. Roads are rutted. Prices are cheaper. While the unification of Europe is bringing sweeping changes, the traditional economy is based on fishing, cork, wine, and textiles. Be sure to balance your look at Iberia with enough Portugal.

While Lisbon's history goes back to the Romans and Moors, its glory days were the 15th and 16th centuries, when explorers such as Vasco da Gama opened new trade routes around Africa to India, making Lisbon one of Europe's richest cities. (These days, in the wake of the 500th anniversary of his 1498 voyage, da Gama has a higher profile.) Portugal's "Age of Discovery" fueled an economic boom, which fueled the flamboyant art boom called the Manueline period—named after King Manuel I (ruled 1495–1521). In the early 18th century, the gold and diamonds of Brazil, one of Portugal's colonies, made Lisbon even wealthier.

Then, on All Saints' Day in 1755, while most of the population was in church, the city was hit by a tremendous earthquake. Candles quivered as far away as Ireland. Lisbon was dead center. Two-thirds of the city was leveled. Fires started by the many church candles raged through the city, and a huge tidal wave blasted the waterfront. Of Lisbon's 270,000 people, 30,000 were killed.

Under the energetic and eventually dictatorial leadership of Prime Minister Marques de Pombal—who had the new city planned within a month of the quake—Lisbon was rebuilt in a

Lisbon

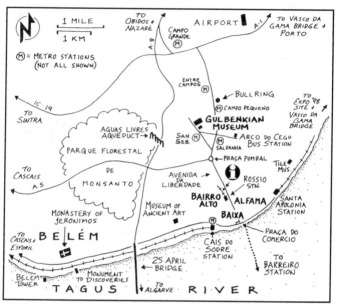

progressive grid plan, with broad boulevards and square squares. Remnants of pre-earthquake Lisbon charm survive in Belém, the Alfama, and the Baírro Alto district.

The heritage of Portugal's Age of Discovery was a vast colonial empire. Except for Macao and the few islands off the Atlantic coast, the last bits of the empire disappeared with the 1974 revolution, which delivered Portugal from the right-wing Salazar dictatorship. Emigrants from former colonies such as Mozambique and Angola have added diversity and flavor to the city, making it more likely that you'll hear African music than Portuguese fado these days.

But Lisbon's heritage survives. The city seems better organized, cleaner, and more prosperous and people-friendly than ever. With its elegant outdoor cafés, exciting art, entertaining museums, a hill-capping castle, a salty sailors' quarter, and the boost given the city after hosting the 1998 World's Fair, Lisbon is a world-class city. And with some of Europe's lowest prices, enjoying Lisbon is easy on the budget.

Planning Your Time

With three weeks in Iberia, Lisbon is worth two days.

Day 1: Start by touring Castle São Jorge at the top of the Alfama, and surveying the city from its viewpoint. Hike down to another fine viewpoint, Miradouro de Santa Luzia, and descend into the Alfama. Explore. Back in the Baixa (bai-shah; "lower city"), have lunch on or near Rua Augusta and walk to the funicular near Praça dos Restauradores. Kick off the described walk through the Baírro Alto with a ride up the funicular. Take a joyride on trolley #28. If it's not later than 14:00, art lovers can Metro or taxi to the Gulbenkian Museum. Consider dinner at a fado show in the Baírro Alto. If one of your nights is a summer Thursday, consider a bullfight.

Day 2: Trolley to Belém and tour the Tower, Monastery, and Coach Museum (note: Belém's sights are closed Mon). Have lunch in Belém. You could spend the afternoon in Sintra touring the Pena Palace and exploring the ruined Moorish castle (to get from Belém to Sintra, return to Lisbon to catch the train to Sintra from Rossio station).

A third day could easily be spent at the Museum of Ancient Art and browsing through the Rossio, Baírro Alto, and Alfama neighborhoods.

The side trip to Sintra is time-consuming and rushes Lisbon. If you'd appreciate more time to absorb the ambience of the city, spend a full two days in Lisbon and do the Sintra side trip on a third day (but not on Mon, when Sintra's Pena Palace is closed).

Orientation

Greater Lisbon has around three million people and some frightening sprawl, but for the visitor, the city can be a delightful small-town series of parks, boulevards, and squares bunny-hopping between two hills down to the waterfront. The main boulevard, Avenida da Liberdade, goes from the high-rent district downhill, ending at the grand square called Praça dos Restauradores. From here the Baixa—the post-earthquake, grid-planned lower town, with three fine squares—leads to the riverfront. Rua Augusta is the grand pedestrian promenade running through the Baixa to the river.

Most travelers focus on the three characteristic neighborhoods that line the downtown harborfront: Baixa (flat, in the middle), the Baírro Alto (literally "high town," Lisbon's "Latin Quarter" on a hill to the west), and the tangled, medieval Alfama (topped by the castle on the hill to the east).

From ye olde Lisbon, Avenida da Liberdade storms into the no-nonsense real world, where you find the airport, bullring, Edward VII Park, and breezy botanical gardens.

Tourist Information

Lisbon's main city TI is in the peach-colored Palacio Foz at the bottom of Praça dos Restauradores (daily 9:00–20:00, tel. 21-346-3314; national underworked TI for Portugal is in same office, tel. 21-346-3658). Other TIs are at the airport (daily 6:00–24:00), Castle São Jorge (kiosk open daily 9:00–13:00, 14:00–18:00), and Belém (kiosk open daily 10:00–13:00, 14:00–18:00, in front of monastery, tel. 21-365-8455). Two good Web sites are www.atl-turismolisboa.pt and www.portugalinsite.pt.

Lisbon's free city map lists all museums and has a helpful inset of the town center. Pick up the free biweekly *Follow Me Lisboa*. Each summer, cheery little "Ask Me about Lisbon" info booths, staffed by eager tourism students, pop up all over town. The TI has a brochure on Gray Line day tours by bus—to Coimbra, Óbidos, Nazaré, Alcobaça, and so on—that includes a better map of Lisbon than the TI's freebie map.

LisboaCard: This card covers all public transportation (including the Metro) and free entrance to most museums (including Sintra sights) and discounts on others, plus discounts on city tours and the Aero-Bus airport bus. You can buy this only at Lisbon's TIs (including the airport TI), not at participating sites. If you plan to museum-hop, the card is a good value, particularly for a day in Belém (covers your transportation and sightseeing), but don't get the card for Sunday, when many sights are free until 14:00, or Monday, when most sights are closed (24-hr card/€12, 48-hr card/€19, 72-hr card/€24; includes excellent explanatory guidebook). You choose the start date and time. Skip Lisbon's Shopping and Restaurant Cards, which unnecessarily complicate your time.

Arrival in Lisbon

By Train: Lisbon has four train stations—Santa Apolónia (to Spain and most points north), Rossio (for Sintra, Óbidos, and Nazaré), Barreiro (for the Algarve), and Cais do Sodre (for Cascais and Estoril). If leaving Lisbon by train, see if your train requires a reservation (boxed "R" in timetable).

Santa Apolónia Station covers international trains and nearly all of Portugal (except the south). It's just past the Alfama. It has ATMs and good bus connections to the town center (buses #9 and #39 go to Praça dos Restauradores; #46 and #90 continue up Avenida da Liberdade—as you exit the station, these bus stops are to your left and run alongside the station). A taxi from Santa Apolónia to any hotel I recommend should cost around €4.

Rossio Station is in the town center (within walking distance of most of my hotel listings, ATM near track 5) and handles trains to Sintra (direct, 4/hr), and Óbidos and Nazaré (both require a transfer at Cacém). Its all-Portugal ticket office on the ground floor is handy (Mon–Fri 7:00–20:00, sells long-distance and international tickets to virtually everywhere except nearby destinations such as Sintra, no CC). You can buy tickets to Sintra upstairs in the lobby in front of the tracks, either at the ticket office or from the simple-to-use machines (select English, pop in coins—about €1.10, TV monitor in lobby lists departure times, usually :07, :22, :37, and :52 in both directions).

Central Lisbon

1. Hotel Lisboa Tejo
2. Albergaria Insulana
3. Pensao Aljubarrota
4. Hotel Metropole
5. Pensao Geres
6. To Pensao 13 da Sorte
7. To Hotel Lisboa Plaza & Ibis
8. Hotel Mundial
9. Armazens do Chiado
   Shopping Center
10. Port Wine Institute
11. Residencial Florescente
12. Canto Camoes Fado
13. La Brasileira & Metro
14. Bus tours depart from here
15. Olisiponia
16. Largo Santa Luzia
17. Museum of Decorative Arts
18. House of Fado Museum
19. To Hotel Britania
20. Hotel Avenida Palace
    & Orion Eden Apt. Hotel
21. Residencia Roma
22. Arco Do Castello
23. Largo Portas do Sol

Barreiro Station, a 30-minute ferry ride across the Tagus River (Rio Tejo) from the dock at Lisbon's Praça do Comércio, covers trains to the Algarve and points south (the €1 ferry ticket is generally sold to you with a train ticket). Note that the same Lisbon dock handles boats to Cacilhas and cruises on the Tejo.

To catch a ferry to the Barreiro train station, go to the two-story white building on the dock that actually looks like a train station (and has an ATM).

Caís do Sodre Station handles the 40-minute rides to Cascais and Estoril.

By Bus: Lisbon's bus station is at Arco do Cego (a 3-block walk from Metro: Saldanha; exiting the station, turn left on Avenida João Crisostomo, then left on busy Avenida da República, look for red "M" for Metro, near McDonald's, bus info: tel. 21-354-5439). A taxi to the center costs about €3.50. The modern bus station has ATMs, a leaflet rack of schedules (near entrance/exit) next to a nifty computer that can display your route, and two info offices—one for buses in Portugal, the other for international routes (both closed Sun). If you plan to leave Lisbon by bus, you can virtually always buy a ticket just a few minutes before departure, but you can also buy it up to seven days in advance if you prefer the peace of mind.

By Plane: Lisbon's easy-to-manage airport is eight kilometers northeast of downtown, with a 24-hour bank, ATMs, a TI (daily 6:00–24:00), reasonable taxi service (€10 to center), good bus connections into town (#44, #45, €0.80), and an airport bus, Aero-Bus #91. The Aero-Bus runs from the airport to Avenida da Liberdade, Praça dos Restauradores, Rossio, and Praça do Comércio (€2.30, 3/hr, 30 min, daily 7:00–21:00, buy ticket on bus). Your ticket is actually a one-day Lisbon transit pass that covers bus, trolley, and funicular rides, but not the Metro (3-day transit pass for €5.50 also sold on bus). If you fly in on TAP airline, show your boarding pass to get a free lift into town on the airport bus (TAP tel. 21-841-6990). Airport info: tel. 21-841-3500; flight info: tel. 21-841-3700.

Getting around Lisbon

A day pass which covers the Metro, lifts, trolleys, and buses costs €2.50 (sold at Metro stations and Carris booths—on Praça da Figueira and behind the Santa Justa elevator). Note that the Lisboa Card covers it all.

By Metro: Lisbon's simple, fast subway is handy for trips to the Gulbenkian Museum, bullfights, Colombo Mall, Expo '98 site, and long-distance bus station. Bring change for the machines, as many stations are not staffed (€0.50 per ride or €1.40 all day, covered by Lisboa Card). Remember to stamp your ticket in the machine. Metro stops are marked with a red "M." *Saida* means exit. If you can't find a Metro map, look in the TI's free *Follow Me Lisboa*.

By Trolleys, Funicular, and Buses: For fun and practical public transport, use the trolleys and the funicular. If you buy your ticket from the driver, one ride costs €0.80 (no transfers). You get two rides for €0.90 if you buy your ticket from a Carris kiosk (on Praça da Figueira or behind the Santa Justa elevator—open daily

8:00–19:30, can mix forms of transportation, doesn't need to do both on same day).

Transit passes cover all public transportation—including the extensive city bus system—except for the Metro (1-day/ €2.30, 3-day/€5.50). Like San Francisco, Lisbon sees its trolleys as part of its heritage and is keeping a few. Trolleys #12 and #28 are here to stay.

By Taxi: Lisbon cabbies are good-humored, abundant, and use their meters. Rides start at €1.60, and you can go anywhere in the center for around €3. Decals on the window clearly spell out all charges in English. Especially if you're traveling with a companion, Lisbon cabs are a cheap time-saver. For an average trip, couples save less than a dollar by taking public transport and spend an extra 15 minutes to get there—bad economics. If time is limited, taxi everywhere. If you're having a hard time flagging one down, ask for a taxi stand (prah-sah dee taxi).

Helpful Hints

Calendar Concerns: Bullfights take place most summer Thursdays in Lisbon and most Sundays nearby. Tuesdays and Saturdays are flea-market days in the Alfama. The national museums are free on Sunday until 14:00 and closed all day Monday.

Pedestrian Warning: Sidewalks are narrow, and drivers are daring; cross streets with care. Lisbon has piles of people doing illegal business on the street. While it's generally safe, if you're looking for trouble, you could find it. For late-night strolling, choose your neighborhood wisely.

Language: Remember to try to start conversations in Portuguese (see "Survival Phrases," near the back of this book). Fortunately, many people in the tourist trade speak English. Otherwise, try Portuguese, French, or Spanish, in that order. Locals call their city Lisboa (LEEZH-bo-ah) and their river the Tejo (TAY-zhoo). Squares are major navigation points and are called *praça* (PRA-sah).

Time-Zone Change: Portuguese time is usually one hour earlier than Spanish time.

Banking: ATMs are the way to go, giving more euros per dollar all over Lisbon (and Portugal). Banks offer fine rates but high fees to change checks or cash (bank hours are generally Mon–Fri 8:30–15:00). American Express cashes any kind of traveler's check at mediocre rates without a commission. Their office is not central (Mon–Fri 9:30–13:00, 14:30–18:30, in Top Tours office at Avenida Duque de Loule 108, Metro: Rotunda, tel. 21-315-5885). Automatic bill-changing machines are available and seductive, offering fair rates but high fees.

Post Office and Telephones: The post office, at Praça dos Restauradores 58, has easy-to-use metered phones (Mon–Fri 8:00–22:00, Sat–Sun 9:00–18:00). The telephone center, on the northwest corner of Rossio Square, sells phone cards and also has metered phones (daily 8:00–23:00, accepts CC).

Internet Access: The TI has a list of the latest. Currently Espaco Agora is the closest to downtown and has the most computers (daily 14:00–19:00, 20:00–24:00, on the waterfront in front of the small Santos train station, a 10-min walk—or short ride on tram #15—west of Praça do Comércio, tel. 21-394-0170).

Travel Agency: Agencies line the Avenida da Liberdade. For flights, Star Turismo is handy and helpful (Mon–Fri 9:30–18:30, closed Sat–Sun, Praça dos Restauradores 14, southwest corner of square, tel. 21-346-0336).

Guides: The city has no regular walking tours, but for a private guide try the Guides' Union (€70/4 hrs, €115/full day, tel. 21-346-7170). Angela da Silva is a good local guide (tel. 21-479-3597, cellular 96-605-9518, e-mail: jsfonseca@mail.pt).

Do-It-Yourself Walking Tours

The Bairro Alto and Chiado Stroll

For a walk worth ▲▲, leave the lower town on the funicular, called Elevator da Gloria, near the obelisk at Praça dos Restauradores. Leaving the funicular on top, turn right to enjoy the city view from Miradouro de São Pedro Alcantara (San Pedro Park belvedere). Wander over to the tile map, which helps guide you through the view, stretching from the castle birthplace of Lisbon on the right to the towers of the new city in the distance on the left. The centerpiece of the park is a bust honoring a 19th-century local journalist. This district is famous for its writers, poets, and bohemians.

If you're into port (the fortified wine that takes its name from Oporto, a city just north of here), you'll find the world's greatest selection directly across the street from the lift at **Solar do Vinho do Porto** (run by the Port Wine Institute, Mon–Sat 14:00–24:00, closed Sun, WCs, Rua São Pedro de Alcantara 45, tel. 21-347-5707). In a plush, air-conditioned living room you can, for €1 to €22 per glass (poured by an English-speaking bartender), taste any of 300 different ports—though you may want to try only 150 or so and save the rest for the next night. Fans of port describe it as "a liquid symphony playing on the palate."

Follow the main street (Rua São Pedro de Alcantara, which turns into Rua Misericordia) downhill a couple of blocks. The grid plan of streets to your right is 16th-century Renaissance town planning—predating the earthquake and grid plan of the lower town by two centuries.

When you reach the small square, Largo Trindade Coelho, the **São Roque Church** will be on your left (8:30–17:00). Built in the 16th century, it's one of Portugal's first Jesuit churches. Wander slowly under its flat, painted ceiling and notice the rich

Pombal's Lisbon

After the earthquake of 1755, Prime Minister Marques de
Pombal rebuilt much of Lisbon. He had served as a diplomat
in London, where he picked up some city-planning ideas—
considered pretty wild by 18th-century Lisbon. (A forceful
figure, Pombal not only rebuilt Lisbon, but also ended the
Inquisition and expelled the Jesuits, who were the intellectual
powers behind the Inquisition.)

Avenida da Liberdade is the tree-lined grand boulevard
of Lisbon, connecting the old town near the river (where most
of the sightseeing action is) with the newer upper town. Before
the great earthquake this was a royal promenade. After 1755 it
was the grand boulevard of Pombal's new Lisbon—originally
limited to the aristocracy. The present street, built in the 1880s
and inspired by Paris' Champs-Élysées, is lined with banks,
airline offices, nondescript office buildings... and eight noisy
lanes of traffic. The grand "rotunda"—as the roundabout
formally known as Praça Marques de Pombal is called—tops
off the Avenida da Liberdade with a commanding statue of
Pombal, decorated with allegorical symbols of his impressive
accomplishments. (A single-minded dictator can do a lot in
27 years.) Beyond that stretches the fine Edward VII Park.
The 20-minute downhill walk from the Rotunda (Metro:
Rotunda) along the 1.5 kilometer-long avenue to the old
town is enjoyable. The black-and-white cobbled sidewalks
are a Lisbon tradition.

Praça dos Restauradores is the monumental square at the
lower end of Avenida da Liberdade. Its centerpiece, an obelisk,
celebrates the restoration of Portuguese independence from
Spain in 1640. (In 1580 the Portuguese king died without a
direct heir. The closest heir was Philip II of Spain—yuck. He
became Philip I of Portugal, ushering in an unhappy 60 years
when 3 Spanish Philips ruled Portugal.) Within a few meters
of the obelisk is the neo-Manueline-style Rossio train station,

side chapels. The highlight is the Chapel of St. John the Baptist
(left of altar, gold and blue), which looks like it came right out
of the Vatican. It did. Made in Rome out of the most precious
materials, it was the site of one papal Mass; then it was shipped
to Lisbon—probably the most costly chapel per square inch ever
constructed. Notice the mosaic floor and the three paintings
that are actually intricate, beautiful mosaics—a Vatican specialty
(designed to avoid damage from candle smoke that would darken

Lisbon's oldest hotel (Hotel Avenida Palace, built to greet those arriving by train), TI, bullfight ticket kiosk, a funicular which climbs to the high town, and a Metro station.

Baixa, between Avenida da Liberdade and the harbor, is the flat, lower city. The grid plan (with many streets named for the crafts and shops historically found there) and most of the five-story facades are Pombal's from just after 1755. Baixa's pedestrian streets, inviting cafés, bustling shops, and elegant old storefronts give the district a certain magnetism. I find myself doing laps in a people-watching stupor. The mosaic-decorated Rua Augusta (with the grand arch near the river framing the equestrian statue of King José I) has a delightful strolling ambience—reminding many of Barcelona's Ramblas. Notice the uniform and utilitarian Pombalan architecture with its decoration limited to wrought iron and tiles. In the years after the earthquake Lisbon did a lot of building without a lot of money.

Midway down the Baixa you'll see the 45-meter-tall **Santa Justa Elevator**. It was built in 1892 (a few years after, and inspired by, the Eiffel tower) to connect the lower town with the high town. While you can no longer enter the Bairro Alto from the skyway at the top, you can still ride the lift for a fine city view (€1.70, daily 7:00–23:45).

The Baixa has three great squares, each ornamented with a statue of a Portuguese king. **Rossio** and **Figueira** squares—congested with buses, subways, taxis, and pigeons leaving in all directions—stand side-by-side at the top. Rossio has been the center of Lisbon since medieval times.

Praça do Comércio, or Trade Square—where the ships used to stop and sell their goods—borders the Baixa at the riverfront. Nicknamed "Palace Square" by locals, for 200 pre-earthquake years it was the site of Portugal's royal palace. It's ringed by government ministries and is the departure point for city tours and the boat across the Tagus. The statue is of King José I, the man who put Pombal to work rebuilding the city.

paintings). The São Roque Museum, with some old paintings and church riches, is not as interesting as the church itself (€1, discount with Lisboa Card, Tue–Sun 10:00–17:00, closed Mon).

After a visit with the poor pigeon-drenched man in the church square (WC), continue downhill along Rua Nova da Trindade (opposite McDonald's). At #20 you can pop into Cervejaria da Trindade, the famous "oldest beer hall in Lisbon," (see "Eating," below) for a look at the 19th-century tiles.

At the next intersection, signs point left to the ruined Convento do Carmo. (Fado aficionados: For orientation purposes, if you'll be coming back to this neighborhood in the evening for fado, note that the recommended fado restaurant, Canto do Camões, is roughly three blocks west of here; for details, see "Nightlife," below). At the intersection, walk downhill to the square. The police guard the headquarters of the National Guard—famous among locals as the last refuge of the prime minister before the people won their democracy in the Revolution of 1974.

On Largo do Carmo, check out the ruins of the **Convento do Carmo**. At first glance the church seems intact, but look closer, through the windows. Destroyed by the 1755 earthquake, its delicate Gothic arches stand as a permanent reminder of that disastrous event.

Next, leave Largo do Carmo walking a block uphill on Travessa do Carmo. At the square take a left (on Rua Serpa Pinto) downhill to Rua Garrett where—in the little pedestrian zone on the right—you'll find a new Metro stop across from an old café.

Coffeehouse junkies enjoy the grand old **A Brasileira** café, which reeks of smoke and the 1930s (open daily). Drop in for a *bica* (Lisbon slang for an espresso) and a *pastel de Belém* (€0.90 cream cake—a local specialty). The statue outside is of the late poet Fernando Pessoa—who used to be a regular at Brasileira.

This district, the **Chiado** (SHEE-ah-doo), is popular for its shopping and theaters. Rua Garrett, lined with fine shops, ends abruptly downhill at the entrance of the six-story shopping complex, Armazens do Chiado. Browse downhill on Rua Garrett, peeking into the classy shops such as the venerable Bertrand bookstore (at #73, English books and a good guidebook selection in room 5). The store's lamps are decorated with the symbol of Lisbon: a ship—carrying the remains of St. Vincent—guarded by two ravens.

To end this walk, catch the subway (Chiado); take Rua do Carmo down to Rossio (facing the mall entrance, it's the road to your left); or rumble downhill into the Armazens mall (eateries on top floor, see "Eating," below). To get from the mall to Baixa—the lower city—take the elevator down (press 0) or the escalators (you'll pass through the Intersports shop on the lower floors—exit through ground level of store).

The Alfama Stroll

For another ▲▲ walk, explore this colorful sailors' quarter, which goes back to Visigothic days. It was a busy district during the Moorish period, and finally the home of Lisbon's fisherfolk (and of the poet Luis de Camões, who wrote, "our lips meet easily high across the narrow street"). The tangled street plan is one of the few aspects of Lisbon to survive the 1755 earthquake, helping make the Alfama a cobbled playground of old-world color. A visit is best during the busy midmorning market time or in the cooler hours in the late afternoon or early evening, when the streets teem with locals. Market days are Tuesday and Saturday on Campo de Santa Clara (8:00–15:00, best in morning).

To get to the castle—the highest point in town—take a taxi or bus #37 from Praça da Figueira. From the castle walk down to the Alfama viewpoint and into the Alfama.

Start at **Castle São Jorge.** Lisbon's castle is boring as far as castles go. But it's the birthplace of the city, it offers a fine view, and it's free (daily 9:00–21:00 or sunset, WCs). Straddle a cannon, enjoy the view and park, and wander the sterile ramparts. Within the castle grounds, **Olisiponia** (the Roman name for Lisbon) is a high-tech syrupy multimedia presentation offering a sweeping video overview of the city's history in English (€3, discount with Lisboa Card, Thu–Tue 10:00–18:00, closed Wed). Near the castle-wall entrance is a little **TI** kiosk (daily 9:00–13:00, 14:00–18:00).

Leave the castle. Across the ramp from the castle entrance/exit is the recommended restaurant Arco do Castello (see "Eating," below). Facing the restaurant, go left and take your first right. From here it's a three-minute walk downhill, through the small square Largo do Contador Mor—which contains the recommended restaurants A Tasquinha and Comidas de Santiago—to another great Alfama viewpoint, at **Largo Santa Luzia** (and another restaurant, Farol de Santa Luzia). This square is a stop for trolleys #12 and #28; some prefer to start their Alfama exploration here and take the steep but worthwhile uphill hike to the castle. Admire the panoramic view from the square's small terrace, Miradouro de Santa Luzia, where old-timers play cards in the shade of the bougainvillea amid lots of tiles. Find the wall of 18th-century tiles that shows the Praça do Comércio before the earthquake. The 16th-century Royal Palace (on the left) was completely destroyed in the quake. For another view, hike left around the church to the scenic catwalk. This is the place for the most scenic cup of coffee in town—at the Cerca Moura's café terrace (kiosk opens at 11:30, Largo das Portas do Sol 4).

The **Museum of Decorative Arts**, next door to Cerca Moura's main café on the square, offers a unique (but nearly meaningless, with its lack of decent English descriptions) stroll through aristocratic households richly decorated in 16th- to 19th-century styles (€4, discount with Lisboa Card, Tue–Sun 10:00–17:00, closed Mon, Largo das Portas do Sol 2, tel. 21-886-2183).

From Largo das Portas do Sol (Cerca Moura bar), go down the stairs (Rua Norberto de Araujo, between the church and the catwalk) into the Alfama. The old wall used to mark the end of Moorish Lisbon. As soon as the stairs end, turn left...down more stairs.

Explore from here until you end up on Rua de São Pedro, a main drag a few blocks below. The Alfama's urban-jungle roads are squeezed into tangled, confusing alleys; bent houses comfort each other in their romantic shabbiness; and the air drips with laundry and the smell of clams and raw fish. Get lost. Poke aimlessly, peek through windows, buy a fish. Locals hang plastic water bags from windows to try to keep away the flies. Favorite saints decorate doors protecting families. St. Peter is big in the Alfama—protector of the fishermen. Churches are generally closed since they share a roving priest. Rua de São Pedro, the fish market and liveliest street around, leads left down to the square Largo do Chafariz de Dentro and the fado museum.

The **House of Fado and Portuguese Guitar** tells the story of fado. Exhibits are in English and the small museum ends with an A/V show and a chance to hear some fado (€2.50, discount with Lisboa Card, Wed–Mon 10:00–13:00, 14:00–18:00, closed Tue, Largo do Chafariz de Dentro, tel. 21-882-3470). A few steps off this square is the recommended Parreirinha de Alfama fado bar (for more on fado, see "Nightlife," below).

To get back downtown: From the Fado museum, you can take a taxi (in front of the museum), or walk a block to the main waterfront drag (facing museum, go to the left around it). This major street, Avenida Infante dom Henrique, runs between the Santa Apolónia train station and Praça do Comércio downtown. From the bus stop, you can take #9 or #39 (both go to Praça dos Restauradores), or #46 or #90 (both continue up Avenida de Liberdade). If you have trouble hailing a taxi, walk five minutes east to the Santa Apolónia station, where a fleet awaits you (about €4 to the center).

Tours—Lisbon

▲▲**Ride a Trolley**—Lisbon's vintage trolleys, most from the 1920s, shake and shiver through the old parts of town, somehow safely weaving within inches of parked cars, climbing steep hills, and offering sightseers breezy views of the city (€0.80). Line #28 is a Rice-A-Roni Lisbon joyride. Trolley #28 stops from west to east include Estrela (the 18th-century late-Baroque Estrela Basilica and Estrela Park—cozy neighborhood scene with pond-side café and a "garden library kiosk"), the top of the Bica funicular (which drops steeply through a rough-and-tumble neighborhood to the riverfront), Chiado square (Lisbon's café and "Latin Quarter"), Baixa (on Rua da Conceicão between Augusta and Prata), the cathedral (Sè), the Alfama viewpoint (Santa Luzia belvedere), Portas do Sol, Santa Clara Church (flea market), and the pleasant and untouristy Graca district. Just pay the conductor as you board, sit down, and catch the pensioners as they lurch at each stop. For a quicker circular Alfama trolley ride, catch #12 on Praça da

Figueira (departs every few minutes, 20-min circle, driver can tell you when to get out for the viewpoint near the castle—about three-quarters through the ride).

City Bus Tours—Several Carris Tours give tired tourists a lazy overview of the city. They're not great, but they're handy, inexpensive, and offered daily year-round. They all start and end at Praça do Comércio, on the west side of the square.

The **Tagus Tour** (which loops around west Lisbon) and the **Orient Express** (which loops east) and are double-decker hop-on hop-off bus tours: you can get off, tour a sight, and catch a later bus. Major stops on the Tagus Tour are the Gulbenkian Museum and Belém sights (runs twice hourly from 9:00–17:00 March–Oct, later in summer, less in winter). The major stops of the Orient Express are Parque das Nações and the Tile Museum (runs hrly 10:15-17:15 March–Oct, less in winter). Both tours use audioguides. And in each case, your ticket functions as a transit pass the rest of the day, covering trams, buses, and lifts (but not the Metro, which is owned by a different company). You can't hopon and hop-off between the two tours. They cost €12.50 apiece. On the **Hills Tramcar** tour, you follow the rails on a 1900s tramcar through the Alfama and Baírro Alto. Scenic ride... sparse information (€17.50, 90-min tour with a live bilingual guide and without stops, 11/day March–Oct, more in summer, less in winter). A two-day ticket for €30 allows you to take all three tours (each about 90 min).

Carris is adding a Sintra and Cristo Rei tour (for about €50). For more information, stop by their office in the yellow bus (with an awning), parked on the west side of Praça do Comércio (can book in advance—just drop by, no CC, discount with Lisboa Card, tel. 21-358-2334).

Tejo River Cruise—Cruzeiros no Tejo runs two-hour trips from the Terreiro do Paço dock off Praça do Comércio, going up as far north as the Vasca da Gama bridge and Parque das Nações and as far east as Belém (€15, discount with Lisboa Card, April–Sept 2/day, at 11:00 and 15:00—confirm time at TI or the kiosk at dock entrance, 4-language narration includes English, hop-on hop-off option at Parque das Nações and Belém sometimes possible on weekends, can buy ticket with cash at kiosk at dock entrance or use CC at dock, drinks included, WC on board, tel. 21-882-0348).

Sights—Lisbon

▲▲▲**Gulbenkian Museum**—This is the best of Lisbon's 40 museums. Gulbenkian, an Armenian oil tycoon, gave his art collection (or "harem," as he called it) to Portugal in gratitude for the hospitable asylum granted him during World War II. This great collection, spanning 2,000 years and housed in a classy modern building, offers the most purely enjoyable museum experience in Iberia. It's cool, uncrowded, gorgeously lit, and easy to grasp, displaying only a few select and exquisite works from each epoch.

Savor details as you stroll chronologically through the ages past the delicate Egyptian, vivid Greek (fascinating coins), and exotic Oriental sections and the well-furnished Louis land. There are masterpieces by Rembrandt, Rubens, Renoir, Rodin, and artists whose names start with other letters. The nubile finale is a dark room filled with Art Nouveau jewelry by the French designer Rene Lalique (€3, free Sun until 14:00, discount with Lisboa Card; Tue 14:00–18:00, Wed–Sun 10:00–18:00, closed Mon, pleasant gardens, good air-con cafeteria, take Metro from Rossio to São Sebastião and walk 200 meters, or €4 taxi from downtown, Berna 45, tel. 21-782-3000, www.gulbenkian.pt).

▲▲**Museum of Ancient Art (Museu Nacional de Arte Antiga)**—This is the country's best for Portuguese paintings from her glory days, the 15th and 16th centuries. (Most of these works were gathered in Lisbon after the dissolution of the abbeys and convents in 1834.) You'll also find the great European masters— such as Bosch, Jan van Eyck, and Raphael—and rich furniture, all in a grand palace. Highlights include the *Temptations of St. Anthony* (a 3-paneled altarpiece fantasy by Bosch, c. 1500); *St. Jerome* (by Dürer); the *Adoration of St. Vincent* (a many-paneled altarpiece by the late-15th-century Portuguese master Nuno Goncalves, showing everyone from royalty to sailors and beggars surrounding Portugal's patron saint); and the curious Namban screens (16th-century Japanese depictions of Portuguese traders in Japan). The museum has a good cafeteria with seating in a shaded garden overlooking the river (€3, free until 14:00 on Sun, free with Lisboa Card, Tue 14:00–18:00, Wed–Sun 10:00–18:00, closed Mon, trolley #15, bus #40, #49, #51, or #60 from Praça da Figueira, Rua das Janeles Verdes 9, tel. 21-391-2800).

▲**National Tile Museum (Museu Nacional do Azulejo)**— This museum, filling the Convento da Madre de Deus, features piles of tiles, which, as you've probably noticed, are an art form in Portugal. The presentation is very low-tech, but the church is sumptuous, and the tile panorama of pre-earthquake Lisbon (upstairs) is fascinating (€2.50, free until 14:00 on Sun, free with Lisboa Card, Tue 14:00–18:00, Wed–Sun 10:00–18:00, closed Mon, 10 min on bus #105 from Praça da Figueira, Rua da Madre de Deus 4, tel. 21-814-7747).

Lisbon's City Museum—This sounds good and is talked up by the TI, but it's way out from the center, comes without a word in English, and is a disappointment.

Cathedral (Sè)—Just a few blocks east of Praça do Comércio, it's not much on the inside, but its fortress-like exterior is a textbook example of a stark and powerful Romanesque fortress of God.

Started in 1150, after the Christians retook Lisbon from the Islamic Moors, its crenelated towers made a powerful statement: The Reconquista was here to stay. St. Anthony—another patron saint of Portugal (but best known as the saint in charge of helping you find lost things)—is buried in the church. In the 12th century his remains were brought to Lisbon on a ship, as the legend goes, guarded by two sacred black ravens...the symbol of the city. The **cloisters** are peaceful and an archaeological work in progress—uncovering Roman ruins (€0.50). The humble **treasury** is worthwhile only if you want to support the church and climb some stairs (€2, free with Lisboa Card, Mon–Sat 10:00–17:00, closed Sun).

Sights—Away from the Center

Parque das Nações—Lisbon celebrated the 500th anniversary of Vasco da Gama's voyage to India by hosting Expo '98. The theme was "The Ocean and the Seas," with an emphasis on the importance of healthy, clean waters in our environment. The riverside fairgrounds are east of the Santa Apolónia train station in an area suddenly revitalized with luxury condos and crowd-pleasing terraces and restaurants. Ride the Metro to the last stop (Oriente—meaning east end of town) to join the riverside promenade. You can go up the Vasco da Gama tower (€2.50, discount with Lisboa Card, daily 10:00–20:00, tel. 21-896-9869) or visit Europe's biggest aquarium, the Oceanario, which simulates four different ocean underwater and shoreline environments (€8.50, discount with Lisboa Card, daily 10:00–20:00). Popular café/bars—such as Bar de Palha—line the waterfront just south of the tower.

Vasco da Gama Bridge—The second-longest bridge in Europe (14 km) was opened in 1998 to connect the Expo grounds with the south side of the Tagus and to alleviate the traffic jams on Lisbon's only other bridge over the river. As the 25th of April bridge (see below) was modeled after the Golden Gate bridge in San Francisco (same company built it and was paid off by years of tolls), this new Vasco da Gama bridge was designed with engineering help from the people building the new San Francisco Bay Bridge.

▲**25th of April Bridge**—At 1.5 kilometers long, this is one of the longest suspension bridges in the world. Built in 1966, it was originally named for the dictator Salazar but was renamed for the date of Portugal's 1974 revolution and freedom. For over 30 years locals could show their political colors by choosing what name to use. While conservatives called it the Salazar bridge, liberals called it the 25th of April bridge. Those who preferred to keep their politics private simply called it "the bridge over the river." When the second bridge over the Tagus opened in 1998, people had a choice: To choose a name...and show their politics. Or continue calling it "the bridge over the river"...which is what they did.

Cristo Rei—A huge statue of Christ (à la Rio de Janeiro), with outstretched arms symbolically blessing the city, overlooks Lisbon from across the Tagus River. It was built as a thanks to God, funded by Lisboetas grateful that Portugal stayed out of World War II. While it's designed to be seen from a distance, a lift takes visitors to the top for a great view (€3, daily 9:00–18:00). Catch the ferry from downtown Lisbon (6/hr, from Praça do Comércio) to Cacilhas then take a bus marked "Cristo Rei" (4/hr, from ferry dock). Because of bridge tolls, taxis to or from the site are expensive. For drivers, the most efficient visit is a quick stop on your way south to the Algarve.

Sights—Lisbon's Belém District

Five kilometers from downtown Lisbon, the Belém District is a stately pincushion of important sights from Portugal's Golden Age, when Vasco da Gama and company made it Europe's richest power. Belém was the send-off point for voyages from the Age of Discovery. Sailors would stay and pray here before embarking. The tower would welcome them home. For some reason, the grand buildings of Belém survived the great 1755 earthquake. Consequently, this is the only place to experience the grandeur of pre-earthquake Lisbon. After the earthquake, rattled and safety-conscious royalty chose to live here (in wooden rather than stone buildings). And the modern-day president of Portugal calls Belém home. To celebrate the 300th anniversary of independence from Spain, a grand exhibition was held here in 1940, resulting in the fine parks, fountains, and monument. Remember, sights are closed on Monday.

Get to Belém quickest by taxi (€5 from downtown), or slower (30 min) and cheaper by trolley #15 (catch at Praça da Figueira or Praça do Comércio) or bus #28 (Praça do Comércio). In Belém, the first stop is the Coach Museum; the second is the monastery. If you miss the first subtle stop (named Belém), you can't miss the second stop, the huge massive monastery. Consider doing Belém in this order: the Coach Museum, pastry and coffee break, Monastery of Jerónimos, Maritime Museum (if interested) and/or lunch at their cafeteria (public access, museum admission not required), Monument to the Discoveries, and Belém Tower. By taxi, start at Belém Tower, the farthest point. Belém also has a cultural center, children's museum, and a planetarium. You'll find eateries at Belém Tower and along Rua de Belém (between the Coach Museum and the monastery).

The little **TI** kiosk (daily 10:00–13:00, 14:00–18:00, tel. 21-365-8455) is directly across the street from the entrance of the monastery. A little red-and-white **Mini Train** does a handy 25-minute hop-on hop-off circuit of the sights—which feel farflung if you're tired—departing nearly every hour from the entrance of the monastery (€2.50, discount with Lisboa Card,

Belém

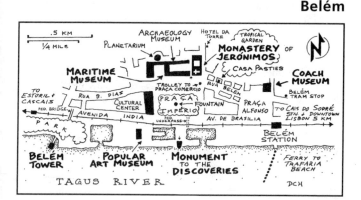

daily except Mon year-round at 10:00, 11:00, 12:00, 14:00, 15:00, 16:00, and 17:00, plus 18:00 and 19:00 June–Sept; can get off to explore a sight and catch the next bus; live guide does tour in Portuguese, English, and French).

▲▲**Coach Museum (Museu dos Coches)**—In 1905 the Queen of Portugal decided to use the palace's riding-school building to preserve this fine collection of royal coaches. Claiming to be the most visited sight in Portugal, it is impressive, with more than 70 dazzling carriages (well-described in English). The oldest is the crude and simple coach used by King (of Spain and Portugal) Philip II to shuttle between Madrid and Lisbon around 1600. Imagine how slow and rough the ride would be with bad roads and no suspension. Study the evolution of suspension—from the first coach, or "Kotze," made in a Hungarian town by that name in the 15th century—and the highly symbolic ornamentation of the coaches. The newly restored "Ocean Coach" stands shiny in the center with figures symbolizing the Atlantic and Indian Oceans holding hands, in recognition of Portugal's mastery of the sea (€3, free Sun until 14:00, free with Lisboa Card, Tue–Sun 10:00–17:30, closed Mon, tel. 21-361-0850).

Rua de Belém leads from the coach museum and the monastery past the guarded entry to Portugal's presidential palace, some fine pre-earthquake buildings, and a famous pastry shop.

Pastry—The **Casa Pasteis de Belém** café is the birthplace of the wonderful cream tart called *pastel del Nata* throughout Portugal. Here they're called *pastel del Belém*. Since 1837 locals have come here to get them warm out of the oven (daily 8:00–24:00, Rua de Belém 88). Sit down. Enjoy one with a *café com leite*. Sprinkle on the cinnamon and powdered sugar.

▲▲▲**Monastery of Jerónimos**—King Manuel (who ruled from 1495) had this giant church and its cloisters built (starting in 1505) with "pepper money"—a 5 percent tax on spices brought back from India—as a thanks for the discoveries. Sailors would spend their last night here in prayer before embarking on their frightening voyages. Here's a tour, starting outside the monastery:

1. South portal: The ornate south portal, facing the street, is a great example of the Manueline style. Manueline—like Spain's Plateresque but with motifs from the sea—bridged Gothic and Renaissance. Henry the Navigator stands in the middle of the door with his patron saint, St. Jerome (above on the left, with the lion). This door is only used when Mass lets out.

As you pass through the entrance, the church (free) is on your right, the cloisters (€3, free Sun until 14:00, free with Lisboa Card) are straight ahead (May-Sept Tue-Sun 10:00–18:30, Oct–April 10:00–17:00, closed Mon, last entry 30 min before closing; pleasant courtyard at Naval Library entrance between monastery and cloisters).

2. Church interior: View the interior from the high altar looking back toward the entry. See how Manueline is a transition between Gothic and Renaissance. While in Gothic architecture huge columns break the interior into a nave with low-ceilinged ambulatories on either side, here the slender palm tree–like columns don't break the interior space, and the ceiling is all one height. Find some of the Manueline motifs from the sea: ropelike arches, the ships, and coral. Exotic new animals—another aspect of the "Age of Discovery"—hide in the capitals. It is, after all, the sea that brought Portugal 16th-century wealth and power and made this art possible.

3. Front of church: Now turn 180 degrees toward the front and see how the rest of the church is Renaissance. Everything but a cupola and the stained glass (replacement glass is from 1940) survived the earthquake. In the main chapel in the apse (at the far front), elephants—who dethroned lions as the most powerful and kingly beasts—support two kings and two queens (King Manuel I is front-left). Walk back on the side with the seven wooden confessional doors (on your right). Notice the ornamental carving around the second one: A festival of faces from newly discovered corners of the world. Ahead of you (near the entry) is the tomb of Vasco da Gama.

4. Tombs: Vasco da Gama's tomb is decorated with richly symbolic carvings: The proud sailboat (in the middle of the side of the tomb) is a Portuguese caravel. This was a technological marvel in its day, with a triangular sail that could pivot quickly to catch the wind efficiently. The sphere is a common Manueline symbol. Some say the diagonal slash is symbolic of the unwritten pact and ambition of Spain and Portugal to split the world evenly. Even the ceiling—a Boy Scout handbook of rope and knots—comes with a whiff of the sea. The second tomb—with literary rather than maritime motifs—is a memorial (he's buried elsewhere) to Portugal's much-loved poet, Camões.

5. Cloisters: Leave the church (turn right, buy a ticket) and enter the cloisters. These cloisters are the architectural highlight of Belém. The lacy lower arcade is textbook Manueline; the simpler top floor is Renaissance. Study the carvings. Upstairs you'll find a bookshop and better views of the church and the cloisters (women's WC upstairs, men's downstairs).

Maritime Museum (Museu de Marinha)—If you're interested in the ships and navigational tools of Portugal's Age of Discovery, this museum, which fills the east wing of the monastery, comes with good English descriptions and is worth a look. Sailors love it (€2.50, free Sun until 14:00, free with Lisboa Card, May-Sept Tue-Sun 10:00–18:00, Oct–April 10:00–17:00, closed Mon; decent cafeteria with separate entrance; as you face planetarium, museum entrance is to your right; Praça do Império).

▲Monument to the Discoveries—This giant riverside monument was built in 1960 to honor Prince Henry the Navigator on the 500th anniversary of his death. Huge statues of Henry, Magellan, Vasco da Gama, and other heroes of Portugal's Age of Discovery line the giant concrete prow of a caravel. Inside the monument, you can ride a lift to a tingly view (€1.90, free Sun until 14:00, free with Lisboa Card, Tue–Sun 9:00–17:00, closed Mon, 5-min audioguide-€1.25, tel. 21-362-0034). Notice the marble map chronicling Portugal's empire building (on the ground leading to the monument). Follow the years as Portuguese explorers gradually worked their way around Africa. Today, all that remains of Portugal's once huge empire is the Azores and Madeira (whose original inhabitants were Portuguese).

▲Belém Tower—The only purely Manueline building in Portugal (built 1515–1520), this white tower protected Lisbon's harbor and today symbolizes the voyages that made Lisbon powerful. This was the last sight sailors saw as they left and the first when they returned, loaded with gold, spices, and social diseases. When the tower was built, the river went nearly to the walls of the monastery and the tower was mid-river. Its interior is pretty bare, but the views of the bridge, river, and Cristo Rei are worth the 120 steps (€3, free Sun until 14:00, free with Lisboa Card, May-Sept Tue–Sun 10:00–18:30, Oct–April 10:00–17:00, closed Mon, exhibitions sometimes held here, tel. 21-362-0034). The floatplane on the grassy lawn is a monument to the first flight across the South Atlantic (Portugal to Brazil) in 1922. The original plane is in Belém's Maritime Museum.

If you're choosing between towers, Monument to the Discoveries is probably the better choice because of its elevator and better view of the monastery. Both towers are interesting to see from the outside whether or not you go up.

Popular Art Museum (Museu de Arte Popular)—This museum takes you through Portugal's folk art one province at a time, providing a sneak preview of what you'll see throughout the country (€1.75, free Sun until 14:00, free with Lisboa Card, Tue–Sun 10:00–12:30, 14:00–17:00, closed Mon, between the monument and the tower on Avenida Brasilia—but it's not the white restaurant in the middle of the pond).

Shopping

Flea Market—On Tuesday and Saturday, the Feira da Ladra flea market hops in the Alfama on Campo de Santa Clara (best in morning). A Sunday market—with coins, books, antiques, and more—is at Parque das Nações (10:00–18:00, in garden Garcia da Horta, Metro: Oriente).

Colombo Shopping Mall—While Lisbon offers decaying but still-elegant department stores, a new shopping center (see below), classy specialty shops, and a teeming flea market, nothing is as impressive as the enormous Centro Colombo, the largest shopping center in Spain and Portugal. More than 400 shops—including the biggest FNAC department store, 10 cinemas, 60 restaurants, and a health club sit atop Europe's biggest underground car park and under a vast and entertaining play center. There's plenty to amuse children here and the place offers a fine look at work-a-day Lisbon (daily 10:00–24:00, pick up a map at info desk, Metro: Colegio Militar takes you right there, tel. 21-711-3636).

Armazens do Chiado—This grand six-floor shopping center connects Lisbon's lower and upper towns with a world of ways to spend money (lively food circus on 6th floor). Amidst other buildings the same height, it doesn't stand out. So here's how to find it: If you approach from Chiado, take Rua Garrett down to the main entrance. From the southwest corner of Rossio, take Rua do Carmo up to the main entry. From the Baixa, head up Rua Assuncão toward the mall where you'll find three subtle entrances on Rua do Crucifixio—through the Intersports store (take their escalators up into the mall), or at #113 or #89 (where small, simple doorways lead to elevators).

Nightlife

Nightlife in the Baixa seems to be little more than loitering prostitutes and litter stirred by the wind. But head up into the Baírro Alto and you'll find plenty of action. The Jardím do São Pedro is normally festive and the Rua Diario de Noticias is lined with busy bars.

The trendy hot spot lately for young locals is the dock district under the 25th of April bridge. The Docas (dock-ash) is a 400-meter-long strip of warehouses turned into restaurants and discos. Popular places include Hawaii, Salsa Latina, Havana, and Friday's (catch a taxi or trolley #15 from Praça da Figueira to the stop Avenida Infante Santo, take overpass, then a 10-min walk toward bridge).

▲▲**Fado**—Fado, which means "fate," is the folk music of Lisbon's backstreets. Since the mid-1800s it's been the Lisbon blues— mournfully beautiful, haunting ballads about lost sailors, broken hearts, and sad romance. To the lilting accompaniment of the Portuguese *guitarra* (like a 12-string mandolin), the singer longs for what's been lost.

These days, the fado songs come with a new casualty— a tourist's budget. Fado has become one of Lisbon's favorite late-night tourist traps, but it can still be a great experience. The Alfama has a few famous touristy fado bars, but the Baírro Alto is better (and safer late at night). Wander around Rua Diario de Noticias and neighboring streets either for a late dinner (after 22:00) or later for just drinks and music. Homemade "fado tonight" signs in Portuguese are good news, but even a restaurant filled with tourists can come with good food and fine fado. Prices for a fado performance vary greatly. Many have a steep cover charge, while others have a minimum purchase. Any place recom- mended by a hotel has a bloated price for the kickback.

Canto do Camões, run by friendly English-speaking Gabriel, is my favorite. It's a great value with good food, music, and an hon- est style of business (open at 20:00, music from 21:00 until around 01:00, €20-or-more meal required, after 22:00 €11 minimum if seats are available, CC, Travessa da Espera 38, from Rua Misericor- dia, go 2.5 blocks west on Travessa da Espera, call ahead to reserve, tel. 21-346-5464, e-mail: canto.do.camoes @clix.pt). The meal is punctuated with sets of three fado songs with different singers. For a snack, a good vintage Porto goes nicely with a plate of *queijo di serra* (sheep cheese) and *pancetta* (salt-cured ham). Relax, spend some time, and close your eyes or make eye contact with the singer. Let the music and wine work together.

A fado bar in the Alfama, **Parreirinha de Alfama,** is known for its owner, singer Argentina Santos, who also does the cooking. People usually eat around 20:30 or 21:00, and Tina starts singing about 21:30 and ends around 01:00 (open nightly, no cover charge for fado, just have dinner and drinks, CC, Beco do Espirito Santo 1, with back to fado museum, Parreirinha is at 2 o'clock, 20 meters up a little alley, take right fork, tel. 21-886-8209).

▲▲▲**Portuguese Bullfight**—The bullring, which was closed for renovation in 2001, will likely re-open in 2002.

If you always felt sorry for the bull, this is Toro's Revenge— in a Portuguese bullfight, the matador is brutalized along with the bull. After an exciting equestrian prelude in which the horseman (*cavaleiro*) skillfully plants barbs in the bull's back while trying to avoid the padded horns, a colorfully clad eight-man team (suicide squad called a *forcado*) enters the ring and lines up single file facing the bull. With testosterone sloshing everywhere, the leader prompts the bull to charge and then braces himself for a collision that can be heard all the way up in the cheap seats. As he hangs onto the bull's head, his buddies then pile on, trying to wrestle the bull to a standstill. Finally, one guy hangs on to el toro's tail and "water-skis" behind him. Unlike at the Spanish *corrida*, the bull is not killed in front of the crowd at the Portuguese *tourada* (but it is killed later).

You'll most likely see a bullfight in Lisbon or Cascais or on the Algarve (Easter–Oct, flyers at TI). In Lisbon's Campo Pequeno, fights are on Thursday at 22:00 mid-June through September (tickets €10–50). The ring is small; there are no bad seats. To sit nearly at ringside, try the cheapest *bancada* seats, on the generally half-empty and unmonitored main floor (Metro: Campo Pequeno).

Note: Half the fights are simply Spanish-type *corridas* without the killing. For the real slam-bam Portuguese-style fight, confirm that there will be *grupo de forcados*. Tickets are nearly always available at the door (no surcharge, tel. 21-793-2143 to confirm). For a 10 percent surcharge you can buy them at the green ABEP kiosk at the southern end of Praça dos Restauradores—this kiosk also sells concert tickets).

Movies—In Lisbon, unlike in Spain, most films are in the original language with subtitles. Many of Lisbon's theaters are classy, complete with assigned seats and ushers. Check the newspaper for what's playing.

Sleeping in Lisbon
(€1.10 = about $1, country code: 351)
Sleep Code: **S** = Single, **D** = Double/Twin, **T** = Triple, **Q** = Quad, **b** = bathroom, **s** = shower only, **CC** = Credit Cards accepted, **no CC** = Credit Cards not accepted, **SE** = Speaks English, **NSE** = No English. Breakfast is included unless otherwise noted.

With a few exceptions, cheaper hotels downtown feel like Lisbon does downtown: tired and well-worn. Singles cost nearly the same as doubles. Addresses such as 26-3 stand for street #26, third floor (which is fourth floor in American terms). If the minibar is noisy, unplug it. For hotel locations, see map on page 244.

Be sure to book in advance if you'll be in Lisbon during its festival—Festas de Lisboa—the last three weeks of June, when parades, street parties, concerts, and fireworks draw crowds to the city.

Finer Hotels in the Center
Central as can be, the Baixa district bustles with lots of shops, traffic, people, buskers, pedestrian areas, and urban intensity.

Near Praça da Figueira: The **Lisboa Tejo** (leezh-boah tay-zhoo) is an oasis, with 58 comfortable rooms and an attentive and welcoming staff (Sb-€70–80, Db-€80–90, prices vary according to room size, 10 percent discount with this book, includes buffet breakfast, CC, air con, laundry service, elevator, Poço do Borratém 4, from southeast corner of Praça da Figueira, walk 1 block down Rua Dos Condes de Monsanto and turn left, tel. 21-886-6182, fax 21-886-5163).

Hotel Mundial, a lesser value, is a massive four-star hotel overlooking a park-like square. It has 255 smallish business-class rooms, doormen, lots of tour groups, and a top-floor Varanda restaurant—with superb city views, especially at night—open to the public (Sb-€105, Db-€120, includes breakfast, CC, air con, free parking, 1 block northeast of Praça da Figueira, Rua D. Duarte 4, tel. 21-884-2000, fax 21-884-2110, e-mail: mundial .hot@mail.telepac.pt).

On Rossio Square: The central **Hotel Metropole**, which keeps its 1920s style throughout its 36 rooms, is elegant. It feels overpriced, but you're paying for its prime location. The smaller back rooms are quieter (Sb-€130–140, Db-€150–170, includes breakfast buffet, CC, air con, elevator, Rossio 30, tel. 21-321-9030, fax 21-346-9166, www.almeidahotels.com, e-mail: metropole @almeidahotels.com).

On Praça dos Restauradores: Hotel Avenida Palace— the most characteristic five-star splurge in town—was built with the Rossio Station in 1892 to greet big-shot travelers back when trains were new and this was the only station in town. The lounges are sumptuous, dripping with chandeliers, and the 82 rooms mix old-time elegance with modern comforts (Sb-€185, Db-€205, superior Db-€230, Db junior suite-€325, Db suite-€400, includes breakfast, CC, air con, laundry service, elevator, free parking but few spaces, hotel's sign is on square, but entrance is at Rua 1 de Dezembro 123, tel. 21-346-0151, fax 21-342-2884, www.hotel-avenida-palace.pt, e-mail: hotel.av .palace@mail.telepac.pt).

Orion Eden Apartment Hotel rents 120 slick and modern compact apartments (with small kitchens) and has a rooftop swimming pool and terrace with city and river views. The building used to be a 1930s cinema, hence the Art Deco architecture and the slightly pie-shaped rooms. Perfectly located at the Rossio end of Avenida da Liberdade, this is a clean, quiet pool of modernity amid the ramshackle charm of Lisbon and an intriguing—though not cheap—option for groups or families of four (Db apartment-€150, 2-bedroom apartment with bed-and-sofa bed combo that can sleep 4 people-€225, breakfast-€8.50, CC, air con, elevator, Praça dos Restauradores 24, tel. 21-321-6600, fax 21-321-6666, e-mail: eden.lisboa@mail.telepac.pt).

Cheaper Pensions

The first four listings are central. The Residencia Roma is a five-minute walk from the center and Pensão Residencial 13 da Sorte is a 10-minute walk away.

On or Near the "Eating Lane" and Rossio Square: Pensão Residencial Gerês, a good budget bet downtown, has 20 bright, basic, cozy rooms with older plumbing. The pension lacks the dingy smokiness that pervades Lisbon's cheaper hotels (S-€40, Sb-€50, D-€45, Db-€50–60, Tb-€75–90, high-end prices June–Oct, CC, no breakfast, Calçada do Garcia 6, uphill a block off the northeast corner of Rossio, tel. 21-881-0497, fax 21-888-2006, Nogueira family speaks some English).

Residencial Florescente rents 72 rooms on the "eating lane," a thriving pedestrian street a block off Praça dos Restauradores. It's an old-world slumber mill, but the rooms are clean (S-€30, Ss-€35, Sb-€45, D-€35, Ds-€40, Db-€55, Twin/b-€60, Tb-€65, no breakfast, CC, most Db with air con, Rua Portas S. Antão 99, tel. 21-346-3517, fax 21-342-7733).

On Rua da Assunção: The Albergaria Residencial Insulana, on a pedestrian street, is very professional, with 32 quiet and comfortable—if a bit smoky—rooms (Sb-€50, Db-€55, extra bed-€10, includes breakfast, CC, elevator, air con, Rua da Assunção 52, tel. 21-342-3131, fax 21-342-8924, www.insulana.cjb.net, e-mail: insulana@teleweb.pt, SE).

Pensão Aljubarrota is a fine value if you can handle the long climb up four floors (nearly 80 steps), narrow hallways, and bubbly black-vinyl flooring. Once you're on top, you'll find small, old, rustically furnished rooms with cute balconies from which to survey the Rua Augusta scene (2-night minimum stay, S-€22.50, D-€35, Ds-€42.50, T-€54, 10 percent discount with cash and this book, all but singles have balconies, CC, Rua da Assunção 53-4, tel. & fax 21-346-0112, Italian Pino and lovely Rita SE).

Up Avenida da Liberdade: Residencia Roma, a sweet little place a block off busy Avenida da Liberdade and two blocks up the street from the Rossio Station, has 24 comfortable rooms and a secure feeling (Sb-€40–45, Db-€53–62, extra bed-€11.50, higher prices apply July–Aug, includes breakfast, CC, air con, back rooms quieter, Travessa da Gloria 22-A, tel. 21-346-0558, call to reserve then send fax with CC number and expiration date, tel. & fax 21-346-0557, e-mail: res.roma@mail.telepac.pt). Some rooms have a kitchen (at no extra cost); breakfast is not included if you use the kitchen.

Pensão Residencial 13 da Sorte is simple but cheery, with 22 rooms and bright tiles throughout (Sb-€37.50, Db-€50, Tb-€58, no breakfast, CC, elevator, just off Avenida da Liberdade near the Spanish Embassy at Rua do Salitre 13, 10-min walk from center, 50 meters from Metro: Avenida, tel. 21-353-9746, fax 21-353-1851, Alexandra SE).

Finer Hotels along Avenida da Liberdade

These listings are a 10-minute walk or short Metro ride from the center. These two places, owned jointly, offer a deal in July and August: Free entrance to Lisbon's museums for guests who stay at least three nights.

Hotel Lisboa Plaza, a four-star gem, is a spacious and plush mix of traditional style with bright-pastel modern elegance. It offers all the comforts, a warm welcome, and a free glass of port with this book (Sb-€122–148, superior Sb-€151–183, Db-€129–164, superior Db-€160–198, Tb-€153–204, superior Tb-€ 98–253, the higher prices apply to spring and fall, superior rooms are larger, suites available, great buffet breakfast-€12, CC, air con, laundry service, nonsmoking floor, parking-€9/day, well-located on a quiet street off busy Avenida da Liberdade, a block from Metro: Avenida at Travessa do Salitre 7, from Metro, walk downhill and turn right at Salitre, tel. 21-321-8218, fax 21-347-1630, www.heritage.pt, e-mail: plaza.hotels@heritage.pt).

Hotel Britania maintains its 1940s-Art-Deco feel throughout its 30 spacious rooms, offering a clean and professional haven on a quiet street one block off Avenida da Liberdade. Run by the Lisboa Plaza folks (above), it offers the same four-star standards—and a free glass of port (Sb-€122–148, superior Sb-€151–183, Db-€129–164, superior Db-€160–198, Tb-€153–204, superior Tb-€198–253, higher prices for spring and fall, breakfast-€12, CC, air con, laundry service, elevator, nonsmoking floor, free street parking or €7.50/day in next-door garage, Rua Rodrigues Sampaio 17, Metro: Avenida, from Metro stop walk uphill on boulevard, turn right on Rua Manuel de Jesus Coelho and take first left, tel. 21-315-5016, fax 21-315-5021, www.heritage.pt, e-mail: britania.hotel@heritage.pt).

Sleeping away from the Center

Hotel Ibis Saldanha, near Lisbon's bus station, offers 116 American-style identical rooms. The Ibis hotel chain offers plain, modern comforts and no stress for a good price (Sb/Db-€58, breakfast-€4, CC, air con, nonsmoking floor, Avenida Casal Ribeiro 23, Metro: Saldanha, 8-min walk from bus station, tel. 21-319-1690, fax 21-319-1699, www.ibishotel.com).

Hotel Ibis Lisboa-Centro is big, concrete, modern, and practical in a soulless area far from the center but near a Metro station (Sb/Db-€54, breakfast-€4, CC, air con, nonsmoking floors, next to Novotel and Metro: Praça de Espanha, Avenida Jose Malhoa, tel. 21-723-5700, fax 21-723-5701, www.ibishotel.com).

In the Alfama: The **Solar do Castelo** has 14 pleasant rooms within the castle walls. It's not central or convenient, but some will find it romantic (Sb-€160, superior Sb-€198, Db-€175, superior Db-€215, CC, air con, nonsmoking rooms, laundry service, Rua das Cozinhas 2, tel. 21-321-8200, fax 21-347-1630, e-mail: solar.castelo@heritage.pt).

In Belém: For a small-town feeling, consider **Hotel da Torre**, which offers 59 rooms next to the monastery—and a couple of blocks from the pastry shop. The best-value rooms are the 10 newly renovated ones, offered at the same price as the other older, but still fine, rooms (Sb-€73, Db-€85, includes breakfast, CC, air con, elevator, double-paned windows, some balconies; facing monastery, it's on the street to the right, Rua dos Jerónimos 8, tel. 21-361-6940, fax 21-361-6946, e-mail: hoteldatorre.belem@mail.telepac.pt).

Eating in Lisbon

Eating between the Castle and the Alfama Viewpoint

(These are listed in order from the castle to the viewpoint.)

Arco Do Castello, an eight-table Indo-Portuguese restaurant, dishes up delicious fish and shrimp curries from Goa, a former Portuguese colony in India. A complete meal for two costs around €25. Top it off with a shot of the Goan firewater, *feni*, made from cashews (Mon–Sat 12:30–15:00, 19:00–24:00, closed Sun, CC, just across from ramp leading into castle, Rua Chão da Feira 25, tel. 21-887-6598).

Largo do Contador Mor is a wispy cobbled square a block above the Miradouro de Santa Luzia and a block below the castle with two good eateries: **A Tasquinha Restaurante**, with great outdoor seating at the top of the square, keeps locals and tourists happily fed with fine plates of grilled sardines (*sardinhas assadas*-€7.50, Mon–Sat 12:00–15:00, 19:00–24:00, closed Sun, Largo do Contador Mor 5, tel. 21-887-6899). Eat fast, cheap, and healthy at **Comidas de Santiago**, a little salad bar with great summer gazpacho (choose 2 salads on small plate for €2.60 or 4 on big plate for €4.30, daily 11:00–18:00, Largo do Contador Mor 21, tel. 21-887-5805).

For a seafood feast, consider dining high in the Alfama at the **Farol de Santa Luzia** restaurant (€14 fixed-price *menu turistico*, Mon–Sat 12:00–15:00, 19:00–24:00, closed Sun, CC, Largo Santa Luzia 5, across from Santa Luzia viewpoint terrace, if they still don't have a sign look for the many window decals, tel. 21-886-3884).

For cheap and colorful dinners, walk past Portas do Sol and follow the trolley tracks along Rua da São Tome to a square called Largo Rodrigues Freitas, where **Nossa Churrasqueira** is busy feeding chicken on rickety tables to finger-lickin' locals with meager budgets (closed Mon).

This gritty chunk of pre-earthquake Lisbon is full of interesting eateries, especially along Rua San Pedro and on Largo de São Miguel. Brighten a few dark bars. Have an aperitif, taste the *branco seco* (local dry white wine). Make a friend, pet a chicken, ponder the graffiti, and pick at the humanity ground between the cobbles.

Eating in Baírro Alto

Lisbon's "high town" is full of small, fun, and cheap places. Just off São Roque's Square you'll find the very simple and cheap **Casa Trans-Montana** (Mon–Sat 12:00–15:00, 19:00–22:00, Sun 19:00–22:00, down the steps of Calcada do Duque at #43). The bright and touristy **Cervejaría da Trindade**, a Portuguese-style beer hall, is full of historic tiles, seafood, and tourists. It's overpriced and in all the guidebooks, but people enjoy the bright and boisterous old-time atmosphere (€15 meals, confirm prices, daily 12:00–24:00, liveliest 20:00–22:00, closed holidays, CC, air con, courtyard, a block down from São Roque at Rua Nova da Trindade 20C, tel. 21-342-3506). You'll find many less-touched restaurants deeper into the Baírro Alto on the other (west) side of Rua Misericordia. See "Fado," under "Nightlife," above, for the best option.

Eating in and near Rossio

The "eating lane" is a galaxy of eateries with good seafood (on Rua das Portas de St. Antão, off the northeast corner of Rossio Square). **Rei da Brasa** is known for its chicken dishes; across the street the simpler **Rei dos Frangos** has the same menu, hours, and owner (daily 12:00–23:00, indoor and outdoor seating, Travessa de Santo Antão 12, a couple steps off the "eating lane," CC, tel. 21-342-7424). **Casa do Alentejo,** specializing in Alentejo cuisine, fills an old ballroom. It's on the second floor of a building that's a cultural and social center for people from the traditional southern province of Portugal living in Lisbon (2-course special of the day-€11, daily 12:00–15:00, 19:00–22:00, Rua das Portas de St. Antão 58).

   Casa Suiça (swee-sah) is a bright, modern, air-conditioned place popular with locals because it's classy but affordable and free of riff-raff. They serve more than pastry—try the light meals, salads, and fruit cups (daily 7:00–21:00, inexpensive at the bar, reasonable at tables, entries on both Rossio and Praça da Figueria squares).

   The sixth floor of **Armazens do Chiado Shopping Center** is a food circus with few tourists in sight, offering a huge selection of fun eateries from traditional Portuguese to Chinese (daily about 10:00–23:30, between the low and high towns, between Rua Garrett and Rua Assuncão). Some of the mall's eateries are actual restaurants (that get quiet from about 15:00–18:00); others

268 Rick Steves' Spain & Portugal

are smaller fast-food counters that share a common eating area and serve all day. **Chimarrão** offers an impressive self-serve pay-by-the-weight salad-and-meat buffet. **Loja das Sopas**, on the opposite end of the floor, offers good soups.

For cod and vegetables prepared faster than a Big Mac and served with more energy than a soccer team, stand or sit at **Restaurant Beira-Gare** (a greasy spoon in front of Rossio train station at the end of Rua 1 de Dezembro, Mon–Sat 6:30–24:00, closed Sun). To get a house-special pork sandwich, ask for a *bifane no pão*.

The Rossio's Rua dos Correeiros is lined with competitive local restaurants. The chain of little **Ca das Sandes** sandwich shops, found here on Correeiros and scattered about town, offer healthy sandwiches, salads, and usually outdoor seating, great for people watching. **Pingo Doce** is a fine supermarket one block west of Rossio (daily 8:30–21:00, kitty-corner from a Ca das Sandes shop, on Rua 1 de Dezembro and Calçada do Carmo).

For a splurge with a view, consider **Varanda de Lisboa**, the restaurant on the top floor of Hotel Mundial. At night when Lisbon's monuments are illuminated, the view is electrifying (allow about €30 per person with wine, daily 12:30–15:00, 19:30–22:00, pianist plays at night, CC, reserve in advance for dinner, particularly Fri–Sat nights, tel. 21-884-2000).

Up Avenida da Liberdade: Cerevejaria Ribadouro is a popular splurge with locals for seafood (€15 meals, daily 12:00–15:00, 19:00–24:00, Avenida da Liberdade 155, at intersection with Rua do Salitre, Metro: Avenida, tel. 21-354-9411). **Quebra Mar** also specializes in seafood. If you sit at the bar (rather than a table), you have the option of getting a *meia dose*—a cheaper half-portion. Note that seafood prices are listed by the kilogram; the waiter will help you determine the cost of a portion (Mon–Sat 12:00–15:00, 18:00–24:00, closed Sun, Avenida da Liberdade 77, near intersection with Praça da Alegria, tel. 21-346-4855).

Drinks

Ginjinha (zheen-zheen-yah) is the diminutive name for a favorite Lisbon drink. *Ginjinha* is a sweet liquor made from the sour cherrylike *ginja* berry, sugar, and schnapps. It's sold for €0.80 a shot in funky old hole-in-the-wall shops throughout town. The only choices are with or without berries (*com* or *sem fruta*) and *gelada* (if you want it poured from a chilled bottle—very nice). In Portugal, when people are impressed by the taste of something, they say, "*Sabe melhor que nem ginjas*" ("It tastes even better than *ginja*"). The oldest *ginjinha* joint in town is a colorful hole in the wall at Largo de Sao Domingos #8 (just off the northeast corner of Rossio square, across from the entrance of the "eating lane"). Another ginjinha bar is on the "eating lane," Rua das Portas de

St. Antão, next to #59 (nearly across the street from recommended Casa do Alentejo).

Transportation Connections—Lisbon

By train to: Madrid (1/day, overnight 22:05–8:25, first class-€65, second class-€51, ticket and bed: €70 in quad, €90 in double, €128 in single; discount with railpass—for example, about €45 for a bed in quad; Rossio station can sell these, no CC; train departs from Santa Apolónia, station takes CC), **Paris** (1/day, 18:05–16:25, 21.5 hrs, departs Santa Apolónia), **Évora** (5/day, 2.5–3.5 hrs, departs Barreiro, 3 are direct, 2 require transfer in Casa Branca; bus is faster), **Lagos** (4/day, 3.5 hrs, departs Barreiro, likely transfer in Tunes), **Faro** (2 fast trains/day, 3.5 hrs, departs Barreiro), **Coimbra** (hrly, 2–2.5 hrs, departs Santa Apolónia), **Nazaré Valado** (4/day, 2.5–3.5 hrs, departs Rossio, transfer in Cacém), **Sintra** (4/hr, 45 min, departs Rossio). Train info: tel. 21-888-4025.

   To Salema: Both the bus and train take about five hours from Lisbon to Lagos. Trains from Lisbon to the south coast leave from the Barreiro station across the Tagus from downtown. Boats shuttle train travelers from Praça do Comércio to the Barreiro train station, with several departures hourly (€1, 30-min ride; note that schedule times listed are often when the boat sails, not when train departs). The 23:10–6:28 overnight train, while no fun, allows you to enjoy the entire day on the Algarve.

   By bus to: Coimbra (12/day, 2.5 hrs, €7.25), **Nazaré** (6/day, 2 hrs), **Fatima** (10/day, 1.5–2.5 hrs, depending on the route), **Alcobaça** (5/day, 2 hrs), **Évora** (12/day, 2 hrs), **Lagos** (8/day, 5 hrs, €12, easier than train, must book ahead, get details at TI). Buses leave from Lisbon's Arco do Cego bus station (Metro: Saldanha, tel. 21-354-5439). Intercentro Lines' buses to **Madrid** (2/day, 8 hrs, day or overnight, €36) leave from the same station (tel. 21-315-9277).

   Flying: You can generally buy a plane ticket to Madrid on short notice for about €150. Flying one-way on a round-trip is a little cheaper.

Driving in Lisbon

Driving in Lisbon is big-city crazy. If you enter from the north, a series of boulevards takes you into the center. Navigate by following signs to Centro, Avenida da República, Praça dos Marques de Pombal, Avenida da Liberdade, Praça dos Restauradores, Rossio, and Praça do Comércio. Consider hiring a taxi (cheap) to lead you to your hotel.

   There are many safe underground pay parking lots (follow the blue "P" signs), but they get more expensive by the hour and can cost €33 per day (at the most central Praça dos Restauradores).

Sights near Lisbon

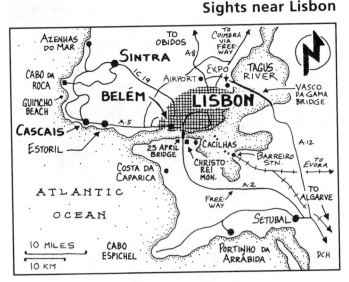

NEAR LISBON: SINTRA, CABO DA ROCA, CASCAIS, AND ESTORIL

For centuries, Portugal's aristocracy considered Sintra the natural escape from Lisbon. Now tourists do, too. Climb through the Versailles of Portugal, the Pena Palace; romp along the ruined ramparts of a deserted Moorish castle on a neighboring hilltop; and explore the rugged and picturesque westernmost tip of Portugal at Cabo da Roca. You can also mix and mingle with the jet set (or at least press your nose against their windows) at the resort towns of Cascais or Estoril.

Planning Your Time

These sights make fine daytrips from Lisbon. Remember that there are two bullrings out here, and it's more likely that your schedule will hit a fight here than in Lisbon. Without a car I'd skip Cabo da Roca and do Sintra, Cascais, and Belém as individual side trips from Lisbon.

By car, the 110-kilometer circular excursion (Lisbon–Belém–Sintra–Cabo da Roca–Cascais–Lisbon) makes for a fine day. Traffic congestion around Sintra can mess up your schedule. Follow the coast from Praça do Comércio west, under the bridge to Belém. Continue west to just before Cascais, where Sintra (11 km) is signposted. Sintra itself is far easier by train than by car from Lisbon. Consider not picking up your rental car until after Sintra.

Drivers who are eager for beach time can leave Lisbon, do

the Sintra circle, and drive directly to the Algarve that evening (4 hrs from Lisbon). From Sintra/Cascais, get on the freeway heading for Lisbon and exit at the Sul Ponte A2 sign, which takes you over the 25th of April bridge and south on A2.

SINTRA

For centuries, Sintra—just 18 kilometers northwest of Lisbon— was the summer escape of Portugal's kings. Those with money and a desire to be close to royalty built their palaces in lush gardens in the same neighborhood. Byron called this bundle of royal fancies and aristocratic dreams a "glorious Eden," and today it's mobbed with tourists. You can easily spend a day in this lush playground of castles, palaces, sweeping coastal views, and exotic gardens.

Tourist Information: Sintra has two TIs, a small one at the train station, and a larger TI a block off the main square (both open daily June–Sept 9:00–20:00, Oct–May 9:00–19:00, tel. 21-923-1157 or 21-924-1623, www.cm-sintra.pt/eng/). Pick up a free map and Sintra guide, packed with travel and sightseeing information. Pick up a schedule for the #434 shuttle bus to the sights. The main TI can arrange *quartos* (rooms in private homes) for overnighters.

Arrival in Sintra: Arriving by train, stop by the station TI for a map. To get to the center by bus, exit station right, and cross the street to get to bus stop #434 (see "Getting Around," below). By car, park it. The main lot is at Volta do Duche, near the center. A small lot is next to the train station. To avoid the traffic alto- gether, park at Pratela do Sintra (the station before Sintra, free parking south of station) and take the train to Sintra.

Planning Your Time

A full day from Lisbon might go like this: Catch an early Lisbon- to-Sintra train (4/hr from Rossio station, 45 min). If you like modern art, visit Sintra's new Museum of Modern Art (near train station). From the station, catch shuttle bus #434 (€3, valid all day) to the main square and TI, and visit the National Palace. For lunch, order a sandwich-to-go from the bakery, Panaderia Reunitas de Sin- tra, across the square from the National Palace. Catch bus #434 up to Pena Palace. Have a picnic lunch in Pena Gardens. Tour palace. Walk down to the Moorish castle and explore. Hike from the Moor- ish castle into town (30-min steep, wooded path; fork in path leads down from within the castle grounds—see map at entry turnstile). Catch train back to Lisbon (before or after dinner in Sintra). Note that the Pena Palace and Museum of Modern Art are closed Mon- day, and the National Palace is closed Wednesday.

Getting around Sintra

Cars are the curse of Sintra. Traffic and parking can be terrible.

But public transportation puts the "glorious" back into Byron's Eden. Bus #434 loops together all the important stops: train station (stop is across street from station); old town/TI/National Palace (stop is at TI); Moorish Ruins; Pena Palace; and back to the station (3/hr, 2/hr in winter, €3 tickets good for 24 hours, buy from driver; first bus starts at 10:20 from station, last one leaves station at 17:15, entire circuit takes 30 min). It's a fairly level 10-minute walk from the station to the old town/TI/National Palace. Taxis don't use a meter but have set fares (e.g., from town center or train station to Pena Palace-€8). If you decide (probably regrettably) to drive to the sights, you'll take a one-way winding loop and be encouraged to park "as soon as you can" or risk having to drive the huge loop again.

Sights—Sintra

National Palace (Palacio Nacional)—While going back to Moorish times, most of what you'll see is from the 15th-century reign of João I and later Manueline work. Although it echoes with Portuguese history and intrigue, the castle is most interesting for Portugal's finest collection of 500-year-old *azulejos* (tiles), its armory, and its fine furnishings (€2, free with Lisboa Card, Thu–Tue 10:00–17:30, closed Wed, no photos; it's the Madonna-bra-white building in the town center, a 10-min walk from the train station).

▲▲Pena Palace (Palacio de Pena)—This magical hilltop palace sits high above Sintra, a steep 15-minute hike above the ruined Moorish castle. Portugal's German-born Prince Ferdinand hired a German architect to build him a fantasy castle, mixing elements of German and Portuguese style. He got a crazy neo-fortified casserole of Gothic, Arabic, Moorish, Disney, Renaissance, and Manueline architectural bits and decorative pieces. (The statue on the nearby ridge is of the architect.) Built in the 1840s, the palace is so well-preserved that it feels as if it's the day after the royal family fled Portugal in 1910 (during a popular revolt making way for today's modern republic). This gives the place a charming intimacy rarely seen in palaces. English descriptions throughout give meaning to the rooms (€3, free with Lisboa Card, Tue–Sun 10:00–18:30, closed Mon, closes at 17:00 off-season). For a spectacular view of Lisbon and the Tagus River, hike for 15 minutes from the palace to the Chapel of Santa Eufemia (the trail's closed but the determined and nimble can climb the fence).

▲▲Moorish Castle (Castelo dos Mouros)—These 1,000-year-old Moorish castle ruins, lost in an enchanted forest and alive with winds of the past, are a castle-lover's dream come true and a great place for a picnic with a panoramic Atlantic view. While built by the Moors, the castle was taken by Christian forces in 1147. What you'll climb on today, while dramatic, was much restored

Sintra

in the 19th century. To get from Sintra to the ruins, hike three kilometers, taxi, or ride bus #434—see "Getting around Sintra," above. The ruins are free (daily 10:00–19:30, closes at 17:00 off-season).

▲**Sintra Museum of Modern Art: The Berardo Collection**—Modern art-lovers rave about Sintra's private modern-art gallery, one of the best in Iberia. The art is presented chronologically and grouped by style in hopes of giving the novice a better grip on post-1945 art (€3, Tue–Sun 10:00–18:00, closed Mon, 500 meters from train station, in Sintra's former casino on Avenida Heliodoro Salgado, exit right from station and go straight—for about 8 min, museum café's entrance is outside building to the right and down the stairs, tel. 21-924-8170, www.berardocollection.com).

Quinta da Regaleira—This neo-Manueline 1912 mansion and

garden, with mystical and masonic twists, was designed by an Italian opera-set designer for a wealthy but disgruntled monarchist two years after the royal family was deposed (€11 for 1.5–2.5 hr tour in English, by reservation only, 12 tours/day in summer, drops to 4/day in winter, max 30 persons, book by calling tel. 21-910-6650 during these hours: Mon–Fri 9:30–13:00, 14:30–15:30—they speak English; the main Sintra TI will call for you on the same day but if it's a weekend, mansion is likely to be booked up; a 10-min walk from downtown Sintra, café, www.regaleira.pt). Ask a local to pronounce Regaleira for you.

Toy Museum—Just for fun, you can wander through a collection of several thousand old-time toys, from small soldiers, planes, cars, trucks, and old trikes to a dolls' attic upstairs. The 20th-century owner João Arbués Moreira started collecting toys when he was 14, and just never quit (€3, free with Lisboa Card, Tue-Sun 10:00–18:00, closed Mon, Rua Visconde de Monserrate, one block in front of National Palace, tel. 21-924-2171, www.museu-do-brinquedo.pt).

Monserrate—Just outside of Sintra is the wonderful garden of Monserrate. If you like tropical plants and exotic landscaping, a visit is time well spent (€3, daily 10:00–17:15, less in winter). Some say that the Pena Gardens (below the palace) are just as good as the more famous Monserrate.

Sleeping and Eating in Sintra
(€1.10 = about $1, country code: 351)

Casa Miradouro is a beautifully restored mansion from 1890. With six spacious, stylish rooms, an elegant lounge, castle and sea views, and a wonderful garden, it's a worthy splurge. The place is graciously run by Frederic, who speaks English with a Swiss accent (Sb-€77–105, Db-€89–118, priciest May–Sept, CC, nonsmoking rooms, closed Jan–Feb, street parking, Rua Sotto Major 55, from National Palace go past Hotel Tivoli Sintra and 400 meters downhill, note that it's a 7-min walk uphill to return to center, tel. 21-923-5900, fax 21-924-1836, www.casa-miradouro.com, e-mail: mail@casa-miradouro.com).

Vila Marques, another elegant old mansion, is funkier, with an eccentric-grandmotherly flair, fine rooms, and a great garden with birds. It's 100 meters behind Hotel Tivoli and 200 meters from the National Palace (D-€40, D/twin-€45, no sinks in rooms, Tb-€100, no CC, Rua Sotto Mayor 1, tel. 21-923-0027, Sra. Marques NSE and does not accept reservations).

Eating: The hardworking, tourist-friendly **Restaurant Regional de Sintra** feeds locals and tourists well (€12.50 meals, Thu–Tue 12:00–16:00, 19:00–22:30, closed Wed, 200 meters from train station at Travessa do Municipio 2, exit station left, go downhill, it's located on the first square—far right corner,

tel. 21-923-4444). The touristy **Restaurante Bristol** serves good meals a block in front of the National Palace (closed Mon, Rua Visconde de Monserrate 16-22, tel. 21-923-3438). At the train station, Pizza Hut's salad bar is an easy place to get a cheap, healthy salad-to-
go for a picnic in Sintra or the ride back to Lisbon.

Transportation Connections—Sintra

To: Lisbon's Rossio Station (4 trains/hr, 45 min), **Cascais** (hrly buses also stop at Cabo da Roca, 45–60 min, bus stop is across street from Sintra train station).

CABO DA ROCA

Wind-beaten, tourist-infested Cabo da Roca is the westernmost point in Europe. It has a little shop, a café, and a tiny TI that sells a "proof of being here" diploma (daily 9:00–20:00). Nearby, on the road to Cascais, you'll pass a good beach for wind, waves, sand, and the chance to be the last person in Europe to see the sun set. If you crave a beach and have a car, Praia Adraga (north of Cabo da Roca) is desolate.

CASCAIS AND ESTORIL

Before the rise of the Algarve, these towns were the haunt of Portugal's rich and beautiful. Today they are quietly elegant, with noble old buildings, beachfront promenades, a bullring, a casino, and more fame than they deserve. Cascais is the more enjoyable of the two; it's not as rich and stuffy and has a cozy touch of fishing village, great seafood, and a younger, less-pretentious atmosphere (TI tel. 21-466-3813). Both are an easy daytrip from Lisbon (4 trains/hr, 40 min from Lisbon's Caís do Sodre station).

THE ALGARVE

The Algarve has long been known as Europe's last undiscovered tourist frontier. But that "jumbo shrimp" statement contradicts itself. The Algarve is well-discovered, and if you go to the places featured in tour brochures, you'll find it much like Spain's Costa del Sol—paved, packed, and pretty stressful. But there are a few great beach towns left, mostly on the western tip, and this part of the Algarve is the south coast of any sun worshiper's dreams.

For some rigorous rest and intensive relaxation in a village where the tourists and the fishermen sport the same stubble, make sunny Salema your Algarve hideaway. It's just you, a beach full of garishly painted boats, your wrinkled landlady, and a few other globetrotting experts in lethargy. Nearby sights include Cape Sagres (Europe's "Land's End" and home of Henry the Navigator's famous navigation school) and the jet-setty resort of Lagos. Or you could just work on a tan and see how slow you can get your pulse in sleepy Salema. If not now, when? If not you, who?

Planning Your Time
The Algarve is your vacation from your vacation. How much time it deserves depends upon how much time you have and how much time you need to recharge your solar batteries. On a three-week Iberian blitz, I'd give it three nights and two days. After a full day of sightseeing in Lisbon, I'd push it by driving four hours around dinnertime to gain an entirely free beach day. With two days, I'd spend one enjoying side trips to Cape Sagres and Lagos and another just lingering in Salema. Plan on an entire day to get from Salema to Sevilla (30-minute bus ride to Lagos, then 5-hour bus ride to Sevilla). With more time, I'd spend it in Salema. Eat all

The Algarve

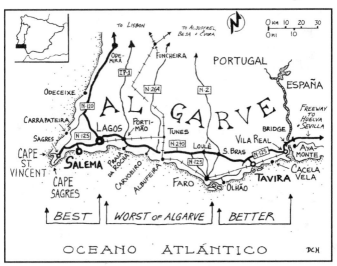

dinners in Salema unless you're fighting bulls in Lagos. The only other Algarve stop to consider is Tavira.

Getting around the Algarve
Trains and buses connect the main towns along the south coast (except on weekends, when service gets skimpy). Buses take you west from Lagos, where trains don't go. The highway makes driving—barring traffic problems—quick and easy. (See "Route Tips for Drivers in the Algarve," at the end of this chapter.)

SALEMA
One bit of old Algarve magic still glitters quietly in the sun— Salema. It's at the end of a small road just off the main drag between the big city of Lagos and the rugged southwest tip of Europe, Cape Sagres. This simple fishing village, quietly discovered by British and German tourists, has a few hotels, time-share condos up the road, some hippies' bars with rock music, English and German menus, a classic beach, and endless sun.

Helpful Hints
Coastal Boat Tours: Local English-speaking guide Sebastian offers a two-hour scenic cruise along the coast. He gives a light commentary on the geology and the plant and bird life as he motors halfway to Cape Sagres and back. Trips include nipping into some cool blue natural caves. Morning trips are best for

Salema

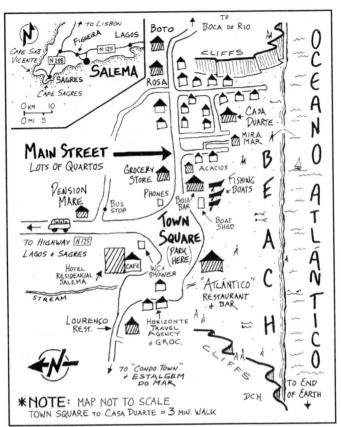

NOTE: MAP NOT TO SCALE
TOWN SQUARE TO CASA DUARTE = 3 MIN. WALK

bird-watching. Kicking back and watching the cliffs glide by, I felt like I was scanning a super-relaxing gallery of natural art. Consider being dropped at (nude) Figueira Beach just before returning to Salema (it's a 20-min walk home to Salema—bring shoes, a picnic, and extra water). Easygoing and gentle Sebastian charges little more than what it costs to run his small boat (€15 per person, daily 10:30 and 13:30 mid June–mid Sept, 2–5 passengers, tel. 28-269-5458 or ask for Sebastian at the beachside fishermen's hut or Pensión Mare).

Travel Agency: Horizonte Travel Agency changes money at fair rates; posts bus and train schedules; sells long-distance bus tickets to Lisbon (same price as bus station); rents cars, mopeds, and mountain bikes; books flights and hotels; offers lots of apartment rentals in Salema; and runs all-day jeep tours to the nature park on the southwest coast (June–Sept Mon–Fri 9:30–19:00, Sat 10:00–19:00, Sun 9:30–13:00; Oct-May Mon–Fri 9:30–13:00, 14:00–18:30, Sat 10:00–14:00, closed Sun, CC, Apartamentos do Mar, Loja 11, Largo da Liberdade, in town center across the stream from Hotel Residencial Salema, tel. 28-269-5855, tel. & fax 28-269-5920; e-mail: horizonte.passeios.turis@mail.telepac.pt, Andrea Fernandes SE).

Changing Money: Salema doesn't have an ATM machine and many places don't take credit cards. Either bring lots of euros, or change money (any kind: dollars, travelers' checks, other currencies) at the Horizonte Travel Agency, Salema Market, or Hotel Residencial Salema.

Taxi: Your hotel can arrange a taxi, or call a taxi direct at cellular 91-938-5139.

Salema Beach Bum's Quickie Tour

Salema has a split personality: The whitewashed old town is for locals, the other half was built for tourists. Locals and tourists pursue a policy of peaceful coexistence. Tourists laze in the sun while locals grab the shade.

Market action: Salema's flatbed truck market rolls in most mornings—one truck each for fish, fruit, and vegetables, and a five-and-dime truck for clothing and other odds and ends. The *1812 Overture* horn of the fish truck wakes you at 8:00. The bakery trailer sells delightful fresh bread and "store-bought" sweet rolls each morning (about 8:00–10:00). And afternoons around 14:30 the red mobile post office stops by.

Fishing scene: Salema is still a fishing village. While the fishermen's hut no longer hosts a fish auction, you'll still see the old-timers enjoying its shade, oblivious to the tourists, mending their nets and arm-wrestling the octopi. In the calm of summer, boats are left out on buoys. In the winter, the community-subsidized tractor earns its keep by hauling the boats ashore. (In pre-tractor days, such boat-hauling was a 10-man chore.) The pottery jars stacked everywhere are octopus traps. Unwritten tradition allocates different chunks of undersea territory to each Salema family. The traps are tied about a meter apart in long lines and dropped offshore. Octopi, thinking these would make a cozy place to set an ambush, climb in and get ambushed. When the fishermen hoist them in, they hang on—unaware they've made their final mistake.

Beach scene: Locals, knowing their tourist-based economy sits on a foundation of sand, hope and pray that sand returns after being washed away each winter. Some winters turn the beach into a pile of rocks. In Portugal, restaurateurs are allowed to build a temporary, summer-only, on-the-beach restaurant if they provide a lifeguard and run the green/yellow/red warning-flag system (red means dangerous). All over the country you'll see lonely beaches with solitary temporary structures housing such beach restaurants. The Atlantico Restaurant got permission to dominate Salema's beach by providing a lifeguard through the summer. And, as is often the case, they've quietly evolved from a temporary to a permanent business. Beach towns must also provide public showers and toilets, such as Salema's Balneario Municipal (daily 14:00–19:00 in summer, showers €0.80, run by Manuela). The fountain in front of it is a reminder of the old days. When water to the village was cut off, this was always open.

On the west end of the beach, you can climb over the rocks past tiny tide pools to the secluded Figuera Beach. While the old days of black widows chasing topless Nordic women off the beach are gone, nudism is still risqué today. Over the rocks and beyond the view of prying eyes, Germans grin and bare it.

Community development: The whole peninsula has been declared a natural park, and further development close to the beach is forbidden. Salema will live with past mistakes, such as the huge hotel in the town center that pulled some mysterious strings to go two stories over the height limit. Up the street is a huge community of Club Med–type vacationers who rarely leave their air-conditioned bars and swimming pools. Across the highway a kilometer or two inland is an even bigger golfing resort with a spa, pool, and tennis (worth exploring by car).

Salema after dark: Salema has several late-night bars, each worth a visit. Consider a Salema pub crawl. *Armarguinha* is a sweet and likeable almond liqueur you might try. The **Boia Bar** offers beachfront drinks and music. Guillerma Duarte's **Atabua Bar** is the liveliest, with the youngest crowd (daily 20:00–02:00 or later, across the street, famous sangria). **A Aventura Bar and Creperie** offers a pleasant atmosphere for sipping drinks and sending e-mail (€4.50/hr, 11:00–02:00, just past the Salema Market).

Sleeping in Salema
(€1.10 = about $1, country code: 351)
Sleep Code: **S** = Single, **D** = Double/Twin, **T** = Triple, **Q** = Quad, **b** = bathroom, **s** = shower only, **CC** = Credit Cards accepted, **no CC** = Credit Cards not accepted, **SE** = Speaks English, **NSE** = No English. When a price range is given, the lowest is the winter rate and the highest is the peak-season summer rate.

Salema is crowded in July, August, and September. The town has three streets, five restaurants, several bars, a lane full of fisherfolk who happily rent out rooms to foreign guests, and a circle of modern condo-type hotels, apartments, and villas up the hillside. Parking is free and easy on the street (beware of the no-parking signs near the bus stop).

For maximum comfort there's no need to look beyond John's Pensión Mare. For economy and experience, go for the *quartos* (rooms—usually with separate private entrances—rented out of homes).

Pensiónes and Hotels

Pensión Mare, a blue-and-white building looking over the village above the main road into town, is the best good, normal hotel value in Salema (Sb-€33–38, Db-€45–60, Tb-€65–75, includes good breakfast, 10 percent discount with this book and cash if arranged in advance, CC, guests-only laundry service €4 per kilo, Praia de Salema, Budens 8650-194, Algarve, tel. 28-269-5165, fax 28-269-5846, www.algarve.co.uk). Two easygoing Brits, John and Alison, run this place, offering seven comfortable rooms, three fully equipped apartments (€50–67, breakfast not available), and a tidy paradise. They speak English better than I do and will hold rooms with a phone call and a credit card. They also rent a gem of a fisherman's two-bedroom cottage on the "*quartos* street" (Db-€75, Qb-€100).

Hotel Residencial Salema, the oversized hotel towering crudely above everything else in town, is a good value if you want a modern, comfortable room handy to the beach. Its 32 red-tiled rooms all have air-conditioning, balconies, and partial views (Sb-€45–65, Db-€50–75, 10 percent discount with this book, extra bed-30 percent more, includes breakfast, CC, elevator, changes money, rents cars and mopeds, closed Nov–March, tel. 28-269-5328, fax 28-269-5329, SE).

Estalagem Infante do Mar is a three-star hotel on top of the cliff. Its 30 rooms are plain but all have balconies, and the views are spectacular (Sb-€43–62, Db-€48–85, extra bed-30 percent more, includes small breakfast, CC, pool, Internet access, laundry service, bar, restaurant, free parking, changes money, has no address except its name, closed Nov–Feb, tel. 28-269-0100, fax 28-269-0109, www.infantedomar.com, mail@infantedomar.com, SE). It's a stiff 10-minute walk uphill. From the Hotel Residencial Salema, cross the bridge and then head up.

Casa Alegria is a colorful apartment with a splash of Santa Fe and a fantastic view (Db/Qb-€75, reserve by calling John of Pensión Mare at tel. 28-269-5165 or Wilfried the owner at tel. & fax 28-269-5020, located at the top of the "*quartos* street").

Quartos and Camping

Quartos abound along the residential street (running left from the village center as you face the beach). Ask one of the locals at the waterfront or ask at the Boia Bar or the Salema Market. Prices vary with the season and plumbing (doubles-€25–45), breakfast is not included, and credit cards are useless. Many places offer beachfront views. It's worth paying extra for *com vista* (view) rooms, since the rooms on the back tend to be dark and musty.

Few *quartos'* landladies speak English, but they're used to dealing with visitors. Many will clean your laundry for about €2.50 or so. If you're settling in for a while or are on a tight budget, park your bags and partner at a beachside bar and survey several places. There are always rooms available for those dropping in. Especially outside of July and August, prices can be soft.

Casa Duarte has five pleasant rooms (4 with views), a communal kitchenette, and two terraces (D-€22.50–35, no CC, tel. 28-269-5206 or their English-speaking daughter Cristina at 28-269-5307; son Romeu, who owns the Salema Market, also SE). From "*quartos* street," turn right at the Clube Recreativo and then left on the paved path. Duarte's is #7, the first building on the right.

The friendly **Acacio family** rents a humble ground-floor double (D-€25–30) and a fine upstairs apartment with kitchenette, balcony, and a great ocean view for up to four people (Tb-€50, Qb-€70, no CC, on "*quartos* street" at #91, tel. 28-269-5473, Silvina NSE).

Maria Helena and Jorge Ribeiro, a helpful young couple, rent two small, simple doubles (D-€22.50, one has tiny view) and a charming tree house–type apartment with a kitchen, fine view terrace, and view toilet for €40 (no CC, Rua dos Pescadores 83, tel. 28-269-5289, SE).

Senhor and Senhora Boto rent two immaculate, comfortable rooms with hillside views (D-€22.50–25) and a spacious two-bedroom sea-view apartment with two terraces (Db-€40–45, Tb/Qb-€50, great value for up to 4 people, no CC). It's at the top of "*quartos* street" at Rua dos Pescadores 4 (walk 5 min up, on the left, tel. 28-269-5265, NSE).

Rosa rents a small double with a big terrace (Db-€30) and a comfortable apartment with balcony that can sleep two couples and a small child. This is a super value at €45, worth the hike and the two-night minimum stay (no CC, near top of hill, 5-min walk from center, Rua dos Pescadores 18, tel. 28-269-5255, NSE).

Campers (who don't underestimate the high tides) sleep free and easy on the **beach** (public showers available in the town center) or at a well-run **campground** with bungalows a kilometer inland, back toward the main road.

Eating in Salema

Fresh seafood, eternally. Salema has six or eight places to eat. Happily, those that face the beach (the three listed below) are the most fun and have the best service, food, and atmosphere.

The **Boia Bar and Restaurant**, at the base of the residential street, has a classy beachfront setting, noteworthy service, and a knack for doing whitefish just right. Their vegetarian lasagna and salads are popular. And their hearty loss-leader breakfast gives you bacon, eggs, toast, coffee, and fresh-squeezed orange juice for the cost of two glasses of orange juice anywhere else in town (daily 10:00–01:00, serving until 22:00; try to arrive for dinner by 19:00, CC, tel. 28-269-5382).

The **Atlantico** is noisier, big, busy, right on the beach, and especially atmospheric when the electricity goes out and faces flicker around candles. It's run by a member of the Duarte family, and the service is friendly. Consider taking your dessert wine or coffee to the beach for some stardust (daily 12:00–24:00, serving until 22:00, CC, tel. 28-269-5142).

The intimate **Mira Mar,** farther up the residential street, is run by gracious Florentine and Dieter, who serve Portuguese fare practically on the beach (daily 12:00–24:00, serving until 23:00, no CC, tel. 28-226-9250).

Restaurante Lourenço, several blocks inland, offers good-value meals, has a local clientele, and makes the best coffee in town (€8 menu, daily 8:00–24:00, no CC, Rua 28 de Janeiro, from Hotel Residencial Salema cross bridge, restaurant is a half-block uphill on your left, tel. 28-269-8622).

Need a break from fish? **Carapau Frances**, in the town square, serves good Greek and Italian food, including cheap pizzas (Wed–Mon 9:00–11:00, 12:00–14:30, 18:00–23:00, closed Tue and Nov–Jan, no CC).

Romeu's **Salema Market** has all the fixings for a great picnic (fresh fruits, veggies, bread, sheep's cheese, sausage, *vinho verde*) to take with you to a secluded beach or Cape Sagres. Helpful Romeu also changes money and gives travel advice (daily 8:00–13:00, 15:00–20:00, on the "*quartos*" street). Another grocery store, **Alisuper**, is just up from the beach on a tiny strip mall next to Horizonte Travel Agency and across from Hotel Residencial Salema.

Drivers who want a classy meal outside of town should consider the elegant **Restaurant Vila Velha** in Sagres or the romantic **Castelejo Restaurante** at Praia do Castelejo (see "Cape Sagres," below).

CAPE SAGRES

This rugged southwestern tip of Portugal was the spot closest to the edge of our flat earth in the days before Columbus. Prince Henry the Navigator, determined to broaden Europe's horizons and spread Catholicism, sent sailors ever farther into the unknown. He lived here at his navigators' school, carefully debriefing ship-wrecked and frustrated explorers as they washed ashore. (TI open Tue–Sat 9:30–13:00, 14:00–17:30, closed Sun–Mon, on main street Rua Comandante Matoso, tel. 28-262-4873.)

Portugal's "end of the road" is two distinct capes. Windy **Cabo St. Vincent** is actually the most southwestern tip. It has a desolate lighthouse that marks what was even in prehistoric times referred to as "the end of the world" (open to the public daily 10:00–17:00, snoop around, peek over the far edge, ask the attendant to spin the light for you). Outside the lighthouse, salt-of-the-earth merchants sell figs, fritters, and seaworthy sweaters (€20 average). **Cape Sagres**, with its old fort and Henry the Navigator lore, is the more historic cape (2 or 3 maritime history exhibits per year, old church, dramatic views). At either cape, look for daredevil windsurfers and fishermen casting off the cliffs.

Lashed tightly to the windswept landscape is the salty town of Sagres, above a harbor of fishing boats and the lavish **Pousada do Infante**. For a touch of local elegance, pop by the *pousada* for breakfast. For €8.50 you can sip coffee and nibble on a warm croissant while gazing out to where, in the old days, the world dropped right off the table. The classy *pousada*, a reasonable splurge with a magnificent setting (Db-€145, tel. 28-262-4222, fax 28-262-4225), offers a warm welcome to anyone ready to pay so much for a continental breakfast.

Restaurant Vila Velha in Sagres is the place to eat if you want to dine really well. Owner Luis speaks English and serves traditional cuisine with a candlelit and dressy ambience. While Vila Velha does fine fish, for some the meaty side of its menu offers a needed break from seafood (€15 meals, next to *pousada*, reservations smart, tel. 28-262-4788). Ask Luis for a glass of his homemade—and complimentary—*ginjinha* (sweet cherry-like liquor) after dinner. A stop here makes sense after tripping out to Cape Sagres.

Sagres is a popular gathering place for the backpacking bunch, with plenty of private rooms in the center and a great beach and bar scene. From Salema, Sagres is a 20-minute drive or hitch, a half-hour bus trip (nearly hourly trips from Salema, check return times), or a taxi ride (€25 2-hr round-trip includes 1 hr free in Sagres).

Many beaches are tucked away on the drive between Salema and Cape Sagres. Most of them require a short walk after you stop along N-125. In some cases you leave your car on access roads or cross private property to reach the beaches—please be considerate. Furnas beach is fully accessible by car. Ingrina and Zavial beaches are accessed by turning south in the village of Raposeira. Many beaches have bars. In Salema, ask at Pensión Mare or the Horizonte Travel Agency for directions to beaches before you head to Sagres.

The best secluded beach in the region is **Praia do Castelejo**, just north of Cape Sagres (from the town of Vila do Bispo, drive inland and follow the signs for 15 min). If you have a car and didn't grow up in Fiji, this really is worth the drive. Overlooking the deserted beach is **Castelejo Restaurante**, which specializes in *cataplanas*, hearty seafood stew that feeds two to three people (April–Oct daily 12:00–22:00, 12 km from Salema at Praia do Castelejo, tel. 28-263-9777).

LAGOS

The major town and high-rise resort on the west end of the Algarve was the capital of the Algarve in the 13th and 14th centuries. The first great Portuguese maritime expeditions embarked from here, and the first African slave market in Europe was held here (understandably not advertised by the local TI, though the slave market does appear on the town map). The old town, defined by its medieval walls, stretches between Praça Gil Eannes and the fort. It's a whitewashed jumble of pedestrian streets, bars, funky craft shops, outdoor restaurants, and sunburned tourists. The church of San Antonio and the adjoining regional museum (€1.90, Tue–Sun 9:30–12:30, 14:00–17:00, closed Mon) are worth a look, but the morning fish market at the Mercado Municipal is more interesting (produce upstairs, closed Sun, on main square, facing marina). The beaches with the exotic rock formations—of postcard fame—begin just past the fort.

Lagos has a small, for-tourists bullfight in its dinky ring from June through September on most Saturdays at 18:30. Seats are a steep €20, but the show is a thriller. Signs all along this touristy coastline advertise this *stierkampf*.

Tourist Information: The TI, a bleak six-minute walk from the bus station, is oddly located on a traffic roundabout (with no parking) on the entrance into town. Although everyone heads seaward, the TI is in the opposite direction—could be worth skipping, especially if you're not lingering in Lagos (Mon–Fri 9:30–13:00, 14:00–17:30, closed Sat–Sun, behind bus station, take Rua Vasco da Gama to the right, and continue straight, on roundabout en route to Portimão, tel. 28-276-3031).

Arrival in Lagos: The train and bus stations are a five-minute walk apart, separated by the marina and pedestrian bridge over a river. Neither the bus station nor the train station has luggage storage.

Coastal Boat Tours: Two companies offer boat tours (roughly April–Nov) and have offices at the marina operated by English-speaking staff. **Bom Dia** offers three different tours by sailboat: a two-hour grotto tour (with a chance to swim), a half-day BBQ cruise (basically a grotto tour with a meal), and a full-day round-trip to Sagres. Check out the possibilities at their ticket office at the marina. Particularly in July and August, book at least a day in advance—by phone or in person (2-hr excursions start at €14.50, no CC, in marina at Lagos 10, WC on board, tel. 28-276-4670 or 91-781-0761, e-mail: bomdiacruises@it.pt). **Dolphin Seafari** offers 90-minute dolphin-watching cruises (5/day, dophin sightings occur on about 80 percent of trips) and 45-minute speedboat tours just for fun (1/day in late afternoon, no CC, big sturdy inflatable lifeboat used for both trips, no WC on board but a WC is in marina near Seafari office, in July–Aug

advisable to book tour 2 days in advance, tel. 28-2792-586
or 91-935-9359).

Sleeping and Eating in Lagos
(€1.10 = about $1, country code: 351)

When a price range is given, the lowest is the winter rate, the
highest is the peak-season summer rate. Lagos is enjoyable for
a resort its size, but I must remind you that Salema is a village
paradise and is only a 20-minute taxi ride (€13.50–16, no meter,
settle price first) or half-hour bus ride away.

Caza de São Goncalo de Lagos, a beautifully decorated
18th-century home with a garden, lovely tile work, parquet floors,
and elegant furnishings, is a fine value. While the downstairs
rooms are relatively plain, upstairs you'll find a plush old-world
lounge, a dreamy garden, and 13 classy old rooms with all the
comforts (Sb-€40–60, Db-€50–70, Qb-€90–100 depending on
room and season, includes breakfast, closed Nov–mid-March,
CC—AmEx only, Rua Candido dos Reis 73, on a pedestrian street
2 blocks off Praça Luis do Camões, a square that's a block behind
the main square, tel. 28-276-2171, fax 28-276-3927, SE).

If you missed the last bus to Salema (leaves Lagos around
20:30), these places are within 100 meters of the bus station:
Pensão Residencial Solar, a good budget bet, has 29 simple,
clean rooms (Sb-€28–45, Db-€40–63, includes breakfast, cheaper
rooms in annex up the hill, CC, elevator, Rua Antonio Crisogono
dos Santos 60, tel. 28-276-2477, fax 28-276-1784, SE). The
big, slick **Albergeria Marina Rio** faces the marina and the busy
main street. Its modern, air-conditioned rooms come with all the
amenities. Marina views come with noise. Quieter rooms are in
the back (Sb-€45–87, Db-€48–90, extra bed €13.50–27, CC,
small rooftop pool, elevator, Internet access, laundry service,
Avenida dos Descobrimentos-Apartado 388, tel. 28-276-9859, fax
28-276-9960, www.marinario.com, e-mail: marinario@ip.pt, SE).

The Club Med–like **youth hostel** is a lively, social, and cushy
experience (dorm bed in quad-€8.50–12.50, 5 Db-€21.50–30,
includes breakfast, kitchen facilities, Internet access, priority given
to hostel members, non-members pay more, Rua Lancarote de
Freitas 50, tel. 28-276-1970, fax 28-276-9684).

Transportation Connections—
Lagos and Salema

Lagos to: Lisbon (5 trains/day, 5 hrs, possible transfer in Tunes;
5 buses/day, 5 hrs), **Évora** (1 bus/day, 5 hrs), **Vila Real St. Antonio** (4 trains/day, 4.5 hrs), **Tavira** (7 trains/day, 3.5 hrs, 2 daily
express trains do it in 2 hrs). Train info: tel. 28-276-2987, bus
info: tel. 28-276-2944.

Lagos to Salema: Lagos is your Algarve transportation

hub and the closest train station to Salema (15 km). Buses go nearly hourly between Lagos and Sagres (30-min ride, last bus departs Lagos around 20:30, fewer buses on weekends); about half the buses go right into the village of Salema—the others drop you at the top of the road into Salema (bus continues to Figueira). From here it's a 20-minute walk downhill into the village.

In Lagos, to get to the bus station from the train station (ignore the "*quartos* women" who tell you Salema is 60 km away), walk straight out of the train station, go left around big building, walk past marina, cross pedestrian bridge and then the main boulevard, and walk straight into the white-and-yellow EVA bus station. If you venture into Lagos, buses to Salema (marked with the final destination, Sagres) also stop on the waterfront. Allow €14 to €17 for a taxi from Lagos to Salema (settle price first). Before heading to Salema, pick up return bus schedules and train schedules for your next destination, particularly if you're going to Sevilla (though as a fallback, stop by Horizonte Travel Agency in Salema to check the posted schedules).

Lagos and Sevilla: The direct bus between Lagos and Sevilla is worth every euro (€15, 2/day, 5 hrs, daily May-Sept, sometimes starts in April and continues into Oct; doesn't run off-season). The bus departs from the Lagos bus station (tel. 28-276-2944) and arrives at Sevilla's Plaza de Armas bus station. Note that Spanish time is one hour later than Portuguese time.

To get from Salema to Lagos, take an early bus (check the schedule; you'll likely have more options if you walk up to the main road) or take a taxi to Lagos (€14-17).

Off-season options: If you're traveling off-season, when the direct Lagos-Sevilla bus doesn't run, getting to Sevilla is a very long day (roughly 8 to 10 hrs). There are two options from Lagos: 1) take buses—with transfers in Faro, Portugal and Huelva, Spain—all the way to Sevilla, or 2) take a train/ferry/bus combination.

The all-bus option is simpler and usually faster, but isn't as good a choice on weekends when bus frequency drops dramatically. You take the bus from Lagos to Faro (7/day, 2 hrs), then catch the bus to Sevilla (2/day, 4 hours with transfer in Huelva). Note that only two buses from Faro run to Sevilla. Get an early start in order to catch a bus from Faro; ideally call (or have a local person call) the Faro bus station (tel. 28-989-9760 or 28-989-9761) to find out the times of the two departures for Sevilla (or see www.eva-bus.com for Lagos-Faro-Huelva bus schedules; from Huelva buses run hourly to Sevilla, 1-hr trip).

Taking a train/ferry/bus combination between Lagos and Sevilla is the most time-consuming of all (about 10 hours) but it's predictable and runs daily year-round (frequency drops on weekends but it's still doable). Take the train from Lagos until the last stop in Vila Real de San Antonio (4/day includes 2 morning departures, allow 4.5 hours with transfer in Tunes or Faro). The Vila Real train station is about a kilometer from the dock (exit straight from station—on Rua Eça de Queiroz, walk about 5 min, turn left on Rua Ayamonte, leads to dock; or take a €3 taxi ride). Ferries run frequently between Vila Real and Ayamonte, Spain (€1, 17/day, 26/day July-Sept, 15 min, last ferry runs about 22:00). Ayamonte is a pleasant border town. The bus station is a 15-minute walk from station; pick up a map and bus schedules from the TI at the Ayamonte dock (Mon-Sat 10:00-13:30, 17:00-20:00, closed Sun, open later and on Sun afternoon in summer, tel. 95-950-2121). To reach the bus station from the dock, angle right though the pedestrian area to Avenida Andalucía, then follow this road past the lake straight to the station (tel. 95-932-1171).

From Ayamonte to Sevilla, catch a direct bus to Sevilla (6/day, fewer on weekends, 2.5 hrs) or transfer at Huelva (10/day, 1 hr, easy transfer). From Huelva, buses run hourly to Sevilla (1 hr). The modern Huelva bus station has ATMs and an English-speaking info office (tel. 95-925-6900). From Huelva, you could take one of four daily trains to Sevilla (2 hrs), but it's simpler to take the bus. Huelva's bus and train stations are connected by a 15-minute walk along Avenida Italia. Sunday schedules are limited and more frustrating. (See "Transportation Connections" near the end of the Sevilla chapter for more specifics.)

TAVIRA

Straddling a river, with a lively park, chatty locals, and boats sharing its waterfront center, Tavira is a low-rise, easygoing alternative to the other, more aggressive Algarve resorts. It's your best east Algarve stop. Because Tavira has good connections by bus and train (it's on the trans-Algarve train line, with nearly hourly departures both east and west), many travelers find the town more accessible than Salema.

The many churches and fine bits of Renaissance architecture sprinkled through Tavira remind the wanderer that 500 years ago the town was the largest on the Algarve (with 1,500 dwellings according to a 1530 census) and an important base for Portuguese adventurers in Africa. The silting up of its harbor, a plague, the 1755 earthquake, and the shifting away of its once-upon-a-time lucrative tuna industry left Tavira in a long decline. Today the town relies on tourism.

Orientation

Tavira straddles the Rio Gilão three kilometers from the Atlantic. Everything of sightseeing and transportation importance is on the south bank. A clump of historic sights—the ruined castle and main church—fills its tiny fortified hill and tangled Moorish lanes. But today the action is outside the old fortifications along the riverside

Tavira

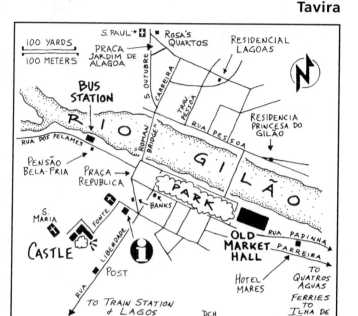

Praça da República and the adjacent shady, fountain- and bench-
filled park. The old market hall is beyond the park. And beyond that
is the boat to the beach island. The old pedestrian-only "Roman
Bridge" leads from Praça da República to the north bank (2 recommended hotels and most of the evening and restaurant action).

Tourist Information: The TI is up the cobbled steps from
the inland end of the Praça da República (daily 9:30–18:00, shorter
hours and closed during lunch and on Sun off-season, depending
on staff availability, Rua Galeria 9, tel. 28-132-2511). Guided town
walks leave from the TI twice daily in summer (€2.50, call TI or
tel. 28-132-1946 for information, reserve 2 days in advance,
particularly July–Aug).

Arrival in Tavira: The train station is a 10-minute walk from
the town center: Leave the station following the yellow "Turismo"
sign and follow this road downhill to the river and Praça da
Republica. The riverside bus station is three blocks from the
town center; simply follow the river into town.

Sights—Tavira
The TI's fine, free map describes a dozen churches with enthusi-
asm. But for most tourists, the town's sights can be seen in a few

minutes. Uphill from the TI you'll find the ruined **castle**, offering only plush gardens and a fine city view (free, Mon–Sat 9:00–17:00). Just beyond the castle ruins is the town's most visit-worthy church, the **Church of Santa Maria**. From there I'd enjoy the riverside park at **Praça da República** and the fun architecture of the low-key 18th-century buildings facing the river. After dinner take a stroll along the fish-filled river, with a pause on the pedestrian bridge or in the park if there's any action in the bandstand.
Beaches—The big hit for travelers is Tavira's great beach island, **Ilha da Tavira**. The island is a long, almost treeless sandbar with a campground, several restaurants, and a sprawling beach. A summer-only boat takes bathers painlessly from downtown Tavira to the island (July–Sept 15 about hrly, timetable available at TI, €1 round-trip, departs 200 meters downriver from the former market hall). It's an enjoyable ride even if you just go round-trip without getting out. Or you can bus, taxi, ride a rental bike, or bake during a shadeless three-kilometer walk out of town to Quatro Aguas, where the five-minute ferry shuttles sunbathers to Ilha da Tavira (runs constantly with demand, last trip near midnight in high season to accommodate diners).

Another fine beach, the **Barril Beach resort**, is four kilometers from Tavira. Walk, rent a bike, or take a city bus to Pedras del Rei and then catch the little train (usually runs year-round) or walk 10 minutes through Ria Formosa National Park to the resort. Get details at the TI.

Sleeping in Tavira
(€1.10 = about $1, country code: 351)
In this beach town, prices shoot up in August.

Residencial Lagoas is spotless, homey, and a block off the river. Friendly, English-speaking Maria offers a communal refrigerator, a rooftop patio with a view made for wine and candles, and laundry washboard privileges (S-€17.50, D-€25, Db-€38, Tb-€43, less off-season, no breakfast, no CC, Rua Almirante Candido dos Reis 24, tel. 28-132-2252). Maria also rents several apartments. Cross the Roman footbridge from Praça da República, follow the middle fork on the other side, and turn right where it ends.

The modern, hotelesque **Residencia Princesa do Gilão** offers bright, modern, riverfront rooms, some with balconies and a view (Db-€40–50, includes breakfast, no CC, Rua Borda de Agua de Aguiar 10, cross the Roman bridge and turn right along the river, tel. & fax 28-132-5171, SE).

Pensão-Residencial Bela Fria is a shiny eight-room place with a rooftop sun terrace overlooking the river. Its simple air-conditioned rooms are quiet, modern, and comfortable (Sb-€25–33, €65 July–Aug; Db-€38–50, €85 July–Aug; includes breakfast, no CC, Rua dos Pelames 1, directly across from bus station, tel. & fax 28-132-5375, e-mail: belafria @hotmail.com, some English spoken).

For quiet, spacious, comfort, **Rosa's Quartos** are tops. Rosa rents 14 big, gleaming, marble-paved rooms on a quiet alley (Db-€25–35, no CC, over bridge and through Jardim da Alagoa square to Rua da Porta Nova 4, opposite St. Paul's church, tel. 28-132-1547, NSE).

For a splurge, consider **Hotel Mare**'s red-tiled and smartly appointed rooms, firm beds, sauna, restaurant, and rooftop terrace. Some rooms on the second floor have balconies overlooking the river (Sb-€23–48, no singles in Aug, Db-€38–67, €82 in Aug, includes breakfast, CC, air con, Rua Jose Pires Padinha, on the TI side of the river just beyond the old market hall, tel. 28-132-5815, fax 28-132-5819, SE).

Eating in Tavira

Tavira is filled with reasonable restaurants. A couple of classy places face the riverbank just beyond the old market hall. A few blocks inland, hole-in-the-wall places offer more fish per dollar.

These places are all within two blocks of the pedestrian Roman bridge, just over the river from the town center. For seafood, I enjoyed the inexpensive and relaxed **Restaurant Bica**, below Residencial Lagoas (see first hotel listing, above). The **Patio**, on a classy rooftop, is worth the extra euros. For Italian cuisine, consider **Patrick's** (good lasagna and curry dishes) and **Aquasul** (pasta, pizza, and more). From the bridge, if you turn left and go upstream through the tunnel you'll find the rickety riverside tables of the popular **Restaurant O Simão** (cheap, tasty grills). **Anazu Pasteleria** is the place to grab breakfast or nurse a late riverside drink (on Rua Pessoa, 1 block east of Roman bridge).

Transportation Connections—Tavira

To: Lisbon (4 trains/day, 5 hrs; 10 buses/day, 5 hrs), **Lagos** (12 trains/day, change in Faro or Tunes, 2–3 hrs), **Sevilla** (2 buses/day, 3.5 hrs, transfer in Huelva; can also hook up with morning Lagos-Sevilla bus in Ayamonte—ask TI or local travel agency for current schedule). Train info: tel. 28-132-2354, bus info: tel. 28-132-2546.

CACELA VELHA

Just a few kilometers east of Tavira (1 km off the main road), this tiny village sits happily ignored on a hill with its fort, church, one restaurant, a few *quartos*, and a beach, the open sea just over the sandbar, a short row across its lagoon. The restaurant serves a sausage-and-cheese specialty fried at your table. If you're driving, swing by, if only to enjoy the coastal view and imagine how nice the Algarve would be if people like you and me had never discovered it.

Route Tips for Drivers in the Algarve

Lisbon to Salema (240 km, 4 hrs): Following the blue "Sul Ponte" signs, drive south over Lisbon's 25th of April Bridge. A short detour just over the bridge takes you to the giant concrete statue of *Cristo Rei* (Christ in Majesty). Continue south past Setubal to the south coast (following signs to Algarve, Vila do Bispo, Sagres, Lagos, and Salema). Just east of Vila do Bispo, you'll hit the tiny road to the beach village of Salema. Decent roads, less traffic, and the glory of waking up on the Algarve make doing this drive at night a reasonable option.

Algarve to Sevilla (240 km): Drive east along the Algarve. In Lagos, park along the waterfront by the fort and the Mobil gas station. From Lagos follow the signs to Faro and then, near Loule, hit the freeway (direction: España) to Tavira. It's a two-hour drive from Salema to Tavira. Leaving Tavira, follow the signs to Vila Real and España. You'll cross over the bridge into Spain (where it's 1 hr later) and glide effortlessly (90 min by freeway) into Sevilla. At Sevilla follow the signs to Centro Ciudad ("city center"), drive along the river, and park (at least to get set up) near the cathedral and tower.

ÉVORA

Deep in the heart of Portugal, in the barren, arid plains of the southern province of Alentejo, historic Évora has been a cultural oasis for 2,000 years. With a beautifully untouched provincial atmosphere, fascinating whitewashed old town, museums, a cathedral, a chapel of bones, and even a Roman temple, Évora stands proudly amid groves of cork and olive trees.

The major sights—the Roman Temple of Diana and early Gothic cathedral—crowd close together at the town's highest point. A subtle but still-powerful charm is contained within the town's medieval wall. Find it by losing yourself in the quiet lanes of Évora's far corners.

The morning market is held on Praça 1 de Maio (daily except Mon). When a bullfight or an occasional American rodeo occur, they're big news. A car goes all over town with a loudspeaker— like an audible poster—announcing the event.

Planning Your Time

With frequent bus connections (15/day, 1.75 hrs) with Lisbon, Évora makes a decent day trip from Portugal's capital city. You can stop by for an overnight en route to or from the Algarve, though connections aren't plentiful, they're sufficient (1 bus/day to Lagos in afternoon, with easy transfer in Albufeira, 5 hrs; or 3 trains/day with 2 transfers, 5 hrs). Drivers can sandwich Évora between Lisbon and the Algarve, exploring dusty droves of olive groves and scruffy seas of peeled cork trees along the way.

With a day in Évora, take the Introductory Walk outlined below, have a quick lunch, see the remaining sights, and enjoy a leisurely dinner. After dinner, stroll the backstreets, ponder life with the retired men on the squares, duck into a students' bar, or follow the 16th-century aqueduct out of town—for 14 kilometers or so.

With more time, take a daytrip—by bus tour, car, or rental bike—to the surrounding countryside to see the prehistoric rock formations (see "Sights near Évora," below).

Tourist Information: The TI is on the main square, Praça do Giraldo 73 (Mon–Fri 9:00–19:00, Sat–Sun 9:00–12:30, 14:00–17:30, tel. 26-670-2671).

Arrival in Évora: The bus station is on Avenida S. Sebastião. To reach the center from the station, it's either a short taxi ride (€2.50) or a 10-minute walk (exit station right, and continue straight all the way into town, passing through the city walls at the halfway point). The train station is on Avenida Dr. Batahona. From the train station to the center, it's a taxi ride (about €3.50) or 25-minute walk straight up Avenida Dr. Batahona, continuing straight—on Rua da República—after you enter the city walls).

Walking Tour: City Tour offers a walking tour of Évora's Roman sights for €18 (daily depending on demand, 2.5 hrs, Alcárcova de Baixa 43, a block from TI, from main square take shopping street—Cinco de Outubro—then first right, tel. 26-674-6970; see "Sights near Évora," below, for their daily excursions). Maria Pires is a good local guide (€73/half day, tel. 91-723-2147).

Introductory Old Town Walk

Évora's walled city is small. These sights are all within a five-minute walk of the main square, Praça do Giraldo. The walk will take about an hour or so, depending on how many sights you visit. If it's a hot day, take this walk early in the morning or late afternoon (before sights close, around 18:00).

Évora was once an important Roman town—from the second century B.C. to the fourth century A.D.—because of its wealth of wheat and silver, its proximity to a river (easy to ship goods), and its location on a trade route to Rome. We'll see Roman sights, though only a few are above ground. Much of Évora's Roman past is buried under the houses and hotels of today (often uncovered by accident when plumbing work needs to be done in basements). The town fell under Moorish rule from the eighth century to the 12th century. And during its glory years (15th–16th centuries), Évora was favored by Portuguese kings, even serving as the home of King John III. From Romans to Moors to kings, this little town has a big history.

The Main Square: Start at Praça do Giraldo, Évora's main square. It was named after Giraldo the Fearless, the Christian knight who led a surprise attack and retook Évora from the Moors in 1165. As thanks, Giraldo was made governor of the town—and the symbol of the city (Évora's coat of arms is a knight on a horse). On this square, all that's left of several centuries of Moorish rule

Évora

❶ SOLAR MONFALIM	❾ ADEGA DE ALENTEJANO
❷ HOTEL SANTA CLARA	❿ REST. COZINHA DE ST. HUMBERTO
❸ RESIDENCIAL POLICARPO	⓫ REST. GUIAO
❹ HOTEL IBIS	⓬ REST. DOM FARTOTE
❺ POUSADA DOS LOIOS	⓭ REST. PAPASANDES
❻ HOTEL CARTUXA	⓮ REST. MOLHOBICO
❼ YOUTH HOSTEL	⓯ PRACA DE SERTORIO
❽ FIALHO REST.	

is their artistry, evidenced by the wrought-iron balconies of the buildings that ring the square (and an occasional distinctive Mudejar "keyhole" window throughout the town).

In the 14th century, the area behind the TI was the Jewish Quarter. Because Christians were prohibited by the Bible from charging interest, Jews did the money-lending, hence the names of the streets such as Rua Moeda (road of money) and Rua de Mercadores (road of merchants).

The Roman triumphal arch that used to stand on this square was demolished in the 16th century to make way for the Church of

St. Antão (at the end of the square). In front of the church is a 16th-century fountain—once an important water source for the town.

The Portuguese King John III lived in Évora for 30 years in the 16th century. The TI is inside the palace where the king's guests used to stay—it was Évora's first hotel. Others weren't treated as royally. A fervent proponent of the Inquisition, the king sanctioned the deaths of hundreds of people who were burned as heretics on this square.

From the Main Square to the Roman Sights and Cathedral: Leave the square on Rua Cinco de Outubro (it's across the square from the Turismo office). The name of the road celebrates the date, October 5, 1910, when Portugal shook off dictatorial rule and became a republic. This little street has been Évora's main shopping street since Roman times (we'll return to it later). Take the first left (at Restaurante Mr. Pickwick's) on Alcárcova de Cima (which in Arabic means "the place with water"). A few steps farther on, you'll see a portion of Roman wall built into the buildings on your right. After this, a series of windows show a longer portion of this wall, which used to surround what is now the inner core of the town. (The wall that presently encircles Évora was built mainly in the 14th century when the town outgrew the Roman walls, and it was fortified in the 17th century when Portugal fought back against Spain, ending a 60-year period of Spanish rule.)

Ahead of you, across the intersection, is the blunt, columned end of a 16th-century **aqueduct** made of granite. You can see the arches of the aqueduct imbedded in shops to your left. Continue straight (on Travessa de Sertorio). The abnormally high sidewalk to your left is another part of the aqueduct.

Keep going straight. Within a block you'll reach a square, Praça Sertorio. The tallest white building on the square is the **town hall**. Go inside (open Mon–Fri 9:00–17:00, sometimes on Sat, closed Sun). Inside on your left are several computers you can use for free Internet access (www.Evora.net). On your right in the corner is an overlook into a dark place. Take a look. When some repair work was done on this building, these Roman ruins were discovered. Labeled the Laconicum, this is part of the **Roman bath**—the sauna where people would meet up and heat up. Through the doorway to the right of this overlook, you'll see more of the excavation, with a map showing the layout of the Roman site. Across from the doorway is a map of other Roman sights in Évora (we'll see all but the last one on this walk).

Exit the Town Hall to the right, to go around the Town Hall building. Across the street (Rua de Olivença), you'll see a Roman tower (once part of the Roman wall you saw earlier) and farther on, the arcaded post office (*Correios*).

Walk alongside the post office and take the first left, on Rua de Dona Isabel. You'll immediately see the **Roman**

arch—Porta de Dona Isabel—that used to be one of the main gates of the Roman Wall.

Wait—don't pass under the arch. Now you're inside the Roman wall. After Giraldo the Fearless retook Évora, the Moors were still allowed to live in the area, but on the other side of this gate, beyond the city walls. That neighborhood is still called Mouraria, for the Moors. They were safe here for hundreds of years, until the crowbar of the Inquisition pried them out in the 16th century.

Pass through the Roman arch and turn right. After a café, you'll pass a little grassy patch (on your right) showing Évora's coat of arms, Giraldo on horseback.

Turn right just after this garden, at the tower—called the Five Corners (*Cinco Quinas*) for its five sides. Walk a block uphill to reach Évora's sight-packed square.

Ahead of you is the Roman temple and fancy Pousada dos Loios. To your right is a public garden (WCs are 50 meters beyond it, down the lane that's left of the tall white reservoir). To your left is the Jardim do Poço restaurant, known for its beautiful garden setting, pricey food, and slow service.

The **Pousada dos Loios**, once a 15th-century monastery, is now a luxurious hotel with small rooms (blame the monks). To the left of the *pousada*, stairs lead down to a church—Igreja dos Loios dos Duques de Cadaval—with an impressive gold altarpiece. Look for the two small trapdoors in the floor flanking the aisle midway up the church. One opens up to a cistern, the other to a bony ossuary. The room to the right of the altar contains tile work, ancient weaponry, and religious art, including a cleverly painted Crucifixion (church open Tue–Sun 10:00–14:30, closed Mon, no photos).

Go to the front of **Roman Temple** (first century A.D.), which was once part of the Roman Forum and the main square during Roman times. Today the town's open-air concerts and events are staged here, against the backdrop of this evocative temple. It's called the Temple of Diana, but now it's thought to have been dedicated to the emperor. (The sign asks you politely in Portuguese not to climb on the temple.)

The Roman Forum sprawled where the **Museum of Évora** stands today. In fact, an excavated section of the Forum is in the courtyard of the museum, along with weighty Roman chunks on the ground floor. Upstairs the museum showcases Portuguese and Flemish art from the 16th to 19th century, along with exhibitions on the top floor and in the basement (€1.50, Wed–Sun 9:00–17:30, Tue 14:00–17:00, closed Mon).

Across the square from the museum is a white building, now used by the university, but notorious as being the **Tribunal of the Inquisition**. Here hundreds or even thousands of innocent people (likely many Moors and Jews) were tried and found guilty. After being condemned, the prisoners were taken in procession

Alentejo: Corks and Jokes

Driving from Lisbon to the Algarve, you'll pass through the
Alentejo region, known for producing cork. Portugal, the
world's leading producer of that wonderful, tasteless, odor-
less seal for wine bottles, produces 30 million corks a day.
Driving through the Alentejo region, you'll see vast fields
of cork oaks. Every seven to nine years the bark is stripped,
leaving a sore red underskin.

The Alentejo region is also known for being extraordi-
narily traditional. Throughout Europe, what a tourist might
see as quaint is seen by city folk as backward. The people of
Alentejo are the butt of local jokes. It's said you'll see them
riding motorcycles in pajamas...so they can better lay into
the corners. Many Portuguese call porno flicks "Alentejo
karate." I met a sad old guy from Alentejo. When I asked
him what was wrong, he explained that he was on the verge
of teaching his burro how to live without food...but it died.
The big event of the millennium in Lisbon was the arrival of
the Alentejanos for Expo '98.

through the streets to be burned on the main square. In front of
this building is a granite sculpture of a coffin with a body inside—
a memorial to those who were killed in the name of God.

The little street to the left of the Inquisition headquarters is
Rua de Vasco da Gama. The globetrotting Gama lived on this
street after he discovered the water route to India in 1498 (his
house, not open to the public, is 30 meters down the street at the
smudged number #15 on your right).

The **cathedral**, behind the museum, was built after Giraldo's
conquest, right smack atop the site of the mosque. (For more on
the cathedral, see "Sights," below.) The first cardinal of this
church was Dom Henrique, who founded the town's university in
1559 (see "Sights," below). Later Dom Henrique became King
Henrique after his great-nephew, the young King Sebastian, died
in North Africa in a disastrous attempt (imagine this) to chase the
Moors out of Africa. Henrique, who ruled only two years before
he died, left no direct descendants. The throne of Portugal passed
to his cousin, King Philip II of Spain, starting a bleak 60-year
period of Spanish rule (1580-1640) and the beginning of Évora's
decline. Note to future kings and queens—leave descendants.

From the Cathedral back to Main Square: Take the little
street, opposite the cathedral's entrance, downhill. It's the shopping street, Rua Cinco de Outubro, which connects Évora's main
sights with its main square. The street is lined with products of the

Alentejo region: cork (even postcards), tile, leather, ironwork, and Arraiolos rugs (made with a distinctive weave in the nearby town of Arraiolos).

On the shopping street, after you pass the intersection with Rua de Burgos, look left to see a blue **shrine** protruding from the wall of a building. The town built it as thanks to God for sparing it from the 1755 earthquake that devastated much of Lisbon. Ahead of you is the main square. The Chapel of Bones is just a few blocks away on your left.

Sights—Évora

▲▲▲**Church of St. Francis and the Chapel of Bones**—To get to the church from the main square, take the road to the left of the imposing Bank of Portugal. At the end of the arcade, turn right on Rua da República. You'll see the church just ahead.

St. Francis wouldn't recognize any of this church as Franciscan. It has a hodgepodge look, partly because the side chapels were bought by different wealthy families who had more money than taste. The huge Baroque chapel to the left of the altar would particularly horrify St. Francis, who valued simplicity.

The entrance to the **bone chapel** is outside, to the right of the church entrance. The cheery message above the chapel reads: "We bones in here wait for yours to join us" (€0.50, €0.25 to take photos, daily 9:00–13:00, 14:30–18:00). Inside the macabre chapel, bones line the walls as five thousand skulls stare blankly at you from walls and arches. This ghoulish foolishness was the work of three monks who thought it would be easier to meditate on the transitoriness of material things in the undeniable presence of death. The bones of the monks responsible for the interior decorating are in the small white coffin to the right of the altar.

After reflecting on mortality, it's almost necessary to have a refreshing, cold drink in the pleasant garden next to the church (as you face entrance, garden is to your right). The kiosk café is next to a goldfish pond. The gardens, bigger than they look, contain an overly restored hunk of the 16th-century Royal Palace. Behind the palace, look over the stone balustrade to see a kids' playground and playfields. Life goes on—make no bones about it.

▲▲**Cathedral**—The cathedral, built in the late 12th century, is a transitional mix of Romanesque and Gothic. The tower to the right is Romanesque (more stocky and fortress-like), and the tower to the left is Gothic (lighter, more windows).

Inside the cathedral, midway down the nave, is a statue of a pregnant Mary. It's thought that the first priests, hoping to make converts out of Celtic pagans who worshiped mother goddesses, thought they'd have more success if they kept the focus on fertility. Across the aisle, Gabriel, added later, comes too late to tell Mary the news she already knows.

Admission to the museum, choir, and cloisters costs €2.50 (church open daily 9:00–12:00, 14:00–17:00; museum/choir/cloisters close at 16:30, no photos, WC under cloister entry). Each corner of the **cloister** bears a carving of one of the four apostles. In the corner closest to the entry, a spiral stairway that leads to the "roof" and a close-up view of the cathedral's crenellations. This common feature of Romanesque architecture literally turned the church into a mighty fortress. A simple chapel niche (on opposite corner from the entry) has a child-size statue of an obviously pregnant Virgin Mary (midway up wall).

The **museum** is notable for art in its first and last room. Center-stage in the first room is an intricate 14th-century puzzle-like ivory statue of Mary (Virgen do Paraiso), her "insides" opened up to reveal the major events in her life. In the last room in a glass case is a sparkling reliquary, containing pieces of the supposed True Cross (in a cross-shape), heavily laden with more than a thousand true gems, rotating to show off every facet.

The sunlit **choir** is glorious (late 15th to early 16th century), from its vantage point overlooking the cathedral to its oak stalls carved with scenes of daily life (hunting boars, harvesting, rounding up farm animals). The huge contraption in the middle is a music stand. Notice the wide edge on the ends of seats. Even the older clerics were expected to stand up for much of the service. But when the seat is flipped up, the edge becomes a ledge, making it possible for clerics to sit while they respectfully stood.

University—Originally known as the College of the Holy Spirit, this was established as a Jesuit university in 1559 by Dom Henrique, the cathedral's first cardinal. Two hundred years later, Marquis de Pombal, the powerful minister of King Jose, decided that the Jesuits had become too rich and powerful. He abolished the Jesuit society in 1759—and confiscated their wealth. The university was closed, and didn't reopen as a university until 1973. To this town of 50,000 people (with 14,000 inside the walls), it's brought 8,000 students, a new vitality, and discos. Now the university is secular, but its emblem is still a dove—the symbol of the Holy Spirit.

The main entrance of the university is the old courtyard on the ground level (downhill from the original Jesuit chapel). Enter the courtyard (free on weekdays and Sat morn, €1.50 Sat 15:00–18:00, Sun 10:00–14:00, 15:00–18:00). Attractive blue-and-white *azulejo* tiles ring the walls and the classrooms, with the theme of the class portrayed in the tiles. You might see students with colorful wide ribbons, denoting their field of learning, wrapped around their notebooks. When the students graduate, they gleefully burn their ribbons in this courtyard as rock music blares outside.

Enter the room directly across the courtyard from the entrance. Here major university events are held, under the watchful eyes of Cardinal Henrique (the painting to the left) and young King Sebastian (to the right).

The university shop to the right of this room gives you a great look at the tiles. In the 16th century this was a classroom for students of astronomy—note the spheres and navigational instruments mingled with cupids and pastoral scenes. Imagine the class back then. Having few books, if any, the male students (no females) took notes as the professor taught in Latin from the lectern in the back. Spitwads were frowned upon.

Behind this courtyard is a smaller courtyard, with a café off its far right corner (Mon–Fri 8:30–19:00, Sat 9:00–12:00, closed Sun). In front of the café is a huge marble fountain where students used to wash their hands. The food is the cheapest in town, and the public is welcome. Strike up a conversation with a student.

Sights near Évora

Near Évora, you'll find **Megalithic sights:** menhirs (standing stones, near Guadalupe and elsewhere), dolmens (rock tombs at Anta do Zambujeiro and Capela-anta de São Brissos), cromlechs (rocks in formation *à la* Stonehenge, at Cromlech dos Almendres), and a cave with prehistoric paintings (Gruta do Escoural). Depending on how much you want to see, you can do a 25- to 70-kilometer loop from Évora by tour (see below), by **car** (list of rental-car agencies available at Évora's TI), or by **bike** (Bike Lab, €1.80/hr, €17.50/day, less for steel bikes, delivers bikes and helmets to your hotel for additional €2.50, no CC, located at Vista Alegre—3 blocks west of city wall and a 15-min walk from TI; ideally reserve at least a day in advance, tel. 26-673-5500, SE).

City Tour offers bus tours of the megaliths (€25, 3 hrs, offered daily depending on demand, no CC, Alcárcova de Baixo 43, from main square head up shopping street—Cinco de Outubro—and take first right, in summer book 2 days in advance; also offers other tours including an €18 walking tour of Évora and a €75 full-day trip to nearby castles, a marble quarry, and ceramic workshop; tel. 26-674-6970, SE).

Sleeping in Évora
(€1.10 = about $1, country code: 351)
Sleep Code: **S** = Single, **D** = Double/Twin, **T** = Triple, **Q** = Quad, **b** = bathroom, **s** = shower only, **CC** = Credit Cards accepted, **no CC** = Credit Cards not accepted, **SE** = Speaks English, **NSE** = No English.

Moderately Priced Hotels
Solar Monfalim has 26 hacienda-type rooms in a central and quiet location (Sb-€65, Db-€80, Tb-€105, includes breakfast,

CC, air con, pleasant breakfast room with balcony, Largo da Misericordia 1, tel. 26-678-0000, fax 26-674-2367, www.monfalimtur.pt, e-mail: reservas@monfalimtur.pt).

Hotel Santa Clara, on a side street, rents 43 tranquil rooms with small bathrooms (Sb-€45, Db-€59, includes breakfast, CC, air con, Travessa do Milheira 19, from Praça do Giraldo, take Rua Pinta Serpa downhill, then right on Milheira; coming from the bus station, turn left on Milheira after you enter city wall, tel. 26-670-4141, fax 26-670-6544, e-mail: hotelsantaclara@mail.telepac.pt).

Residencial Policarpo, in a 16th-century building, has a homey feel, with 20 simple rooms tucked around a courtyard (S-€28, Ss-€43, Sb-€50, D-€35, Ds-€48, Db-€55, Tb-€67, includes breakfast, no CC, double-paned windows, air con, terrace, fireplace, parking, 2 entrances: Rua da Freiria de Baixo 16 and Rua Conde da Serra, near university, tel. & fax 26-670-2424, e-mail: incoming.alentejo@policarpo.net).

Hotel Ibis, a cheap chain hotel, has 87 identical, Motel 6–type rooms an eight-minute walk from the center, just outside the city walls (Sb/Db-€45–50, breakfast-€4, CC, air con, elevator, parking, Quinta da Tapada, tel. 26-674-4620, fax 26-674-4632, www.ibishotel.com).

Splurges

The elegant **Pousada dos Loios** has everything but large rooms. Once a 15th-century monastery, it's now a luxury hotel with 30 smallish rooms, many fine public spaces, courtyards, and a small swimming pool (Db-€185, suites available, cheaper Nov–Mar, includes breakfast, CC, air con, elevator, free parking, Convento dos Loios, across from Roman Temple, reserve with Central Booking Office at tel. 21-844-2001, fax 21-844-2085, www .pousadas.pt, e-mail: guest@pousadas.pt).

Hotel Cartuxa, though not as central as the pousada, has 85 far-more-spacious rooms, lower prices, a swimming pool big enough to swim in, and a sprawling garden bordered by the city wall (Sb-€115, Db-€130, includes breakfast, CC, air con, elevator, parking-€4, attached restaurant/bar, Travessa da Palmeira 4/6, 5-min walk from center, tel. 26-673-9300, fax 26-673-9305, www.hotelcartuxa.com, e-mail: hotelcartuxa@mail.telepac.pt).

Hostel

Évora's **hostel**, just a couple years old, still feels new. It's glorious as hostels go, with a central location, rooftop terrace, 16 doubles, and 16 multi-bed rooms, all with bath (84 beds total, Db-€25–31 per person, dorm bed-€11–13.50, prices vary with season, non-members pay a little extra per night, includes breakfast, air con, elevator, lockout 11:00–14:00 for cleaning, 2 blocks off town square, Rua Miguel Bombarda 40, tel. 26-674-4848, fax 26-674-4843). It's wise to book in advance; contact the Central Booking Office at 21-359-6000, by fax at 21-359-6001, or at www.pousadasjuventude.pt, e-mail: reserveas@movijovem.pt).

Eating in Évora

Fialho is a local favorite, where you can dine without chewing up your budget (closed Mon, Travessa Mascarhenas 14, from main square go right alongside church—Rua João de Deus—for a 5-min walk, take first left after garden square, tel. 26-670-3079).

The atmospheric **Adega de Alentejano** is like an above-ground wine cellar that feels as large as a beer hall. A huge clay wine cask crowds the entry. Inside, locals enjoy traditional dishes at great prices (Mon–Sat 12:00–15:00, 19:00–22:00, closed Sun, no CC, use door to right of apparent entrance, Rua Gabriel Victor do Monte Pereira 21, from main square go right alongside church—on Rua João de Deus, then take third left, tel. 26-674-4447). **Molhóbico**, which does Alentejo cuisine with a Spanish flair on a small square, is romantic (closed Sun, Rua de Aviz 91, at intersection with Travessa do Serpe, coming from center go through Roman arch—on Rua de Dona Isabel—and continue straight for 4 blocks, tel. 26-674-4343).

Eating near Praça do Giraldo: A couple of central but touristy places known for traditional cuisine are **Restaurante Cozinha de St. Humberto** (closed Thu, pricey, Rua da Moeda 39, tel. 26-670-4251, a block off Praça do Giraldo) and **Restaurante Guião** (closed Mon, Rua da República 81, between the main square and Church of St. Francis, tel. 26-670-3071). For local atmosphere, eat at **Dom Fartote** just off the main square (daily 12:00–15:00, 19:00–24:00, Rua Romano Romalha 11, tel. 26-677-8100).

Popular **Papasandes** offers great, cheap, filling salads and sandwiches—but no air conditioning. If it's hot, get the food—even salads—to go (Mon–Sat 9:00–24:00, Sun 13:00–24:00, Rua Alcárcova de Baixo 23, from main square Praça do Giraldo, take the shopping street toward the cathedral, then first right).

Transportation Connections—Évora

To: Lisbon (by bus: 15/day, 1.75–2.5 hrs; by train: 4/day, 2.5 hrs including ferry from Barreiro Station to Lisbon), **Lagos** (by bus: 1/day, 5 hrs, transfer in Albufeira; by train: 3/day, 5.5 hrs with transfers at Casa Branca and Funcheira), **Madrid** (2 buses/day, 7.5–10 hrs, buy 1 day in advance to insure a seat; the 7.5-hr bus is overnight), **Sevilla** (1 bus/day on Wed, Fri, Sat, and Sun, 7.5 hrs).

CENTRAL PORTUGAL:
COIMBRA AND NAZARÉ

While the far north of Portugal has considerable charm, those with limited time enjoy maximum travel thrills on or near the coast of central Portugal. This is an ideal stop if you're coming in from Salamanca or Madrid or are interested in a small-town side trip north from Lisbon.

The college town of Coimbra (3 hrs north of Lisbon by train, bus, or car) is Portugal's Oxford and its easiest-to-enjoy city. Browse through the historic university, fortresslike cathedral, and lively Old Quarter of what was once Portugal's leading city.

Nazaré, an Atlantic-coast fishing-town-turned-resort, is black-shawl traditional and beach friendly. You'll be greeted by the energetic applause of the surf, widows with rooms to rent, and big plates of steamed shrimp. Have fun in the Portuguese sun in a land of cork groves, eucalyptus trees, ladies in seven petticoats, and men who stow cigarettes and fishhooks in their stocking caps.

Several other worthy sights are within easy daytrip distance of Nazaré. You can drop by the Batalha Monastery, the patriotic pride and architectural joy of Portugal. If the spirit moves you, the pilgrimage site at Fatima is nearby. Alcobaça has Portugal's largest church (and saddest romance). And Portugal's incredibly cute walled town of Óbidos is just down the road.

Planning Your Time

Few Americans give Portugal much time. Most do Lisbon and the south coast. On a three-week trip through Spain and Portugal, Coimbra and Nazaré each merit a day. There's another day's worth of sightseeing in Batalha, Alcobaça, and Fatima. If you're connecting Salamanca or Madrid with Lisbon, I'd do it this way (for specifics see Salamanca's and Coimbra's "Transportation Connections").

By Car
Day 1: Leave Salamanca early, breakfast in Ciudad Rodrigo, early afternoon arrival in Coimbra, tour university and old cathedral.
Day 2: Shop and browse the Old Quarter, lunch at Batalha, tour church, visit Fatima, evening in Nazaré.
Day 3: Make the 16-kilometer side trip from Nazaré to Alcobaça (town, monastery, wine museum). Spend afternoon back in Nazaré with a look at Sitio and beach time. Seafood dinner.
Day 4: Visit Óbidos on your way to Lisbon. Arrive in Lisbon by noon.

By Train
Day 1: You have only one option and it's miserable: the 04:38–08:25 Salamanca–Coimbra train connection (5-hr trip, 1 hr gained in Portugal). Spend the day seeing Coimbra.
Day 2: Catch morning bus from Coimbra to Nazaré. Set up and relax in Nazaré, Sitio, and on the beach. Seafood dinner.
Day 3: Do the triangular loop (Nazaré–Batalha–Alcobaça–Nazaré) by bus.
Day 4: Train into Lisbon.

COIMBRA
Don't be fooled by Coimbra's drab suburbs. Portugal's most important city for 200 years, Coimbra (KWEEM-bra) remains second only to Lisbon culturally and historically. It served as Portugal's leading city while the Moors controlled Lisbon. Only as Portugal's maritime fortunes rose was landlocked Coimbra surpassed by the ports of Lisbon and Porto. Today Coimbra is Portugal's third-largest city (pop. 100,000) and home to its oldest and most prestigious university (founded 1290). When school is in session, Coimbra bustles. During school holidays, it's sleepy. It's got a great Arab-flavored Old Quarter—a maze of people, narrow streets, and tiny *tascas* (restaurants with just a few tables).

Orientation
Coimbra is a mini-Lisbon—everything good about urban Portugal without the intensity of a big city. I couldn't design a more enjoyable city for a visit. There's a small-town feeling in the winding streets set on the side of the hill. The high point is the old university. From there, little lanes meander down like a Moroccan medina to the main pedestrian street. This street (named Visconde da Luz at the top, turning into Rua de Ferreira Borges halfway down) runs from the square Praça 8 de Maio to the Mondego River, dividing the old town into upper (Alta) and lower (Baixa) parts.

From the Largo da Portagem (main square by the river) everything is within an easy walk. The Old Quarter spreads out like an amphitheater—timeworn houses, shops, and stairways all

Coimbra

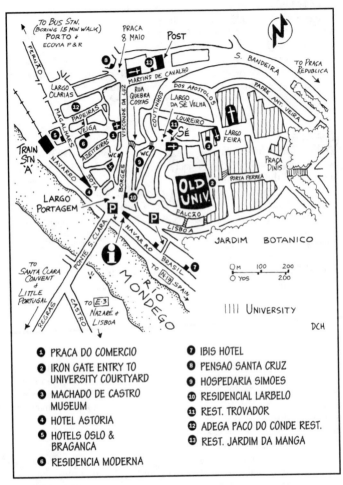

① PRAÇA DO COMERCIO
② IRON GATE ENTRY TO UNIVERSITY COURTYARD
③ MACHADO DE CASTRO MUSEUM
④ HOTEL ASTORIA
⑤ HOTELS OSLO & BRAGANCA
⑥ RESIDENCIA MODERNA
⑦ IBIS HOTEL
⑧ PENSAO SANTA CRUZ
⑨ HOSPEDARIA SIMOES
⑩ RESIDENCIAL LARBELO
⑪ REST. TROVADOR
⑫ ADEGA PACO DO CONDE REST.
⑬ REST. JARDIM DA MANGA

lead up to the university. The best views are looking up from the far end of Santa Clara Bridge and looking down from the observation deck of the university. The TI and plenty of good budget rooms are within several blocks of the train station.

Tourist Information

Pick up a map and the monthly cultural calendar at the helpful English-speaking TI at Largo da Portagem (June–Sept Mon–Fri 9:00–19:00, Sat–Sun 10:00–13:00, 14:30–17:30; Oct–May

Mon–Fri 9:00–18:00, Sat–Sun 10:00–13:00, 14:30–17:30, entrance on Navarro, tel. 23-985-5930, www.turismo-centro.pt, e-mail: rtc-coimbra@turismo-centro.pt). Here you can get bus schedules (printed out for you) and information on sights in central Portugal. Other TIs with similar hours are on Praça Dinis (tel. 23-983-2591) and Praça da República (tel. 23-983-3202; both near the university). While there are no regular walking tours, the TI has a list of private guides (such as Cristina Bessa at tel. 23-983-5428, €75 per half day).

Helpful Hints

The Abreu travel agency sells bus tickets to Salamanca and beyond (Mon–Fri 9:00–12:30, 14:30–18:30, Sat 9:00–12:30, closed Sun, CC, Rua da Sota 2, near train station A, tel. 23-985-5520); if you're heading to Salamanca, the bus is a far better option than the train (for more info, see "Transportation Connections—Coimbra," below). ATMs and banks (Mon–Fri 8:30–15:00) are plentiful. Avis has an office in train station A (Mon–Fri 8:30–12:00, 15:00–19:00, closed Sat–Sun, tel. & fax 23-983-4786, www.avis.com) and Hertz is at Rua Padre Estevão Cabral (tel. 23-983-4750).

Arrival in Coimbra

By Train: There are two Coimbra train stations, A and B. Major trains (e.g., from Lisbon and Salamanca) stop only at B (big). From there, you can take a free three-minute shuttle train to the very central A station (free, included with ticket that got you to B-train station). To find out exactly which train to take to get to the A station, go to the *informações* office and ask at the ticket window: *"Comboio* [kom-boy-oo] *para Coimbra?"* Local trains (e.g., to Nazaré) stop at both stations. Station B has an ATM in an outside wall of the station, opposite the end with the café. Taxis wait across the tracks (about €3 to Station A or your hotel). Station A has a helpful English-speaking information office (*informações*) with schedules, tucked away in a waiting room (daily 9:00–14:00, 15:00–19:00, tel. 23-983-4998). Across the street from Station A are two Multibanco ATMs.

By Bus: The bus station, on Avenida Fernão de Magalhaes (tel. 23-985-5270), is a boring but easy 10-minute walk from the center. Exit the bus station to the right and follow the busy street into town or take a taxi (€2). Local buses are expensive (€1.10), and by the time bus #35 comes along, you could already have walked downtown. (If you need only inter-bus schedules, the much more central TI will print timetables for you.) If you're heading for the bus station to leave Coimbra by bus, take Avenida Fernão de Magalhaes past its intersection with Cabral and look on the left—the Neptuno café marks the station's subtle entrance.

Do-It-Yourself Orientation Tour of Coimbra's Old Quarter

Coimbra is a delight on foot. You'll find yourself doing laps along the straight (formerly Roman) pedestrian-only main drag. Do it once following this quickie tour:

Start at **Santa Clara Bridge**. The bridge has been a key bridge over the Mondega River since Roman times. For centuries it had a tollgate (*portagem*). Cross the bridge for a fine Coimbra view, a lowbrow popular fairground, and free parking.

The square, **Largo da Portagem** (at the end of the bridge on the Coimbra side), is a great place for a coffee or a pastry. Pastelaria Briosa's pastries are best.

Stroll down the **pedestrian street**. After a gauntlet of cloth- ing stores, take the stairs (to your left) leading to a terrace over- looking the square below (public WC on stairwell). The square is the pleasant **Praça do Comércio** (shaped like a Roman chariot racecourse—and likely to have been one 2,000 years ago) and the heart of the old town. Look at your map. The circular street pat- tern outlines the wall used by Romans, Visigoths, Moors, and Christians to protect Coimbra. Historically the rich could afford to live within the protective city walls (the "Alta" or high town). Even today, the Baixa, or low town, remains a poorer section, with haggard women rolling their wheeled shopping bags, children running barefoot, and men lounging on the square like it's their life's work. Return to the pedestrian street.

Across the street from the overlook, steps lead up through an ancient arched gateway—Arco de Almedina—into the old city and to the old cathedral and university. We'll go there later.

Farther along the pedestrian drag, stop at the picturesque corner just beyond the cafés (where the building comes to a triangular corner). The steep road climbs into Coimbra's historic ghetto (no Jewish community remains).

You'll know if it's graduation time if graduation photos are displayed in photographers' windows. Check out the students decked out in their traditional university capes (displaying rips on the hem for girlfriends) and color-coded sashes (yellow for medicine, red for law, and so on).

The pedestrian street ends at Praça 8 de Maio with the **Church of Santa Cruz** and its ornate facade. The shiny "neck- lace" on the angel behind the trumpeter is actually electrified to keep pigeons from dumping their corrosive load on the tender limestone.

People (and pigeons) watch from the terrace of the recom- mended **Café Santa Cruz** (to the right of church). Built as a church but abandoned with the dissolution of the monasteries in 1834 (the women's room is in a confessional), this was the 19th-century haunt of local intellectuals. There's also a great

Self-Service Restaurant Jardim da Manga directly behind the church at a little park with a fountain (see "Eating," below). Beyond the cafeteria is the covered market (Mon–Sat 8:00–14:00).

Backtrack to **Arco de Almedina** (literally "gate to the *medina*") and climb into the old town. If you can't make it to Morocco, this dense jungle of shops and markets may be your next-best bet. Part of the old-town wall, this is a double gate with a 90-degree kink in the middle for easier defense. The two square holes in the ceiling, through which boiling oil would be poured, turned attacking Moors into fritters. Shops here show off the fine local blue-and-white ceramic work called *faiança*. (If you're tired and it's hot, end the walk here, or catch a taxi—from the train station—to the university.)

You're climbing the extremely steep **Rua de Quebra Costas**—"Street of Broken Ribs." At one time this lane had no steps and literally was the street of broken ribs. During a strong rain this becomes a river. A few steps uphill is the old cathedral. Beyond that is the university. After you pass the cathedral, you'll see a building with signs pointing out opposite ways to reach the university. Go right for the old university (after a stiff climb, go up the stairs to reach the Iron Gate).

Sights—Coimbra's Old University

Coimbra's 700-year-old university was modeled after Bologna's university (Europe's first, A.D. 1139). It's a stately, three-winged former royal palace (from when Coimbra was the capital), beautifully situated overlooking the city. At first, law, medicine, grammar, and logic were taught. Then, with Portugal's seafaring orientation, astronomy and geometry were added. While Lisbon's university is much larger, Coimbra's is still the country's most respected university.

Cost and Hours: A combo ticket for the two university sites that cost money to see—the Grand Hall and King John's Library—is €4 (otherwise €2.50 per site, May–Sept daily 9:00–19:00, Oct–April daily 9:30–12:00, 14:00–17:00). Consider taking a taxi to the Iron Gate and sightseeing Coimbra downhill.

Iron Gate—Find the gate to the old university (on Praça da Porta Ferrea). Before entering, stand with your back to the gate (and the old university) and look across the stark modern square at the fascist architecture of the new university. In what's considered one of the worst cultural crimes in Portuguese history, the dictator Salazar tore down half the old town of Coimbra to build these university halls. Salazar, proud that Portugal was the last European power to hang onto its global empire, wanted a fittingly monumental university here. After all, Salazar—along with virtually all people of political importance in Portugal—was educated in Coimbra. If these bold buildings are reminiscent of Mussolini's

EUR in Rome, perhaps it's because they were built in part by Italian architects for Portugal's little Mussolini.

Coimbra's Old University

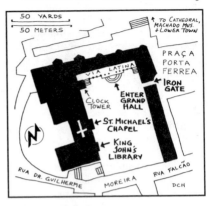

OK, now turn and walk through the Iron Gate. Traditionally, freshmen, proudly wearing their black capes for the first time, pass through the Iron Gate to enroll. But to get out they find an Iron Gate gauntlet of butt kicks from upperclassmen. Walk into the...

Old University Courtyard—The statue in the square is of King John III. While the university was established in 1290, it went back and forth between Lisbon and Coimbra (back then, university students were adults, privileged, and a pain to have in your town). In 1537 John III finally established the school permanently in Coimbra (away from Lisbon). Standing like a good humanist (posing much like England's Renaissance King Henry VIII), John modernized Portugal's education system Renaissance-style. But he also made the university the center of Portugal's Inquisition.

Survey the square with your back to the gate. The dreaded sound of the clock tower's bell—named the "baby goat" for its nagging—called the students to class. On several occasions the clapper has been stolen. No bell...no class. No class...big party. A larger bell (the "big goat") rings only on grand and formal occasions.

The university's most important stops all face this square: the Grand Hall (up the grand stairway on the right between you and the clock tower), St. Michael's Chapel (straight ahead, through the door, then to the left), and King John's Library (across the square, farthest door on left, flanked by columns).

The arcaded passageway (upstairs) between the Iron Gate and the clock tower is called Via Latina, from the days when only Latin was allowed in this part of the university. Purchase your ticket at the end of Via Latina immediately under the tower (but beforehand read first paragraph of "View Catwalk," below). See the following sights in any order you like.

The Grand Hall (Sala dos Capelos)—Enter from the middle of Via Latina. This is the site of the university's major academic ceremonies, such as exams and graduations. This was originally the throne room of the royal palace. Today the

rector's light-green chair sits thronelike in front. While students
in their formal outfits filled the benches, teachers sat along the
perimeter, and gloomy portraits of Portuguese kings looked
down. Since there is no clapping during these formal rituals,
a brass band (on the platform in the back) would punctuate
the ceremonies with solemn music. Tourists look down from
balconies above the room.

View Catwalk: Continue around the Grand Hall and out
onto the narrow observation deck for the best possible views of
Coimbra. (The viewpoint will likely be open, but may be closed
if there aren't sufficient staff to monitor the "only 10 people on
the balcony at a time" rule. If you're interested in the Grand
Hall only because of this view, before paying admission, ask, "*A
varanda esta aberta?*"—Is the veranda open?)

From the viewpoint, scan the old town. Remember, before
Salazar's extension of the university, this old town surrounded
the university. The Baroque facade breaking the horizon is the
"New" Cathedral—from the 16th century. Below that, with the
fine arcade, is the Machado de Castro Museum, housed in the
former bishop's palace and sitting on a Roman site (see below).
And below that, like an armadillo, sits the old cathedral. If you
see any noisily painted yellow and blue windows, it marks a
república. Traditionally, Coimbra students (from the same distant
town) lived together in groups of about a dozen in communal
houses called *repúblicas*. Today these function as tiny fraternities—
some are highly cultured, others are mini–Animal Houses. Look
beyond the houses to the Mondego River, the longest entirely
Portuguese river. Over the bridge and above the popular fairgrounds is the 17th-century Santa Clara Convent—at 180 meters,
the longest building in Coimbra.

St. Michael's Chapel—This chapel is behind the 16th-century
Manueline facade (enter through the door to the right of the
facade—once inside, push the door on the left marked *capela*, free
admission). The architecture of the church interior is Manueline;
notice the golden "rope" trimming the arch before the altar. The
decor is from a later time. The altar is 17th-century Mannerist, with
steps unique to Portugal (and her South American colonies) symbolizing the steps the faithful take on their journey to heaven. The
2,100-pipe 18th-century German-built organ is notable for its hori-
zontal "trumpet" pipes. Unique to Iberia, these help the organist
perform the allegorical fight between good and evil—with the hori-
zontal pipes trumpeting the arrival of the good guys. Finally, above
the loft in the rear are the box seats for the royal family.

The **Museum of Sacred Art**, farther down the corridor,
will likely still be closed for renovation in 2002. When it reopens,
a painting of John the Baptist will again point the way to art that
nuns and priests find fascinating. The museum was created in

1910 to keep the art in Coimbra when the new republic wanted
to move all the art to Lisbon. (Also in the corridor, you'll find
the café and WCs.)

King John's Library—This grand library displays 30,000 books
in 18th-century splendor. The zealous doorkeeper locks the door
at every opportunity to keep out humidity. Buzz to get into this
temple of thinking. You might have to wait outside (until other
tourists who are inside are ready to leave). Inside, at the "high
altar," stands its founder, the Divine Monarch John V. The reading tables inlaid with exotic South American woods (and ornamented with silver ink wells) and the precious wood shelves (with
clever hide-away staircases) are reminders that Portugal's wealth
was great—and imported. Built Baroque, the interior is all wood.
Even the marble is just painted wood. Look for the trompe l'oeil
Baroque tricks on the painted ceiling. Gold leaf (from Brazil) is
everywhere, and the Chinese themes are pleasantly reminiscent
of Portugal's once-vast empire. The books, all from before 1755,
are in Latin, Greek, or Hebrew. Imagine being a student in
Coimbra 500 years ago. As you leave, watch how the doorman
uses the giant key as a hefty doorknob.

More Sights—Coimbra

Machado de Castro Museum—The museum may be closed for
restoration in 2002, but check to be sure. Housed in the old bishop's palace, it contains ceramics, 14th-to-16th-century religious
sculpture (mostly taken from the dissolved monasteries), and a
Roman excavation site. Upstairs, look for the impressive 14th-
century *Cristo Negro* carved in wood (this may still be undergoing
restoration). Until a decade ago when this statue was cleaned (and
the black—from candle soot—came off), it was considered to be a
portrait of a black Christ. Just before you return downstairs, enjoy
the views from the top-floor arcade.

The Roman building, criss-crossed with empty tunnels, in the
basement provided a level foundation for an ancient Roman forum
that stood where the museum does today. At the entry read the
Latin-inscribed Roman stone: bottom line—Aeminiens, referring
to the people who lived in Roman Coimbra, then called Aemi-
nium; fifth line—the fourth-century emperor of the day, Constan-
tio; and the second line—a reference perhaps to an early alliance
of barbarian tribes from the North Atlantic. Notice the few economical "plug-on" Roman busts—from the days when they'd keep
the bodies but change the heads according to whomever the latest
emperor was. The museum sometimes houses art exhibitions here
in the Roman tunnels or on the ground floor (€3, includes any
exhibitions, Tue–Sun 9:30–12:30, 14:00–17:30, closed Mon, free
Sun morning). Visit this before or after the old university, since
both are roughly at the same altitude.

Old Cathedral (Sè Velha)—Same old story: Christians push out Moors (1064), tear down their mosque, and build a church. The Arabic script on a few of the stones indicates that rubble from the mosque was used in the construction. The facade of the main entrance even feels Arabic. Notice the crenellations along the roof of this fortresslike Romanesque church; the Moors, though booted out, were still considered a risk.

The three front altars are each worth a look. The main altar is a fine example of Gothic. The 16th-century chapel to the right is one of the best Renaissance altars in the country. The apostles all look to Jesus as he talks, while musical angels flank the holy host. To the left of the high altar, the Chapel of St. Peter shows Peter being crucified upside down. The fine points of the carving were destroyed by Napoleon's soldiers.

The giant, holy water font shells are a 19th-century gift from Ceylon, and the walls are lined with 16th-century tiles from Sevilla.

On the right just before the transept is a murky painting of a queen with a skirt full of roses. She's a local favorite with a sweet legend. Against the wishes of the king, she always gave bread to the poor. One day, when he came home early from a trip, she was busy doling out bread from her skirt. She pulled the material up to hide the bread. When the king asked her what was inside (suspecting bread for the poor), the queen—unable to lie— lowered the material and, miraculously, it was only roses.

The peaceful cloister (entrance near back of church) is the oldest Gothic cloister in Portugal. Its decaying walls, neglected courtyard, and overgrown roses offer a fine framed view of the cathedral's grassy dome (church is free, cloisters cost €0.80; church hours: Mon–Thu 10:00–18:00, Fri 10:00–14:00, Sat 10:00–17:00, cloister closes from 13:00–14:00; the public is welcome to come to Mass, ask TI for schedule).

Little Portugal (Portugal dos Pequenitos)—This is a children's (or tourist's) look at the great buildings and monuments of Portugal in miniature, scattered through a park a couple of blocks south of town, across the Santa Clara Bridge (€4, daily March–June 10:00–19:00, July–mid-Sept 9:00–20:00, mid-Sept–Feb 10:00–17:00).

Kayaks, Cruises, and Adventure Sports—O Pioneiro takes you from Coimbra to Penacova (25 km away) by minibus and leaves you with a **kayak** and instructions on getting back. It's a three-hour paddle downstream on the Rio Mondego to Coimbra (€15, 10 percent discount with this book, daily April–mid-Oct, 1- and 2-person kayaks available, book by phone, meet at park near TI, tel. 23-947-8385 to reserve, best time to phone is 20:00–22:00, SE). Most people stop to swim or picnic on the way back, so it often turns into an all-day journey. For the first 20 kilometers you'll go with the flow, but you'll get your exercise paddling the last five flat kilometers.

If you'd rather let someone else do the work, Basofias boats **cruise** up and down the river daily in summer (€8, 3/day but none on Mon, fewer off-season, 75 min, depart in afternoon from dock across from TI, get schedule at TI, tel. 23-982-6815).

Capitao Dureza specializes in **adventure sports**—at your own risk: rappelling, rafting, and canyoning (book by tel. & fax 23-342-7772).

Sights—Near Coimbra
▲**Conimbriga Roman Ruins**—Portugal's best Roman site is impressive...unless you've been to Rome. Little remains of the city, in part because its inhabitants tore down buildings to throw up a quick defensive wall against an expected barbarian attack. Today this wall cuts crudely through the site. Highlights are the fine mosaics of the Casa dos Fonts (under the protective modern roofing) and a delightful little museum (€3, site open daily 9:00–18:00; museum open 10:00–16:30, closed Mon). The ruins are 15 kilometers south of Coimbra on the Lisbon road. On weekdays two buses leave for the ruins each morning from Coimbra's A Station (AVIC bus stop is on the riverside just in front of the station) and return late afternoon (€1.50, 30-min trip). Buses run twice per hour to Condeixa but leave you 1.5 kilometers from the site. Check bus schedules at the Coimbra TI.

Sleeping in Coimbra
(€1.10 = about $1, country code: 351)
Sleep Code: **S** = Single, **D** = Double/Twin, **T** = Triple, **Q** = Quad, **b** = bathroom, **s** = shower only, **CC** = Credit Cards accepted, **no CC** = Credit Cards not accepted, **SE** = Speaks English, **NSE** = No English. Breakfast isn't included unless noted.

The listings are an easy walk from the central A station and Santa Clara Bridge. For the cheapest rooms, simply walk from the A station a block into the old town and choose one of countless *dormidas* (cheap pensions). River views come with traffic noise.

Hotels
Hotel Astoria gives you the thrill of staying in the city's finest old hotel for a painless price (Sb-€65–80, Db-€80–95, depending on season, extra bed-€25–30, includes breakfast, 10 percent discount by showing this book at check-in, CC, air con, elevator, fine Art-Deco lounges, plush breakfast room, public parking opposite hotel €5/day, central as can be at Avenida Navarro 21, tel. 23-985-3020, fax 23-982-2057, e-mail: astoria@almeidahotels.com, SE). Rooms with river views cost nothing extra.

Hotel Oslo rents 33 good business-class rooms a block from the A station. Rooms are small but hint of Oslo (Sb-€38–45, Db-€50–60, third person-€10 extra, includes breakfast buffet with view of old Coimbra, also a top-floor view bar that sometimes has free fado show for guests on Sat nights at 21:00, CC, air con, free parking, Avenida Fernão de Magalhaes 25, tel. 23-982-9071, fax 23-982-0614, e-mail: hoteloslo@sapo.pt, SE).

Ibis Hotel is a modern high-rise. Its orderly little rooms come with all the comforts and American Motel 6 charm. Well-located on a riverside park, it's three blocks past the Santa Clara Bridge and the Old Quarter (Sb/Db-€36–41, breakfast extra, CC, easy €2.90/day parking in basement, elevator, some smoke-free rooms, Avenida Emidio Navarro, tel. 23-985-2130, fax 23-985-2140, e-mail: h1672@accor-hotels.com, SE).

Hotel Braganca's ugly lobby disguises 83 clean, comfortable, but sometimes smoky rooms (ask to sniff several) with modern bathrooms (Sb/shower-€33, Sb/tub-€50, Db/shower-€50, Db/tub-€63, save money by requesting a shower, or *chuveiro*, includes breakfast, CC, air con, elevator, free parking in small lot if space available, Largo das Ameias 10, next to A station, tel. 23-982-2171, fax 23-983-6135, e-mail: hbraganza@mail.telepac.pt, SE). To minimize street noise, ask for a quieter room in the back.

Pensions and Cheaper Options

Residencial Moderna hides 16 delightful little rooms overlooking a pedestrian street. Many rooms come with a balcony (ask *com varanda*) and parquet floors (Db-€30–40, 10 percent discount with this book, no CC, air con, inexpensive parking nearby, Rua Adelino Veiga 49, 3rd floor, a block from A station, tel. 23-982-5413, fax 23-982-9508, Fernandes family NSE).

Pensão Santa Cruz overlooks the charming and traffic-free square called Praça 8 de Maio at the end of the pedestrian mall. It's a homey place, with 15 rooms van Gogh would paint. You'll find lots of stairs, dim lights, and some balconies worth requesting (D-€12.50–20, Db-€17.50–€27.50, most expensive July–Aug, prices are soft so ask for relief if you need it, no CC, Praça 8 de Maio 21, 3rd floor, tel. & fax 23-982-6197, www.pensaosantacruz.com, e-mail: mail@pensaosantacruz.com, Walter, Anna, and Oswald SE).

On Largo da Portagem, in front of the bridge, **Residencial Larbelo** is run-down but mixes frumpiness and former elegance. The old-fashioned staircase, elegant breakfast room, and weary management take you to another age (Sb-€20, Db-€25–30, depending on season and plumbing—shower cheaper than bath, breakfast-€1.30, CC—Visa only, Largo da Portagem 33, tel. 23-982-9092, fax 23-982-9094, NSE).

Hospedaria Simões is a last resort. It's buried in the heart of the old town, just below the old cathedral. Run by the Simões

family, it offers 18 clean, well-worn rooms, but only eight have
real windows; ask for a *quarto com janela* (Sb-€15, Db-€17.50, Tb-
€22.50, Qb-€28, piles of stairs, fans, no breakfast, no CC, from
Rua Ferreira Borges, go uphill through old gate toward cathedral,
take first right, Rua Fernandes Thomas 69, tel. 23-983-4638).

The youth hostel, **Pousada de Juventude**, on the other
side of town in the student area past the Praça da República, is
friendly, clean, and well-run, but is no cheaper than a simple *pensão* (€9.50 for members, €11.50 for non-members, less off-season,
4-bed rooms, closed 12:00–18:00, Rua Antonio Henriques
Seco 14, tel. 23-982-2955, SE).

Eating in Coimbra

Restaurant Trovador, while a bit touristy, serves wonderful food
in a classic and comfortable ambience, with entertaining dinner
fado performances nearly nightly after 21:00. It's the place for
an old-town splurge (daily menu €27.50, Mon–Sat 12:00–15:00,
19:30–22:30, closed Sun, CC, facing the old cathedral, reservations
necessary to eat with the music—ask for a seat with a music view,
tel. 23-982-5475).

Boemia Bar, a happy student place, serves €5 grilled-pork
meals near the old cathedral, behind Restaurant Trovador
(Mon–Sat 19:00–24:00, closed Sun).

Adega Paço do Conde knows how to grill. Choose your
seafood or meat selection from the display case, and it's popped
on the grill. Students, solo travelers, and families like this homey
place (€5 meals, Mon–Sat 11:00–23:00, closed Sun, Rua Paço do
Conde 1, CC, from Praça do Comércio, take the last left—Adelino
Veiga, opposite the church, and walk 2 blocks to small square—
Largo do Paço do Condo, tel. 23-982-5605, Alfredo SE).

For a quick, easy, and cheap meal with locals next to a cool
and peaceful fountain, slide a tray down the counter at **Self-
Service Restaurant Jardim da Manga** (€6 meals, Sun–Fri
8:00–23:00, closed Sat, in Jardim/Garden da Manga, behind
Church of Santa Cruz, tel. 23-982-9156).

For an acceptable meal on a great square, eat at **Restaurant
Praça Velha** (don't let the waiters con you, daily 8:00–01:00,
Praça do Comércio 72).

The **Santa Cruz Café**, next to the Church of Santa Cruz,
is Old World elegant, with outdoor tables offering great people
watching over the Praça 8 Maio.

Picnics: Shop at the municipal *mercado* behind the Church
of Santa Cruz (Mon–Sat 8:00–14:00, closed Sun), or at hole-in-
the-wall groceries in the side streets. The central "supermarket"
Minipreço—behind the A station—is disappointing, selling fruit
only in large quantities and lacking real juice. But in case they
have something you want, they're open long hours (Mon–Sat

8:30–20:00, Sun 9:00–13:00, 15:00–19:00). The well-maintained gardens along the river across from the TI are picnic-pleasant.

Transportation Connections—Coimbra

By bus to: Alcobaça (2/day, 90 min), **Batalha** (3/day, 75 min), **Fatima** (9/day, 1 hr), **Nazaré** (5/day, 1.75 hrs, €6.50), **Lisbon** (17/day, 2.5 hrs), **Évora** (12/day, 8.25 hrs), **Lagos** (14/day, 10 hrs with 1 change). Bus info: tel. 23-985-5270. Frequency drops on weekends, especially Sunday.

By train to: Nazaré/Valado (6/day, 3.5 hours, transfer in Figueira de la Foz, bus is better). Train info: tel. 23-983-4998 (www.cp.pt).

To Salamanca: One **train** per day departs at 20:25 and drops you in Salamanca at 02:22 in the morning (5 hrs, 1-hr time difference). The far better option is the direct **bus** (1/day Tue–Sat, 11:00–18:15, 6 hrs, 1-hr time difference, worth the €17 even if you have a railpass). To guarantee a place, book two days in advance. You can buy your ticket by phone or in person at the Abreu travel agency in Coimbra (Mon–Fri 9:00–12:30, 14:30–18:30, Sat 9:00–12:30, closed Sun, CC, Rua da Sota 2, near train station A, tel. 23-982-7011, e-mail: jpeters.coimbra@abreu.pt, helpful James SE) more easily than at Coimbra's bus station (Intercentro, tel. 23-985-5270, NSE).

NAZARÉ

I got hooked on Nazaré when colorful fishing boats littered its long, sandy beach. Now the boats motor comfortably into a new harbor a 30-minute walk south of town, the beach is littered with frolicking families, and it seems most of Nazaré's 10,000 inhabitants are in the tourist trade. But I still like the place.

Even with its summer crowds, Nazaré is a fun stop offering a surprisingly good look at old Portugal. Somehow the traditions survive, and the locals are able to go about their black-shawl ways. Wander the backstreets for a fine look at Portuguese family-in-the-street life. Laundry flaps in the wind, kids play soccer, and fish sizzle over tiny curbside hibachis. Squadrons of sun-dried and salted fish are crucified on nets pulled tightly around wooden frames and left under the midday sun. Locals claim they are delightful—but I don't know. Off-season Nazaré is almost empty of tourists—inexpensive, colorful, and relaxed, with enough salty fishing-village atmosphere to make you pucker.

Nazaré doesn't have any blockbuster sights. The beach, tasty seafood, and funicular ride up to Sitio for a great coastal view are the bright lights of my lazy Nazaré memories.

Plan some beach time here. Sharing a bottle of *vinho verde* (new wine, a specialty of central Portugal) on the beach at sundown is a good way to wrap up the day.

Orientation

Nazaré faces its long beach, stretching from the new harbor north to the hill-capping old town of Sitio. Leaving the bus station, turn right and walk a block to the waterfront and survey the town. Scan the cliffs. The funicular climbs to Sitio (the hilltop part of town). Also to your right, look at the road kinking toward the sea. The building (on the kink) with the yellow balconies is the Ribamir Hotel, next to the TI. Just beyond the Ribamir you'll find the main square (Praça Sousa Oliveira, with banks and ATMs) and most of my hotel listings.

Sitio, which feels like a totally separate village sitting quietly atop its cliff, is reached by a frequent funicular (€0.60). Go up at least for the spectacular view.

Tourist Information: The TI faces the beach a block south of the main square (May–June daily 10:00–13:00, 15:00–19:00, July–Aug daily 10:00–22:00, Oct–April daily 10:00–13:00, 15:00–18:00, tel. 26-256-1194). Ask about summer activities, bullfights in Sitio, and music on the beach (Sat–Sun 22:00).

Internet Access: Try the Cultural Center Library (Mon–Fri 9:30–13:00, 14:00–19:00, Sat 15:00–19:00, on main road along beach en route to harbor) or the post office (Mon–Fri 9:00–12:30, 14:30–18:00, on Rua Mouzinho Albuquerque, about 5 blocks inland, also has metered phones).

Sights—Nazaré

Nazaré Fashions: Seven Petticoats and Black Widows—Nazaré is famous for its women who wear skirts with seven petticoats. While this is mostly just a creation for the tourists, there is some basis of truth to the tradition. In the old days, women would sit on the beach waiting for their fishermen to sail home. To keep warm during a cold sea wind and stay modestly covered, they'd wear several petticoats in order to fold layers over their heads, backs, and legs. Even today, older and more traditional women wear short skirts made bulky by several—but not seven—petticoats.

Black outfits are worn by a person in mourning. Traditionally, if your spouse died you wore black for the rest of your life. This tradition is still observed, although in the last generation, widows began remarrying—considered quite racy at first.

The Beach—Since the harbor was built in 1986, boats are no longer allowed on the beach. Before that they filled the squares in the winter and the beaches in the summer. Today it's the domain of the beach tents—a tradition in Portugal. In Nazaré, the tents are run as a cooperative by the old women you'll see sitting in the shade ready to collect €6 or more a day. The beaches are groomed and guarded. Flags indicate danger level: red (no one in the water), yellow (wading is safe), green (no problem). If you see a mass of children parading through town down to the beach,

Nazaré

① RIBAMAR HOTEL REST.   ⑤ CASA DO FRANGOS REST.
② ALBERGARIA MAR BRAVO   ⑥ RESTAURANTE AQUARIO
③ RESIDENCIAL A CUBATA   ⑦ OFICINA REST.
④ HOTEL MARE

they're likely from a huge dorm in town that provides poorer kids from this part of the country with a summer break.

Funicular to Sitio—Nazaré's funicular was built in 1889—the same year as the Eiffel Tower—by the same disciple of Eiffel who built the much-loved elevator in Lisbon. Ride up the lift (called *Ascensor*); it goes every 15 minutes (€0.60 each way, runs 7:15–24:00, every 15 min 7:30–21:30, otherwise every half-hour, WCs at base). Notice how the locals get off while it's still moving. Walk to the staggering Nazaré viewpoint behind the station at the top, then the main viewpoint past the many vendors at the promontory (wave to America). Sitio feels different. Its people are farmers, not fishing folk.

Activities—Sitio stages Portuguese-style **bullfights** on Saturday nights from July through early September (tickets from €10 at kiosk in Praça Sousa Oliveira). Sitio's **NorParque** is a family-friendly **water park** with a pool, slides, and Jacuzzi (June–Sept

10:00–19:00, confirm hours at TI). A **flea market** pops up near
Nazaré's town hall every Friday (9:00–13:00, at the inland end of
the street the bus station is on) and the colorful **produce market**
bustles in the morning (daily 8:00–12:00, Oct–May closed Mon,
kitty-corner from bus station).

Sleeping in Nazaré
(€1.10 = about $1, country code: 351)
Sleep Code: **S** = Single, **D** = Double/Twin, **T** = Triple, **Q** = Quad,
b = bathroom, **s** = shower only, **CC** = Credit Cards accepted, **no
CC** = Credit Cards not accepted, **SE** = Speaks English, **NSE** =
No English.

You should have no problem finding a room, except in
August, when the crowds, temperatures, and prices are all at
their highest. You'll find plenty of hustlers meeting each bus and
Valado train and waiting along the promenade. Even the normal
hotels get into the act during the off-season. I've never arrived
in town without a welcoming committee inviting me to sleep in
their *quartos* (rooms in private homes).

I list a price range for each hotel: The lowest is for winter
(roughly Jan–March), the sky-highest for mid-July through August.
The rest of the year (approximately April–mid-July and Sept–Dec)
expect to pay about midrange. You will save serious money if you
arrive with no reservations and bargain. Even the big professional
places are down on their knees for 10 months of the year.

Ribamar Hotel Restaurant has a prime location on the
waterfront, with an Old World, hotelesque atmosphere, including
24 rooms with dark wood and four-poster beds (Sb-€25–45, Db-
€33–63, prices flexible, includes breakfast, attached restaurant,
parking-€5, €10 in Aug, CC, some balconies, TV, good restaurant downstairs, Rua Gomes Freire 9, tel. 26-255-1158, fax 26-
256-2224, some English spoken). Look for the yellow awnings
and balconies.

Albergaria Mar Bravo, next to Ribamar, is on the main
square and the waterfront. Its 16 comfy rooms are great—
modern, bright, and fresh, with balconies—but the staff is not
genuinely friendly (Sb-€40–85, Db-€60–97, depending on view
and month, great view breakfast room, CC, air con, elevator,
Praça Sousa Oliveira 67-A, tel. 26-256-9160, fax 26-256-9169,
e-mail: marbravo@clix.pt, SE).

Residencial A Cubata, a friendly place on the waterfront
on the north end, has 22 small, comfortable rooms and older
bathrooms (Sb-€25–50, Db-€33–75, depends on view and season,
includes breakfast, 10 percent discount with this book if you pay
cash, CC, free parking, noisy bar below—though they've recently
added soundproofing, Avenida da República 6, tel. 26-256-1706,
fax 26-256-1700, some English spoken). For a peaceful night,

forgo the private balcony, take a back room (saving some money), and enjoy the communal beachfront balcony.

Hotel Mare, just off the Praça Sousa Oliveira, is a big, modern, American-style hotel with 36 rooms, some tour groups, and a roof-top terrace (Sb-€45–75, Db-€50–90, Tb-€55–105, includes break-fast, CC, all with air con and balconies, double-paned windows, elevator, free parking lot, Rua Mouzinho de Albuquerque 8, tel. 26-256-1122, fax 26-256-1750, e-mail: hotel.mare@mail.telepac.pt, SE).

Quartos: I list no dumpy hotels or cheap pensions because the best budget option is *quartos*. Like nowhere else in Iberia, locals renting spare rooms clamor for your business here. Except perhaps for weekends in August, you can stumble into town any day and find countless women hanging out on the street (especially around the bus station) with fine modern rooms to rent. I promise. The TI's partial list of *quartos* totals 200. If you've got a backpack, they've got a room. Their rooms are generally better than hotel rooms—for half the cost. Your room is likely to be large and homey, with old-time-elegant furnishings (with no plumbing but plenty of facilities down the hall) and in a quiet neighborhood, six short blocks off the beachfront action. I'd come into town and have fun looking at several places. Hem and haw and the price goes down. **Nazaré Amada** rents four fine rooms (average price for Db-€20, €30 July–Sept, Rua Adriao Batalha, garage, cellular 96-257-9371, SE).

Eating in Nazaré

In this fishing village even the snacks come from the sea. *Percebes* are local boiled barnacles, sold as munchies in bars and on the street. Merchants are happy to demonstrate how to eat them and let you sample one for free. They're great with beer in the bars.

Vinho verde, a northern Portugal specialty, is a very new wine—picked, made, and drunk within a year. It's refreshing and a bit like champagne without the bubbles, Generally white, cheap, and on every menu, it goes great with shellfish. *Amendoa amarga* is the local amaretto.

Nazaré is a fishing town, so don't order *hamburguesas*. Fresh seafood is great all over town, more expensive (but affordable) along the waterfront, and cheaper farther inland. Waiters will sometimes bring you food (such as olives or bread) that you didn't order. Just wave it away or else you'll pay for it.

A restaurant lane—Travessa do Elevador—leads from the town square to the base of the funicular. Among the many hard-working places here, I like **Restaurante Aquario** (daily 12:00–15:00, 18:00–23:00, closed Wed off-season, Largo das Caldeiras 14, a short block off the main square).

The family-run **Oficina** serves home-style seafood dishes, not fancy but filling, in a friendly setting that makes you feel

like you're eating at someone's kitchen table (daily 12:00–
15:00, 19:00–22:00, Rua das Flores 33, off Praça Dr. Manual
Arriaga; facing the restaurant Casa dos Frango, take street
immediately left).

Chicken addicts can get roasted chickens to go at **Casa
dos Frango** (daily 9:30–13:00, 15:30–20:30, Praça Dr. Manual
Arriaga 20), while picnic gatherers can head for the covered
mercado across from the bus station (daily 8:00–12:00, closed
Mon Oct–May).

Restaurante O Luis in Sitio serves excellent seafood and
local cuisine to an enthusiastic crowd in a cheery atmosphere.
While few tourists go here, friendly waiters make you feel welcome. This place is worth the trouble if you want to eat well in
Nazaré: Ride the lift up to Sitio and walk five minutes to Praça de
Toros (€10 dinners, daily 12:00–24:00, air con, CC, from funicular take steps down to main drag, turn right on main drag and
walk to bullring, take street downhill left of bullring, Rua Dos
Tanques 7, tel. 26-255-1826).

Transportation Connections—Nazaré

Nazaré's bus station is in the center, on Avenida Vieria Gumaraes,
a block inland from the waterfront. The nearest train station is
at Valado (5 km toward Alcobaça, connected by semi-regular
€1.10 buses and reasonable, easy-to-share €6 taxis). To avoid
this headache, consider using intercity buses instead of trains.
If you're heading to Lisbon, trains and buses work equally well.
While the train station is five kilometers from Nazaré and a trip
to Lisbon requires a transfer in Cacém, you'll arrive at Lisbon's
very central Rossio station (near recommended hotels). Lisbon's
bus station is a Metro (or taxi) ride away from the center.

Nazaré/Valado by train to: Coimbra (6/day, 3.5 hrs, change
at Foz da Figueira; see bus info below), **Lisbon** (7/day, 3 hrs).
Train info: tel. 26-257-7331.

Nazaré by bus to: Alcobaça (stopping at Valado, 13/day,
20 min), **Batalha** (8/day, 1 hr, some change at São Jorge), **Óbidos**
(6/day, 1 hr; bus is better than train), **Fatima** (3/day, 90 min),
Coimbra (6/day, 1.75 hrs; bus is better than train), **Lisbon** (5/day,
2 hrs). Buses are scarce on Sunday. Bus info: tel. 26-255-1172.

**Daytripping from Nazaré to: Alcobaça, Batalha, Fatima,
or Óbidos:** Traveling by bus you can see both Alcobaça and
Batalha in one day (but not on Sun, when bus service is sparse).
Alcobaça is easy to visit on the way to or from Batalha (and both
are connected by bus with Óbidos). Ask at the bus station or TI
for schedule information and be flexible. Fatima has the fewest
connections and is farthest away. Without a car, for most, Fatima
is not worth the trouble. A taxi from Nazaré to Alcobaça costs
about €10.

Nazaré Area

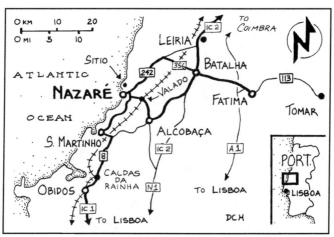

BATALHA

The only reason to stop in the town of Batalha is to see its great monastery. Considered Portugal's greatest architectural achievement and a symbol of its national pride, the Batalha (which means "battle") Monastery was begun in 1388 to thank God for a Portuguese victory that kept it free from Spanish rule (€3, daily 9:00–18:00, Oct–March until 17:00, tel. 24-476-5180).

Tourist Information: The TI, located across from the monastery, has free maps and information on buses (daily 10:00–13:00, 15:00–19:00, Oct–March 10:00–13:00, 14:00–18:00, Praça Mouzinho de Albuquerque, tel. 24-476-5180). Batalha's market day is Monday morning (behind the monastery).

Arrival in Batalha: If you take the bus to Batalha, you'll be dropped off within a block of the monastery and TI. There's no official luggage storage, but you can leave luggage at the monastery's ticket desk while you tour the cloisters.

Sights—Monastery of Santa María

Monastery Exterior—The equestrian statue outside the church is of Nuno Alvares Pereira, who commanded the Portuguese in the battle and masterminded the victory. Before entering the church, study the carving on the west portal (noticing the angels with their modesty wings).

Founder's Chapel—This chapel (near the church entrance) holds several royal tombs, including Henry the Navigator's. Tucked in the wall, Henry wears the church like a crown on his head.

Cloisters—Pay before entering. The greatness of Portugal's Age of Discovery shines brightly in the royal cloisters, which combine the simplicity of Gothic with the elaborate decoration of the Manueline style.

Chapter Room—This is famous for its fine and frighteningly broad vaults. The ceiling was considered so dangerous to build (it collapsed twice) that only prisoners condemned to death were allowed to work on it. Today unknowing tourists are allowed to wander under it. It's the home of Portugal's Tomb of the Unknown Soldier. The adjacent refectory holds a small museum of World War I memorabilia, and the long hall dotted with architectural scraps used to be the monks' dorm.

Keep your ticket, exit the first cloister to a square, follow signs to the right (WC is to the left), and you'll reach the…

Unfinished Chapels—The chapels were started for King Duarte around 1435 to house the tombs of his family and successors. Never finished, the building—with the best Manueline details you see here—is open to the sky. Across from the elaborate doorway are the tombs of King Duarte and his wife, their recumbent statues hand in hand, blissfully unaware of the work left undone.

Transportation Connections—Batalha
By bus to: Nazaré (5/day, 1 hr), **Alcobaça** (10/day, 30 min), **Fatima** (3/day, 30 min), and **Lisbon** (6/day, 2 hrs). Expect fewer buses on Sunday. By car, Batalha is an easy 16-kilometer drive from Fatima. You'll see signs from each site to the other.

FATIMA
On May 13, 1917, the Virgin Mary, "a lady brighter than the sun," visited three young shepherds and told them peace was needed. World War I raged on, so on the 13th day of each of the next five months Mary dropped in again to call for peace. On the 13th of October, 70,000 people witnessed the parting of dark storm clouds as the sun wrote "God's fiery signature" across the sky. Now, on the 13th of May, June, July, September, and October, and on the 19th of August, thousands of pilgrims gather at the huge neoclassical **basilica of Fatima** (evening torchlit processions for 2 nights, starting the night before, usually the 12th and 13th). In 1930 the Vatican recognized Fatima as legit, and in 1967, on the 50th anniversary, 1.5 million pilgrims—including the Pope—gathered here. Fatima welcomes guests. Near the basilica is the TI (April–Sept daily 10:00–13:00, 15:00–19:00, Oct–March daily 10:00–13:00, 14:00–18:00, Avenida Jose Alves Correia da Silva, tel. 24-953-1139).

The impressive **Basilica do Rosário** stands in front of a mammoth square lined with parks. (Dress modestly to enter the basilica.) Surrounding the square are a variety of hotels, restaurants, and tacky souvenir stands.

Visitors may want to check out two museums (both open daily 9:30–18:30 and cost about €6). The **Museo de Cera de Fatima** is a series of rooms telling the story of Fatima one scene at a time with wax figures (English leaflet describes each vignette). The **Museu-Vivo Aparicões**, a low-tech sound and light show, tells the same story (worthless without English soundtrack playing—ask). While the wax museum is better, both exhibits are pretty cheesy for those who are inclined not to take Fatima seriously.

Apart from the 12th and 13th of most months, cheap hotel rooms abound. Buses go from Fatima to **Batalha** (3/day, 30 min), **Leiria** (15/day 30 min), and **Lisbon** (12/day, 1.5–2.5 hrs, depending on route); service drops on Sunday.

ALCOBAÇA

This pleasant little town is famous for its church, the biggest in Portugal and one of the most interesting. I find Alcobaça more interesting than Batahla.

Tourist Information: The English-speaking TI is across the square from the church (daily 10:00–13:00, 15:00–19:00, Nov–April closes at 18:00, Praça 25 de Abril, tel. 26-258-2377).

Arrival in Alcobaça: If you arrive by bus, it's a five-minute walk to the town center and monastery: Exit right from the station (on Avenida Manuel da Silva Carolino), take the first right, and continue straight (on Avenida dos Combatentes).

Sights—Alcobaça

▲▲**Cistercian Monastery of Santa María**—This abbey church— the best Gothic building and the largest church in Portugal—is a clean and bright break from the heavier Iberian norm. It was started in 1178 after this area was reconquered from the Moors. It became one of the most powerful abbeys of the Cistercian Order and a cultural center of 13th-century Portugal. The abbey, clean and simple, is designed to be filled with hard work, prayer, and total silence. The abbey and cloisters cost €3 (worthwhile €1 English leaflet, free info at TI, April–Sept daily 9:00–19:00, Oct–March 9:00–17:00, tel. 26-258-2377).

Nave and Tombs of Dom Pedro and Ines: A long and narrow nave leads to two finely carved Gothic tombs (from 1360) in the transepts. These are of Portugal's most romantic and tragic couple, Dom Pedro (King Peter I) and Dona Inês de Castro. They rest feet-to-feet in each transept so that on Judgment Day they'll rise and immediately see each other again. Pedro, heir to the Portuguese throne, was in love with the Spanish aristocrat Inês. Concerned about Spanish influence, Pedro's father, Alfonso IV, forbade their marriage. You guessed it—they were married secretly. The angry father-in-law, in the interest of Portuguese independence, had Inês murdered. When Pedro became king

(1357), he ripped out and ate the hearts of the murderers. And even more interesting, he had Inês' rotten corpse exhumed, crowned it, and made the entire royal court kiss what was left of her hand. Now that's *amore*. The carvings on the tomb are just as special. Like religious alarm clocks, the attending angels are poised to wake the couple on Judgment Day. Study the relief at the feet of Ines: Heaven, Hell, and jack-in-the-box coffins on Judgment Day. Napoleon's troops vandalized the tombs.

More Tombs and Relics in the Sacristy: Near the king's tomb, step into the Hall of Tombs for more deceased royalty. Behind the high altar is the sacristy. In the round room decorated with painted wooden sculptures, the little glassed-in hollows in the statues and beams hold relics (tiny bits of bones or clothing) of the monks who died in the monastery.

Cloisters: Pay before entering. Circle the cloister counter-clockwise. Cistercian monks built the abbey in 40 years, starting in 1178. They inhabited it until 1834 (when the Portuguese king disbanded all monasteries). Cistercian monks spent most of their lives in silence and were allowed to speak only when given permission by the abbot.

Kitchen: The 18th-century kitchen's giant three-part oven could roast seven oxen simultaneously. The industrious monks rerouted part of the River Alcoa to bring in running water. And how about those hard surfaces?

Refectory or Dining Hall: This is opposite the fountain in the cloister used by the monks to wash up before eating. Imagine the hall filled with monks eating in silence as one reads from the Bible atop the "Readers' Pulpit."

Hall of Kings: Located just before you reenter the nave, this hall features statues of most of Portugal's kings and tiled walls telling the story of the building of the monastery.

▲**Mercado Municipal**—The Old World is housed happily here under huge steel-and-fiberglass domes. Inside, black-clad, dried-apple-faced women choose fish, chicks, birds, and rabbits from their respective death rows. It's an Old World Safeway, with figs, melons, bushels of grain, and nuts. Buying a picnic is a perfect excuse to drop in (Mon–Sat 9:00–13:00, closed Sun, best on Mon). It's a five-minute walk from the TI or bus station; ask a local, "*Mercado municipal?*"

▲▲**National Museum of Wine (Museu Nacional do Vinho)**— This museum, a kilometer outside Alcobaça (on the road to Batalha and Leiria, right-hand side), offers a fascinating look at the wine of Portugal (€1.50, May–Sept Tue–Fri 9:00–12:30, 14:00–17:30, Sat–Sun 10:00–12:30, 14:00–18:00, closed Mon; Oct–April Mon–Fri 9:00–12:30, 14:00–17:30, closed Sat–Sun, tel. 26-258-2222; your car is safer parked inside the gate). Run by a local cooperative winery, the museum teaches you everything you never wanted to know about Portuguese wine in a series of rooms that used to be fermenting vats. With some luck you can get a tour—much more hands-on than French winery tours—through the actual winery.

Transportation Connections—Alcobaça
By bus to: Lisbon (5/day, 2 hrs), **Nazaré** (12/day, 30 min), **Batalha** (4/day, 30 min), **Fatima** (3/day, 75 min, more frequent with transfer in Batalha). Bus frequency drops on Sunday. A taxi to the Valado train station costs €4; to Nazaré, €8.50.

ÓBIDOS
This medieval walled town was Portugal's "wedding city"—the perfect gift for a king to give to a queen who has everything. (Beats a toaster.) Today it's preserved in its entirety as a national monument surviving on tourism. Óbidos is crowded all summer, especially in August. Filter out the tourists and see it as you would a beautiful painted tile. It's worth a quick visit.

Postcard perfect, the town sits atop a hill, its 13-meter-high 14th-century wall corralling a bouquet of narrow lanes and flower-bedecked, whitewashed houses. Óbidos is ideal for photographers who want to make Portugal look prettier than it is. Walk around the wall and peek into the castle (now an overly-impressed-with-itself *pousada*, Db-€183, CC, tel. 26-295-9105, fax 26-295-9148).

Wander the back lanes and lose yourself in this lived-in open-air museum of medieval town nonplanning. Study the centuries-old houses and drop by the churches. St. Mary's Church, on the town square, gleams with lovely 17th-century *azulejo* tiles. The small Municipal Museum, also on the square, is not worth the €1.50 unless you enjoy stairs, religious art, and Portuguese inscriptions. Outside the town walls are a 16th-century aqueduct, a windmill, and a small produce market.

Óbidos is tough on the average tourist's budget. Pick up your picnic at the small grocery store just inside the main gate (on the street heading downhill), the larger grocery near the TI on Rua Direita, or the tiny market just outside the town wall.

Orientation
Tourist Information: There are two TIs. One is a city TI at Óbidos' main gate (daily Mon–Fri 9:30–19:30, Sat–Sun 10:00–13:00, 14:00–18:00, off-season closes 18:00 weekdays, 17:00 weekends, tel. 26-295-9231). The other TI (Região de Turismo do Oeste), on the main street—Rua Dereita—covers the region (Sun–Fri 9:30–19:00, Sat 10:00–13:00, 14:00–18:00, Oct–April 9:30–18:00, in the middle of town).

Arrival in Óbidos: Ideally take a bus to Óbidos and leave by either bus or train. If you arrive at the train station, you're faced with a 20-minute uphill hike into town (a killer with luggage). The bus drops you off much closer (go up the steps and through the archway on the right). There's no official place to store luggage.

Sleeping and Eating in Óbidos

To enjoy the town without tourists, spend the night. Two reasonable values in this overpriced toy of a town are the hotelesque **Albergaria Rainha Santa Isabel** (Sb-€48–63, Db-€57–70, third person-€15 extra, includes breakfast, CC, air con, elevator, on the main 1-lane drag, Rua Direita, tel. 26-295-9323, fax 26-295-9115, e-mail: arsio@oeste.online.pt, SE) and **Casa do Poço**, with four dim, clean rooms around a bright courtyard (Db-€58, Tb-€73, includes breakfast, Travessa da Mouraria, in old center near castle, tel. 26-295-9358, fax 26-295-9282, SE).

For less-expensive intimacy, try a *quarto*. Signs advertise rooms for rent all over town. **Lelia and João Fonseca da Silva** rent two good rooms (D-€25, 100 meters in from the town gate on the low road, Rua Josefa d'Óbidos, tel. 26-295-9113, NSE).

Eating: At **Restaurant O Barco**, professionals Mariana and Walter serve international and Portuguese cuisine with a French accent (€12.50, Tue–Sun 12:30–14:30, 19:30–22:00, closed Mon, walk down from St. Mary's Church, Largo Dr. Joao Lourenco, tel. 26-295-0925).

Transportation Connections—Óbidos

To: Nazaré (5 buses/day, 1 hr), **Lisbon** (3 buses/day, 75 min; 7 trains/day, 2 hrs, transfer in Cacem), **Alcobaça** (6 buses/day, 1 hr), **Batalha** (4 buses/day, 2 hrs). Fewer buses run on Sunday.

Route Tips for Drivers in Central Portugal

Lisbon to Coimbra: This is an easy 2.5-hour straight shot on the slick Auto-Estrada A1 (toll: €11). You'll pass convenient exits for Fatima and the Roman ruins of Conimbriga along the way. Leave the freeway on the easy-to-miss first Coimbra exit and then follow the "centro" signs. Four kilometers after leaving the freeway you'll cross the Mondego River. Take Avenida Fernão de Magalhaes directly into town; you'll find free parking near the Ponte de Santa Clara (bridge), on the side opposite the city center. Most hotels are near the train station and this bridge.

Óbidos to Lisbon: Don't drive into tiny, cobbled Óbidos. Ample tourist parking is provided outside of town. From Óbidos, the tollway zips you directly into Lisbon. For arriving and parking in Lisbon, see that chapter. If going to Sintra, follow signs to Cascais as you approach Lisbon.

APPENDIX

Iberian History

The cultural landscape of modern Spain and Portugal was shaped by the various civilizations that settled on the peninsula. Iberia's sunny weather and fertile soil made it a popular place to call home.

The Greeks came to Cadiz around 1100 B.C., followed by the Romans, who occupied the country for almost 1,000 years, until A.D. 400. Long after the empire crumbled, the Roman influence remained and could be found in things like cultural values, materials, building techniques, and even Roman-style farming equipment, which was used well into the 19th century. And, of course, there was wine.

Moors (711–1492)

The Moors—North Africans of the Muslim faith who occupied Spain—had the greatest cultural influence on Spanish and Portuguese history. They arrived on the Rock of Gibraltar in A.D. 711 and moved north. In the incredibly short time of seven years, the Moors completely conquered the peninsula.

The Moors established their power and Muslim culture in a subtle way. Non-Muslims were tolerated and often rose to positions of wealth and power; Jewish culture flourished. Rather than brutal subjugation, the Moorish style of conquest was to employ their sophisticated culture to develop whatever they found. For example, they encouraged wine-making, although for religious reasons they themselves weren't allowed to drink alcohol.

The Moors ruled for more than 700 years. Throughout that time, pockets of Christianity remained. Local Christian kings fought against the Moors whenever they could, whittling away at the Muslim empire, gaining more and more land. The last Moorish stronghold, Granada, fell to the Christians in 1492.

The slow, piecemeal process of the Reconquista split the peninsula into the independent states of Portugal and Spain. In 1139 Alfonso Henriques conquered the Moors near present-day Beja in southern Portugal and proclaimed himself king of the area. By 1200 the Christian state of Portugal had the borders it does today, making it the oldest unchanged state in Europe. The rest of the peninsula was a loosely-knit collection of smaller kingdoms. Spain's major step toward unity was in 1469, when Fernando II of Aragon married Isabel of Castile. Known as the "Catholic Monarchs," they united the other kingdoms under their rule.

The Golden Age (1500–1700)

The expulsion of the Moors set the stage for the rise of Portugal and Spain as naval powers and colonial superpowers. The Spaniards, fueled by the religious fervor of the Reconquista, were interested in spreading Christianity to the newly-discovered New World. Wherever they landed, they tried to Christianize the natives—with the sword, if necessary.

The Portuguese expansion was motivated more by economic concerns. Their excursions overseas were planned, cool, and rational. They colonized the nearby coasts of Africa first, progressing slowly around Africa to Asia and South America.

Through exploration (and exploitation) of the colonies, tremendous quantities of gold came into each country. The aristocracy and the clergy were swimming in money. It was only natural that art and courtly life flourished during this Golden Age.

Slow Decline

The fast money from the colonies kept Spain and Portugal from seeing the dangers at home. Great Britain and the Netherlands also were becoming naval powers, defeating the Spanish Armada in 1588. The Portuguese imported everything, stopped growing their own wheat, and neglected their fields.

During the centuries when science and technology in other European countries developed as never before, Spain and Portugal were preoccupied by their failed colonial politics. In the 18th century Spain was ruled by the French Bourbon family. (This explains the French Baroque architecture that you'll see, such as La Granja near Segovia and the Royal Palace in Madrid.) Endless battles, wars of succession, revolutions, and counterrevolutions weakened the countries. In this chaos there was no chance to develop democratic forms of government. Dictators in both countries made the rich richer and kept the masses underprivileged.

During World War I Portugal fought on the Allied side and Spain stayed neutral. In World War II both countries were neutral, uninterested in foreign policy as long as there was quiet in their own states. In the 1930s Spain suffered a bloody and bitter civil war between fascist and democratic forces. The fascist dictator Francisco Franco prevailed, ruling the country until his death in 1975.

Democracy in Spain and Portugal is still young. After a bloodless revolution, Portugal held democratic elections in 1975. After 41 years of a fascist dictatorship, Spain finally had elections in 1977.

Today socialists are in power in both countries. They've adopted a policy of balance to save the young democracies and fight problems such as unemployment and foreign debts—with moderate success. Today Spain and Portugal are members of the European Union. Though not considered wealthy or powerful, both countries are prospering, thanks in part to you and tourism.

Art

The "Big Three" in Spanish painting are El Greco, Velázquez, and Goya.

El Greco (1541–1614) exemplifies the spiritual fervor of much Spanish art. The drama, the surreal colors, and the intentionally unnatural distortion have the intensity of a religious vision.

Diego Velázquez (1599–1660) went to the opposite extreme. His masterful court portraits are studies in realism and cool detachment from his subjects.

Goya (1746–1828) matched Velázquez's technique but not his detachment. He let his liberal tendencies shine through in unflattering portraits of royalty and in emotional scenes of abuse of power. He unleashed his inner passions in the eerie, nightmarish canvases of his last, "dark" stage.

Not quite in the league of the Big Three, Murillo (1617–1682) painted a dreamy world of religious visions. His pastel, soft-focus works of cute baby Jesuses and radiant Virgin Marys helped make Catholic doctrine palatable to the common folk at a time when many were defecting to Protestantism.

You'll also find plenty of foreign art in Spain's museums. During its Golden Age, Spain's wealthy aristocrats bought wagonloads of the most popular art of the time—Italian Renaissance and Baroque works by Titian, Tintoretto, and others. They also loaded up on paintings by Rubens, Bosch, and Brueghel from the Low Countries, which were under Spanish rule.

In the 20th century Pablo Picasso (see his stark, antiwar *Guernica* mural in Madrid), Joan Miró, and surrealist Salvador Dalí made their marks. Great museums featuring all three are in or near Barcelona.

Architecture

The two most fertile periods of architectural innovation in Spain and Portugal were during the Moorish occupation and in the Golden Age. Otherwise, Spanish architects have marched obediently behind the rest of Europe.

The Moors brought Middle Eastern styles with them, such as the horseshoe arch, minarets, and floor plans designed for mosques. Islam forbids the sculpting or painting of human or animal figures ("graven images"), so artists expressed their creativity with elaborate geometric patterns. The ornate stucco of Granada's Alhambra, the elaborate arches of Sevilla's Alcázar, and decorative colored tiles are evidence of the Moorish sense of beauty. Islamic and Christian elements were blended in the work of Mozarabic (Christians living under Moorish rule) and Mudejar (Moors living in Spain after the Christian reconquest) artists.

As the Christians slowly reconquered the country, they turned their fervor into stone, building churches both in the heavy, fortress-of-God Romanesque style (Lisbon's cathedral) and in the lighter, heaven-reaching, stained-glass Gothic style (Barcelona, Toledo, and Sevilla). Gothic was an import from

France, trickling into conservative Spain long after it swept through Europe.

The money reaped and raped from Spain's colonies in the Golden Age spurred new construction. Churches and palaces were built using the solid, geometric style of the Italian Renaissance (El Escorial) and the more ornamented Baroque. Ornamentation reached unprecedented heights in Spain, culminating in the Plateresque style of stonework, so called because it resembles intricate silver filigree work. Portugal's highly ornamented answer to Plateresque is called Manueline. Lisbon's Belém Tower is its best example.

In the 18th and 19th centuries, innovation in both countries died out. Spain's major contribution to modern architecture is the Art Nouveau work of Antonio Gaudí early in the 20th century. Most of his "cake-left-out-in-the-rain" buildings, with asymmetrical designs and sinuous lines, can be found in Barcelona.

Bullfighting—Legitimate Slice of Spain or Cruel Spectacle?

The Spanish bullfight is as much a ritual as it is sport. Not to acknowledge the importance of the bullfight is to censor a venerable part of Spanish culture. But it also makes a spectacle out of the cruel killing of an animal. Should tourists boycott bullfights? I don't know.

Today bullfighting is less popular among locals. If this trend continues, bullfighting may survive more and more as a tourist event. When the day comes that bullfighting is kept alive by our tourist dollars rather than the local culture, then I'll agree with those who say bullfighting is immoral and that tourists shouldn't encourage it by buying tickets. Consider the morality of supporting this gruesome aspect of Spanish culture before buying a ticket. If you do decide to attend a bullfight, here is what you'll see.

While no two bullfights are the same, they unfold along a strict pattern. The ceremony begins punctually with a parade of participants around the ring. Then the trumpet sounds, the "Gate of Fear" opens, and the leading player—el toro—thunders in. An angry half-ton animal is an awesome sight, even from the cheap seats.

The fight is divided into three acts. Act 1 is designed to size up the bull and wear him down. The matador (literally "killer"), with help from his assistants, attracts the bull with the shake of the cape, then directs the animal past his body, as close as his bravery allows. The bull sees only things in motion and red. After a few passes the picadors enter, mounted on horseback, to spear the swollen lump of muscle at the back of the bull's neck. This lowers the bull's head and weakens the thrust of his horns. (In the 19th century horses had no protective pads and were often killed.)

In Act 2, the matador's assistants (banderilleros) continue to enrage and weaken the bull. The banderillero charges the charging bull and, leaping acrobatically across its path, plunges brightly-colored barbed sticks into the bull's vital neck muscle.

After a short intermission, during which the matador may, according to tradition, ask permission to kill the bull and dedicate the kill to someone in the crowd, the final, lethal Act 3 begins.

The matador tries to dominate and tire the bull with hypnotic cape work. A good pass is when the matador stands completely still while the bull charges past. Then the matador thrusts a sword between the animal's shoulder blades for the kill. A quick kill is not always easy, and the matador may have to make several bloody thrusts before the sword stays in and the bull finally dies. Mules drag the bull out, and his meat is in the market mañana. Rabo del toro (bull-tail stew) is a delicacy.

Throughout the fight, the crowd shows its approval or impatience. Shouts of "*¡Olé!*" or "*¡Torero!*" mean they like what they see. Whistling or rhythmic hand-clapping greets cowardice and incompetence.

You're not likely to see much human blood spilled. In 200 years of bullfighting in Sevilla, only 30 fighters have died (and only one was actually a matador). If a bull does kill a fighter, the next matador comes in to kill him. Even the bull's mother is killed, since the evil qualities are assumed to have come from the mother.

After an exceptional fight, the crowd may wave white handkerchiefs to ask that the matador be awarded the bull's ear or tail. A brave bull, though dead, gets a victory lap from the mule team on his way to the slaughterhouse. Then the trumpet sounds, and a new bull barges in to face a fresh matador.

A typical bullfight lasts about three hours and consists of six separate fights—three matadors (each with their own team of picadors and banderilleros) fighting two bulls each. For a closer look at bullfighting by an American aficionado, read Ernest Hemingway's classic, *Death in the Afternoon.*

The Portuguese bullfight is different from the Spanish bullfight. For a description, see the Lisbon chapter. In Portugal, the bull is not killed in front of the crowd, though it is killed later.

Festivals and Public Holidays

Spain and Portugal erupt with fiestas and celebrations throughout the year. Semana Santa (Holy Week) fills the week before Easter with processions and festivities all over Iberia, but especially in Sevilla. To run with the bulls, be in Pamplona—with medical insurance—the second week in July.

This is a partial list of holidays and festivals. Some dates haven't yet been set. For more information, contact the Spanish or Portuguese National Tourist Offices (listed in this book's

Introduction) and check these Web sites: www.whatsonwhen
.com, www.holidayfestival.com, www.whatsgoingon.com, and
www.festivals.com.

Jan 1	New Year's Day, Spain & Portugal
Jan 6	Epiphany, Spain
Early Feb	La Candelaria (religious festival), Madrid (Spain)
Late Feb	Carnival (Mardi Gras), Portugal
Feb 28	Day of Andalucía (some closures), Andalucía (Spain)
Easter	Holy Week and Easter, Spain & Portugal
April 16–21	April Fair, Sevilla (Spain)
April 25	Liberty Day (parades, fireworks), Portugal
May–June	Algarve Music Festival, Algarve (Portugal)
May 1	Labor Day (closures), Spain & Portugal
May 2	Day of Autonomous Community, Madrid (Spain)
May 13	Pilgrimage to Fatima, Fatima (Portugal)
Mid-May	Feria del Caballo (horse pageantry), Jerez (Spain)
May 15–25	San Isidro (religious festival), Madrid (Spain)
June 10	Portuguese National Day, Portugal
June 13	St. Anthony's Day, Lisbon (Portugal)
June 13	Pilgrimage to Fatima, Fatima (Portugal)
June	Lisbon's Festival, Lisbon (Portugal)
Mid-June	Corpus Christi, Spain
Late June	La Patum (Moorish battles), Barcelona (Spain)
June 24	St. John the Baptist's Day, Spain
June 29	St. Peter's Day, Lisbon (Portugal)
Late June–	International Festival of Music and Dance,
Early July	Granada (Spain)
July	(second week) Running of the Bulls,
	Pamplona (Spain)
July 13	Pilgrimage to Fatima, Fatima (Portugal)
Aug	Gràcia Festival, Barcelona (Spain)
Aug 6–15	Verbena de la Paloma (folk festival), Madrid (Spain)
Aug 15	Assumption (religious festival), Spain & Portugal
Aug 19	Pilgrimage to Fatima, Fatima (Portugal)
Sept 13	Pilgrimage to Fatima, Fatima (Portugal)
Mid-Sept	Our Lady of Nazaré Festival, Nazaré (Portugal)
Mid-Sept–	Autumn Festival (flamenco, bullfights),
mid-Oct	Jerez (Spain)
Late Sept	La Mercé (parade), Barcelona (Spain)
Oct 5	Republic Day (businesses closed) , Portugal
Oct 12	Spanish National Day, Spain
Oct 13	Pilgrimage to Fatima, Fatima (Portugal)
Nov 1	All Saints' Day, Spain & Portugal
Nov 9	Virgen de la Almudena, Madrid (Spain)
Mid-Nov	International Jazz Festival, Madrid (Spain)
Dec 1	Independence Restoration Day, Portugal
Dec 6	Constitution Day, Spain

Dec 8	Feast of the Immaculate Conception, Spain & Portugal
Dec 13	Feast of Santa Lucia, Spain
Dec 25	Christmas, Spain & Portugal
Dec 31	New Year's Eve, Spain & Portugal

Numbers and Stumblers

- Europeans write a few of their numbers differently than we do: 1 = 1 , 4 = 4 , 7= 7. Learn the difference or miss your train.
- Europeans write dates as day/month/year (Christmas is 25/12/02).
- Commas are decimal points, and decimals are commas. A dollar and a half is 1,50. There are 5.280 feet in a mile.
- When pointing, use your whole hand, palm downward.
- When counting with fingers, start with your thumb. If you hold up your first finger to request one item, you'll probably get two.
- What we Americans call the second floor of a building is the first floor in Europe.
- Europeans keep the left "lane" open for passing on escalators and moving sidewalks. Keep to the right.

Let's Talk Telephones

This is a primer on telephoning in Europe. For specifics on Spain and Portugal, see "Telephones" in the Introduction.

Dialing Direct

Making Calls within a European Country: What you dial depends on the phone system of the country you're in. About half of all European countries use area codes; the other half uses a direct-dial system without area codes.

If you're calling within a country that uses a direct-dial system (Spain, Portugal, Belgium, France, Italy, Switzerland, Norway, and Denmark), you dial the same number whether you're calling within the city or across the country.

In countries that use area codes (such as Austria, Britain, the Czech Republic, Finland, Germany, Ireland, the Netherlands, and Sweden), you dial the local number when calling within a city, and you add the area code if calling long-distance within the country. Example: The phone number of a hotel in Munich is 089/264-349. To call it in Munich, dial 264-349; to call it from Frankfurt, dial 089-264-349.

Making International Calls: You always start with the international access code (011 if you're calling from America or Canada, or 00 from virtually anywhere in Europe), then dial the country code of the country you're calling (see list on next page).

What you dial next depends on the particular phone system of the country you're calling. If the country uses area codes, you drop the initial zero of the area code, then dial the rest of the area code and the local number. Example: To call the Munich hotel from Spain, dial 00, 49 (Germany's country code), then 89-264-349.

Countries that use direct-dial systems (no area codes) differ in how they're accessed internationally by phone. For instance, if you're making an international call to Spain, Portugal, Italy, Norway, or Denmark, you simply dial the international access code, country code, and phone number. (Example: The phone number of a hotel in Madrid is 91-521-2900. To call it from Portugal, dial 00, 34—Spain's country code, then 91-521-2900.) But if you're calling Belgium, France, or Switzerland, you drop the initial zero of the phone number. Example: The phone number of a Paris hotel is 01 47 05 49 15. To call it from Madrid, dial 00, 33 (France's country code), then 1 47 05 49 15 (the phone number without the initial zero).

Calling America or Canada from Europe: Dial the international access code (00 for most of Europe, exceptions noted in list below), then dial 1, the area code, and local phone number. Example: Our number here at Europe Through the Back Door (in Edmonds, WA) is 425/771-8303. To call us from Europe, dial 00-1-425-771-8303.

International Access Codes
When dialing direct, first dial the international access code of the country you're calling from. Virtually all European countries use "00"; the only exceptions are Finland (990) and Lithuania (810). For both the United States and Canada, it's "011."

Country Codes
After you've dialed the international access code, dial the code of the country you're calling.

Austria—43	Greece—30
Belgium—32	Ireland—353
Britain—44	Italy—39
Canada—1	Morocco—212
Czech Rep.—420	Netherlands—31
Denmark—45	Norway—47
Estonia—372	Portugal—351
Finland—358	Russia—7
France—33	Spain—34
Germany—49	Sweden—46
Gibraltar—350	Switzerland—41
(9567 from Spain)	United States—1

Dial Away . . .
United States/Canada to Spain: 011–34–nine-digit number
United States/Canada to Portugal: 011–351–nine-digit number

Spain or Portugal to United States/Canada: 00–1–area code–
  seven-digit number
Spain to Portugal: 00–351–nine-digit number
Portugal to Spain: 00–34–nine-digit number
Long Distance within Spain or within Portugal: Whether dialing
  across the street or across the country, use the nine-digit number.
Spain or Portugal to Tangier, Morocco: 00–212–39–six-digit
  number
United States/Canada to Tangier, Morocco: 011–212–39–
  six-digit number
Spain to Gibraltar: 9567–five-digit number
Portugal to Gibraltar: 00–350–five-digit number
United States/Canada to Gibraltar: 011–350–five-digit number
Directory Assistance: In Spain, dial 1004 for local numbers and
  025 for international numbers (expensive). In Portugal, dial 118
  for local numbers and 177 for international numbers. (Note:
  In Spain a 608 or 609 area code indicates a mobile phone.)

Calling-Card Operators
It's cheaper to call direct, but some travelers prefer to use their
calling cards (AT&T, MCI, or Sprint).

	AT&T	MCI	SPRINT
Spain	900-990-011	900-99-0014	900-99-0013
Portugal	800-800-128	800-800-123	800-800-187
Morocco	002-110-011	002-110-012	———
Gibraltar	8800	———	———

U.S. Embassies
Madrid, Spain: Serrano 75, tel. 91-587-2200, www.embusa.es/cons
/services.html
Lisbon, Portugal: Avenida das Forcas Armadas, tel. 21-727-3300,
www.american-embassy/pt
Gibraltar: Call embassy in Madrid (above).
Casablanca, Morocco: 8 Boulevard Moulay Youssef, tel. 22/26-
45-50, www.usembassy-morocco.org.ma

Metric Conversion (approximate)

1 inch = 25 millimeters	32 degrees F = 0 degrees C
1 foot = 0.3 meter	82 degrees F = about 28 degrees C
1 yard = 0.9 meter	1 ounce = 28 grams
1 mile = 1.6 kilometers	1 kilogram = 2.2 pounds
1 centimeter = 0.4 inch	1 quart = 0.95 liter
1 meter = 39.4 inches	1 square yard = 0.8 square meter
1 kilometer = 0.62 mile	1 acre = 0.4 hectare

Climate

First line, average daily low temperature; second line, average daily
high; third line, days of no rain.

J	F	M	A	M	J	J	A	S	O	N	D

SPAIN
Madrid

35°	36°	41°	45°	50°	58°	63°	63°	57°	49°	42°	36°
47°	52°	59°	65°	70°	80°	87°	85°	77°	65°	55°	48°
23	21	21	21	21	25	29	28	24	23	21	21

Barcelona

43°	45°	48°	52°	57°	65°	69°	69°	66°	58°	51°	46°
55°	57°	60°	65°	71°	78°	82°	82°	77°	69°	62°	56°
26	23	23	21	23	24	27	25	23	22	24	25

Almeria (Costa del Sol)

46°	47°	51°	55°	59°	65°	70°	71°	68°	60°	54°	49°
60°	61°	64°	68°	72°	78°	83°	84°	81°	73°	67°	62°
25	24	26	25	28	29	31	30	27	26	26	26

PORTUGAL
Lisbon

46°	47°	50°	53°	55°	60°	63°	63°	62°	58°	52°	47°
57°	59°	63°	67°	71°	77°	81°	82°	79°	72°	63°	58°
16	16	17	20	21	25	29	29	24	22	17	16

Faro (Algarve)

48°	49°	52°	55°	58°	64°	67°	68°	65°	60°	55°	50°
60°	61°	64°	67°	71°	77°	83°	83°	78°	72°	66°	61°
22	21	21	24	27	29	31	31	29	25	22	22

MOROCCO
Marrakesh

40°	43°	48°	52°	57°	62°	67°	68°	63°	57°	49°	42°
65°	68°	74°	79°	84°	92°	101°	100°	92°	83°	73°	66°
24	23	25	24	29	29	30	30	27	27	27	24

Basic Spanish Survival Phrases

English	Spanish	Pronunciation
Hello.	Hola.	oh-lah
Do you speak English?	¿Habla usted inglés?	ah-blah oo-stehd een-glays
Yes. / No.	Sí. / No.	see / noh
I don't speak Spanish.	No hablo español.	noh ah-bloh ay-spahn-yohl
I'm sorry.	Lo siento.	loh see-ehn-toh
Please.	Por favor.	por fah-bor
Thank you.	Gracias.	grah-thee-ahs
Goodbye.	Adiós.	ah-dee-ohs
Where is a...?	¿Donde hay un...?	dohn-day ī oon
...hotel	...hotel	oh-tel
...youth hostel	...albergue de juventud	ahl-behr-gay day hoo-behn-tood
...restaurant	...restaurante	ray-stoh-rahn-tay
...supermarket	...supermercado	soo-pehr-mehr-kah-doh
Where is the...?	¿Dónde está la...?	dohn-day ay-stah lah
...train station	...estación de trenes	ay-stah-thee-ohn day tray-nays
...tourist information office	...Oficina de Turismo	oh-fee-thee-nah day too-rees-moh
Where are the toilets?	¿Dónde están los servicios?	dohn-day ay-stahn lohs sehr-bee-thee-ohs
men / women	hombres / mujeres	ohm-brays / moo-heh-rays
How much is it?	¿Cuánto cuesta?	kwahn-toh kway-stah
Write it?	¿Me lo escribe?	may loh ay-skree-bay
Cheap(er).	(Más) barato.	(mahs) bah-rah-toh
Is it included?	¿Está incluido?	ay-stah een-kloo-ee-doh
I would like...	Quería...	keh-ree-ah
We would like...	Queríamos...	keh-ree-ah-mohs
...a ticket.	...un billete.	oon bee-yeh-tay
...a room.	...una habitación.	oo-nah ah-bee-tah-thee-ohn
...the bill.	...la cuenta.	lah kwayn-tah
one	uno	oo-noh
two	dos	dohs
three	tres	trays
four	cuatro	kwah-troh
five	cinco	theen-koh
six	seis	says
seven	siete	see-eh-tay
eight	ocho	oh-choh
nine	nueve	nway-bay
ten	diez	dee-ayth
At what time?	¿A qué hora?	ah kay oh-rah
now / later	ahora / más tarde	ah-oh-rah / mahs tar-day
today / tomorrow	hoy / mañana	oy / mahn-yah-nah

Basic Portuguese Survival Phrases

Hello.	**Olá.**	oh-**lah**
Do you speak English?	**Fala inglês?**	**fah**-lah een-**glaysh**
Yes. / No.	**Sim. / Não.**	seeng / now
I'm sorry.	**Desculpe.**	dish-**kool**-peh
Please.	**Por favor.**	poor fah-**vor**
Thank you.	**Obrigado[a].**	oh-bree-**gah**-doo
Goodbye.	**Adeus.**	ah-**deh**-oosh
Where is...?	**Onde é que é...?**	**ohn**-deh eh keh eh
...a hotel	**...um hotel**	oon oh-**tehl**
...a youth hostel	**...uma pousada de juventude**	oo-mah poh-**zah**-dah deh zhoo-vayn-**too**-deh
...a restaurant	**...um restaurante**	oon rish-toh-**rahn**-teh
...a supermarket	**...um supermercado**	oon soo-pehr-mehr-**kah**-doo
...the train station	**...a estação de comboio**	ah ish-tah-**sow** deh kohn-**boy**-yoo
...tourist information	**...a informação turistica**	ah een-for-mah-**sow** too-**reesh**-tee-kah
...the toilet	**...a casa de banho**	ah **kah**-zah deh **bahn**-yoo
men / women	**homens / mulheres**	aw-maynsh / mool-**yeh**-rish
How much is it?	**Quanto custa?**	**kwahn**-too **koosh**-tah
Cheap(er).	**(Mais) barato.**	(mīsh) bah-**rah**-too
Is it included?	**Está incluido?**	ish-**tah** een-kloo-**ee**-doo
I would like...	**Gostaria...**	goosh-tah-**ree**-ah
...a ticket.	**...um bilhete.**	oon beel-**yeh**-teh
...a room.	**...um quarto.**	oon **kwar**-too
...the bill.	**...a conta.**	ah **kohn**-tah
one	**um**	oon
two	**dois**	doysh
three	**três**	traysh
four	**quatro**	**kwah**-troo
five	**cinco**	**seeng**-koo
six	**seis**	saysh
seven	**sete**	**seh**-teh
eight	**oito**	**oy**-too
nine	**nove**	**naw**-veh
ten	**dez**	dehsh
At what time?	**A que horas?**	ah keh **aw**-rahsh
now / soon / later	**agora / em breve / mais tarde**	ah-**goh**-rah / ayn **bray**-veh / mīsh **tar**-deh
Today.	**Hoje.**	**oh**-zheh
Tomorrow.	**Amanhã.**	ah-ming-**yah**

For 336 more pages of survival phrases for your next trip to Iberia, check out *Rick Steves' Spanish & Portuguese Phrase Book and Dictionary*.

Road Scholar Feedback for SPAIN & PORTUGAL 2002

We're all in the same travelers' school of hard knocks. Your feedback helps us improve this guidebook for future travelers. Please fill this out (or use the on-line version at www.ricksteves.com/feedback), attach more info or any tips/favorite discoveries if you like, and send it to us. As thanks for your help, we'll send you our quarterly travel newsletter free for one year. Thanks! Rick

Of the recommended accommodations/restaurants used, which was:

Best _____

      Why? _____

Worst _____

      Why? _____

Of the sights/experiences/destinations recommended by this book, which was:

Most overrated _____

      Why? _____

Most underrated _____

      Why? _____

Best ways to improve this book:

_____

_____

I'd like a free newsletter subscription:

_____ Yes _____ No _____ Already on list

_____
Name

_____
Address

_____
City, State, Zip

_____
E-mail Address

Please send to: ETBD, Box 2009, Edmonds, WA 98020

Faxing Your Hotel Reservation

Use this handy form for your fax (or find it online at
www.ricksteves.com/reservation). Photocopy and fax away.

One-Page Fax

To: _____ @ _____
      hotel   *fax*

From: _____ @ _____
        name   *fax*

Today's date: ___ / ____ / ___
               day *month* *year*

Dear Hotel _____,

Please make this reservation for me:

Name: _____

Total # of people: _____   # of rooms: _____   # of nights: _____

Arriving: ___ / ____ / ___ My time of arrival (24-hr clock): _____
           day *month* *year*   (I will telephone if I will be late)

Departing: ___ / ____ / ___
            day *month* *year*

Room(s): Single___ Double___ Twin___ Triple___ Quad___

With: Toilet___ Shower___ Bath___ Sink only___

Special needs: View___ Quiet___ Cheap___ Ground Floor___

Credit card: Visa___ MasterCard___ American Express___

Card #: _____

Expiration date:_____

Name on card: _____

You may charge me for the first night as a deposit. Please fax, e-mail, or
mail me confirmation of my reservation, along with the type of room
reserved, the price, and whether the price includes breakfast. Please
inform me of your cancellation policy, also. Thank you.

_____
Signature

_____
Name

_____
Address

_____
City   **State**   **Zip Code**   **Country**

_____
E-mail Address

INDEX

FREE-SPIRITED TOURS FROM

Rick Steves

Great Guides

Big Buses

Small Groups

No Grumps

Best of Europe ■ **Village Europe** ■ **Eastern Europe** ■ **Turkey** ■ **Italy** ■ **Britain**
Spain/Portugal ■ **Ireland** ■ **Heart of France** ■ **South of France** ■ **Village France**
Scandinavia ■ **Germany/Austria/Switzerland** ■ **London** ■ **Paris** ■ **Rome**

Looking for a one, two, or three-week tour that's run in the Rick Steves style? Check out Rick Steves' educational, experiential tours of Europe.

Rick's tours include much more in the "sticker price" than mainstream tours. Here's what you'll get with a Europe or regional Rick Steves tour...

- **Group size:** Your tour group will be no larger than 26.

- **Guides:** You'll have two guides traveling and dining with you on your fully guided Rick Steves tour.

- **Bus:** You'll travel in a full-size 48-to-52-seat bus, with plenty of empty seats for you to spread out and read, snooze, enjoy the passing scenery, get away from your spouse, or whatever.

- **Sightseeing:** Your tour price includes all group sightseeing. There are no hidden extra charges.

- **Hotels:** You'll stay in Rick's favorite small, characteristic, locally-run hotels in the center of each city, within walking distance of the sights you came to see.

- **Price and insurance:** Your tour price is guaranteed for 2002. Single travelers do *not* pay an extra supplement (we have them room with other singles). ETBD includes prorated tour cancellation/interruption protection coverage at no extra cost.

- **Tips and kickbacks:** All guide and driver tips are included in your tour price. Because your driver and guides are paid salaries by ETBD, they can focus on giving you the best European travel experience possible.

Interested? Call (425) 771-8303 or visit www.ricksteves.com for a free copy of Rick Steves' 2002 Tours booklet!

Rick Steves' Europe Through the Back Door
130 Fourth Avenue North, PO Box 2009, Edmonds, WA 98020 USA
Phone: (425) 771-8303 ■ Fax: (425) 771-0833 ■ www.ricksteves.com

FREE TRAVEL GOODIES FROM

EUROPEAN TRAVEL NEWSLETTER

My *Europe Through the Back Door* travel company will help you travel better *because* you're on a budget—not in spite of it. To see how, ask for my 64-page *travel newsletter* packed full of savvy travel tips, readers' discoveries, and your best bets for railpasses, guidebooks, videos, travel accessories and free-spirited tours.

2002 GUIDE TO EUROPEAN RAILPASSES

With hundreds of railpasses to choose from in 2002, finding the right pass for your trip has never been more confusing. To cut through the complexity, ask for my 64-page *2002 Guide to European Railpasses.* Once you've narrowed down your choices, we give you unbeatable prices, including important extras with every Eurailpass, **free:** my 90-minute *Travel Skills Special* video or DVD; your choice of one of my 16 country guidebooks and phrasebooks; and answers to your "top five" travel questions.

RICK STEVES' 2002 TOURS

We offer 18 different one, two, and three-week tours (180 departures in 2002) for those who want to experience Europe in Rick Steves' Back Door style, but without the transportation and hotel hassles. If a tour with a small group, modest family-run hotels, lots of exercise, great guides, and no tips or hidden charges sounds like your idea of fun, ask for my 48-page 2002 Tours booklet.

YEAR-ROUND GUIDEBOOK UPDATES

Even though the information in my guidebooks is the freshest around, things do change in Europe between book printings. I've set aside a special section at my website (www.ricksteves.com/update) listing *up-to-the-minute changes* for every Rick Steves guidebook.

Call, fax, or visit www.ricksteves.com to get your...

- ☑ **FREE EUROPEAN TRAVEL NEWSLETTER**
- ☑ **FREE 2002 GUIDE TO EUROPEAN RAILPASSES**
- ☑ **FREE RICK STEVES' 2002 TOURS BOOKLET**

Rick Steves' Europe Through the Back Door

130 Fourth Avenue North, PO Box 2009, Edmonds, WA 98020 USA
Phone: (425) 771-8303 ■ Fax: (425) 771-0833 ■ www.ricksteves.com

Rick Steves' Phrase Books

Unlike other phrase books and dictionaries on the market, my well-tested phrases and key words cover every situation a traveler is likely to encounter. With these books you'll laugh with your cabby, disarm street thieves with insults, and charm new European friends.

Each book in the series is 4" x 6", with maps.

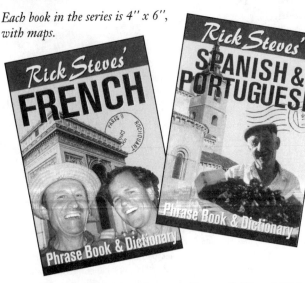

RICK STEVES' FRENCH PHRASE BOOK & DICTIONARY
U.S. $6.95/Canada $10.95

RICK STEVES' GERMAN PHRASE BOOK & DICTIONARY
U.S. $6.95/Canada $10.95

RICK STEVES' ITALIAN PHRASE BOOK & DICTIONARY
U.S. $6.95/Canada $10.95

RICK STEVES' SPANISH & PORTUGUESE PHRASE BOOK & DICTIONARY
U.S. $8.95/Canada $13.95

RICK STEVES' FRENCH, ITALIAN & GERMAN PHRASE BOOK & DICTIONARY
U.S. $8.95/Canada $13.95

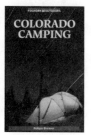
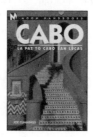

MOON HANDBOOKS

provide comprehensive coverage of a region's arts,
history, land, people, and social issues in addition
to detailed practical listings for accommodations,
food, outdoor recreation, and entertainment. Moon
Handbooks allow complete immersion in a region's
culture—ideal for travelers who want to combine sightseeing with insight for an extraordinary travel experience
in destinations throughout North America, Hawaii,
Latin America, the Caribbean, Asia, and the Pacific.

WWW.MOON.COM

Rick Steves shows you where to travel
and how to travel—all while getting the most value
for your dollar. His Back Door travel philosophy
is about making friends, having fun, and avoiding
tourist rip-offs.

Rick has been traveling to Europe for more
than 25 years and is the author of 22 guidebooks,
which have sold more than a million copies. He
also hosts the award-winning public television
series *Rick Steves' Europe.*

WWW.RICKSTEVES.COM

ROAD TRIP USA

Getting there is half the fun, and Road Trip USA
guides are your ticket to driving adventure. Taking
you off the interstates and onto less-traveled, two-
lane highways, each guide is filled with fascinating
trivia, historical information, photographs, facts
about regional writers, and details on where to
sleep and eat—all contributing to your exploration
of the American road.

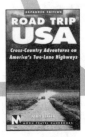

*"[Books] so full of the pleasures of the
American road, you can smell the upholstery."*
                                    ~**BBC radio**

WWW.ROADTRIPUSA.COM

FOGHORN OUTDOORS guides are for campers, hikers, boaters, anglers, bikers, and golfers of all levels of daring and skill. Each guide focuses on a specific U.S. region and contains site descriptions and ratings, driving directions, facilities and fees information, and easy-to-read maps that leave only the task of deciding where to go.

"Foghorn Outdoors has established an ecological conservation standard unmatched by any other publisher." ~Sierra Club

WWW.FOGHORN.COM

TRAVEL SMART guidebooks are accessible, route-based driving guides focusing on regions throughout the United States and Canada. Special interest tours provide the most practical routes for family fun, outdoor activities, or regional history for a trip of anywhere from two to 22 days. Travel Smarts take the guesswork out of planning a trip by recommending only the most interesting places to eat, stay, and visit.

"One of the few travel series that rates sightseeing attractions. That's a handy feature. It helps to have some guidance so that every minute counts." ~San Diego Union-Tribune

CiTY·SMaRT™ guides are written by local authors with hometown perspectives who have personally selected the best places to eat, shop, sightsee, and simply hang out. The honest, lively, and opinionated advice is perfect for business travelers looking to relax with the locals or for longtime residents looking for something new to do Saturday night.